D0655974

The Politics of Race

EDITORIAL ADVISERS

BRITISH POLITICAL SOCIOLOGY YEARBOOK

VOLUME 2

The Politics of Race

EDITED BY IVOR CREWE

CROOM HELM LONDON

Printed and bound
in Great Britain by
Redwood Burn Limited
Trowbridge & Esher

CONTENTS

ACKNOWLEDGEMENTS

For the second year in succession I am heavily indebted to my friend and colleague, Tony Fox, for undertaking the great bulk of the work necessary for the preparation of the bibliography.

INTRODUCTION

The central purpose of this second volume of the *British Political Sociology Yearbook* remains the same as that expressed in the Preface to the first: to strengthen the state of political sociology *in* Britain by gathering together original work on the political sociology *of* Britain. The principles along which this volume is organised are also the same as the last. The *Yearbooks* are thematic, not eclectic, the focus in this case being the political sociology of race relations in modern Britain. Overall content is deliberately structured to include reports of fresh empirical research, of innovation of method, and of new developments in concepts and theory, as well as a comprehensive bibliography and other reference material. But the *Yearbook* is not what the Americans call a 'reader,' namely, a large, tightly integrated compendium of the better work in an area done in the (mainly) recent past. The emphasis here is on advances in the field across a broad front and although serious attention is paid to balance and coverage, no claim to a systematic survey of the field is made. The aim is both to reflect and serve the current intellectual preoccupations of specialists in the area, and a certain untidiness in matters of symmetry and coverage is therefore inevitable.

In one sense the *Yearbook* can be regarded as filling the vacuum created by the absence of any academic journal devoted to the political sociology of Britain. It seeks to bring to the attention of a specially interested audience hitherto unpublished research and scholarship. Work that would otherwise have to be published in journals not primarily devoted to the interests of political sociologists concerned with Britain, is made more prominent, it is hoped, through the existence of the *Yearbook*. Indeed, the editor sees the *Yearbook* as having a special role to play for the high quality research that might not find any wider audience through 'the usual channels': dissertations and doctoral theses, smaller projects, and research by members of polytechnics, the smaller university departments, and institutions not formally part of higher education, all come into this category. The *Yearbook* is not simply a contribution to the study of British politics, but is intended to be a medium of communication amongst political sociologists, especially those who feel, for reasons to do with the institutions in which they work, cut off from others with similar intellectual concerns.

In another more obvious sense, however, the *Yearbook* is quite unlike an academic journal. By necessity papers are generally solicited, although uncommissioned contributions are very welcome and the hope is that their numbers will increase as this series becomes better known.

The next volume of the *Yearbook* will focus on participation and will be edited by Colin Crouch. Any researchers who would like to contribute to the volume should contact him at the London School of Economics.

In the course of this volume various contributors complain about the superficial level of academic research undertaken until now on the politics of race relations in Britain. In a broad survey of the 'state of the discipline' Brier and Axford make what turns out to be a common criticism: political scientists, they argue, have largely confined their interest to narrow areas at the micro-level, of which the impact of race in the election campaigns of particular wards or constituencies is a prime example. A glance through this volume's bibliography lends credence to the complaint: impressionistic descriptions of local racialist campaigns by maverick candidates and studies of turnout and party choice amongst specific immigrant communities are clearly more numerous than their relative importance warrants. And yet there is still much to be done within the circumscribed area of race and elections: studies so far have all been confined to the single community, the only exception being a variety of attempts to relate the racial and other demographic and economic characteristics of constituencies with parliamentary election results. But as more than one contributor points out, this exercise is fraught with inferential pitfalls. A statistical association between the size of the immigrant community and the size of the electoral 'swing' across a set of constituencies proves very little about the politics of immigrants or native-born, and at best does no more than raise interesting questions, to which only the sample survey at the individual level can provide convincing answers. A conventional national political survey of one or all immigrant groups would be inappropriate, however, as well as impractical (on which see Airey and Jowell's chapter), but a systematic survey of ethnically similar groups in different communities is surely long overdue. Abrams' five-town study of racial prejudice points the way in this regard (see his chapter in E.J.B. Rose, *Colour and Citizenship*, 1969).

Where else should political sociologists turn? Axford and Brier, concerned about the neglect of macro-level analysis, stress the need for conceptual frameworks which would help us to understand the place of racial conflict in the British political system as a whole and to make international comparisons. Sociologists have provided a number of alternative perspectives from which to view Britain's particular 'pattern of dominance' and its likely development in the future (see Sami Zubaida, *Race and Racialism*, 1970) — Marxist categories, pluralist assumptions, host-stranger analogies and colonial-native models — although the focus has been upon social integration, or discrimination and exploitation, and the political system (although not the exercise of power) has been a muted theme. Schutz and Scott contribute an additional perspective, an adaptation of Louis Hartz's 'fragment theory,' which is particularly relevant to those states created and dominated by permanent immigrants (settlers), usually after a breakaway from the imperial government of their country of origin. Schutz and Scott examine community relations in Northern Ireland and draw parallels with the situation in Rhodesia, a comparison that has its critics in this volume (see Nelson's chapter). The view that social conflict in Northern Ireland takes a typically racial form, of a settler-native rather than a caste or imperial-native variety, will by no means be generally accepted, although it has already received some support (see, for example, Robert Moore in *Race*, 1972, and Liam de Paor, *Divided Ulster*, 1970).

Those political scientists who do consider the role of racial conflict in a political system usually refer to the exploitation of popular racial prejudice by elites wishing to further their own political ends. Axford and Brier take a different tack, and inspired by Habermas' work on legitimacy in advanced industrial democracies, suggest that elite political groups, otherwise in conflict, have by tacit consensus eliminated race from the national political agenda; left to their own devices racial minorities have not the resources to put it back on. Lawrence reaches similar conclusions but on the basis of his empirical work in Nottingham proceeds to argue that this benign neglect has extended to the racial fears of the white working class and has been a major contributor to the growing disillusion with conventional party politics amongst the British electorate. The evidence is circumstantial only, however; Lawrence's highly plausible case is an obvious candidate for further research in which greater use is made of the time-series data now becoming available on the basis of the regular opinion polls conducted over the last decade.

By its nature a Yearbook is likely to reflect the strengths and weaknesses of its professional audience. The major part of this volume is devoted to strictly empirical studies of the grassroots, and in this respect it is open to the earlier criticisms levelled against the work of social scientists. But the research reported here breaks important new ground. There are three chapters on the politics of different racial minorities, in which the question of their political integration arises in one form or another. Le Lohé's painstaking detective work on the local election turnout and voting patterns of Bradford's Pakistani community turns up some real surprises. Turnout amongst the (registered) Pakistani community is generally higher than that of their native neighbours. In the one ward with a Pakistani Labour candidate, a substantial 'swing' towards the Conservatives, well against the trend throughout the rest of Bradford, fails to be attributable to a white backlash as commonly supposed at the time. It transpires that Pakistani voters refused to support their co-national Labour candidate and switched *en masse* to the Conservative. Is all this not impressive testimony to the Pakistani community's thorough integration into Bradford's local party politics? The answer is a resounding no: the white Conservative won because his Pakistani Labour opponent originally came from East Pakistan (now Bangladesh) whereas the great majority of Pakistani voters were born in West Pakistan!

Alderson's historical survey of the politics of Anglo-Jewry and his case study of the February 1974 election campaign in the 'Jewish' constituencies of North London raises questions about the existence of a 'Jewish vote.' The true picture is complicated. Evidence of a homogeneous partisanship capable of switching rapidly and massively in response to an issue relating exclusively to their ethnic status (i.e. the situation Le Lohé describes in Bradford) is hard to come by in the case of the Jewish community. The impact of the Conservative Government's postponement of arms sales to Israel during the Yom Kippur War, for example, would appear to have been small, although sufficient to tip the balance in a highly marginal seat. But the Jewish vote is distinctive in the sense that support for the Conservatives always appears to have been less than would be forthcoming from non-Jews of a similar occupational status, which by the 1970s is, on average, very high. Jewish sensitivity to their minority and outsider status, in Alderson's phrase, being 'not quite British,' may be the explanation.

Phizakalea's study of English and West Indian adolescents also produces a complex pattern of results. On the surface there appears to be little significant difference between the two groups: *both* display widespread feelings of political powerlessness (a low level of 'political efficacy'). But on closer examination it sppears that whereas the white schoolchildren explained their sense of political helplessness in class terms, their West Indian counterparts articulated similar feelings in racial terms. Moreover, whereas a sense of political inefficacy tended to be accompanied by a lack of *personal* confidence amongst the whites the relationship amongst the West Indian respondents was much weaker: a substantial minority was psychologically confident but politically disaffected, potential recruits perhaps for militant black political movements operating outside the conventional channels.

Three further chapters deal with aspects of racism among the majority population, of which two (Nelson's study of Protestant Loyalists and Scott's research on a local branch of the National Front) adopt 'participant observer' techniques. This might be thought ironic in the light of the usual assumption that such approaches are particularly suitable for studying the behaviour of 'strangers,' such as ethnic minorities. But it was because the attitudes of their subjects are commonly regarded as strange, indeed labelled as extremist or deviant, that an ethnomethodological approach was employed. Both studies call the supposed deviancy into question. Nelson shows how Loyalist ideology, including their justification of discrimination against Catholics (where it is perceived at all), contains little notion of racial superiority or distinctiveness, either implicitly or explicitly. Instead it is largely understood by its own supporters in terms of a strictly applied liberal constitutionalism. Scott is at pains to show how most members of the National Front in 'Fettlerbridge' joined almost by chance and for reasons that had far more to do with private frustrations and domestic crises than with any worked out personal political position. Members who possessed some kind of coherent racialist ideology did so after rather than before joining the National Front, and then only in the unusual and unpredictable circumstance of remaining a member for some time. King and Wood adopt a very different approach in their attempts to locate the social and ideological sources of 'Powellism.' But their re-analysis of national poll data leads to similar conclusions to those reached by Scott. Powellites could be characterised as beither socially unrepresentative nor ideologically coherent.

Finally, Jowell and Airey discuss the practical problems of undertaking survey research on race relations, based on their extensive experience in this area at Social and Community Planning Research. They show that there are commonsense as well as practical aids for dealing with many of the problems peculiar to sampling and interviewing racial minorities in Britain and to asking either white or coloured respondents about racial prejudice and discrimination. There are few solutions that are entirely satisfactory but at least the likelihood of major error can be substantially reduced. They show that rigorous empirical research on the political sociology of race relations in Britain is possible. This *Yearbook* will, it is hoped, encourage more of it to be done.

Ivor Crewe

THEORETICAL PERSPECTIVES

1. THE THEME OF RACE IN BRITISH SOCIAL AND POLITICAL RESEARCH

Alan Brier and Barrie Axford

This paper is concerned with the theoretical problems for political sociology which are raised by relationships between racial minorities in Britain and the formal political institutions, in the sense that these are conventionally understood in political science. It is not concerned with the definition of race as a sociological category, but makes use of an intentionally loose working conception which is available in the growing literature of race relations in this country.[1] The use of the term race does, however, have the intention, in what follows, of restricting the area of discussion by its implied rejection of analyses based upon minority situations, or immigration, as independent explanations.

For sociologists of race relations, the area presents both a serious problem and a closely related metaproblem. A problem exists in the sense conveyed by John Rex that '. . . race relations challenges the consciences of sociologists in a way that probably no other problem does,'[2] and a metaproblem exists in terms of prolonged debate about the ability of existing sociological categories to explain race relations in colonial, 'Third World' and metropolitan societies. Although few scholars may have found themselves in a dilemma quite so traumatic as Robert Blauner, who felt as though he was 'balancing on a tightrope between sociological analysis that deals with the complexity of social reality and a radical commitment that speaks to the necessity of changing those relations,'[3] there is little doubt that questions about the normative stance and scholastic role adopted by researchers reflect increasing concern with the nature and purpose of academic inquiry into race relations.

Whereas debate about the role of the (white) scholar has prompted a certain amount of genuine soul searching,[4] little progress has been made with the problem of theoretical adequacy. As Sheila Allen has pointed out, the burden of research has either been excessively atheoretical and individualistic with an 'emphasis on attitudes and the dynamics of prejudice,' or posited at a theoretical and macrostructural level in which 'race or colour as a factor in political and economic relations'[5] is ignored. Overall, the field of sociological research into race relations seems to be peopled by a body of uneasy confrères, some of whom are concerned with immediate practical problems — e.g. the identification of prejudice and its elimination by means of liberal education and good community relations; and others who present a range of theoretical alternatives covering the ground from economic determinism to what Rex calls 'crude empiricist phenomenology,'[6] and taking in that author's own appeal for a 'truly political economy' which comprehends the dynamics of imperialism and colonial exploitation. That sociologists of race are deeply divided as to the nature and value of their work is apparent, as is the extremely unsatisfactory state of theorising about race relations, but at the risk of attributing agreement where little exists, it does appear that all approaches are informed by one basic similarity — they all acknowledge that race relations need to be explained as an important and sensitive area of social relations.

The same is not true in British political science. For the most part, the treatment of race in accounts of British government and politics is conspicuous not so much by its absence — for a number of studies in the last decade have documented, if in a rather cursory manner, the fact that immigration and race relations constitute an 'issue of high potential'[7] — as by a predilection to deal with the subject only insofar as study of it serves to highlight the working of some institution of government and the policy process,[8] or where it intrudes upon the (until recently) neat map of electoral politics.

In this latter realm the focus of inquiry has been on the impact of black populations on white electoral behaviour and upon the effects of the electoral mobilisation of black voters. By and large, descriptive case studies and inferences drawn from survey analysis or aggregate data come to the same conclusion, most recently reiterated by Richard Rose, that 'while race relations present substantial political problems in Britain, these problems are not yet electoral, because of the overwhelming preponderance of the white population.'[9]

Of course the disruptive potential of New Commonwealth Immigration (a euphemism derived from the Census) has never been doubted. Butler and Stokes report that among their sample in 1964 and 1966 more than half felt 'very strongly' about immigration, and a further third felt 'fairly strongly.'[10] A more recent study on public opinion and colour issues demonstrates yet again the enduring hostility of white Britons to black immigration.

'A majority of the public has been consistently hostile to further immigration and a somewhat smaller majority has consistently favoured the repatriation of at least some of the coloured immigrants already in Britain.'[11]

Despite such evidence the issue has failed to make a long term and widespread impact on the party balance. The effects of electoral participation by black voters, however, are still subject to vague and tentative assertions. Writing about the 1970 General Election, Deakin and Bourne indicate that the swing towards the Conservatives slowed up considerably in areas of substantial immigrant settlement,[12] reinforcing the widely held belief that New Commonwealth voters are usually to be found supporting the Labour Party. They also note that 'what is striking about the participation of minorities is that it took place in wholly

3

orthodox style. The effect of the votes which were cast was to add one variation to the existing pattern, not to create a new aberration from it,'[13] thereby suggesting a tendency towards absorption into 'formal' British politics which may not accord with actual realities. In fact one of the few hard facts to emerge from discussions about the electoral effect of black participation is that black candidates seem to produce an adverse reaction in the white electorate even when they stand on a major party platform and urge fellow immigrants to vote for the party and not the (black) candidate.[14]

Thus, in accounts detailing the complexities of electoral politics in Britain race is generally acknowledged to produce only a marginal effect. In much the same way students of local politics, particularly those given to producing tracts in the 'community studies' genre, have failed to treat with questions of race relations in any but the most cursory manner.[15] Yet even those infrequent studies which actually set out to talk about 'race *and* local politics' rarely offer profound insights into the dynamics of race relations in local settings.

In sum, the virtual non-appearance in electoral politics, the limited political mobilisation of black people and the low level of racial conflict in local communities has been explained as a result of a fortuitous party political consensus to exclude race from interparty conflict; of the greater salience of other issues; of the good sense and liberal nature of the British people, or, alternatively, of their inability to distinguish between political party stances on immigration and race issues. The language and electoral registration difficulties experienced by black people have also been mentioned, as have the alien nature of the British political process and the dearth of leadership in the black community. It is typical of these explanations that they rarely question the 'unimportance' of race, which, although an 'issue of high potential' has had little political effect; and that they should attribute such factors as the limited use made of British political institutions by blacks, to shortcomings in the minority community. In an essay on the Sikh turban issue in Wolverhampton, David Beetham, following De Witt John, places the responsibility for the low involvement of blacks in the political institutions of the host community squarely on the shoulders of the black community leadership.[16] At no time does he suggest that the poor political integration of black minorities and the mode of the 'thematisation' (Habermas' term for the according of recognition and legitimation to a political issue) of race in formal politics may be due to causes arising in the political system itself.

It is not suggested that race does not impinge on formal politics at all, or that it is not thematised. Indeed, the very existence of an immigration issue and the response of successive governments to hostile public opinion, resulting in legal restrictions on New Commonwealth immigration, bear witness to its appearance in formal political debate. The party political consensus to ensure that racial conflict does not

4

invade the ritual of electoral competition is itself part of a unique thematisation of race, and so is the setting up of an elaborate framework of community relations organisations like the Community Relations Councils.

A Methodological Digression on the February 1974 General Election

There is, then, a somewhat paradoxical contrast between the literature of race relations, in which changing situations of conflict potential are frequently described, and studies of voting and elections in Britain, where if the question of race is mentioned at all, it is usually to stress its lack of visible relationship with measures of voting behaviour. It is possible that the explanation lies in the immigrant's fear of becoming politically prominent, as Michael Banton suggests[18] or perhaps in his indifference to the electoral process, and his unwillingness to make differential use of it. It is also surprising that there is apparently very little sign of electoral effects due to white reaction to the arrival and concentration of black immigrants in distinctive residential areas.[19]

When it is not confirming that immigration did not play a noticeable part in the campaign, and a rather lesser part than in 1970,[20] the Nuffield College study of the February 1974 election notes that apart from a continued reluctance by electors to support black candidates of any party 'immigration itself seems to have played little or no part in the results.'[21]

This conclusion is based, as usual, upon an examination of the swings in relevant constituencies, but in testing for effects which are likely to be numerically small, swing has serious disadvantages as a measure of behaviour, since it includes several sources of variation which cannot be controlled statistically.[22] Two other aggregate analyses of earlier elections have, however, identified significant partial correlations between concentrations of New Commonwealth Immigrants and aspects of voting, when controlling for the effects of class. P. Davies and K. Newton have established that turnout in Birmingham wards in local elections in the 1960s varied 'consistently . . . with the class, housing and age structure of electorates, and to a lesser but still significant extent with their percentage of coloured immigrants.[23] J.S. Rasmussen in relating a series of variables to the Labour share of the vote in constituencies in four 'regions,' obtained partial correlations with the percentage of New Commonwealth Immigrants, when class was held constant. He thus obtained a positive partial correlation in the South, and negative coefficients for the North, Central and Celtic Fringe regions. This is in fact the only such study to report significant residual effects of this kind.[24]

These two investigations have been distinguished because their results to some extent contradict the findings of the analysis of swings, by taking into account more information and by a simpler measure-

Table 1* Multiple Regression Equations with Turnout and Party Votes as Dependent Variables

Dependent Variable	Constant	Coefficients for Variables										Multiple Correlation
		1	2	3	4	5	6	7	8	9	10	
Turnout												
Coefficient	74.28	0.10	-0.07	0.06	0.07	0.07	-0.58	0.04	0.05	-0.17	-0.26	R = .66
t – value	7.72	0.60	0.67	0.21	4.24	1.33	6.04	2.10	1.63	3.49	1.18	
R^2 if variable deleted	-	.43	.43	.43	.39	.43	.36	.42	.42	.41	.43	
% Conservative												
Coefficient	-12.72	0.17	0.61	1.52	0.05	1.14	0.48	0.13	0.17	-0.13	0.53	R = .71
t – value	0.57	0.44	2.60	2.48	1.31	9.83	2.18	2.61	2.27	1.10	1.04	
R^2 if variable deleted	-	.51	.50	.50	.50	.36	.50	.50	.50	.50	.50	
% Labour												
Coefficient	101.29	-0.10	-1.25	-0.74	-0.05	-1.57	0.39	-0.18	-0.84	0.29	-1.52	R = .84
t – value	3.93	0.23	4.64	1.05	1.15	11.72	1.53	3.16	9.94	2.19	2.57	
R^2 if variable deleted	-	.71	.69	.71	.71	.59	.71	.71	.62	.70	.70	
Liberal												
Coefficient	-82.38	1.22	1.02	0.97	0.20	0.59	-0.54	0.11	0.33	-0.05	1.20	R = .61
t – value	2.93	2.51	3.47	1.26	4.04	4.03	1.92	1.79	3.59	0.37	1.86	
R^2 if variable deleted	-	.36	.35	.37	.34	.34	.37	.37	.35	.37	.37	

* See footnote to Table 2.

Table 2*   Multiple Regression Equations with Logarithmic Transformation of Variable 10 (% New Commonwealth Immigrants)

Dependent Variable	Constant	Coefficients for Variables										Multiple Correlation
		1	2	3	4	5	6	7	8	9	10	
Turnout												
Coefficient	75.70	0.07	-0.05	0.07	0.07	0.06	-0.56	0.04	0.05	-0.23	0.10	R = .65
t – value	7.67	0.42	0.48	0.26	4.25	1.13	5.89	1.79	0.54	6.96	0.43	
R² if variable deleted	-	.43	.43	.43	.40	.43	.37	.42	.42	.34	.43	
% Conservative												
Coefficient	13.14	-0.14	0.47	1.17	0.05	0.95	-0.43	0.09	0.20	-0.24	2.86	R = .74
t – value	0.60	0.37	2.14	1.99	1.40	8.13	2.01	1.94	2.82	3.31	5.55	
R² if variable deleted	-	.55	.54	.54	.54	.46	.54	.54	.54	.53	.51	
% Labour												
Coefficient	71.37	0.22	-1.01	-0.25	-0.05	-1.34	0.37	-0.14	-0.89	0.27	-3.48	R = .85
t – value	2.81	0.50	3.95	0.36	1.22	9.90	1.48	2.77	10.98	3.17	5.83	
R² if variable deleted	-	.73	.72	.73	.73	.65	.73	.72	.63	.72	.70	
% Liberal												
Coefficient	-60.82	1.00	0.83	0.61	0.20	0.42	-0.52	0.09	0.37	-0.02	2.53	R = .63
t – value	2.15	2.66	2.94	0.79	4.11	2.79	1.91	1.52	4.07	0.21	3.80	
R² if variable deleted	-	.39	.38	.39	.36	.38	.39	.39	.36	.39	.37	

*   Note to Tables 1 and 2

The variables are numbered as follows in these Tables:

1	% Males	2 % Aged 65 +	3 % Aged 15-19	4 % Owner occupation	5 % SEGs 1, 2, 3, 4, 13
6	% SEG 11	7 % in Manufacturing	8 % in Agriculture	9 % shared occupation of housing	10 % New Commonwealth origin

ment of voting behaviour. They do not suggest interpretations of their findings, beyond a need for further investigation. Each investigation also made use of multiple regression methods, although the results have mostly been expressed in terms of partial correlation. To continue this method of investigation a confirmatory study has been attempted of some of the results from the General Election of February 1974. The illustrative findings to be discussed are in themselves highly tentative and preliminary, but will serve to demonstrate the difficulty of reliance upon null-hypothesis testing only as a means of advancing an argument.

Clearly, aggregate data analysis cannot differentiate between some of the suggested explanations of individual motivations in relating race to voting, but it can deal with hypotheses at a constituency level. As such, it seems appropriate to an investigation of overall electoral effects or 'backlash' behaviour, but is unable to estimate the voting behaviour of the immigrant communities themselves.

Drawing upon previous experience in constructing efficient statistical predictions of party votes using social-structural variables, the following indicators of class, age and housing structures were employed.

(1) The percentage of males in the population;

(2) The percentage of the population aged sixty-five and over;

(3) The percentage of the population aged fifteen to nineteen years;

(4) The percentage of household tenures which were owner-occupied;

(5) The percentage of households in shared dwellings;

(6) The Registrar General's socioeconomic groups 1, 2, 3, 4 and 13, expressed as a percentage of economically active males, as an indicator of middle class occupations. These groups consist of professional workers, employers and managers;

(7) Socioeconomic group 11, unskilled manual workers expressed as a percentage of economically active males;

(8) The percentage of those in employment in manufacturing, construction, gas, electricity and other industries;

(9) The percentage employed in agriculture.

The source in each case was the *Census 1966: United Kingdom General and Parliamentary Constituency Tables*,[25] and the results calculated in time for this publication use the values only for those constituencies which were more than 90 per cent unchanged by the redistribution of boundaries.

The 1966 Census constituency tables also contain the means of calculating the percentage of the population of New Commonwealth origin, which was taken as an indicator of areas of concentrations of coloured immigrants.

The results of multiple regression of the various parties' shares of the constituency vote and of the percentage turnout on these ten variables are shown in Table 1.

In these models the conclusion, indicated by testing the null-hypotheses that there is no partial relationship between the prediction which we are interested in and these dependent variables, is that except in the equation for the Labour vote, the percentage of New Commonwealth Immigrants does not have a significant independent effect. As has been noted in other studies, it is the Labour vote which is most conveniently predicted from a regression equation using variables of this kind, and it is apparent that the contribution of the immigrant variable, while attaining a reasonable level of statistical significance, is a small one when compared with variables relating to socioeconomic structure. A better model of turnout is obtainable (for which R = .657) if the Liberal share of the vote is included among the predictors, and in this case only three additional variables, % SEG 11, % owner-occupied households and % shared households, are needed. The most difficult variable to predict from the present set of variables is, not surprisingly, the Liberal vote.

The percentage of the population who are immigrants of New Commonwealth origin is a highly skewed variable, however, so that linear regression using simple percentages will be considerably influenced by extreme values. In fact, over 50 per cent of caluclated values for individual constituencies were less than 1 per cent and only 18 observations were greater than 3 per cent. Examination of the simple relationships between this variable and the four dependent variables considered in Table 1 yielded the following regression equations:

Turnout	=	$80.40 - 0.89$	% NCO	(N = 345	r = $-.32$)
% Conservative	=	$36.85 + 0.44$	% NCO	(N = 345	r = $+.06$)
% Labour	=	$38.76 - 0.32$	% NCO	(N = 345	r = $-.03$)
% Liberal	=	$24.10 - 0.43$	% NC)	(N = 279	r = $-.09$)

Whereas the equations obtainable by excluding from consideration all values for the precentage of New Commonwealth origin less than 1.0 were:

Turnout	=	$82.23 - 1.31$	% NCO	(N = 104	r = $-.57$)
% Conservative	=	$43.22 - 1.16$	% NCO	(N = 104	r = $-.31$)
% Labour	=	$30.96 + 1.66$	% NCO	(N = 104	r = $+.29$)
% Liberal	=	$26.54 - 1.01$	% NCO	(N = 102	r = $-.32$)

The situation is complicated by the known measurement and other errors involved in the 1966 10 per cent Sample Census, and one should suspect heterogeneity in the data, perhaps of the regional kind suggested by Rasmussen, as well as non-linearity in these relationships. The former has not yet been investigated, but the latter is incorporated into the results shown in Table 2, in which a logarithmic transformation has been made of the racial composition variable, so that the model is now log-linear in this variable. The contrasts between the two attempts at multiple regression analysis immediately raise questions of interpretation. The partial effect of the concentration of coloured immigrants is now indicated as statistically significant in each of the

9

prediction equations for party shares of the vote, although in the case
of turnout the effect remains insignificant. Also, the coefficients for
the Conservative and Liberal vote equations are positive and that for
the Labour vote is negative. The marginal effect indicated is still
relatively a small one, but the overall fit of the model is clearly improved by the logarithmic transformation of the immigrant variable.

The form of non-linearity suggested by the improved fit of the log-
linear model is one in which the higher values of the racial indicator are
associated with a diminishing marginal effect on the party votes. It is
tempting to interpret this as a modified backlash effect, since the
effect is to increase Conservative and Liberal shares of the vote in these
areas. But the bivariate regressions for concentrations of 1 per cent or
more suggest the transformation employed now overestimates the non-
Labour vote and underestimates the Labour share in areas with the
highest immigrant concentration. It is now constituencies corresponding to the middle of the transformed distribution which are better
estimated than by the equations in Table 1.

The problems associated with an unguided search for statistical
significance are now clear to see. There is no way, except by statistical
fit, of deciding which of the contradictory conclusions indicated above
is to be preferred. Without an adequate theoretical basis, it is impossible
to use multiple regression or allied techniques to distinguish chance
findings from genuine significance, when large numbers of variables are
considered together.[26] It is not possible either to dispose of the question of assication between race and voting simply in terms of linear
additive models.

The results discussed are highly provisional, and may be invalidated
on further investigation on at least four grounds. They may reflect a
bias in the set of constituencies considered, which has been generated
on grounds of convenience and availability of data, or they may be
subject to systematic measurement error in the 10 per cent Sample
Census. Further, lack of homogeneity may be suspected in the data but
the problem remains of finding an adequate rationale for subdivisions.
Finally the relationships observed may be attributable to some other
unconsidered source. But they do serve to illustrate the disutility of
'data-dredging' approaches to the problem. What is needed is a more
rigorous form of hypothesis.

Explanations of Elite Consensus

It was argued earlier that the surprising feature of the appearance of
race in formal politics in Britain was that its unique mode of thematisation should have passed almost entirely unremarked. *Almost* entirely,
because, in fact, a number of commentators have remarked on the
establishment of the 'elite consensus' to remove the issue from political
debate by instituting what amounts to a dual policy of immigration

control and community relations. Hannan Rose, writing about the 1971 Commonwealth Immigration Act, speculated on the wave of increasingly restrictive laws passed during the 1960s, and concluded that 'perhaps the parties were trying to neutralise the issue and remove it from political concern by establishing the question of immigration as one that had been solved,'[27] but he does not consider the motivations behind the community relations policy. It is left to Ira Katznelson to undertake a critical study of the response of the political system to the demands of black groups within it. He too identifies the existence of a 'consensus to exclude' race from politics and sees it as the basis for a policy whereby the black population 'is indirectly linked to the policy through quasi-colonial buffer institutions.'[28] Katznelson explains the need for such a policy in terms of the system's need to maintain legitimacy. In his scenario, buffering institutions like the CRC and the Race Relations Board are instruments of social control designed to depoliticise race and ensure that New Commonwealth Immigrants remain a marginal group politically and socially isolated from the rest of the population. However, while such an approach represents a considerable advance on previous attempts to deal with the politics of race, it is incomplete. Katznelson does not discuss the reasons for the particular form of indirect linkages that he identifies, he merely emphasises that they serve to isolate (and alienate) the black population. This is not sufficient. Why, after all, should political élites seek to remove race from the political arena, with the professed intention of defusing potentially conflictual situations, and at the same time set up buffer institutions which, if Katznelson and others are correct, function in such a way as to frustrate black demands and drive them to form political organisations outside the ambit of 'normal' politics?

As Philip Mason, a former director of the Institute of Race Relations, objects, 'the government of the day, the Civil Service and Parliament . . . [has been found] frequently insensitive, often complacent and pompous, often reluctant to make any change, sometimes legally pedantic, but never cynically determined on this kind of policy. On the contrary . . . it has always been taken for granted . . . that it was against the interests of this country that there should be a section of society which is easily identified, which is discriminated against and which is alienated from government and from the majority.'[29]

It may also be considered strange that a desire to avoid a race-polarised politics should be coupled with indirect incorporation when more usual mechanisms of linking individuals and groups to the policy — vote maximising political parties, the myriad groups of the pluralistic universe and the electoral system itself — are available for use. An unwillingness to countenance the conflicts of interest in race relations and immigration as political questions provides one answer to this point, for party and parliamentary leaders must surely have taken into account the likelihood of great passion being generated should political parties attempt to maximise the immigration issue for their own electoral ends. Likewise specific attempts to recruit black voters and activists would doubtless affect a party's support among sections of the white electorate. Another response might be framed in terms of the 'strangeness' of the British political system to black people, which necessitates the most sophisticated and humane approach to incorporation vested in the community relations strategy. In this way, it is held, the sensibilities of immigrant and host communities are not violated and integration proceeds peacefully. Such explanations are plausible but they remain unconvincing. To restate the arguement: it is held that there exists an élite consensus to exclude racial questions from formal politics, with the intention of promoting racial peace and good community relations. The 'political' expression of this consensus has been a dual policy of, on the one hand, increasingly restrictive immigration policies, meant to appease the white electorate; and on the other hand, the establishment of bodies designed to counter prejudice and facilitate host-immigrant links over a wide area. As a result, black people will be gradually incorporated into the society and polity and racial harmony will be preserved.

There are however some discordant notes to be struck. Immigration control is aimed at greatly inhibiting the numbers of New Commonwealth Immigrants entering Britain. In achieving this unequivocal objective it has been very successful. The aims of the community relations policy are rather more equivocal, though still clear enough for the goals of assimilation and integration of immigrants into British society and policy to be discernible. It is with regard to these aims that certain caveats must be introduced. Although it may be acknowledged that to expect total racial assimilation in Britain would be to expect a kind of social mobility and absorption which is not commonly found in an advanced society characterised by class divisions,[30] the absence of wide-scale assimilation is perhaps odd in view of the pious intentions expressed by leaders of statutory bodies in the Community relations field.[31]

Nor can this lack of assimilation be attributed to a rejection of British culture and institutions by black people. A host of publications have made it clear that for the vast majority of West Indian immigrants – who after all have been greatly 'Anglicised' in their cultural practices – Britain represented, not a strange and alien new world, but the mother country and the 'New Jerusalem.'[32]

The tendency to adopt an assimilationist outlook was strong among such people, and even in the United States, where a militant 'black identity' movement has sharply challenged long held assumptions about race relations, 'until recently blacks remained, with notable exceptions, firm supporters of the assimilationist tradition.'[33]

Equally, the notion that the low levels of assimilation can be blamed solely on the race prejudice of the white population is open to doubt.

It is true that widespread prejudice exists, and its nature, extent and consequences have been well documented.[34] However, at least in the narrow political realm with which this paper is concerned it is not demonstrated that antipathetic attitudes are necessarily translated into prejudiced behaviour,[35] and the existence of hostile attitudes alone is insufficient to explain such factors as low black participation in politics and the virtual non-appearance of the race issue. Conversely, it is useless to advance the thesis that race is not politicised because of the colour-blind response of white Britons. There is considerable evidence to suggest that ambivalence characterises the feelings of many white Britons towards black people.[36]

This ambivalence is not being resolved in favour of more tolerant attitudes by the activities of the community relations committees and other voluntary bodies. If the tension apparent in white attitudes, and sometimes in white behaviour does indicate the potential for race-polarised politicis in Britain, why is it that the community relations machinery has dealt with it only in peripheral ways? Thus the CRC's promotion of 'forceful integration,' as Dilip Hiro points out, means simply 'organising inter-racial dances, international exhibitions of food and dress and the like' which often attract only 'non-representative members of different races.'[37]

As to assimilation into the formal politics of Britain, it seems likely that such absorption as has taken place[38] would have occurred even in the absence of community relations policies and structures. Although Nicholas Deakin and Jenny Bourne state that 'There is no reason in principle why immigrant participation should not come to be accepted as legitimate, as it has been in the case of the Irish,'[39] the fact is that neither the actions of the major political parties – which refuse to treat with race as a legitimate conflict area, or with black people as potential voters and activists – or the workings of the community relations structures seem likely to enhance the prospect of participation based on absorption. Indeed, the very likelihood of direct participation by blacks is excluded by the ethics of the community relations structure. It is with regard to this fact that most accusations have been made. In 1968, Michael Dummett attacked the NCCI[40] and its local committees for diverting the activities of immigrants into non-political directions to prevent the development of an effective protest movement.[41] More recently Ira Katznelson has pressed the same attack against the Community Relations Commission and its local formations.[42] If the broad assimilation of black people into politics is stymied by the community relations structure, so too is the expression of a political pluralism based on racial group demands and identity. Thus not only the politics of assimilation by means of more usual mechanisms of incorporation, but also the legitimate politics of racial pluralism are inhibited by the present mode of incorporation. The result may be the emergence of a politics based on some form of black

13

identity which rejects the institutionalised consensus and intrudes on formal politics in ways likely to deepen the tension and ambivalence already remarked upon.

To the volume of criticism against the community relations policy and structures it might be objected that they have had insufficient time to effect a radical change in race relations. However, there is no way in which this can be argued for or against, except by polemic. Similarly, any argument which attempts to explain the virtual non-appearance of race as an issue in British politics by reference to the time factor ignores not only the changing and increasingly complex dimensions of the situation, for example those concerned with the so-called Second Generation Immigrants, or more accurately 'Black British,'[43] but also the increasingly alarmed tone of comment about the state of race relations and the potential for conflict which it displays. The prognosis might be for a race-polarised politics, the development of a politics based on assimilation,[44] and the expression of racial demands in a politics based on cultural pluralism. None of these is unequivocally realised at present.

The point of the review of evidence so far is to establish a minimal level of agreement over the existence in Britain of a consensus, at least at elite level, over the substance of the proper relationship between race and formalised politics. An attempt has been made to show that other available critical analyses of this situation in the form of theories of the institutionalisation of racism, or of élite conspiracy, point to the existence of such a consensus, but do little to examine or explain its content. This is not an unfamiliar state of affairs in current social theory, in which partial or otherwise mystifying formulations have the effect of diverting attention towards inessentials, nor is it intended to imply that the theory of race and politics presents an especially good example of such theoretical inversion. But, to reiterate, the major difficulty lies in finding an explanation of both the existence and the content of this consensus, which is by no means confined to practising professional politicians or civil servants, but has its counterpart and extension in current work on race relations.

The essential character of this consensus is, as Chris Mullard[45] forcefully argues, that of a systematic separation of 'issues' while retaining an apparently radical analytical rubric of 'the race problem.' Consciously or (as is more usually the case) unconsciously, the designation of the problem area of 'race relations' as an area for legislation and administrative action, can serve to present a partial view of the nature of the social situation which obscures essential characteristics as much as it renders possible the recognition of authentic problems and relationships. Under such a rubric, issues for solution are likely to be subjects for short-range amelioration, which may often prove to be exacerbated instead. Mullard argues the point polemically to point up the contrast between official tolerance and experienced discrimination by the black community in Britain, and the ambiguous role of the established machinery for conciliation. The experience of many of those concerned with institutions of mediation seems to have been that they have become instead a focus for the exposure and expression of what is often simply destructive conflict and frustrations. The treatment of race relations in Britain *is* 'of a piece,' but it consists of a series of attempts to separate what are really inseparable phenomena. Characteristic examples of the style are the White Paper of August 1965, which attempted to separate the issues of reducing the rate of 'coloured' immigration and the problem of improving relations between the existing immigrant and host communities, and the Commonwealth Immigrants Act of 1968. It became apparent in the latter case that arguments about the potential buffering role of Asians of East African origin, arising from their economic skills and familiarity with European culture and the English language, did little to reduce the fears of a government concerned with the reduction of citizenship rights bestowed in the immediate post-colonial period.[46]

For some writers who wish to sustain the subject area of race relations the characteristic separation of related issues is part of an articulated analytical position. Thus, the immigrant-host distinction which was proposed early in the study of race relations in Britain, suggested as a focus the problems of migration and cultural assimilation, but in a way which would be most likely to identify as problems, factors specific to the particular groups being studied. It would then be necessary to differentiate clearly not only between black and white, in the style of much romantic polemic, but also between many variants of cultural divergence, corresponding to a variety of ethnic minorities. The well-known critique of this mode of analysis, in the Sparkbrook study,[47] while serving to identify instead communities of interest between all racial groups when caught in the traps of poverty and inadequate housing, still tends to focus on a too specific and localised perspective, and has even, in its way, contributed a kind of analytical basis for the formulation of limited goals for amelioration of neighbourhoods.

The effect of the powerful prevailing consensus is, however, to divert attention from the somewhat obvious economic basis for the process of immigration, in the labour requirements of British industry. A. Sivanandan's brief analysis provides a starting point for discussion of an alternative mode of explanation, but seems to present too simplistic and deterministic a view to avoid the difficulty of much writing of this character, of appearing to be rapidly overtaken by events. In his view, Britain, unlike Germany or South Africa, has proved unable to satisfy the requirements of a capitalistic economy, conceived as increasingly in the hands of monopoly capital, for a 'buffer' of easily disposable labour which can be conveniently employed in times of growth and disposed of in recessions. The South African system is formulated upon

15

a holistic philosophy in which there is no contradiction between the ideology of exploitation and the ideology of discrimination, while the *gastarbeite* system in West Germany entertains within a liberal democratic ethos, a kind of contract labour which does not entail citizenship rights. Britain, by contrast:

> '. . . the history of post-war race relations . . . is the history of second-class production factors. At first impoverished by war and forced to resort to labour-intensive modes of production, Britain turned to her colonies to provide the manpower she required . . . If they had to be afforded citizenship, it was a small price to pay. She was after all, the Mother Country and it behoved her to do no less. . . . By the end of the fifties, however, the haze of empire had receded, the boom was well-nigh over, and the economy was turning away from labour-intensive production — and Notting Hill had happened. The system of *laissez-faire* discrimination, which had hitherto helped to regulate the inflow of cheap labour, was no longer adequate. And the social problems created by an increasingly racialist society were laid at the door of "the alien wedge" . . . If "they" could not be sent back, "they" must at least be kept out; the State would take a hand. Hence the Commonwealth Immigration Act of 1962 which, in addition to stemming "the immigrant tide" also inaugurated the era of institutional racism. Racial exploitation may continue in the hands of free market forces, but the State had given its imprimatur.'[48]

This argument represents an important blend in the analysis of a developing institutionalised racism and a suggested explanation of this development. Unfortunately, it is not clear how far the argument might be held to be falsified by renewed interest in migrant workers' rights in Germany, by apparently radical changes in the holistic ideology of apartheid, or on a more specific level by further legislation to extend the definition of discrimination in Britain in order to take account of the recent judicial ruling permitting a working mens' club to ban a black snooker player from membership. More important, it is not clear whether Sivanandan regards the racial character of the 'second-class production factors' as accidental or necessary to the process described.

However, his discussion does identify in addition the key role of the 'liberal democratic ethos,' which we have earlier termed the content of the elite consensus on British race relations. The ideology of racism, he argues, serves to conceal the interests of monopoly capitalism until it is itself revealed as a symptom of the deeper malaise, the inability of monopoly capitalism to be accommodated within the liberal ethos. Institutional liberalism is, in effect, the remaining, although characteristic, bulwark against thoroughgoing repression in the form of repatriation and withdrawal of rights. For the time being, however, repatriation and other drastic 'solutions' are repudiated not only on the pragmatic grounds

16

that history cannot be unmade, and no other country of origin can in many cases be found prepared to accept rejected migrants, but also because they offend the concerns of official liberalism.

Further, this formulation, while establishing that the problem is not to be traced to metaphysical tensions between performance and prescription, still in reality re-poses the question asked earlier, and does not do more than hint at possible answers. Why should the historical tradition take this particular form in Britain, and not some other? Part of the argument is admittedly that institutional liberalism is fighting a losing battle against growing racism embodied in legislation, and in the behaviour of immigration officers, police and the judiciary. From this an interpretation of the origin of institutionalised attitudes can at least be inferred. However to this extent the analysis proposed seems unduly deterministic and unidirectional. Taking a broader perspective, it is not obvious that thoroughgoing repression is improbable or infeasible in a developed complex industrial society, in the same way that military repression seems to be as sustainable as the universal bogey of socialism and liberalism alike, fascist dictatorship.[49] Without becoming committed to an interpretation of these forms of behaviour as regression or retreat into the irrational, it is easy to concede that liberalism in various manifestations has a poor defensive record against them. The comparison may be legitimately raised since it is introduced in Sivanandan's own argument. It does, nevertheless, do less than justice to the complexities of the situation revealed by the still very limited amount of basic research carried out, for example, by those social scientists who have been concerned with the dimensions and extent of racial prejudice in Britain.

In this research, as has been noted earlier, the methodological controversies seem in general to suggest a situation of structured ambivalence on the part of most white Britons towards the other races.

An Alternative Perspective — Habermas on System Crises

To introduce at this point a different theoretical analogy, it does seem that a useful terminology can be derived instead from recent works by Jurgen Habermas, formerly of the University of Frankfurt, addressing himself to the character of crises under 'late capitalism.' Some explanation of the context of the argument is required, but in what follows the notion to be extracted for further use is that of the existence of contradictions which for various reasons cannot be thematised because for them to be so would undermine the operating assumptions of late capitalism. Habermas has, in effect, been concerned with a theory of crisis management, or the possibility of postponement of different types of crisis, in a way which can best be understood as an application of the kind of general programme of philosophical investigation established in *Knowledge and Human Interests*.[50]

A recent summary of the relevant ideas in English[51] begins from

Marx's conception of economic crisis as a crisis-ridden process of economic growth, and raises the question whether late capitalism follows the same pattern of development as classical, competitive, capitalism or whether the crisis tendencies inherent in an earlier period are no longer a threat to the continuation of the system. Following a formulation by Offe, Habermas[52] analyses the structural features of late capitalism, the stage of capitalism in which oligopolistic market structures and an interventionist state reduce the pre-eminence of the market as a steering mechanism and fill the increasing functional gaps in the market, in terms of three systems. The economic system is increasingly dominated by the monopolistic and public sectors, which display rapid progress in production. The political/administrative system attempts to regulate the overall economic cycle by a series of crisis avoidance strategies, determined by a 'didactically demanded compromise between competing imperatives, steady growth, stability of money value, full employment and balance of trade.'[53] The legitimation system, representing an aspect of what Habermas elsewhere terms the sociocultural system, is affected by the collapse of the 'basic bourgeois ideology of fair exchange' and is required to legitimate a government apparatus which increasingly intervenes on its own initiative in the production process. The universality of civil rights and suffrage obtained by the earlier universalistic bourgeois ideology presents a problem of legitimation independently of general elections which is resolved through formal democracy. To prevent the thematisation of the inevitable conflict between administratively socialised production and a still private form of acquiring the produced values, a legitimation process is required that elicits mass loyalty without encouraging mass participation. At the same time class conflict is kept latent in its essential areas by the 'immunisation' of the original conflict zones in the economic system. To each of these systems there corresponds a crisis mode, which may occur at the level of the system itself, in the style of the classic economic crisis of Marxist theory, and appears as a crisis of individual subjectivity. Habermas appears to consider some crises as capable of temporary, or even indefinite solution in an almost hierarchical way. The capability in late capitalism of regulating economic crises, with a resultant tendency to class compromise, leads on to a crisis of rationality or efficiency in the political/administrative system, as it struggles with the problems of preventing economic crisis from disturbing growth. The result may be a deficit of legitimation in which the scope for manipulation is narrowly delimited, while the cultural system remains resistant to administrative control. The state may attempt to make the administrative system independent of the formation of legitimising will, but is limited by the degree of structural dissimilarity between administration and cultural tradition. From this point of view, the reason why late capitalist societies bother to retain formal democracy is that purely administrative variants in the form of a conservative authoritarian welfare state or a fascist system of permanent mobilisation are less compatible with the demands of the sociocultural system than a party state based on mass democracy. The thesis is then advanced that only if the sociocultural system were incapable of being randomly functionalised to support the administrative system would difficulties in legitimation reach crisis proportions, so that if a crisis in legitimation does occur, it must be founded on a crisis of individual motivation.[54]

Habermas' method of linking the sociocultural system with other systems with reference to their crisis potential rather than the normative stability, seems to provide a more useful general perspective from which to approach the specific problem of elite consensus over race relations. Equally his analysis of the achievement of motivation through civil and family/vocational privatism, is not by itself very dissimilar from less general analyses of class formations in British sociology, although its interpretation and context differ radically. Anthony Giddens, for example, insists upon the misleading character of technocratic theories of contemporary society, and of the right and propensity to strike as a 'focal element in maintaining the orientation to economism which allows for the persistence of the prevailing system of industrial authority, and more generally for the continuing separation of economy and polity which Marx rightly noted as a distinctive feature of capitalist society.'[55] The formulation of these problems is, of course, considerably more complex and problematic than this brief survey can suggest, but it does provide a more general basis for the understanding of the theory of race and politics.

Habermas' account of class compromise appears to suggest a greater degree of permanence than a British perspective would find acceptable, but it is clearly not regarded as an inevitable or guaranteed long term situation. Instead, it remains a means of proceeding from a Marxist problematic, as a starting point, to his particular concern with the reunification of philosophical enquiry. There appears to be no great difficulty in including the problem of attitudes to race within the general framework of techniques of crisis avoidance. While retaining Sivanandan's analysis of the functional nature of racism, it is possible to account for the ambivalence of white British attitudes in terms of a contradiction between an insistence, at least in the sociocultural system, on economic equality for all races, in the normal sense of job opportunities, and a failure to require a comparable general equality in housing or political power.[56] Thus, while not identical in content with the similar operation of consciousness of class compromise through specific industrial militancy and civil and family privatism, it is identifiable as a similar process. Also, a similar duality is certainly apparent in the treatment of migrant workers in Western Europe.

Conclusion

To restate our position directly, attitudes and behaviour in the politics of race in Britain often appear ambivalent and contradictory in character. Yet they are sufficiently regular and observable to be noticed by writers of radically different persuasions, and are even embodied in much formal analysis of the problem of race in this country. The contradictory character of attitudes gives rise to argument about the extent of racism, institutional or otherwise, in Britain, but need not do so since this feature in itself may be understood as functional for the attempted management of legitimation crises, in Habermas' sense. The attitudes noted serve to retain racial tension as a displacement mechanism but to keep its expression within manageable limits by particularising different aspects of the problem for separate treatment. We are claiming here a function of these characteristic British attitudes which is similar to that which is postulated in some research on the United States for 'buffering' institutions which mediate between black and white communities. Such institutions do not appear to have yet established themselves significantly in Britain, while the simple concept of buffering still appears too weak to account for the form and development of specific kinds of racism. The emphasis when the approach is is applied to Britain is upon sponsored bodies such as the Community Relations Commission and Community Relations Committees while in the United States such groups are perhaps only lately beginning to supplement more autonomous and spontaneous forms of institutions, but both are regarded as instruments of social control.[57]

There are several advantages to the mode of analysis suggested here. It provides, for those who wish to use it, a means of interpreting the activities and attitudes of researchers with the area of race relations, and additionally suggests that much of the polemic which characterises this group of specialists is remarkably idle, being based on an undialectical conception of the area of study.[58] In particular the dispute over the utility of the concepts of race and class in the context of studies of race relations may now appear unfruitful. The designation of problems as racial in character may serve in a sense to obscure their origin in the formation of under-classes, but it is not necessary to proceed to reduce one range of explanations entirely to the terms of the other. Equally, the argument from degrees of institutionalisation of particular racisms, fails to provide any means of integration with general sociological theory.

On the other hand, there is no need to resort, as Katznelson has done in possibly the only fully developed framework for the comparative analysis of the politics of race relations which has yet appeared, to a Weberian position in which, in an apparently content-free manner, cross national differences in the appearance of issues can be subsumed under a study of the differing overlaps and combinations of class, status and power.[59] There are admittedly difficulties in specifying content in Habermas' formulation, to which it does not seem an adequate response to leave the answer to empirical research or the unfolding of historical categories. However, such difficulties do appear to be of a different order from the need to reinforce other kinds of explanations by special historical pleading, as in the identification of a 'British sense of fair play' or the importation of *ad hoc* theories into the influential 'stranger' and role-typing hypotheses when additional difficulties arose.[60]

To confront, finally, a more serious objection to the analysis suggested here, the argument that there has been a kind of élite consensus in Britain which has the effect of minimising the appearance of the issue of race in formal politics may appear to be equivalent to using as a starting point for the establishment of an imminent contradiction the non-appearance of that contradiction.. It may be that we are perversely ignoring the institutionalisation of racism proposed in Sivanandan's perspective. The problem, however, remains that although it is possible to analyse the manifestations of racism at various levels in British politics, it still characteristically presents itself, or is presented, as something else. The mode of recognition of the problem is such as to attempt to immunise it as a conflict area, which is a process which seems best comprehensible in the general Habermasian framework. In this, the objective is eventually to identify the conditions of appearance, wholly or in part, of some crucial thematised contradictions.

NOTES

1.   However unsatisfactory, this terminology has already become the basis for an extensive literature. See for example S. Zubaida (ed.), *Race and Racialism*, Tavistock, London, 1970, especially papers by J. Rex and M. Banton; also M. Banton, *Race Relations*, Tavistock, London, 1967 and J. Rex, *Race, Colonialism and the City*, Routledge & Kegan Paul, London, 1973, especially Part III, Chs. 16 & 17.
2.   John Rex, 'The Concept of Race in Sociological Theory' in S. Zubaida, *op. cit.*, p. 35.
3.   Robert Blauner, *Racial Oppression in America*, Harper and Row, New York, 1972, p. viii.
4.   See for example Lee Bridges, 'Race Relations Research: From Colonialism to Neo-Colonialism? Some random Thoughts,' *Race*, vol. XIV, no. 3, 1973, pp. 331-41.
5.   Sheila Allen, 'Immigrants or Workers?' in Zubaida, *op. cit.*, p. 101.
6.   J. Rex, *Race, Colonialism and the City*, p. 194.
7.   D. Butler and D. Stokes, *Political Change in Britain*, Macmillan, London, 1969, pp. 349-54.
8.   Hannan Rose, 'The Immigration Act 1971: A Case Study in the Work of Parliament,' *Parliamentary Affairs*, Vol. 26, No. 1, 1972, pp. 69-91 emphasises the apparent muddle and lack of any clear policy direction.

9.   R. Rose, 'Britain: Simple Abstractions and Complex Realities' in R. Rose (ed.), *Electoral Behaviour: A Comparative Handbook*, The Free Press, New York, 1974, p. 523.

10.   *Loc. cit.*

11.   Donley T. Studlar, 'British Public Opinion, Colour Issues, and Enoch Powell: A Longitudinal Analysis,' *British Journal of Political Science*, Vol. 4, part 3, 1974, p. 378.

12.   N. Deakin and J. Bourne, 'Powell, the Minorities and the 1970 Election,' *Political Quarterly*, vol. 41, no. 4, p. 407. Nicholas Deakin's earlier work in this area is presented in *Colour and the British Electorate*, Pall Mall, London, 1965.

13.   Deakin and Bourne, p. 409.

14.   As for example in the case of Dr David Pitt in the Clapham constituency. An account of the campaign in Clapham can be found in Deakin and Bourne, pp. 410-13.

15.   For example, G.W. Jones' study of Wolverhampton borough politics makes little play with the problems of racial origin which were apparent in that locality during the 1960s. See *Borough Politics*, Macmillan, London 1969. M.J. Speirs and M. Le Lohé, 'Pakistanis in the Bradford Municipal Election of 1963,' *Political Studies*, vol. 12, 1964, discuss the appearance of independent candidates in relation to power struggles within the local Pakistani community.

16.   See De Witt John, *Indian Workers Associations in Britain*, Oxford University Press, London, 1969, and D. Beetham, *Transport and Turbans: A Comparative Study in Local Politics*, Oxford University Press, London, 1970, pp. 67-9.

17.   See J. Habermas, 'Legitimation Problems in Late Capitalism,' *Social Research*, vol. 14 (4), Winter 1963, p. 648.

18.   M. Banton, *Racial Minorities*, Fontana/Collins, London, 1972, pp. 175-6.

19.   See P. Davies and K. Newton, 'The Social Patterns of Immigrant Areas,' *Race*, vol. XIV, no. 1, 1972, pp. 43-57, and J. Doherty, 'The Distribution and Concentration of Immigrants in London,' *Race Today*, Dec., 1969. pp. 227-31.

20.   D. Butler and D. Kavanagh, *The British General Election of February 1974*, Macmillan, London, 1974, pp. 24, 60, 139-42. Cf. D. Butler and M. Pinto Duschinsky, *The British General Election of 1970*, Macmillan, London, 1971, pp. 341, 406-8. This points out additionally that Powellite candidates did not perform notably better than other Conservatives, in terms of swing.

21.   M. Steed in Butler and Kavanagh, p. 335.

22.   National uniformity of swings must logically imply non-uniformity of probabilities of transition between different component voter states, the estimation of which is subject to serious difficulties. Constituencies have to be assigned to categories which may or may not be justified by the required statistical homogeneity, in order that estimation may proceed. See W.L. Miller, 'Measures of Electoral Change using Aggregate Data,' *Journal of the Royal Statistical Society*, Series A, vol. 135, part 1, pp. 122-41.

23.   'An Aggregate Data Analysis of Turnout and Party Voting in Local Elections,' *Sociology*, vol. 8, no. 2, 1974, p. 228.

24.   'The Impact of Constituency Structural Characteristics upon Political Preferences in Britain,' *Comparative Politics*, vol. 6, no. 1, 1973, pp. 123-45. Significance values are not appropriate in the original, but an unexplained contrast between the partial correlation of Labour vote and immigrant percentage calculated separately for rural and urban constituencies gives rise to some doubts about the status of these findings, which may be due to nothing more than statistical ill-conditioning. For a critique of this paper, and a fresh analysis which finds no significant aggregate-level relationship between immigrant settlement and the vote, see Ivor Crewe and Clive Payne, 'An Ecological Regression Model of the Two-Party Vote Ratio in 1970,' in *British Journal of Political Science* (forthcoming).

25.   General Register Office, HMSO, London, 1969. The unchanged constituencies following the redistribution were indicated in material from the BBC Election Unit for the February 1974 election, and voting figures were taken from *The Times Guide to the House of Commons*, London, 1974.

26.   The larger the number of variables, the greater the probability that at least one coefficient will be found significant purely by chance in multiple regression. See, for example, R.J. and T.H. Wonnacott, *Econometrics*, Wiley, New York, 1970, p. 66. For the variables in the present study, stepwise multiple regression produced consistent results, but for presentation Tables 1 and 2 are based upon standard multiple regression technique.

27.   H. Rose, 'The Politics of Immigration After the 1971 Act,' *Political Quarterly*, vol. 44, no. 2, p. 184.

28.   Ira Katznelson, *Black Men, White Cities*, Oxford University Press/Institute of Race Relations, London, 1973, p. 145.

29.   P. Mason, *Race Relations*, Oxford University Press, London, 1970, p. 306, cited in M. Banton, *Racial Minorities*.

30.   For an elaboration of this point and the question of ethnic assimilation, see M. Parenti, 'Assimilation and Counter-Assimilation: From Civil Rights to Black Radicalism,' in P. Green and S. Levinson (eds.), *Power and Community*, Pantheon, New York, 1969.

31.   The Birmingham Community Relations Officer included in the central core of his committee's work: 'To be constantly in touch with significant opinion within the immigrant community, relating to their needs and wishes, in order to be able to interpret their needs to the community as a whole'; *and* 'To assist by all means possible the host community to think through the significance of the changes that have taken place in the "racial balance" of the city's population and to help the community to become sufficiently sensitive to these changes.' quoted in M. Hill and R. Issacharoff, *Community Action and Race Relations*, Oxford University Press/Institute of Race Relations, London, 1971, p. 169.

32.   See, for example, D. Hire, *Black British, White British*, Penguin Books, Harmondsworth, 1973, and the portraits included in D. Humphreys and G. John, *Because They're Black*, Penguin Books, Harmondsworth, 1971.

33.   Parenti, *op. cit.*, p. 181.

34.   A basic source, and one that made a considerable impact on first publication is W.W. Daniel, *Racial Discrimination in Britain*, Penguin, Harmondsworth, 1968.

35.   See J.W. Prothero and C.W. Grigg, 'Fundamental Principles of Democracy: Bases of Agreement and Disagreement,' *Journal of Politics*, vol. 22, 1960.

36.   See, for example, E.J.B. Rose and associates, *Colour and Citizenship: a report of British Race Relations*, Oxford University Press, London, 1969, pp. 551-604, and Christopher Bagley, *Social Structure and Prejudice in Five English Boroughs*, Institute of Race Relations, London, 1970. This ambivalence is also reflected in the attitudes of party leaders. See A. Weintraub, 'Race and Local Politics in England: A Case Study of Willesden,' paper presented at the American Political Science Association Conference, September 1973, a revised version of which appears in this *Yearbook*.

37.   D. Hiro, *op. cit.*, p. 233.

38.   In the 1970 General Election, Deakin and Bourne report of the wards in the London constituency of Paddington North that figures derived from a head count at polling stations suggest that 'in this area of high immigrant concentration a high proportion of black people voted.' *Op. cit.*, p. 408. In another paper, Deakin suggests also that 'local Labour parties began at the end of the fifties and into the early sixties to function . . . as a channel for the upward mobility of West Indian elites, and as a socializing instrument for a number of rank and file.' He further indicates that this trend has not been maintained. See N. Deakin, ' 'Ethnic Minorities in Urban Politics: Some Reflections on the British Case,' *New*

23

Atlantis, vol. 2, no. 1, 1970, p. 145. The number of black candidates either standing for major parties or minority platforms in elections remains small. In 1970, the number was seven. See 'Notes on the General Election,' *New Community*, vol. 3, no. 4.

39.   N. Deakin and J. Bourne, *op. cit.* p. 410.

40.   The National Committee for Commonwealth Immigrants, a body set up on 1 April 1964 to provide advice and information to the government, and also to foster the formation of local and regional organisations, now succeeded by the Community Relations Commission.

41.   M. Dummett, 'Immigrant Organisations,' background paper for a talk given at the *Third Annual Race Relations Conference*, Queen Elizabeth College, London, 19-20 September 1968.

42.   I. Katznelson, *op. cit.*

43.   See, for example, C. Mullard, *Black Britain*, Allen and Unwin, London, 1973, pp. 175-7.

44.   If the American experience is illustrative, the likelihood of assimilation is small. There, incorporation of urban blacks via more bureaucratised forms of linkage has resulted in what Katznelson calls an 'urban counter-revolution' with the assimilationist ideal increasingly discredited. See I. Katznelson, 'Urban Counterrevolution,' in R.P. Wolff (ed.), *1984 Revisited*, Knopf, New York, 1973.

45.   *Op. cit.*, pp. 89-116.

46.   These points are taken from A. Sivanandan, 'Race, Class and Power,' *Race*, vol. XIV, no. 4, 1973, pp. 389-90.

47.   John Rex and Robert Moore, *Race, Community and Conflict: a study of Sparkbrook*, Oxford University Press for the Institute of Race Relations, 1967.

48.   *Loc. cit.* Author's quotation marks. The argument is pointed up by accounts of the periods of immigration, e.g. C. Peach, *West Indian Migration to Britain: a social geography*. Oxford University Press for the Institute of Race Relations, London, 1968, which emphasises the fall-off when employment prospects in Britain declined.

49.   Cf. Erich Fromm, *The Fear of Freedom*, Routledge and Kegan Paul, London, 1942; and the discussion of 'herrenvolk democracy' in P.L. van den Berghe, *Race and Racism: a comparative perspective*, Wiley, New York, 1967, p. 29.

50.   *Erkenntnis und Interesse*, Suhrkamp, Frankfurt, 1968; *Knowledge and Human Interests*, translated by J.J. Shapiro, Heinemann, London, 1972, with the addition of a useful appendix reprinted from a different source, which provides a densely packed but brief summary of Habermas' position. See also, W. Dallmayr (ed.), *Ma terialen zu Habermas' 'Erkenntnis und Interesse,'* Suhrkamp Suhrkamp, Frankfurt, 1974.

51.   'What Does a Crisis Mean Today? Legitimation Problems in Late Capitalism,' *Social Research*, vol. 40, no. 4, 1973, pp. 643-67, originally in *Merkur,* April-May, 1973.

52.   Cf. *Legitimationsprobleme im Spätkapitalismus*, Suhrkamp, Frankfurt, 1973, p. 15.

53.   *Social Research*, 1974, pp. 646-7.

54.   See also, 'Können Komplexe Gesellschaften eine vernünftige Identikät ausbilden?' in Jurgen Habermas and Dieter Heinrich, *Zwei Reden*, Suhrkamp, Frankfurt, 1974, pp. 23-84.

55.   *The Class Structure of the Advanced Societies*, Hutchinson, London, 1973, p. 268 and Ch. 14, esp. the section on 'the relevance of class analysis,' pp. 269-74.

56.   Cf. a 1968 Gallup Poll cited in Banton, *Racial Minorities*, p. 115.

57.   Ira Katznelson, 'Urban Counterrevolution,' 1973, and, with a bewildering array of conceptual and other sources, 'Participation and Political Buffers in Urban America,' *Race*, vol. XIV, no. 4, 1973, pp. 465-80.

58.   Cf. A. Kirby, 'New Directions at the I.R.R.,' Appendix in C. Mullard, *Black Britain*; A. Sivanandan, *Race and Resistance – the I.R.R. Story*, Race Today Publications, London, 1974; and John Rex's strictures on British 'neo-Durkheimianism' in 'The Future of Race Relations Research in Britain,' *Race*, vol. XIV, no. 4, 1973, pp. 481-4.

59.   *Black Men, White Cities*, 1973.

60.   Reference here is intended to the seminal but almost wholly atheoretical volume by Rose and associates, *Colour and Citizenship*; and to Banton, *Race Relations*.

2. PATTERNS OF POLITICAL CHANGE IN FRAGMENT REGIMES: NORTHERN IRELAND AND RHODESIA

Barry Schutz and Douglas Scott

Colonialism in general, and British colonialism specifically, has helped to generate a wide spectrum of social and political phenomena in the modern world. Not only have new societies been created from the fabric of the European social order, but often bloody and prolonged conflict has ensued between colonial settlers and the peoples native to a territory. Some colonial societies have become enmeshed in this chronic disorder without fully achieving either statehood or nationhood, at least in terms of internationally recognised independence.

The historically colonial status of Ireland both before and during the period of union with Great Britain (1800-1920)[1] is an example of intra-European colonial conflict. Indeed, historians and analysts of British colonialism seem to have forgotten Ireland when establishing typological frameworks, despite the obvious fact that Ireland was for centuries a seedbed for the attitudes and methods of imperialism and colonialism.[2] In contrast to Ireland, Britain's oldest colony (ca. 1100-1920) is the relatively recent example of Rhodesia, established in 1889, in which the settler-native conflict has strained, to the point of rupture, its links with the mother country. Though offshoots of different periods of British imperial ambitions, Ireland and Rhodesia are illuminating case studies of settler societies in disagreement with their nation of origin over the anticipated fruits of traditional colonial policy.

The legacy of British colonial rule has also been felt among nations that have actually achieved independence, both within and outside the framework of the Commonwealth. In the nineteenth century Britain gave a measure of self-government to both the Anglo-Scottish Canadians and the French Canadians, which constituted a *de facto* partitioning of Canada into clearly identifiable ethnic groups. Today the ethnic division manifests itself in conflicts over language, reinforced to some extent by religion and the regional concentration of the French Canadians. The consequence of these 'mutually reinforcing loyalties' is that the regime remains under severe pressure from a significant section of its population.[3]

The case of India, however, demonstrates a different British colonial legacy. Instead of recognising the needs and differences among the various ethnic groups on the subcontinent, Britain united 'India' by its military strength and built a colonial infrastructure. Colonial government was withdrawn when India achieved self-government, leaving a vacuum that split the regime along religious lines — Hindu and

Moslem. Extensive political reorganisation in India has additionally created new administrative units based on regional languages that have reinforced the previous cleavage. Language and national divisions within Pakistan have subdivided that country, with neighbouring India holding the balance of military power in support of certain Indo-Pakistani groups.

European colonialism has reached its fullest form in South Africa, where the European-derived minority exercises oppressive domination over the indigenous majority.[4] Rhodesian society has a similar structure and set of priorities, though it is built upon the subjection of an even greater relative majority of native peoples. Also, the British involvement has been even more pervasive and recent than in South Africa.

From this classificatory perspective a comparative analysis of the political development of Rhodesia and Northern Ireland can be made. Each of these political cultures represents an offspring of an era of British imperialism and colonialism and each has been stamped with a fragment of the British society at a given point in history. As a result of the motives and methods which brought them into being and sustained their growth, Northern Ireland and Rhodesia exist today as civil societies divided by disparate mores and life styles and pregnant with fundamental upheaval.

Sequential Development

In order to distinguish analytically the comparative sequences and actors' roles, it is necessary to use the initiation of the Industrial Revolution as a demarcation point.[5] If imperial and colonial policies predate the Industrial Revolution, as was the case in Ireland, the time frame is much longer and the proposed conceptual distinction can be seen more clearly. The imperial leadership network, for example, revolves to a large extent around the British monarch and his court. Direct imperial commissions — whether political, military or economic — emanate from the monarchy's national and international strategic calculations. As parliamentary power in monetary affairs increases in relation to that of the monarchy, legislative elites begin to intervene more directly in imperial and colonial decision making.

The introduction of a wider circle of political actors involves simultaneously the inclusion of social and economic elites in the expanded network, because of overlapping statuses. Once political structures are imposed or created, imperial economic interests (City of London investors, planners, etc.) are not far behind. Indeed, they are usually encouraged by the monarchy and political leaders because of the need for financial resources necessary for the maintenance of a great power position in Europe. The relationship between political and economic elites is further reinforced by the fact that Trading Companies are established with royal charters.

Thus, prior to the Industrial Revolution the infrastructure for later economic exploitation was built jointly by political and economic interests. In turn, the extent to which the settlers served such interests differentiates imperial from colonial development. From the perspective of the imperial political leaders, planting the home country flag on new territory constitutes the primary political setting. If economic resources are derived from, rather than given to, the new territory, imperial rulers will tolerate a considerable amount of autonomy in local development. Ultimately, this independence provides a real impetus toward colonial development, not possible in the initial imperial phase.

However, if such policies postdate the Industrial Revolution, as was the case in Rhodesia, then dividing lines between imperial and colonial actors and constitutions are not as clear-cut as in the case of Ireland. The political, economic and social development that occurred over several centuries in Ireland took only decades in Rhodesia. Nevertheless, as with pre-industrial imperialism, the imperial/colonial developmental sequence follows a discernible pattern.

Imperial leadership revolves around the monarchy, although that role grows increasingly symbolic and formal in the period after the inception of the Industrial Revolution. Political parliamentary elites acquire greater power and authority in determining imperial policies. Rather than embarking upon the crude military intrusions of the earlier period, the more recent imperial actors are administrators trained in Britain to carry out their 'sacred civilising duties' in the empire. Buttressed by the pervasive influence of missionaries who represent the diverse sects and religions of the imperial source, the major Catholic-Protestant cleavage in pre-industrial society is relaced by a cluster of competing missionary groups more appropriate to an emergent market society.

Investors are more concerned with profits in the later epoch. Chartered companies established for imperial purposes are no longer mere extensions of monarchical and mercantilist interests, but instead are corporate economic entities organised to weld together political and strictly economic pursuits. The settlers themselves are not merely social flotsam and jetsam, but are skilled human surplus created by the industrialising process of the nineteenth and twentieth centuries. The aspirations of these floating lower middle to middle class workers help initially to develop imperial control, but ultimately create confusion between their imperial ties and their specifically colonial aspirations. Often in the brief period since their settlement their interests coincide with those of the imperial elites; but increasingly they do not. The decisive dissonance comes from the application of policies relating to the native peoples.

Orientations Toward Political Development

There is no scarcity of literature concerned with political and economic development by historical sequence. Marx and Engel's categories are still basic to sociohistorical analysis and often provide at least heuristic, and sometimes accurate, perspectives on the development of civil society.[6] Yet Marx, Engels and even Lenin have little to say about the sequential distinction between imperialism and colonialism. Their assumption that the two are intimately related has obscured a difference that contemporary Marxists have been concerned to isolate and analyse.[7]

Of developmental analyses only Samuel Huntington's refers to the European experience and setting of the new settlers. In so doing he is suggesting the imperial/colonial connection, at least in institutional terms. Huntington's main argument is that the United States is not politically modern, even if it has achieved a modern level of economic development. Furthermore, he suggests that if typological comparisons are to be made, South Africa, Rhodesia and Algeria are the societies with which the United States has the most in common structurally. Thus, returning to the examples of the interaction of imperialism and colonialism with which this essay is concerned, British colonial policy appears at the root of such diverse phenomena as Rhodesia and the Irish and American national experiences.

The Durham Commission's Report of the colonial dilemma in Canada in 1838 has furnished a convenient point of departure for tracing the fundamental tenets of colonial policy, particularly toward the process of decolonisation. The Durham Formula derives from the visit of Britain's Lord Durham to Canada in 1838 in an effort to conciliate the grievances of both the English speaking settlers of Upper Canada, mainly Ontario, and those of the French speaking Quebecois. A policy for developing a large amount of authority to these two local citizenries was then devised. It emerged in the nineteenth century as a solution to the demands for home rule posed by various colonial extensions of the home country.

The Durham prescription responded specifically to the failure of policy in the American colonies. The colonisation of Ireland, in its first phase, predated the Durham Formula by about four hundred years, and the ensuing settlement policy of the second phase by over two hundred years. The Durham Formula, then, was intended to prevent the recurrence of Irelands and Americas but was never applied to Ireland itself. So while successes and failures with the Irish colonial experience tended to influence British policy toward subsequent colonial establishments, the reverse situation did not obtain. By the time Durham and Wakefield had reorganised the direction of British colonial policy in the middle of the nineteenth century, the specific problems of the Irish question had acquired their own dynamics.

Despite this, however, there are salient similarities in the historical cases of Rhodesia and Northern Ireland in terms of British colonial application. In each, Britain relied upon the loyalties of at least some of its emigrating subjects to maintain imperial control over the land and the indigenous people, and in each case the emigrant colonials acquired over time their own separate political interests with regard to both. Finally, in each case the 'settlers' elevated their elite status, which had been based on explicit loyalty to the Crown, into a claim for *de jure* local domination through the instrumentality of quasi-autonomous institutions that, however, stopped short of national independence.

The Idea of Fragment

The particular dynamics of imperial/colonial regimes are well illuminated by the set of concepts expressed by Louis Hartz and four colleagues in Hartz's edited volume, *The Founding of New Societies*.[8] Hartz's first premise is that a set of societies has been founded by social fragments of European countries: fragments that have lodged themselves in new, unfamiliar and often hostile environments. The societies presented in the volume are each of European origin but are implanted outside continental Europe. But there does not seem to be any reason for excluding the transplantation of European fragments to other European territories, particularly in peripheral and insular territories such as Ireland.[9]

The concept of fragment is an archetype: it represents a 'before-and-after' abstraction, an analytic exaggeration of developmental sequence in modern social history.[10] The empirical societies that it attempts to abstract are often generalised as 'settler societies,' although the fragment type refers specifically to settlement in a historical context — i.e. settlement *from* Europe, and settlements that 'founded new societies' and indeed new nationalisms.[11]

Our purpose is not solely to review the historical meaning of the concept of fragment or to review additionally its variant types, but rather to explore the possibility of using this concept (a) in comparing selected aspects of political development in Northern Ireland and Rhodesia, and (b) in measuring the sequential distinctions between imperialism and colonialism. Because of this focus on sequential development, the fragment construct will be reviewed here in that hypothesised sequence and not as it has been elaborated logically by Hartz and others. Therefore, the *quasi-fragment* would *precede* the fragment *per se*, just as imperialism precedes colonialism. Elaborations such as dual fragments can develop only after these sequences.

Quasi-Fragment

The notion of quasi-fragment is related directly to the distinction between imperialism and colonialism. The quasi-fragment is a European settlement that is totally dependent on the official sanction and support of the imperial power. As such it does not effectively generate its own ethos: it relies on whatever economic, social and political changes the parent country dictates. Quasi-fragments tend to be smaller in absolute size than the typical developed fragment and are usually unable to claim legitimacy of rule over the native peoples in the eyes of the imperial power. They are more likely to have to contend with a relatively mobilised, organised and developed indigenous population than are the full fragments. And, most importantly, the quasi-fragment remains almost fully attached to the home country's economic infrastructure. Unlike the full fragment, the quasi-fragment does not develop an elaborated division of labour within itself. Its mission is to manage, administer and coerce the natives in imperially sponsored projects. Cases of quasi-fragments can be viewed typologically in terms of scale and size. Thus a range can be comprehended extending from the small administrative cadres operating in such areas as West Africa, where the climate and conditions do not tend to attract European settlers, all the way to the Algerian, Kenyan and perhaps Angolan/Mozambique cases where the quasi-fragment even acts out its expectation of national independence, although never emerging as a full fragment.

Fragment

The quasi-fragment, as an imperial imposition, has the potential for enlargement into a full fragment through the development of imperialism into colonialism. This process of 'fragmentation'[12] is characterised by the presence of certain common conditions: (1) political and economic modernisation taking place in a European nation-state; (2) the migration by a portion of that society to a territory undergoing exploration and imperial domination by the European nation-state; (3) the implantation in the new territory of an ethos derived from the European social experience,[13] and (4) the consequent 'establishment' of a colonial society by old and new settlers. Establishment is ascertained by: (1) the degree of determination of the settlers to remain in the colony, often in the face of adverse conditions; (2) the durability of the European fragment ethos; (3) the characteristic presence of reproducable social units, i.e. families, and (4) the birth of a new generation on the soil of the new territory, i.e. the emergence of 'sabras.'[14] This process tends to generate among the settlers an increasing sense of political and economic (although not usually cultural) separateness from the home country. The separation tends to follow this developmental sequence: (1) pursuit and acquisition of greater political autonomy from the home country; (2) pursuit of greater economic benefits where the objective is economic self-sufficiency; (3) the achievement of political independence (uni- or bilaterally), and (4) the development of a new nationalism based on the fragment ethos. Economically and politically the fragments evolve from a state of dependency on the home country to one of competition with it.

As a part detached or broken off from the whole, the term 'fragment' connotes wholeness in and of itself. This assumption is conveyed by Hartz, perhaps with the purpose of stressing the social and cultural homogeneity of the settlers in contrast to the home country's social structure and to the diverse societies of native peoples in the new territory. The cleavages that do exist in the fragment are subsumed under social and cultural consensus deriving from the peculiar circumstances and fragmentation.

Fragment homogeneity, deriving from social class in the home country, is further enhanced by conditions in the new environment. But as the subjective sense of fragment cohesion grows, so the awareness of separation from the mother country intensifies. This process is jointly perceived by settlers, imperial decision makers and natives. It is this burgeoning discrepancy of interests between the fragment and the home country which distinguishes imperialism from colonialism.

Moreover, while the settlers are seen as a social whole by themselves, the imperial authorities and the natives, cleavages must objectively be inherent from the first moment on the new soil. To survive economically and socially, they must develop a division of labour. And since these fragments have been modern groups, they would not easily accept the establishment of a subsistence economy. Hence, even a more feudally directed fragment would have to organise a society with distinct levels. And, of course, a post-feudal fragment would by economic necessity have to throw up farmers, trappers, labourers, shopkeepers, bankers, manufacturers, administrators and import-export operators. It is only from such diversity that a consensus is derived and the bases laid for the greater conflict with both native peoples and imperial authorities.[15]

Apart from a division of labour there are the cleavages that might be expected to result from subsequent immigration. Hartz suggests, however, that the fragment-type society exhibits an almost unique capacity for absorption. Besides native peoples and culturally distinct imported labourers, the settlers bolster and expand their new society with additional immigrants from their own and other European homelands. Of course, even if the new immigrants are from the home country (as is the tendency, for reasons relating mainly to common language), they come from different social classes, different regions, and, fundamentally, from a different historical epoch. It is clear that the hypothesised contrast between the cultural source and the fragment has an empirical basis. Nonetheless, in the main these new immigrants must, to an exacting extent, conform to the fragment way of life. And in most cases, they do. They migrated out of a willingness to conform to new surroundings, capable of ensuring them, in return, some modicum of material and mental fulfillment.

Ireland

Historic Divisions

In a recent autobiography[16] Terence O'Neill, the Prime Minister of Northern Ireland from 1963-9, made reference to the 'planters' and the 'Gaels,' when describing one of the types of divisions among the people of Northern Ireland. In using those terms to characterise the contemporary population of Ulster, O'Neill is recalling events not of one or two generations removed, but rather the period in Anglo-Irish history in which the transition from English imperialism to English colonialism occurred, the early seventeenth century. During that period, a more persuasive ruling mechanism was established which was coupled with the military defeat of provincial Irish chiefs. A fragment of another society (Scotland) was introduced into the province of Ulster. It is the transition from imperialism to colonialism in Anglo-Irish history as well as the division between Ulster and the other three historic provinces which makes more comprehensible some of the underlying causes of contemporary events.

The Quasi-Fragment

From the perspective of this essay, English rule in Ireland up to the ascension of the Stuart monarchy to the English throne (1603) can be termed the period of the quasi-fragment regime. The emergence of English authority structures in Ireland from the Normans through the Tudors was characterised by repeated cycles of expansion and contraction. Until the military victories in Elizabeth's rule eliminated the strong provincial Irish Gaelic chiefs, especially in Ulster, English policy had been to rely on English administrators as well as a few powerful Anglo-Irish families to maintain England's presence.

Many unsuccessful attempts were made to develop a social infrastructure upon which to increase English authority. The simple fact was that the English did not have sufficient resources to coordinate the necessary military, social and political policies. For the early Norman and English monarchs the 'conquest' of Ireland was undertaken for the purpose of protecting royal political and military alliances; it was important that Ireland not be used by England's enemies as a military base. Because of the cost to the English in terms of money and manpower, the conquering of Ireland became an impossible goal. At best a kind of positive neutralisation was established.

Although political institutions were established in Ireland paralleling those created in England, they were but a thin veneer of controlling mechanisms placed on top of an Irish Gaelic society. The ruling Gaelic political nobility were in many cases displaced, but they were not driven out of the local area. If they were not allowed to maintain their political status, the Norman aristocracy was nevertheless willing to

33

acknowledge the Gaelic chiefs as a social elite, the equals of the Normans.[17] The outcome was that Anglo-Norman leaders were absorbed into Irish Gaelic society by the simple process of marriage to the daughters of the Irish leaders, which has led a contemporary historian to quip that '. . . the most successful of the first Norman leaders symbolised the consolidation of his gains by marrying into the Gaelic aristocracy.'[18] The lack of coherent political policy *vis-à-vis* Ireland was further manifested by the fact that social and economic development was not clearly coordinated with the objective of strengthening political institutions. The Anglo-Normans were modernisers only in their social and economic policies.[19]

Nonetheless, while such development was taking place, the imperial political hold on the island was slipping because of the absorption of rulers into Gaelic society. There was no plan that called for the continual development and supervision of the existing political institutions. The lack of continuity between political and military policy also weakened political authority by the '. . . drainage of men and supplies from Ireland to the wars in Scotland and Wales, as well as the fatal attraction which the wars against France on Continental soil were beginning to have on the Kings of England.'[20]

The English, in fact, had become involved in 'quasi-fragment' rule. Political structures and authorities reflected the internal political needs of the imperial Anglo-Norman and English monarchs with little heed to the Gaelic context in which they would operate. There was no planned coordination with the needs of the local Norman nobility, with the inevitable result that throughout most of the fouteenth century the advantage lay with the Irish chieftain. They were busily reconquering lost land and thereby greatly reducing the ability of the imperial settlers to sustain themselves. In fact, because of the adverse turn of events, a reverse migration took place: settlers were returning from outlying areas to the 'English Pale' or to England.[21] For long periods of time it became impossible to provide the imperial rulers and settlers with military support. Perpetual problems with Scotland and France were the first priority for England's military and financial resources, which meant that incursions into Ireland had to be limited in scope and duration.

The Fragment

The political institutions created through the quasi-fragment government of Ireland by the monarchy had been found wanting. They required too many resources and needed constant military support. A new infrastructure had to be built which would create allegiance to the throne such that Catholic enemies of the monarchy would not consider Ireland as a potential ally. Emigration from England, and more especially from Scotland, was to be the instrument used to create stability and ensure political allegiance in Ireland, special consideration being given to the province of Ulster. Three types of emigration policies can be discerned:

(a) Land in Counties Antrim and Down was given to government supporters (Scots) who encouraged emigration from Scotland to Ulster.

(b) A plantation system was established whereby large tracts of land were given to Protestant landlords for settlement.

(c) The charter company of the City of London was given land (Londonderry and its environs) on which it was to settle people.

To the Anglican-Roman Catholic division created by Henry VIII was now added another religious group, the Scots-Presbyterians, with their own distinctive culture and traditions that, despite their Celtic origins, set them apart as an ethnic group whose national identification was explicitly Scottish.

Seventeenth century Anglo-Irish history occupies a special place in the memories of each generation of Catholics and Protestants in Northern Ireland. The events of that century are like an arsenal of weapons which must continually be displayed by one side or the other to demonstrate that there is absolutely no change in either side's effective defences. In 1609, James I instituted the 'plantation' of Ulster which, in the conceptual schema of this essay, suggests the dividing line between imperial domination and colonial development. The Scottish planters transformed the North of Ireland by wholehearted settlements such as never had been seen before. Their tenacity is the root of Terence O'Neill's ability to label the current population of Northern Ireland as either 'planters' or 'Gael.'[22]

In terms of Protestant historical memory, the military battles won by the forces of William of Orange in 1689 and 1690, in the siege of Derry and the Battle of Boyne against the Catholic forces of the returning James II, who had left his sanctuary in France, could have happened during this century. The several yearly Protestant celebrations, including 12 July and the re-enactment of the Battle of Scarva (County Down), are vivid demonstrations of the intensity of feelings of Protestants and Catholics and constant reminders of their relative power positions.

Population pressure and economic deprivation were causes for rural disorder and violence between Catholics and Protestants during the last half of the eighteenth century. The most permanent historical mark of this period was the founding of the Orange Order in 1795 in the Ulster County of Armagh to protect Protestants from organised groups of marauding peasant Catholics as well as to prevent Catholic acquisition of land. Although established in Ulster, the Orange Order initially attracted its membership from the Church of Ireland, and it was not until the 1930s that Presbyterians joined members of the established church in its active support.

This new unity was prompted, paradoxically, by disputes between two prominent Presbyterian clergymen [23] but can largely be attributed to the political mobilisation of the Catholic population. The Orange Order fostered a reinvigorated consensus among Protestants in the fragment society of Ulster which remains fundamentally intact to this day. From early reactive beginnings it became the bulwark of support for the development of the Ulster Unionist Party, such that until very recently it would have been unthinkable for a member of the Northern Ireland government not to be a member.

The nineteenth century was the period of opposition formation by both Protestant and Catholics. The latter were led by several outstanding figures, two of whom were especially prominent: Daniel O'-Connell and Charles Stewart Parnell. The former fought for Catholic emancipation and repeal of the Act of Union which had joined England and Ireland in 1800-1. O'Connell won the first battle and lost the second, but not before he had permanently wedded Irish nationalism and Roman Catholicism in the minds of both Protestant and Catholic alike. The extent to which he had mobilised the Catholic population can be seen in accounts of the County Clare by-election of 1828 in which he put himself forward as a candidate and was victorious despite the fact that he was legally prohibited from sitting in Parliament if he won the seat.[24]

O'Connell's victory over a Protestant pro-emancipationist member of the government in the by-election of 1828 in County Clare was a decisive display of organisational power. This victory was the principal cause of an Orange revival that saw gentry and peasant renew their alliance, which had been severely weakened during the tenure of the Secretary of Ireland, Sir Robert Peel. The tenor of letters sent to Peel by landlords of Protestant and Orange sympathies is indicated by the following excerpt: 'The present state of things cannot be endured. The Romans are united as one man, and common safety will justify counter-association against the chance or dread of commotion.'[25]

The sectarian violence that beset Ulster between 1880 and 1893 is attributable to a change in leadership tactics on the part of the Irish nationalists, from respect for British parliamentary institutions to their obstruction.[26] If Daniel O'Connell joined religion and nationality, it was Charles Stewart Parnell who created the first fully unified Irish nationalist opposition in British parliamentary politics by adding political partisanship to the equation. He mobilised Roman Catholic electoral support, taking full advantage of the various reform acts of 1867, 1872 and 1884 to rebuild a Nationalist Party capable of halting proceedings of the House of Commons as well as demanding ultimately that one or the other of the two British parties embrace an Irish Home Rule position.

The General Election of 1880 was fought by Parnell on the broad issue of land reform. This made exceptionally good tactical sense because the land issue was critical if future economic crises were to be avoided. Memories of the Great Famine only a few decades past were especially salient to nationalists of all kinds, '. . . from moderate home rulers to extreme republicans.'[27] As President of the Irish National Land League, he focused Irish attention on the 'bread-and-butter' issue of the day. The electoral success of 1880 allowed Parnell to shift the focus away from the land issue to Home Rule.

The Land League was replaced by a new organization, the National League, dominated by the parliamentary party and providing it with effective electoral machinery. The movement consolidated under Parnell's leadership in preparation for the next general election.[28]

The election of 1885 set the geographic and political parameters firmly in place on both the 'Irish' and 'Ulster' questions. Despite Gladstone's victory in England, the Liberal Party had been virtually eliminated from Irish politics, since it returned no members to the House of Commons. Conservatives under the banner of Ulster Unionism were returned only in the Ulster counties and the two Dublin University seats. The regional strength of Irish Unionism was now clearly defined. The strength of Parnell's election victory also, and most importantly, defined and helped to determine the character of the threat to Ulster Unionism itself. Of the thirty-three members Ulster sent to the House of Commons, the Unionists carried sixteen while the nationalists captured seventeen. F.S.L. Lyons summarises the consequences of the election:

'On the one hand, by exhibiting the province as evenly divided in its political loyalties, they led Home Rulers, Irish as well as British, to underestimate the strength and tenacity of Ulster Unionism and therefore to assume that while Unionism might be coerced it did not need to be conciliated. And, on the other hand, the Unionists themselves, confronted with this irrefutable evidence of the enemy in their midst, were naturally driven to exaggerate the siege mentality to which, for historical reasons, they were already prone and to answer the implied menace to their security by even tighter organization and even greater intransigence.'[29]

The interposition of the Ulster Unionists, supported by the British Conservatives, between the Irish Nationalists and the British Liberals assured a redefinition of the meaning of Home Rule. They had fought Nationalists demands for a Dublin parliament by embracing Liberal Party suggestions that the North and South each have a legislative body. If the logic of partition was to be accepted, it seemed natural to preserve the historic province of Ulster as a single unit. However, the Census of 1911 showed that the population of the province had a slight Protestant majority, but that the rate of population growth favoured the Catholics. Therefore, it seemed obvious to the Unionists that to preserve their power in areas of their highest concentration, a 'partition' of Ulster was in order. The six northeastern counties, eliminating the large nationalist majorities in the counties of Donegal, Monaghan and Cavan, would secure Unionist dominance. And thus, born of political gerrymandering, the modern configuration of Northern Ireland came into being.

Partition

The irony of the period from 1885-1920 was that the harder the loyalists fought against Home Rule in the form of an Irish parliament, the greater the likelihood that British politicians would subdivide the island and create two Home Rule parliaments. Much to the dismay of the various Nationalist groups not only was the island partitioned into sub-areas with Catholic and Protestant majorities but the power of the fragment would remain and be further solidified because they helped draw the new territorial boundaries. By retaining six of Ulster's nine counties the British substate had a built-in Protestant majority in the rato 65-35 per cent.

By the end of the 1960s dissension in Northern Ireland had increased such that the violence that marked the period between 1885 and 1914 was being repeated. Parliamentary hegemony by the Protestants during the fifty-two years (1920-72) of their uninterrupted rule only increased the narrow 'fragment mentality' to the point where the third Prime Minister of Northern Ireland could openly state that virtually all Catholic citizens were axiomatically disloyal toward the British connection. Such thinking meant that it was virtually impossible to conceive of oppositions being created that would cross sectarian lines to any substantial extent. Further, such a viewpoint saw all Catholic opposition as monolithic: an unending war against the provincial government. The fragment regime found that it was simply too easy to use the sectarian cleavage to obtain its support from all classes of Protestants. There was no reason to appeal for support by any other means.

British military 'intervention' in 1969 and suspension of the Stormont Parliament in 1972 brought about the first hard look taken by both Labour and Conservative governments in London at the Ulster situation. The outcome was the establishment of a new Northern Ireland Assembly whose executive had to include both Protestants and Catholics. In reality the Secretary of State for Northern Ireland, a member of the British Cabinet, might be considered a super-executive, overseeing the power sharing of the provincial parliament. To paraphrase Arend Lijphart, the British are attempting to establish a 'guided' consociational democracy. It was impossible for Protestant *and* Catholic elites to generate overarching cohesion by themselves for the stability of the province — it had to be imposed and regulated by the British government.

The Rhodesian Case

The permutations of the 'fragment' archetype which have already been discussed relate equally to the Rhodesian experience. Rhodesia was founded by Rhodes' Pioneer Column in 1889. While most of them did not remain, the settler society was established by imperial design after the African resistance of 1896-7. From 1897 to 1921, whole family units of English speaking whites immigrated into the colony to settle. Most of them were farmers, others were mainly small workers who mined the deposits of gold which were scattered about. By 1921 the cultural, racial and class nature of the society had been established. The pattern of immigration was to be maintained henceforth, and the white Rhodesians expressed their preference with a decisive vote for internal self-government. They had already perceived — seemingly correctly at that point — that they were a proper *British* colony, firmly on the Durham track toward political autonomy.

But how British were they? In fact, the Pioneer Column and the more important 1897-1921 immigrants were predominantly African born. By 1911 over 44 per cent of the white population in Rhodesia were South African or Rhodesian born, and by 1931 this had increased to 64 per cent. Most of those not born in southern Africa had moved there from Britain and had been residing there for some time. Since virtually none could have been born in Rhodesia before 1889, South Africa tended to be their country of origin. Further, less than 20 per cent of those South African born immigrants to Rhodesia were of the South African Dutch Reform Church. Thus, the vast majority of these South African born Rhodesian immigrant settlers were British rather than Afrikaner.

It has often been assumed that the Pioneer Column and their accompanying British South African Police, commissioned by Rhodes under the direction of Frank Johnson, had been the foundational settlement of white Rhodesia. It has also been assumed that this occupation force was essentially British by birth. However, a questionnaire conducted by the (Southern) Rhodesian Archives in 1940 among surviving pioneers, British South African Police, or their relatives, questions this assumption.[31] Forty-nine per cent of the Police responding indicated South African birth. Only about 42 per cent of the Pioneers were born in the United Kingdom. Of those born in South Africa the vast majority were born in the Cape Colony, which tended to be the main residential area of British South African life, especially of those in the British South African elite. The first organised whites to enter and occupy Rhodesia were more British South African than British in terms of country or area of origin. Furthermore, about one-third of these earliest white settlers left within two years after arriving. By 1940, about half of the Pioneers and 60 per cent of the Police had either died or moved to South Africa. Hence, the idea that this Pioneer Column were the founders of the new Rhodesian society remains true only at the level of symbolism.

Rhodesian social foundations are thus intricately tied to the lines of development in white South Africa. L.M. Thompson has suggested that South Africa possessed two, ostensibly coeval, fragments.[32] Measured by size (vis-à-vis the indigenous population), this might be a questionable hypothesis. First, there were always more Afrikaners than British; second, the Dutch migration and settlement predated that of the British by over 150 years; and third, communication patterns between the Dutch settlers and Holland were effectively cut off almost from inception, while the British settler communications with the mother country remained relatively intense after colonisation in 1820.

By this analysis, it might be inferred that while the Afrikaners were congealing into full fragment status by the mid-nineteenth century, the British South Africans remained an imperially dependent quasi-fragment. However stubborn might be the early British settlers in South Africa, they ultimately looked to local imperial authority and the Crown for real as well as symbolic leadership and governance.[33] This dependence sufficiently distinguishes them from the Afrikaners who looked to no one but themselves — economically, politically and culturally.

Despite this apparent British South African shortcoming in political authority and identity, the British imperial authorities operated under the assumption that South Africa was a repetition of Canada and that, therefore, power would eventually be devolved to the British settlers.[34] This 'imperial inertia' was ultimately elaborated in a sort of colonial multiplier effect. By mistaking British South Africa for British Canada, the British set a precedent which would prove to be disastrous. Eventually they were to ignore their mistake in South Africa (and Natal where the Durham Formula was conceived to apply to almost a handful of British settlers) and repeat the same blunder in Rhodesia in the disastrous experiment of the Central African Federation.[35] If responsible government could be given to a few thousand white Natalians in 1856, then why not to a few thousand white Rhodesians in 1923?[36]

In essence, then, the social foundation of white settler Rhodesia immigrated between 1897 — the year in which the African resistance was suppressed — and 1923, the year in which white Rhodesia opted for 'responsible government' rather than incorporation into the Union of South Africa. During this period the European population of Rhodesia increased from about 4,000 to over 34,000.

Moreover, in 1911 there were only 551 females to every 1,000 males, but by 1921 this ratio had risen to 771:1000. And in 1911 64 per cent of the male population were between the ages of twenty and forty-four, whereas in 1921 only 43 per cent were in that age bracket. Thus, much of the population increase between 1911 and 1921 was due to natural increase, with a much larger proportion of the European population being children. Finally, in 1921, 38.2 per cent of the white population in Rhodesia were married compared with 36.2 per cent in South Africa and 36.4 per cent in Great Britain. This is a significant statistic, since the male/female balance was such that about 44 per cent of the white population in Rhodesia were female. From this perspective one can see the beginnings of a functioning conscious society.

Rhodesia's white settlers in November, 1922, opted for 'responsible government' rather than incorporation into the Union of South Africa. The latter course would have removed the settler colony's debts to the British South African Company as well as ensured development within the framework of the South African economy. However, such a choice would have permitted Rhodesians as little cultural identity as the Natalians in South Africa.

From 1923 to the Second World War, the Rhodesian fragment consolidated and developed. The European population increased from over 34,000 to about 65,000 in 1941 and to over 82,000 in 1946. Selectivity in immigration was rigorously enforced in order to preserve the apparent rationale for self-government and 'Britishness.' Non-British Europeans, and especially Afrikaners, were actively reduced to less than 5 per cent of the total European immigrants throughout this period. British ethnic origin was a primary attribute of the 'desirable' immigrant, although a capacity to speak English was generally acceptable. During the early years of the Nazi terror Rhodesia had an excellent opportunity to take in European refugees — predominantly Jewish — but the Prime Minister, Sir Godrey Huggins, feared that they would dilute Rhodesia's British foundation. Thinking in increasingly antiquated imperial terms, Huggins sensed the global dimensions of the British Empire and, therefore, the high rates of mobility of British subjects. European refugees, on the other hand, would be stateless and would thus become a more permanent public element in Rhodesia. But perhaps all of these reasons revolved around the dilemma of race and class relations. With more whites than supervisory posts available, the rigid stratification of Rhodesian society would be upset, with unpredictable consequences for the settlers' privileged position.

After World War II the question of independence and dominion status loomed large for the Rhodesian settlers. To the south, the Afrikaners had mobilised an effective political organisation which took power in 1948. The consequences for British interests in South Africa, including the British South Africans themselves, were in doubt. In the meantime, the deposits in the Copper Belt in Northern Rhodesia were being mined with profitable proficiency by firms based on British and American capital. And inside Southern Rhodesia, tobacco was rapidly becoming the base industry for the development of a more elaborate infrastructure which would decide the extensive chromium, asbestos and coal deposits as well. Finally, the claims of Africans, particularly those in wage labour, were beginning to be heard. Ordinary racialist suppression of mobility could no longer suffice as a means of maintaining social and economic place in the Rhodesian settlers' plural society.

Fragment status was already theirs, but the Rhodesians by a margin of about two to one voted to forego immediate dominion status in order to build on a broader economic base. By this reasoning, the Central African Federation came into being in 1953. Along with the extension of the settler's domain across the Zambesi into Northern Rhodesia and Malawi [37] came the reality of white minority rule over six million additional Africans. In order to establish a framework which could politically absorb this problem, the British government and the colonial settlers under Huggins devised a federal format and a graduated qualified franchise into which an anticipated African bourgeoisie could move. With the advent of African nationalism in the north, this arrangement was furnished with the conceptual label of 'partnership.'

The terms of the Federation contained a clause which would put off any formal independence from Britain until a ten-year period had elapsed. The Federation would be reviewed in 1963, and then formal independence would follow. Britain was withdrawing from Africa as well as Asia, and had hoped that the Rhodesians would be the last settler colony to receive the benefits of the Durham Formula. The Rhodesians understood this and planned accordingly. Their comprehension of Britain continued to be imperial. They still thought of themselves as a civilised outpost for the mother country and a counter to Afrikaner as well as African barbarianism in southern central Africa. But they wanted and fully expected independence from Britain as a white-settler-ruled state. What was good for the Afrikaners had to be good for the Rhodesians. But the way for Afrikaner rule was prepared in the Union of 1910, [38] and this was 1953-63. The Durham Formula had been reinterpreted: the British imperial decline now necessitated a socially and culturally plural commonwealth. By 1963 the Federation was in disarray and the Rhodesians were gathering political momentum for a unilateral break with the home country. The British were in the midst of wholesale decolonisation in Africa, and power was being devolved to native elites. African nationalist demands had been mounting for a majoritarian political solution in Rhodesia, and the British, with increasing economic dependence upon South Africa, were attempting to 'muddle through.' In 1961 a referendum had approved a constitution which would give the Africans a small piece of the electoral pie and the Rhodesians their ostensible independence. The settlers had had enough waiting. They threw out the establishment United Federal Party and elected the right wing 'independence now'-oriented Rhodesian Front. Within three years the Federation was buried and the second RF Prime Minister, Ian Smith, led the settlers to declare unilateral independence from the British and self-declared rule over 95 per cent of the colony's population. [39]

The white Rhodesians had felt betrayed by the British. The British

could not understand the settlers' dismay. And the Africans were
forced to choose between the lesser of two evils. None of these groups
could comprehend the others. The Rhodesians imagined that they were
still in an imperial orbit. The British could not fathom settler arrogance
in 'going it alone.' And the Africans were as mistaken as the settlers in
expecting help from a *former* imperial power. No one's expectations
were fulfilled and tripartite acrimony and violence persists as a result.

Harold Wilson's expectation that the settlers would fold within
weeks after minimal sanctions were applied indicated the distance in
time and space which now existed between parent and child. Rhodesian
expectations that Britain, even under Labour, would quickly see the
error of its ways and reach a settlement with Ian Smith furnished
similar evidence from the other side. And the African nationalists' conviction that their imperial guardians would intervene on their behalf
betrayed their own historical separation from global reality. Between
1965 and 1972 these actors in the decolonisation process continued
to carry hopes for a solution to the problem. Only recently has the
hard reality dawned.

The Rhodesian survival of sanctions generated another myth — that
of their own national cohesion. Forgetting the imbalance of their
economic pluralism, they created fantasies about their gritty endurance
while living at their customary privileged level. As usual, the Africans
took the brunt of the impact while the South Africans offered financial
and political support to the White Rhodesians.[40] Pushed into the rear
of white Rhodesian consciousness was the uncomfortable fact that
there had been no population increase at all after 1961. Both immigration and emigration and birth and deaths have been offsetting, while at
the same time the African population has increased by about one
million. The European/African ratio now stands at approximately one
to twenty-three. And the smaller Asian and Coloured populations are
likewise increasing.[41]

The separation of the Rhodesian fragment was to be confirmed
with the election of a Conservative government in Britain in 1970. The
Home-Smith talks effectively reached such an agreement, thus putting
off the threat of African majority rule, in Smith's lifetime at least.
After that there would probably be no British interest in enforcement
anyway. But one of the conditions was a thorough testing of the agreement amongst the *whole* population. Despite Rhodesian white distress
at this development, a commission was formed under Lord Pearce to
carry out the task in early 1972. Every sector of the African population
including many of salaried chiefs who were the regime's extension into
the rural areas,[42] rejected the terms of the agreement. In Gwelo, some
parts of Salisbury and some rural areas there were physical manifestations of this disapproval. The Pearce Commission returned a verdict of
'no acceptance' by the African population and has effectively put off
British legalisation of UDI for the time being. Moreover, the Com-

mission's presence brought the matter to something of a head and has apparently recharged Rhodesian African nationalism both inside and outside the borders.

Rhodesia's quarter-million whites (a generous estimate) are now entering a new phase of self-doubt. As indicated above, they are not increasing in numbers in either absolute terms or relative to the indigenous population. Their economic problems have been eased not only by South Africa but by Britain, the United States, Japan and a number of European states. Yet sanctions of a sort remain, and the Rhodesian economy continues to lose foreign exchange. African nationalist (Zimbabwean) guerillas have since late 1972 shown greater expertise and effectiveness, and this can only further undercut settler confidence. Despite these apparent setbacks, the Rhodesian Front has modernised racial domination in Rhodesia and has furnished these ex-colonial settlers with an organisational bastion for maintaining their privileged position and power in Rhodesia.[43]

Rhodesia's status, however, is ultimately subordinate to the entrenched Afrikaner fragment. South Africa has achieved the position of a dominant power in southern and central Africa, and so Rhodesia furnishes a buffer against threats to the South African position. As a part of a greater subordinate state system, Rhodesia's international position is dependent politically and economically upon South Africa. If the South African regime judges that its interests might be better served by transforming Rhodesia into another Botswana, then there would be little that the Rhodesians could do about it. While there is little likelihood of this option being pursued by South Africa in the near future, the situation does point up the continuing dependency of the Rhodesian Europeans. In this sense the Rhodesians remain a British South African quasi-fragment within the context of a *South African* subordinate state system. Their existence as a tiny oligarchy dominating an enormous native population remains imperially determined by the very fragment from whom they escaped in the first place.

Fragment Dynamic: Patterns of Social Communications

If there is a dynamic in fragment development, it lies in its characteristic patterns of social communications.[44] One of the sharpest distinctions that can be made between imperialism and colonialism involves the extent and cause of emigration from the home country to the new territory. Such movement of population can depend on any one or a combination of the following conditions:

(1)   The political, social and economic conditions in the home country may force citizens to leave.

(2)   The home country might force people to leave.

(3)   The home country might develop a conscious policy which

44

encourages its citizens to emigrate.

(4)   The institutional base in the new territory is sound enough to encourage emigration.

Furthermore, the nationalism and national consciousness which develop in the new territory after the fragment's migration from the parent country is capable of measurement in terms of levels of frequency and intensity in communications and exchange within the society, and between the members of one society and another. It is assumed that there already exists a clustered pattern of communications derived from the historical past and from a common class identification, and that it is only reinforced and intensified in the new environment. Even if some class diversity exists among the first established settlers, based on social stratification in the homeland, it tends to break down within the fragment in the new society.

Fragment unity upon implantation, the rapid construction of a new nation, and the unifying challenge of the environment all tend to reinforce intrafragment communication. After the establishment of the new settler society, the ethos begins to rigidify. Communications with the country of origin are drastically reduced. Ideological orientation soon becomes fixed and conservative in the absence of the competitive challenge of new social classes which characterised the parent country. Without the dynamic flow of European-centred change, the fragment ethos increasingly acquires a sense of inwardness as well as a political conservatism. Once the native peoples are suppressed, there is no longer the perception of a significant internal threat, and thus expansion, consolidation and development remain as the only challenges to social equilibrium.

For analysis from the fragment perspective, four distinct variables stand out: (1) historical time; (2) proximity to parent country; (3) size of fragment relative to indigenous population; and (4) the impact of contiguous territories.

Historical Time: Social communication and interaction is greatly determined by facilities for transport and exchange as well as by class structure. In older fragments there tends to be a more rigid pattern of social communication, generally articulated in feudal societal arrangements as in the cases of Quebec and the Ibero-American settlements. Moreover, these fragments, like the Dutch in South Africa, were isolated from their European roots because of the difficulty of travel and communications from the home country to the new territory. Later fragments were able to maintain more frequent and intense contact with the home country due to the development of more advanced forms of transport and communications.

Proximity to Parent Country: Generally the greater the distance of the fragment from the home country, the less is the frequency and intensity of social communications between them, and thus the greater is the tendency for the fragment ethos to be fixed and conservative in relation to the changes occurring in the home country. As a corollary to the proximity variable, it would appear that the later the fragmentation occurs, the less significant is the impact of distance. Thus, Australia's communications and transport links with Britain are probably as strong as Canada's even though her distance from the home country is much greater, because the establishment of the settler society in Australia took place at a time when modes of transport and communication were undergoing revolutionary development.

Relative Size: This variable refers to the size of the settler group *vis-à-vis* the native population. The larger the relative size of the fragment, the greater the tendency for the fragment to develop independent means of communication and interaction, distinct from the home country and the indigenous peoples. Thus Australian settlers would interact and communicate more among themselves than would the New Zealanders who, being smaller in perceivable absolute and relative size, would find greater need for maintaining contact with the home country and for accommodating themselves to the indigenous population.

The Irish quasi-fragment and the Ulster full fragment, as well as the British fragments established in South Africa and Rhodesia, were greatly influenced by the historical timing of their settlement. The Irish incursions occurred far earlier than the first British experience in South Africa in 1820, though a Dutch settlement of the Cape was contemporaneous with the Scottish plantation of Ulster.[45] Therefore, because of the time lag, British settlements in Africa were more concertedly English in cultural identification, more imperially conscious, and more establishmentarian in religious preference.

For the Irish, of course, geographic proximity compensated for historical distance. Conversely, for British settlements in South Africa, distance from the homeland did much to undo the sense of identification which the newness of the settlement could have ensured. Transport and communication patterns, therefore, were consciously intensified during the Second Industrial Revolution of the late nineteenth century when the Pioneer Column and their followers occupied Rhodesia. In Ireland proximity functioned naturally to permit the Presbyterians of Ulster and Plantation Protestants of the three other provinces to maintain a sustaining level of social, economic and political communications with their Scottish and English origins, a level that was never achieved by the newly implanted Rhodesian fragment.

As a result, for example, Labour's nationalisation policies after World War II were accepted by the Northern Ireland fragment regime, despite their ideological indigestibility, because of their source in the 'British' homeland. The Rhodesians, for their part, have steadfastly resisted most policy changes originating from Britain since they achieved self-government in 1923.[46]

The third variable, relative size, is also important to the comparative analysis of Ireland and Rhodesia. Although the Protestant fragment of Northern Ireland is a majority by a ratio of about three to two, they comprise only 20 per cent of the population of the entire island. But by any measure the ratio of Protestants to Catholics is far closer to parity than that of Europeans to Africans in Rhodesia and South Africa. Currently, there is approximately one European to every twenty-three Africans in Rhodesia proper, and no more than sixteen per cent are white in South Africa and Rhodesia together. But in terms of fragments, the Afrikaner fragment is larger than the British South African fragment and is more exclusive in its social communications than is the latter. It has always been the British South Africans who have suggested such concepts as 'partnership' and 'qualified franchise,' while the more confident Afrikaners put forth 'apartheid.'

Thus, from the perspectives of historical time, proximity and relative size, the Protestant fragment of Northern Ireland resembles as much the Dutch/Afrikaner fragment of South Africa as the British South African quasi-fragment and their offshoot, the Rhodesian fragment. The Protestant incursion into Ireland occurred earlier in time, was closer to the home country, and has been characterised by a relatively larger population *vis-à-vis* the indigenous peoples. As a result, communication has been more closely linked to the home country and has been more frequent and intense among the fragment themselves. The Rhodesians have had to rely more upon the earlier settled and more numerous Afrikaners in the suppression of the native peoples and in the pattern of separation from the home country.

Contiguous Territories: Proximity can also be analysed through the historical and societal inputs of territories contiguous with the fragments. The two cases in question, especially, are conceptually illuminated by the focus on this variable in regard to both the fragment and the indigenous peoples. In Northern Ireland the latter occupied an entire island with its own political identity, while the source of both the quasi-fragment and fragment was the British isles proper, which, if not contiguous, constituted the nearest 'foreign' land. Rhodesia's contiguity with South Africa has shaped its development, and the presence of African Zambia to the north could alter her future. The South African connection has been the most enduring for the Rhodesian fragment and has been the primary ingredient of its political, as distinct from cultural, identity.

The partition of Ireland in 1920-1 into six northeastern counties and a twenty-six county Irish Free State placed a legal border between the fragment and the majority of the indigenous population. At the outset of the new regime in Northern Ireland, popular loyalties were divided along religious, political and national lines. Protestant Unionists who had vigorously opposed home rule now supported the autonomy of their new government and the British connection while Catholic

Nationalists repudiated the 'six-county' regime and identified with the Irish Free State.

The hostility of Catholics on both sides of the border to the Northern regime, coupled with the Civil War in the South, '. . . enabled the Unionists to appropriate loyalty and good citizenship to themselves and to use the national flag (Union Jack) as a party emblem.'[47] The fact that the Catholic population sought support from the government of a contiguous territory and that their political behaviour was directly influenced by the Free State seemed to underscore the need to preserve fragment consciousness in all its aspects.

In Rhodesia, the first settlers were predominantly South African in birth, and nearly unanimously so in residence. The emergence and growth of Rhodesian fragment nationalism also derived from the southern border as Afrikaner nationalism has fed directly into the Rhodesian Front movement in both its anti-imperial and anti-native contexts. Under present circumstances even the military foundations of fragment supremacy in Rhodesia are sustained in South Africa.

In both cases, origins and conflicts are traced to links with contiguous territories. The British military intervention in Northern Ireland and the South African involvement in Rhodesia each reveal the fundamental roles which these two countries played in the establishment and perpetuation of the dominant fragment societies in Northern Ireland and Rhodesia. And just as these countries continue to buttress the fragments, the territories contiguous on the other borders supply the political and demographic impetus for the subordinated indigenous peoples in the fragment's national territory. As a quasi-fragment, early English settlers were dependent upon imperial rule and therefore had no illusions about independence. But the Plantation fragment of the seventeenth century was motivated to migrate by their own economic disadvantages in Scotland, by their dissenting religious propensities and by imperial population policies. They were already disinclined to accept wholeheartedly the imperial conception of their political status. Consequently, there was a real basis for divergence of interests which was instrumental in separating imperial and colonial phases of Irish evolution and in generating conflict between colonial 'planters' and native Gaels.

In South Africa the British quasi-fragment revealed no separatist tendencies in the nineteenth century. However, the burgeoning Rhodesian fragment, from the beginning, felt shackled by the prominent official status of the British South Africa Company. Their early agitation for greater representation in the colonial legislature[48] grew to a movement toward 'Responsible Self-Government' under the perceived provisions of the Durham Formula. Britain, however, preferred to see imperial investments secured through Rhodesian attachment to the Union of South Africa. This imperial-colonial cleavage was a continuation of the earlier cleavage regarding BSAC vs. settler representation.

But it was brought to a head by the referendum on the issue. Settler preference for self-government and non-affiliation with the Union of South Africa indicated their ultimate desire for independent dominion status similar to that of Australia, Canada or New Zealand.

Thereafter British imperial interests increasingly viewed an amalgamation of Southern Rhodesia with Northern Rhodesia as desirable, especially because of the productive copper deposits of the latter. The Afrikaner political breakthrough in South Africa in 1948 provided an issue for imperial and colonial cooperation on this design and by 1953 the Central African Federation became a reality.[49] Most white Rhodesians thought that the Federation was a timely economic consolidation toward the achievement of dominion status. Their expectations were that within ten years an enlarged Rhodesia, in the form of the Federation, would rank with Canada and Australia as a Commonwealth dominion.

These expectations were deferred, however, by British political imperatives in Africa, and by 1960 the Federation was being dismantled without provisions for a fragment-controlled Rhodesia. British policy makers were paying more attention to indigenous nationalist movements, and the Rhodesians were shocked into countermobilisation. This, of course, led to the establishment of an illegal but ostensibly effective independence on 11 November 1965.

Both the Northern Ireland and Rhodesian fragments experienced crises of autonomy through confrontations with Britain in the 1960s and 1970s. The crises coincided with a significant parallel in leadership which occurred in both societies — the premiership of Terence O'Neill in Northern Ireland from 1963 to 1969 and that of Garfield Todd in Southern Rhodesia from 1953 to 1958. Both men were selected by their single party dominant governments for the purpose of replacing leaders who had dominated both party politics and national policy making for more than twenty years.[50] Further, the eventual undoing of each of these leaders and their sympathisers came from the mobilisation of indigenous oppositions which severely threatened fragment supremacy. Although neither O'Neill nor Todd was especially positive toward these movements, each was aware of the need for fundamental reform in order to ensure continued tranquillity between the fragment and the indigenous people. This aroused open hostility among the rooted residential interests in Northern Ireland and Rhodesia. Despite being removed and replaced by weaker men, connected to these same interests, both O'Neill and Todd continued to be viewed by the fragment elites as disloyal to their cause. Ultimately, of course, the interim appointments of James Chichester-Clark in Northern Ireland and Edgar Whitehead in Rhodesia were also terminated because of continuing divisions among the leadership.

Terence O'Neill had lived much of his life and been educated in England, from which his political attitudes were derived. After serving in the British forces, he went to Northern Ireland with the thought of seeking a seat in the Westminster Parliament, thus continuing in the O'Neill 'British tradition.' When he found that he could not expect nomination for the Imperial Seat, he accepted nomination for the local Stormont Parliament. But, unlike his predecessor, he did not have a 'grass roots' attachment to Ulster politics.

As Prime Minister, O'Neill conceived of himself as a reformer in his personal conduct toward the Catholic community and the Irish Republic. In the North he visited Catholic institutions, such as schools and hospitals, and spoke before joint meetings of Protestants and Catholics.[51] And, of course, to the extreme displeasure of the Unionist right wing, he initiated the North-South Prime Ministerial meeting. In a 'presidential' sense he had wide support in both Protestant and Catholic communities, but it was impossible to translate that support into parliamentary seats during the 1969 Stormont election. The mutually reinforcing cleavages dividing the Province generally reasserted themselves to his disadvantage.

In Rhodesia, Sir Edgar Whitehead, who succeeded Todd in 1958, instituted such legislation as the Law and Order Maintenance Act, the foundation for the repressive policies later carried out by the Rhodesian Front Government. Whitehead's continual association with the increasingly disdained British political image led to his government's surprising downfall in the 1962 General Election and to its replacement by the Rhodesian Front, which had campaigned on the issue of 'independence now, unilaterally if necessary.' After two years of uncertainty under Winston Field, the Rhodesian Front selected Ian Smith to lead the Rhodesian fragment into independence in order ro secure their domination over the African population.

Thus, in both Northern Ireland and Rhodesia the fragment response intensified because each lost faith in the imperial protector. In Rhodesia they overthrew what they perceived as the unholy instruments which the unfathomable home country was foisting upon them in order to rob them of what they saw as their birthright — continued supremacy over the natives.

In Northern Ireland supremacy was defined in terms of political autonomy within the United Kingdom, a condition previously subscribed to by both the Conservative and Labour governments. Because the Imperial Parliament had never intervened in Northern Ireland affairs since the creation of the Northern government, a faction of the Unionist Party considered that such a right had lapsed, despite language to the contrary in the Government of Ireland Act of 1920. To this group, generally led by the former Cabinet Minister, William Craig, British intervention would call for a UDI response on the part of the Unionist ruling elites. The equivalent declaration by Ian Smith in Rhodesia seemed to them to be a worthy precedent.

The sectarian violence which began in 1969 brought British military intervention into the North because the Unionist government could not maintain public order. Since the first enthusiastic Catholic reception of British military presence, however, British troops have come to be viewed as supporters of the Unionist regime. The formulation of policies for limited social reform preceded the recognition that political change was needed, thus making the British army the only stabilising instrument in the society. Because of right-wing pressures on the Unionist leaders and the upsurge of the IRA, the Conservative government in Britain had to suspend the Northern Ireland Constitution and supplant the Stormont Parliament. Rule from Britain and the continued sectarian violence have again reinvigorated fragment consciousness. Organisations for the political, social, psychological and military defence of Ulster proliferate daily. In 1974 both the Rhodesian and Northern Ireland fragments remain prisoners of their own self-proclaimed autonomy and isolation.

Conclusion

By viewing political development in Northern Ireland and Rhodesia in terms of the imperial/colonial sequence and from the perspective of fragment analysis, significant comparative insight into very complex social and political phenomena can be gained. The distinction between imperialism and colonialism, and between the quasi-fragment and the fragment, in the Rhodesian context indicates that white Rhodesia was imperially designed by Cecil John Rhodes and economic interests in the City of London. But at the same time, Rhodesia was sociologically a colonial extension of the British South African quasi-fragment. In its own evolution, the Rhodesian fragment cut its imperial ties and applied its fundamental colonial knowledge to its own political dilemma, the need to maintain supremacy over the native population. The same sociological, historical and political ties to Britain that affect the leadership's conceptions of the status of Northern Ireland. The spectrum seems to be bounded by UDI and total integration into the United Kingdom. Regardless of whether and to what extent fragment power will be preserved, fragment consciousness is unlikely to recede.

NOTES

We would like to thank Professor Joanna V. Scott for critical assistance in reviewing this paper. We wish to acknowledge the editorial and clerical assistance of the Institute of Government and Public Affairs and the Center for Afro-American Studies at UCLA.

1.   Despite the fact that Britain and Ireland were 'united' in 1800, we maintain that it still retained its colonial status until partition.

2.   For a proper corrective by Irish political historians, see David Thornley, 'Historical Introduction,' in Basil Chubb, *The Government and Politics of Ireland*, Stanford University Press, Stanford, California, 1970, pp. 1-42; also the impressive collection of essays in T.W. Moody and F.X. Martin (eds.), *The Course of Irish History*, The Mercier Press, Cork, 1967. The essay by G.A. Hayes-McCoy in that volume directly addresses out point. See 'The Tudor Conquest (1534-1603),' pp. 174-88.

3.   For an excellent comparative analysis of 'mutually reinforcing cleavages' and regime stability see Richard Rose and Derek Unwin, 'Social Cohesion, Political Parties and Strains in Regimes,' in *Comparative Political Studies*, vol. 2, no. 1, April 1969, pp. 7-67.

4.   'Indigenous majority' includes here Coloureds who certainly are indigenous to South Africa and the Asians who certainly are not.

5.   Lipset and Rokkan have provided us with a useful perspective in using the Industrial Revolution as well as the National Revolution as broad analytic categories. See S.M. Lipset and S. Rokkan, 'Cleavage Structures, Party Systems, and Voter Alignments: An Introduction,' in Lipset and Rokkan (eds.), *Party Systems and Voter Alignments*, The Free Press, New York, 1967, pp. 1-64.

6.   See especially Shlomo Avineri (ed.), *Karl Marx on Colonialism and Modernization*, Doubleday Anchor, New York, 1969; and Robert C. Tucker, *The Marxian Revolutionary Idea*, W.W. Norton, New York, 1968.

7.   See especially Giovanni Arrighi, *The Political Economy of Rhodesia*, Mouton, The Hague, 1967; and Arghiri Emmanuel, 'White Settler Colonialism and the Myth of Investment Imperialism,' *New Left Review*, 73, May-June 1972, pp. 35-57.

8.   Louis Hartz (ed.), *The Founding of New Societies*, Harcourt, Brace, New York, 1964. The collaborators are Kenneth McRae (Canada), Richard Morse (Latin America), Richard N. Rosecrance (Australia), and Leonard M. Thompson (South Africa).

9.   For example see the suggestion of Richard Rose, *Governing Without Consensus*, Beacon Press, Boston, 1971, chapter III.

10.   The term 'modern' has been susceptible to confusion. We use it here to cover the period during the impact of the political thought of Machiavelli and others who theorised in terms of the nation-state. For a more thorough discussion, see Reinhard Bendix, 'Tradition and Modernity Reconsidered,' in *Comparative Studies in Society and History*, IX, April 1967, pp. 292-346.

11.   Hartz, *op. cit.*, pp. 11-16.

12.   'Fragmentation' here refers to the process whereby the quasi-fragment transforms itself into or is supplanted by the fragment. It also refers to the elaboration of the 'colonial fragment' into a 'national (independence) fragment' connoting the unfolding of a traditional political culture. The same term is used by other students of socially and culturally plural societies in describing the cleavages between the societal groups in those societies. See for example Alvin Rabushka and Kenneth Shepsle, *Politics in Plural Societies*, Charles Merrill, Columbus, 1972. In this sense the term 'fragment' is as confusing as the term 'plural.' However, we shall adhere to Hartz' use of 'fragment' and 'fragmentation' to avoid further misunderstanding.

13.   Hence a transplanted feudal ethos will remain strikingly feudal in contrast to the evolving European ethos, e.g. Quebec and Latin America; a liberal fragment ethos in the United States or Canada; and a radical ethos in Australia.

14.   'Sabra' is a Hebrew term used to describe those Israeli citizens actually born on Israeli soil. If Israel is perceived as a fragment society, then the 'sabra' can be understood as the legitimation of that fragment's existence.

15.   It is suggested here that there is a cross-cutting developing nexus between the fragment sectors and the imperial authorities against native interests on the one hand, and between the native elites and the imperial authorities against the fragment sectors on the other.

16.   See Terence O'Neill, *The Autobiography of Terence O'Neill*, Rupert Hart-Davis, London, 1972.

17.   F.X. Martin, 'The Anglo-Norman Invasion,' in T.W. Moody and F.X. Martin (eds.), *The Course of Irish History*, Mercier Press, Cork, 1967, p. 139.

18.   Thornley, *op. cit.*, p. 56.

19.   Martin, *op. cit.*, pp. 139-41.

20.   *Ibid.* p. 141.

21.   J. F. Lydon, 'The Medieval English Colony,' in Moody and Martin (eds.), *op. cit.*, p. 156.

22.   Not all planters were Scottish. Sir Basil Brooke's (the third Northern Ireland Prime Minister) family derive from an English 'servitor' granted lands under the original Ulster Plantation.

23.   See Andrew Boyd, *Holy War in Belfast*, 2nd edition, Anvil Books, Tralee, 1970, pp. 1-10.

24.   J.H. Whyte, 'The Age of Daniel O'Connell,' in Moody and Martin (eds.), *op. cit.*, p. 253.

25.   Senior, *op. cit.*, p. 221.

26.   T.W. Moody, 'Fenianism, Home Rule and the Land War,' in Moody and Martin (eds.), *op. cit.*, pp. 282-3.

27.   *Ibid.*, p. 285.

28.   *Ibid.*, p. 289.

29.   F.S. Lyons, *Ireland Since the Famine*, Weidenfeld & Nicholson, London, 1971, p. 286.

30.   From Southern Rhodesia Census Report, 1911 and 1931, Government Printer, Salisbury, 1911, 1931.

31.   From the Questionnaire entitled, 'The 1890 Pioneer Corps and the British South Africa Company's Police,' a form to be filled in by Pioneers or, in case of decease, by his dependants or relatives, and returned to the Government Archivist. For additional details on the substance and method of this questionnaire see B.M. Schutz, 'The Theory of Fragment and the Political Development of White Settler Society in Rhodesia' (unpublished Ph.D. dissertation, University of California at Los Angeles, 1972), p. 114.

32.   See Leonard M. Thompson, 'The South Africa Dilemma' in Hartz (ed.), *op. cit.*, pp. 178-218.

33.   See John S. Galbraith, *Reluctant Empire: British Policy on the South African Frontier, 1934-1854*, University of California Press, Berkeley, 1963.

34.   See Leonard M. Thompson, 'The South Africa Dilemma,' in Hartz (ed.), Little, Brown, Boston, 1966, pp. 4-17.

35.   Kenneth Kirkwood's analysis of the 'imperial inertia' of British colonial policy in his essay on 'Darwin and Durham: Some Problems of Race and Politics in the Multi-Racial Societies of the British Commonwealth and Colonial Empire,' in *Man, Race and Darwin*, Oxford University Press, Oxford, 1960, pp. 95-107 is especially keen on this point.

36.   See Claire Palley, *The Constitutional History and Law of Southern Rhodesia 1888-1965*, Clarendon Press, Oxford, 1966, pp. 16-26.

37.   The inclusion of Northern Rhodesia and Nyasaland was essentially an agreement between imperial and colonial interests. As colonial *protectorates*, these two territories were essentially under imperial control. Southern Rhodesia, on the other hand, had opted for and been granted internal self-government, thus achieving clear-cut colonial status with only circumscribed links to the imperial Centre.

38.   Thompson, *op. cit.*

39.   See especially James Barber, *Rhodesia: The Road to Rebellion*, Institute of Race Relations, Oxford University Press, London, 1967 and Frank Clements, *Rhodesia: The Course to Collision*, Pall Mall, London, 1969.

40.   See R.B. Sutcliffe, 'The Political Economy of Rhodesian Sanctions,' *The Journal of Commonwealth Studies*, vol. VII, July 1969, pp. 113-25.

41.   *1969 Rhodesian Population Census, Volume I, The European, Asian, and Coloured Population*, Government Printer, Salisbury, 1969.
42.   See A.K. Weinrich, *Chiefs and Councils in Rhodesia*, University of South Carolina Press, Columbia, S.C., 1971.
43.   See Herbert Adam, *Modernizing Racial Domination*, University of California Press, Berkeley, 1971, for this perspective in the South African case. Larry W. Bowman, 'Organization, Power, and Decision-Making within the Rhodesian Front,' *Journal of Commonwealth Political Studies*, VII, July 1969, pp. 145-65, provides data to support the Adam thesis in regard to Rhodesia.
44.   Rosecrance, *op. cit*. See especially Karl Deutsch, *Nationalism and Social Communication,* John Wiley and Sons, Inc., New York, 1953, for the basic statement on the role of social communications in the development of nationalism.
45.   Conor Cruse O'Brien, 'Violence in Ireland, Another Algeria?', *New York Review of Books*, XVII, 4 September 1971, pp. 17-19, for a comparison between Afrikaners and the Ulster Protestants in terms of Calvinist orientation; attitude to the land; attitude to the Church; the militant tendency toward violent defence; and the symbolic commemoration of these.
46.   An additional variable may be the role of class whereby social communications between fragment and home country might involve a specific class or regional cultural context, e.g. where primary communication and travel is between Northern Ireland and Scotland and between Ulster Protestant and Scottish non-elites; or, in Rhodesia, where communication and travel is more specifically English and middle class.
47.   J.L. McCracken, 'Northern Ireland,' in Moody and Martin (eds.), *op. cit.*, p. 316.
48.   First the settlers moved for parity with BSAC representatives; then for majority (achieving this by 1911). See Palley, *op. cit.*, pp. 191-201.
49.   The Federation included the two Rhodesias and Nyasaland. This political form was selected because it reflected the ostensible enhanced status of the indigenous peoples, although they were then to be regarded as 'junior partners' at best. See Patrick Keatley, *The Politics of Partnership*, Penguin Books, Baltimore, 1963.
50.   Lord Brookeborough (Sir Basil Brooke) was head of the Ulster Unionist Party and Prime Minister of Ulster from 1943 to 1963, while Lord Malvern (Sir Godfrey Huggins) was head of the United Federal Party (amongst its many names) and Prime Minister of Southern Rhodesia from 1933 to 1953. Lord Malvern also served as Prime Minister of the Central African Federation from 1953 to 1956.
51.   O'Neill, *op. cit.*, includes many accounts of such visits as well as the historical meetings with Sean Lemass and Jack Lynch.

3. RACE, ELECTIONS AND POLITICS[1]

Daniel Lawrence

According to one leading commentator, colour did not become a major factor in British politics until 1964.[2] In fact, the presence of black people in this country has been the subject of both political debate and government action for centuries. As early as 1596 an Act of the Privy Council expressed the view that 'there are of late divers blackamoors brought to this realm, of which kinds there are already too manie' and ruled that they 'should be sent forth of the land.'[3] In the eighteenth century a similar solution was proposed for the mainly freed but unemployed slaves who had become concentrated in the common lodging houses for the destitute in the St Giles area of London and, in 1787, 351 of them were shipped off (along with 60 white prostitutes) to Sierra Leone.[4] In 1919, following a spate of racial disturbances in a number of British ports, there were once again calls for the repatriation of coloured people.[5] At about the same time the concern expressed by trade unionists, over what they alleged to be unfair competition from coloured seamen, resulted in the Aliens Order of 1920, and the Special Restriction (Coloured Alien Seamen) Order of 1925, which not only limited the entry of non-white seamen into Britain but also helped create a situation in which it became extremely difficult for those already here to find employment. Yet more political involvement in race relations came with the 1935 British Shipping (Assistance) Act, which required shipowners receiving subsidies to give preferential treatment to seamen of British nationality.[6] These examples clearly demonstrate that neither black people themselves, not political concern over their presence here, are as new to Britain as is often supposed. Indeed the extent of Britain's involvement in the slave trade, and colonialism and imperialism more generally, makes it inconceivable that it could have been otherwise.

Nevertheless, it is perhaps only since the 1950s that matters relating to race relations have become of major and continuing political significance. This is primarily because before that time non-white British subjects made little use of the traditional right of free entry which accompanied their duty to owe allegiance to the Crown. But, as the exercising of that right became increasingly frequent, so political concern over Britain's open door policy became more pronounced. No more than ten years after some Conservatives had expressed concern lest the implicit distinction in the category 'citizen of the United Kingdom and Colonies' (contained in the Labour Government's 1948 British Nationality Act) might enable it to be used at some future date to introduce an 'artificial distinction' between British subjects, there had developed a powerful lobby within the Conservative Party pressing for just such a distinction to be invoked to restrict the entry of coloured British subjects to this country.[7] By June of 1962 the members of that lobby had their way, and the Commonwealth Immigrants Act removed the right of free entry which for centuries before had been enjoyed by all British subjects. The Act did not receive the support of the Parliamentary Labour Party. Yet, shortly after returning to office in 1964, it went even further than the Conservative Government and introduced a ceiling on the number of entry vouchers to be issued under the Act in any one year. There can be no doubt that both measures were introduced in response to what politicians saw as a growing and irresistible clamour for control amongst the electorate.

During the years that followed, immigration continued to be an extremely controversial issue. Peter Griffiths, on an openly racial platform, and in defiance of the national swing, won Smethwick in the 1964 general election for the Conservatives. In 1968, at a time of particular hardship for Kenyan Asians holding British passports, legislation was rushed through Parliament to prevent them from using their passports to enter Britain freely — an action subsequently condemned by no less a body than the International Commission of Jurists. It was in the same year that Enoch Powell made his dramatic entry on to the race relations scene. His extraordinarily well-publicised speeches precipitated his expulsion from the Conservative Shadow Cabinet, and thousands of white workers demonstrated (and in a few instances even went on strike) in support of his views.

Given his obvious importance, the race issue has attracted surprisingly little attention from political sociologists. They have particularly neglected the electoral behaviour of those very black people whose presence in Britain has been the subject of so much controversy. This is probably because most students of voting behaviour are more interested in explaining and predicting the outcome of elections than understanding the relationship between political behaviour and social structure. And, of course, since coloured immigrants are not sufficiently numerous to make any direct difference to the outcome of an election in more than a few constituencies, a psephological rather than a sociological orientation does render their electoral behaviour fairly uninteresting. The greater interest shown in the impact of the race issue on the voting behaviour of native whites reflects the fact that the presence of even a small number of immigrants can still make a significant contribution to a result. As Deakin and Bourne rightly note:
' . . . Elections have been the occasion for speculation on the response of the white majority: immigrants have been seen chiefly as a stimulus which promotes certain sections of Labour supporters into defecting to the Conservatives.'[8]

No less striking than the lack of interest in the race issue amongst political sociologists is the conclusion reached by those who have examined it. They seem agreed that in spite of its political importance the race issue has only rarely affected the outcome of an election in any crucial way. Indeed the case of Smethwick in 1964, when Peter Griffiths defeated Patrick Gordon-Walker, is perhaps the sole instance in which it is generally held that the race issue was decisive. In their Nuffield Election Study, Butler and King conclude that it made no appreciable difference to the swing in the great majority of constituencies in which coloured immigrants were found in 1964 and, in his special Appendix, Steed argues that immigration problems had no general effect on the election.[9] Contrary to the expectations of many commentators, the race issue was even less prominent in 1966 – so much so that Deakin begins his account of the Election by stating:

'The issue of coloured immigration cannot be shown to have had any significant political impact at the British General Election of 1966, in terms of voting behaviour. This conclusion needs to be stated baldly at the beginning of any analysis of the long term implications of the result of the election for race relations in Britain, since it falsifies the prophecies made after the last General Election by so many observers including the present writer.'[10]

In spite of the intervention of Enoch Powell in the 1970 Election, and the extensive publicity given to his charge that the British people had been misled over immigration figures, with the astonishing implication that there were traitors in the Civil Service, the race issue is generally held not to have been a central issue. Deakin and Bourne, for example, argue that 'despite the publicity given to Mr Powell and Mr Benn, the general public appear to have been less interested in the issue than the mass media'[11] and that 'by the close of the campaign, race did not appear to have stablished itself as a central issue.'[12] Butler and Pinto-Duschinsky advance a similar view.

'Despite the deterioration in race relations since 1966, and Mr Powell's powerful speeches on immigration during the campaign, the 1970 Election was not marked by the bitterness, the racial slogans or the obscenities that were apparent in a few constituencies in 1964 . . . it is unlikely that coloured immigration swayed many white voters in 1970.'[13]

This conclusion about the comparative electoral impotence of the race issue is puzzling when set alongside the fact that politicians have obviously found the issue extremely troublesome. For this reason, it will be helpful to begin the discussion of the relationship between race, elections and politics with some general observations on the role of issues in the determination of electoral behaviour.

Although it is now firmly established that electors are poorly informed spectators who differ from politicians in their view of political issues this does not mean that issues play no part in the shaping of their party preferences. Even those issues which fail to evoke a strong direct response from voters may still affect their behaviour indirectly. For example, electors may focus not on actual policies but on the apparent consequences of policies and in this way credit or blame governments for conditions over which they have no control. However, 'race' is generally agreed to be one of those exceptional issues that has evoked a strong and clearly discernible response from the elctorate. As a result, it is held to have the potential to make a marked impact on electoral behaviour. One possible explanation of why this potential appears not to have been realised is to be found in Butler and Stokes' *Political Change in Britain*. They emphasise that the influence of an issue depends not just on whether or not it 'excites genuine and strong attitudes in significant parts of the electorate' but also on the nature of the links which are thought to exist between the issue and the major political parties.

> 'The sharpest impact on party strength will be made by issues which simultaneously meet three conditions, that is to say by issues on which attitudes are widely formed, on which opinion is far from evenly divided and on which the parties are strongly differentiated in the public's mind.'[14]

They go on to suggest that despite the widespread opposition to coloured immigration the race issue has 'never exercised anything like its potential impact on the party balance, because the public has failed to differentiate the party positions.'[15] As support for this conclusion they cite a number of findings from their own study of public opinion: for example, that as many as 61 per cent of their respondents saw no difference between the parties' policies on the issue of immigration control.[16]

To find that relatively few members of the electorate distinguish between the parties in this respect is not entirely unexpected. Since control over Commonwealth immigration was first introduced in 1962 the positions of the Labour and Conservative parties have certainly converged. Moreover, both parties have been internally divided on the desirability of some of the particular restrictive measures which have been brought in. There is also evidence that both major parties have tried to play down the race issue during elections.[17] One of the effects of this may have been to blur still further the slight remaining differences between the parties — differences, it may be added, which would probably be known to, and fully understood by, only the small and politically well-informed section of the electorate.

Far from providing an adequate explanation of the allegedly small electoral impact of the race issue, however, the finding that the majority of the electorate do not distinguish between the parties' policies on race actually undermines the very conclusion it is held to explain. Although the Labour and Conservative positions on race and immigration have undoubtedly converged since 1962, significant (albeit minor) differences have remained. This has, not unreasonably, encouraged political commentators to continue to think of Labour as the more liberal of the two main parties. But, less reasonably, they seem to have assumed that these minor differences are recognised and thought to be significant by the electorate as a whole. This failure to comprehend the nature of the public's knowledge and understanding of policies is, perhaps, attributable to a 'subtle bias' which Butler and Stokes suggest arises from the fact that elite observers have little real contact with the general public: 'the politician, the journalist and the political scientists all tend to encounter people whose interest in politics is grossly unrepresentative of their fellow citizens.'[18] In this instance, the bias has led to the already noted tendency for elections to be seen as an occasion for speculation on how much the race issue has caused Labour voters to defect to the Conservatives. In particular, it has resulted in comparisons of the swing in constituencies with varying proportions of coloured people in an effort to establish whether or not the race issue has produced significant shifts in party allegiances. The underlying assumption of such comparisons has been that since most electors are firmly opposed to coloured immigration there will be a tendency for the swing to the Conservatives to be greater (or the swing to Labour less great) in constituencies with large numbers of coloured immigrants. If the race issue has not been electorally significant it is assumed that there will be no marked difference in the swing. I shall suggest below that this kind of exercise is misleading for several reasons. At this stage it is sufficient to note that it is misleading because, from as early as 1964, the majority of the electorate did not consider the Conservatives' policy on race to be any more or less appropriate than Labour's. As a consequence, the 'swing test' of the significance of the race issue is clearly unreliable.[19]

Deakin's use of the 'swing test' in the case of the 1966 General Election amply illustrates this point. He notes that:

'In seats significantly affected by immigration the swing to Labour was 3.8 per cent, compared with 2.6 per cent for the United Kingdom as a whole. More important, in the West Midlands, the area widely regarded as being the most likely to produce deviant results as a consequence of resentment on the immigration issue, the swing to Labour was also significantly above the national average — 3.7 per cent. Moreover, of the 51 seats identified by A.J. Allen and Associates for the *Economist* as being chiefly affected 18 were held by the Conservatives at the Dissolution but no less than 13 of these fell to Labour at the Election.'[20]

His conclusion is that 'the issue of coloured immigration *cannot be shown to have had* any significant political impact at the British General Election, in terms of voting behaviour' (my italics). His implication, however, is that it *did not have* any significant impact. My own view is that a comparison of swings cannot tell us anything useful about the role of the race issue one way or the other. For 52 per cent of those interviewed by Butler and Stokes in 1966, in areas of high immigrant concentration, there seemed to be no difference between the two major parties on the race issue; for 11 per cent a vote for Labour would be the obvious decision, and only for the remaining 37 per cent would it make sense to vote Conservative.

But, even if more of the electorate had distinguished between the parties on the race issue, the swing could still not have told us anything about the electoral impact of the race issue. It is possible, for example, that an average swing could have masked a large immigrant swing to Labour as well as a large white working-class swing to the Conservatives.[21] Furthermore, it cannot be assumed that racialist appeals are potentially significant in only those constituencies with high immigrant populations. They may also have a strong appeal in areas in which a section of the electorate simply fears the possibility of an immigrant influx. Once allowance is also made for variations at a constituency level in terms of the composition of the electorate, the parties represented (major and minor), the positions adopted on the race issue by particular candidates, the importance of other issues (local and national) and so on, then it is obvious that such a crude measure as the swing cannot tell us anything about the role of any particular issue in an election campaign. It cannot be *demonstrated* that the race issue was influential in 1966, but examining the pattern of swings does not allow us to conclude that it was uninfluential. It may be that a markedly exceptional swing provides *prima facie* grounds for judging the race issue important in certain circumstances (for example, the campaign in Smethwick in 1964), but on the whole it is simply not possible to derive such conclusions from a study of swing patterns.

Deakin, of course, does not rely solely on the 'swing test' to support his conclusion about the comparative irrelevance of the race issue in 1966.

'National Opinion Polls found that only one person in twelve ranked immigration as the most important issue facing the country, and one third placed it last in significance in a list of seven issues . . . even in Smethwick immigration ranked some way below housing.'[22]

Similar evidence was used by Deakin and Bourne in their discussion of the 1970 Election.

'In four Gallup surveys carried out in the month before the election, no more than 10 per cent of the sample ever selected immigration as the most urgent problem facing the country and in the final poll, two days before the election only 8 per cent mentioned immigration, the cost of living issue having captured far more attention.'[23]

Nevertheless, even this apparently direct evidence on the relevance of the race issue does not allow us to conclude that it lacked impact in the 1966 and 1970 Elections. It is doubtful, for example, if the term 'immigration' adequately sums up what it is about the race issue which most concerns many members of the electorate. More obviously, questioning respondents about the most urgent or important questions facing *the country*, does not necessaily indicate what it is that they see to be the most pressing problems facing *them*. There is also a possibility that some respondents will answer questions such as these, not in terms of what *they* think is the most urgent problem, but rather in terms of what the reporting of the campaign by the mass media has suggested to them is generally considered to be the most important.

However, these several possible specific flaws mask a more fundamental one. What the questions attempt to measure is not the actual significance of the race issue (or even the more specific issue of immigration) but the extent to which the race issue *in itself* is an issue of concern to the electorate. The form taken by the pollsters' questions makes no allowance for the possibility that the race issue may be important not only in isolation, but also because of its real or imagined relationship to other issues. There is no way in which questions asking people to rank issues in importance, or to state which issue they judge to be the most urgent, can begin to measure the combined or interactive effect of the race issue. If, for example, some electors are concerned about immigration because they believe it will exacerbate the housing crisis, there is no way in which this far from exceptional kind of view will be revealed by the type of questions which have been put to the electorate by the pollsters.

It is difficult to overstate the importance of this point, for the flaw characterises not only the questions used by opinion pollsters, but also the analyses of the relationship between race and elections so far discussed. This is not to deny that in particular instances race may not stand out as a separate issue. But, for most people, it is probably intimately related, whether consciously or unconsciously, to other issues. Furthermore, there is no reason to suppose that the nature of the relationship with other issues need be as simple as in the example of race and housing already mentioned. It seems more likely that the relationship will be complex and something not even understood by electors themselves. In other words, even if it could be shown that the race issue had made no great electoral impact as an independent issue, it could still be argued that it may have made a substantial influence on electoral behaviour indirectly. Unfortunately, since indirect influences are not easily demonstrated much of what follows must be speculative. However, even if the particular argument advanced is not considered convincing, it does seem that it is in this general direction that further research and analysis must go if the relationship between race, elections and politics is to be fully understood. I shall suggest that, whether or

61

not the race issue has been directly responsible for changes in party allegiances, coloured immigration and the resultant race issue may have made a significant contribution to the more general disillusionment with party politics and politicians evident in some quarters of the electorate; that it may have helped reduce the enthusiasm with which many recent votes have been cast for the two main parties; and also that it may have increased the likelihood of support going to minor parties — especially, but not necessarily, those with distinctive positions on race relations and immigration.

There is now considerable evidence that many electors do not believe there is any fundamental difference between the two major parties. For almost twenty-five years the Gallup Poll has been asking its respondents: 'Do you think that there is any really important difference between the parties or are they all much the same?' (or 'all much of a muchness'). The pattern of replies obtained over this period is summarised in the accompanying diagram.[24] It shows that since 1951 there has been a marked decline in the proportion of respondents who believe there to be an important difference between the parties.[25] Moreover, the 1970 Election seems to have been fought with only half of those interviewed believing there to be anything very significant to choose between them.[26]

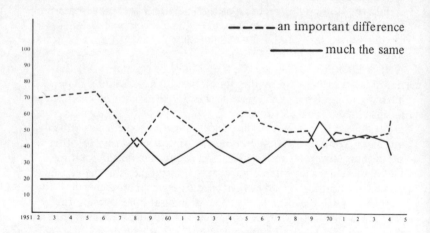

'Do you think that there is any really important difference between the parties or are they all much the same?' (or 'much of a muchness').

Survey evidence also exists to support the view that many members of the electorate are disillusioned with both politicians and party politics. In 1966, 57 per cent of an NOP sample agreed with the statement: 'Politicians these days are out of touch with ordinary people' and an identical proportion claimed most politicians were more interested 'in the good of their party' than 'in the good of the country as a whole.'[27] In 1968, a large proportion of an NOP sample agreed with a similar series of cynical statements. For example, 57 per cent alleged: 'Most politicians are in it for what they can get out of it'; 66 per cent asserted: 'Most politicians care more about their party than their country'; and as many as 78 per cent were prepared to believe that: 'Most politicians will promise anything to get votes.'[28]

It is possible that disillusionment may have reached a peak in the late 1960s as an NOP poll for Granada TV in November 1972 found smaller proportions agreeing with the kind of statements used in their 1968 study. Even so, 40 per cent were still prepared to assert that: 'Most politicians are in it for what they can get out of it' and 62 per cent felt that: 'Most politicians will promise anything to get votes.' There are also other indications that a widespread disillusionment with our party political structure may have continued into the 1970s. One obvious example is the trend in turnouts at general elections. In 1950 the turnout was 84 per cent. By 1970 it had fallen fairly consistently to 72 per cent and, even after allowance is made for the fact that the 1970 Election was held in June with a slightly older register, there can be no doubt that a real decline had occurred.[29] Even the relatively high turnout of 79 per cent in the February 1974 Election was significantly below that of 84 per cent for the February 1950 Election held with an equally new register. It can also be argued that the reversal of the downward trend in 1974 supports rather than undermines the view that there is a widespread disillusionment with our party political structure. For, whilst it is true that more votes were cast in 1974 than in 1970, there was a marked fall in the number of votes cast for the two major parties.[30] This would seem to reflect an increasing dissatisfaction with the electoral and political ascendency of Labour and Conservative, rather than any returning confidence in the party political structure they have dominated so completely for decades.[31]

I do not intend to discuss the extent to which this widespread belief in the essential similarity of the two major parties, and disillusionment with party politics and politicians, is justified. However, in order to appreciate the relevance of such views to the race issue, it is necessary at least to note some of the factors which may account for their development. The first is that the difference in the composition of the Parliamentary Labour and Conservative parties has narrowed considerably.[32] As a result, working-class electors are now less likely to be able to identify with many Labour MPs — and certainly working-class electors are more likely than their middle-class counterparts to complain about disappearing party differences and politicians being out of touch with the problems of ordinary people.[33] A convergence in the positions of the two major parties also seems evident in the field of policy.[34] Of course disenchantment with party politics is not necessarily ideological in character and those who complain about the two major parties may be more concerned with their level of competence than with whether or not they are sticking to ideologically based policies. Nevertheless, in the present climate, apparent political somersaults and U-turns are more likely to be seen as evidence that politicians do not keep their promises than that they are sufficiently wise to shift their positions as circumstances demand. Britain's economic and other difficulties have no doubt contributed to and further compounded this feeling of disenchantment. As was noted earlier, electors often make sense of the complexity of party politics by focusing not on the details of policy alternatives but on the apparent consequences of any particular party being in office. In this way, a party may receive praise or blame for a state of affairs over which it may have had little direct control. Over the past decade or so, however, electors have probably been attributing blame very much more often than praise. On a whole range of issues ranging from permissiveness to the general price of inflation of recent years, there is clear evidence of a widespread dissatisfaction with the *status quo*.[35] There is also evidence that most people feel Britain has now lost its place as one of the leading nations of the world.[36] The fact that many of these things which members of the electorate define as our most serious economic and social problems have not been solved by a succession of governments makes it more likely that politicians in general, rather than any particular political party, will be held responsible for them − or at least judged not to be capable of providing solutions to them. Moreover, the marked tendency of governments to blame their predecessors for unpopular conditions probably reinforces this since it makes the assigning of blame (or praise) to any one party much more difficult.

There can be no doubt that the particular issue of Commonwealth immigration has contributed to this general feeling of disillusionment with party politics. It is an issue on which most members of the electorate have always had a clear-cut view. Butler and Stokes, for example, found that over 80 per cent of their three samples (questioned in 1963, 1964, and 1966) felt that 'too many immigrants had been let into the country' and such findings are in close accord with the results of a whole series of opinion polls and other studies.[37] One conclusion which electors could and many undoubtedly did draw from the influx of immigrants was that politicians were out of touch with the wishes and day to day problems or ordinary people − particularly those living in areas of high immigrant concentration. Of course it is true that immigration control was introduced in response to the clamour for it from the electorate. But by the time the first Commonwealth Immigration Act was introduced in 1962 there were already about one million coloured people in Britain and many felt that the legislation had come too late to be of very much value. The further restrictions brought into force in 1965, 1968 and 1971 may be seen as a recognition on the part of politicians that this was what many native whites wanted, but the changes will often have been interpreted by electors as clear signs that too little was done too late by politicians, rather than that the situation was always being closely controlled. It has already been noted that most electors do not believe that there is much difference between the parties on the race issue. In part, this reflects the fact that their policies have converged, and that in the course of election campaigns they have tended to play down what differences do exist. But it is probably also due to the fact that many members of the electorate simply feel that successive governments have failed to get to grips with what they see as a very pressing problem: a view which seems to be reflected in the arguments of those who now favour not only immigration control, but also a policy of repatriation. It may be added that the failure of politicians to deal with coloured immigration in a way which satisfied the majority of the electorate may have had a heightened significance, since the fundamental shift in the status of the immigrants, from former colonial subjects to full citizens of the UK, symbolised the decline of Britain as a world power. No longer did Britain rule over hundreds of millions of coloured people in her colonies. On the contrary, British people were now expected to treat as equals at home those who only a short time before had been the subject peoples of their great Empire.

In short, whether or not the race issue has had any direct impact on election results in other than a few exceptional cases, there are good grounds for supposing that both in its own right, and through its relationship with other issues, it may over a period of years have made a sizeable contribution to what seems to be a growing disenchantment with politicians and party politics more generally. Whether or not it has actually shifted much support from one party to another in most elections, the race issue may very well have played a part in increasing the number of non-voters and also undermined the confidence and enthusiasm with which many other electors cast their votes. And, despite the fact that the race issue did not figure prominently in the 1974 Election, it is possible that it could have helped increase the size of the Liberal vote at the expense of the Labour and Conservative parties. This is not to suggest that the Liberal position on race relations and immigration is any closer to the views of the electorate than that of the other major parties. Nor is it to suggest that votes were cast for the Liberals in 1974 because some electors felt that they would adopt a tougher line on the race issue than the other parties. However, it remains possible that the Liberals benefited indirectly from the race issue in so far as their improved position seems to have been primarily

a result of disillusionment with the other major parties: a disillusionment which stems in part from the way in which they have handled the
race issue. Were the race issue to have had only a direct and independent effect on electoral behaviour then only parties with a clear-cut and
tough position (like the National Front) might have benefited. Since
its impact also operates indirectly and in interaction with other issues,
however, it may have been of advantage to less obvious political groups.
In the case of the Liberals, it could be that they picked up the votes of
many disillusioned electors primarily, and perhaps only, because they
emphasised the extent to which they represented the sole feasible way
of breaking away from the domination of the two other parties.

The obvious appeal of Enoch Powell to many voters since his
dramatic intervention in the debate on immigration control provides
further support for the foregoing analysis. He alone of senior politicians
has given the impression of being prepared to speak out against those in
both parties who have allowed immigration to take place on a scale
which most electors judge unacceptable. His expulsion from the
Shadow Cabinet in 1968 helped establish him in the eyes of many
people as a man prepared to commit political suicide, if necessary, in
pursuit of those political ends he felt vital for the survival of the kind
of Britain he loved. The style of his speeches, and the manner in which
he has been condemned by the leading politicians of all major parties,
has cast him in the role of the one politician of stature capable of
appreciating how ordinary people are feeling, who is also prepared to
fulfil his duty to speak out on their behalf. The simple and superficially
plausible arguments advanced in his speeches, in which he has portrayed himself as the mouthpiece of his constituents, must have proved
especially gratifying to those who have lost confidence in other politicians. That those who support Powell often know little of the detailed
content of his speeches (or his position on other issues) is of no great
consequence, for his main attraction seems to be as a man prepared to
stand up for the ordinary citizen against the party battalions. His repatriation proposal (whilst, in fact, hopelessly impracticable) has the
advantage of appearing straightforward (and even humane) in contrast
to the indecisive and vague proposals on race relations offered by other
leading figures — figures who to many seem incapable of seeing the race
problem in the same stark, clear-cut and 'realistic' way they see it
themselves. To many of those who have grown tired and cynical of
party politicians, Powell's identification with and apparent concern for
ordinary people is probably sufficient to earn him their support.

I have argued that to understand the role played by the race issue it
must be treated not only as an independent variable with a potential to
affect electoral behaviour directly, but also as one in which interaction
with other issues and factors can have a significant *indirect* impact on
voting behaviour. That there is any need to make this point reflects the

extent to which enquiries into electoral behaviour are often conducted
in a more or less mechanical fashion without serious attention being
paid to the social situation of voters. Relationships are frequently
established between party choice and such variables as socioeconomic
position, age and sex, but rarely are party preferences investigated as
manifestations of the (changing) social situations of particular groups of
men and women. For this reason, our understanding of voting behaviour is still very limited. And, since mechanically established correlations
are often the only kind of evidence on which explanations are based,
it is inevitable that they are frequently little more than intuitive in
character. This is true even in the case of the well-established and crucial relationship between party choice and socioeconomic position. No
doubt encouraged by the apparent consistency in voting behaviour, as
well as the fact that party support divides so clearly along class lines,
there has been a marked tendency to assume both that most voters see
the choice between the parties as clear-cut, and that the meaning of
most of the votes cast by electors is self-evident. Most members of the
working class obviously vote Labour because it is (and is seen by them
to be) the party of the working class, and most members of the middle
and upper classes vote Conservative because that party represents (and
is seen by them to represent) their class interests. What is not self-
evident is the significance of the votes cast by those who, like working-
class Conservatives, deviate from the class pattern. But it is often
assumed that, for the large majority, the significance of Labour and
Conservative voting can be easily discerned in the different class
characteristics of those who vote Labour and Conservative. Yet, as
Butler and Stokes have pointed out, 'our evidence about the nature of
the link remains oddly limited.'

> 'First, too little attention has been paid to the beliefs that link class
> to party in the voter's mind; the system of ideas, the attitudes,
> motives and beliefs which lie behind the observed differences have
> been largely neglected. Second, treatments of class alignments have
> tended to be static in their approach.'[38]

Now if our understanding of such a well-established link as that between class and party is still 'oddly limited,' it is inconceivable that we
will come to understand the complications introduced by the race
issue if we do no more than calculate swings and ask respondents what
they think are the most important problems facing the country. Clearly,
any serious attempt to determine how a new factor in British politics
like race has affected, and will affect, electoral behaviour must be
incorporated within a much wider examination of the voting behaviour
and changing social situation of those affected by it. What follows, is an
attempt to do so with data collected in the course of a study of race
relations in Nottingham. This evidence alone cannot be used as the
basis for widespread generalisations since those interviewed are not in

any sense representative of the electorate as a whole. The samples were drawn from a specially constructed sampling frame of adult males living in a central city area in which there was a large proportion of Commonwealth immigrants. However, it is quite possible that the findings obtained are not markedly different from those that would have emerged had comparable investigations been conducted in similar constituencies elsewhere.[39]

Sixty per cent of the immigrant respondents were West Indian (the vast majority from Jamaica) and the remainder were from India (22 per cent) and Pakistan (18 per cent). Most had come to Britain for negative rather than positive reasons. Though their migration was 'voluntary,' few would have left home had economic circumstances not been so difficult. Moreover, many would have preferred to go to other countries had it been possible. They came to Britain, in all but a handful of cases, not to settle but to work for a time and then return and, even though they had spent many years in Britain when interviewed, a majority still did not intend to settle permanently. Few had found Britain as they expected and most did not feel welcome here. Indeed, most still saw themselves very much as outsiders — some even more so than when they arrived. Few of the immigrants were well qualified. They were mainly employed in manual (predominantly unskilled and semi-skilled) jobs in a limited range of industries and were earning wages significantly below the national average for manual workers. Most expressed satisfaction with their jobs and the vast majority were extremely realistic in their employment aspirations. Nevertheless, resentment often dominated the part of the interview dealing with employment. It stemmed, in most cases, not from personal job dissatisfaction but the conviction that racial discrimination was widespread. Similar expressions of resentment were common when housing was discussed. Although the vast majority of immigrants lived in what most would judge to be substandard housing, most seemed to be fairly satisfied with it. Resentment arose from the conviction that racial discrimination was prevalent and made it more difficult for immigrants to get council houses and buy their own homes. On the whole, most of the immigrant respondents were very apprehensive about their own future and that of their children in Britain, and very doubtful about the possibility of ever eliminating racial discrimination.

Whereas all of the coloured people interviewed were immigrants, most of the white respondents had been born in Nottingham or its immediate environs and as many as 70 per cent had lived in Nottingham all of their lives. It is therefore hardly surprising that most of them felt they had a prior claim on jobs and houses. Like the immigrants, most of the native whites were manual workers (almost half were unskilled or semi-skilled), earned wages significantly below the national average and also lived in accommodation which would generally be held to be substandard. In comparison with most of those living in the countries from which the immigrants had come the native whites might well be judged relatively affluent. However, in comparison with the indigenous population of the country as a whole, they are certainly underprivileged. Most of them belong to the group my Nottingham colleagues, Coates and Silburn, have termed 'the forgotten Englishmen' in their book on poverty.[40] They are not in danger of starving but neither do they enjoy, or have much prospect of enjoying, the secure and comfortable existence which many of the immigrants believed typical of everyone in this country. They subsist, by national standards, on low wages or mean pensions, and this is the main reason why they live in the inner zone of the city. There they live what is effectively a different kind of life from that which is taken for granted by so many of those who live in the pleasant suburbs that ring the city. It is they (and those like them elsewhere) who are hit hardest by inflation, our chronic housing problem, and the anxiety and loss of dignity and self-respect which so often accompanies material deprivation. They comprise, in short, one of the most vulnerable sections of the indigenous population and, in many respects, those most likely to feel threatened by highly visible competitors for scarce resources. Consistent with this, most of the native whites interviewed argued that English people ought to receive priority in the allocation of council houses and in the field of employment. Like the immigrants, however, they too were very apprehensive about the future of race relations Indeed, as many as 74 per cent of them thought that there could be a repetition of Nottingham's 1958 racial disturbances.

Majorities in both samples had voted in the most recent general election held prior to the interviews — that of 1966. However, 27 per cent of the immigrant respondents were unregistered: usually because they did not know of, or understand, the registration procedure. The incidence of both registration and voting varied with the length of stay, educational level and socioeconomic position of the immigrants. It was the poorly educated, unskilled and recently arrived amongst them who were least likely to have been registered or, if registered, to have failed to vote. Failure to register or vote seems to have been indicative of a more general lack of enthusiasm for politics. For example, only 52 per cent of those who had not been interested in politics in their home countries had voted, compared with as many as 80 per cent of those who had been politically active. Yet even amongst the voters the level of interest and involvement in *British* politics was low. Only two immigrant respondents were members of political parties and, at least as measured by familiarity with the names of political figures, there was evidence of considerable political ignorance. But this low level of interest in *British* politics does not necessarily reflect a similar level of interest in other political matters. Indeed as many as 61 per cent of the immigrant respondents said they had been interested in politics in their country of origin and, whereas less than 2 per cent were members of

British political parties, the corresponding membership figure for parties at home was 20 per cent. This would suggest that it is the feeling of being an outsider in this country, rather than a lack of political consciousness, which determines the low level of involvement in British politics for many immigrants.

Almost all of the immigrant respondents who turned out at the 1966 Election voted Labour. Only amongst the Indian respondents was there any sign of a significant non-Labour vote and, with 27 per cent of them voting Conservative, they behaved in almost identical fashion to the white voters. Most of those in both samples who had voted in 1966 had also voted in 1964. In this instance too the immigrants were less likely to have been registered and the proportion of them who had cast a vote was smaller than amongst the whites. Moreover, the way in which the votes were distributed between the parties was very similar to the pattern which obtained for 1966. In both samples clear majorities had voted Labour, and again there was greater minority support for the Conservatives amongst the indigenous voters. Amongst the immigrants it was again most noticeable amongst the Indians. Respondents were also asked about their behaviour in the previous Council election and their replies followed the same pattern as for the 1964 and 1966 General Elections. The only difference in this case was that a greater proportion in both samples had abstained.

As expected, most of the native whites who had voted Labour in 1966 said that they had done so because they believed (at the time) that it represented the interests of the working class. For example:

'I've always voted Labour. I've always been a working-class man and I've been led to believe that Labour are working-class.'

'I think it's because I was born into it, and I don't see why a working-class man should vote the opposite side of the fence.'

Only 18 per cent of the immigrants who voted Labour gave similar replies. Rather more (38 per cent) saw their self-interest primarily as coloured immigrants rather than members of the working class.

'Well I hear — I don't know if it's true — that the Conservatives don't like the coloured people and don't want us here. But the Labour they do a lot for us so I give them my vote.'

'I heard Wilson say some things about coloured people and they wasn't bad — they was friendly.'

A further 16 per cent of the native whites claimed to have voted Labour for little other than force of habit and, although not a single immigrant answered the question in this way, 12 per cent (all Jamaicans) said they voted Labour in Britain because they had always voted Labour at home — which is tantamount to voting from force of habit. The only other significant way in which the answers of the Labour voters differed is that 14 per cent of the immigrants (but none of the indigenous voters) said that they had no particular reason for voting Labour. Very often this meant that they had blindly followed someone else's advice.

The most interesting aspect of these answers is undoubtedly the fact that, compared to the white voters, relatively few of the immigrants said that they had voted Labour because it represented their interests as members of the working class. But, in this particular instance, presenting the findings for the immigrants as a whole masks a marked difference between the West Indians on the one hand and the Indians and Pakistanis on the other. For, whilst the Indians and Pakistanis gave reasons to do with their position as coloured immigrants as frequently as the West Indians, they also gave reasons to do with class as frequently as the whites. It was the West Indians amongst the immigrants who scarcely ever expressed themselves in class terms.

When respondents were asked about their future voting intentions there were signs that the fairly consistent pattern which had obtained in 1964 and 1966 might be beginning to break down. The most obvious indication amongst the native white respondents was how many of them had become uncertain about voting Labour. For whilst the support for the Conservative Party had shown only a small increase, support for the Labour Party had slumped. Even so, it was amongst the immigrants that disenchantment with the Labour Party was most marked. The proportion of immigrant voters who had supported Labour in 1966 was as high as 93 per cent. The proportion of those interviewed who said that they would vote Labour 'if there was a General Election tomorrow' was as small as 23 per cent. Most striking, apart from this, was the large proportion who said that they did not know how they would vote – or that they would definitely not be voting. Obviously questions about future voting intentions may be worth little as predictors of actual electoral behaviour except when they are put at a time when an election is imminent – but they are interesting as rough and ready indicators of the extent of really solid support that a party enjoys. Looked at in this way, it suggests that the Labour Party cannot any longer be certain of the support of nearly all coloured immigrant voters – or even most white working-class voters.

Something of what the respondents felt about the choice offered to them at elections was established through a series of questions put to them in the course of the interviews. The first questions was: 'What would you say are the main differences between the Labour and Conservative parties?' By implying in the wording of the question that significant differences did exist, respondents may have been discouraged from suggesting that this was not the case. On the other hand, it does render the fact that so many did make such an assertion all the more striking. As many as 23 per cent of the immigrants and 39 per cent of the native whites voiced opinions of this kind.

'When they want to get elected then they make promises and seem different — but when they get in then there's no difference at all.'

'There's no difference. A dog is a dog whether white or black. A change in colour does not alter the fact that it's a dog. They just bark differently.'

'No difference at all — they're both rotten.'

'There isn't one — they both line their own pockets.'

'As they are now there's not much difference between the parties. Once they're elected into power they forget all their promises. I've no faith in politicians at all.'

A further 35 per cent of the immigrants and 8 per cent of the whites said that they were not familiar with any differences between the parties. Thus nearly 60 per cent of the immigrants and 47 per cent of the natives said that they could not distinguish between the parties or did not believe there was anything significant between them to distinguish.

A second question put to all respondents was: 'Do you think it makes much difference *to the country* which of them wins an election?' As many as 46 per cent of the white indigenous respondents and 35 per cent of the immigrants said that they did not think it did.

'No, because no matter who's in they're going to pull each other to pieces and bash the working man.'

'No. They only promise to do different things so that the public will vote them in. Once in power they do exactly the same as each other.'

'How will it make a difference — you tell me — they're just the same.'

'No — both parties make a mess of it. The only real difference is that the Conservatives kept quieter about it.'

'It doesn't make any difference to the country. It only makes a difference to a party leader and his followers.'

A further 21 per cent of the immigrants, and 4 per cent of the native whites said that they did not know whether or not it made any difference. In other words, half of the whites and well over half of the immigrants were not convinced that the election of one party rather than the other made any appreciable difference to the country.

The third question in the sequence was: 'Do you think it makes much difference *to you personally* which of them wins an election?' Once again, the most striking feature of the replies was how few of the respondents thought that it did. As many as 61 per cent of the whites and 42 per cent of the immigrants said that it made no difference.

Moreover, a further 14 per cent of the immigrants said that they did not know whether or not it made any difference to them.

'No, quite honestly. They both hammer the working man. If they can't tax him on drinks they will on cigarettes or something else. They'll get at him somehow.'

'It should do — but it doesn't. If the Labour party was what it's supposed to be it should help the working man — but it's just the same as the other.'

'No — I'm not sure really why I vote Labour. You have to accept things. I do my duty and vote.'

'No. We should be better off under Labour but we aren't.

'It doesn't affect me brother. I just keep going.'

Finally, in this sequence of questions, all respondents were asked: 'Would you say there is any difference in the attitudes of the Labour and Conservative parties towards coloured immigrants?' As many as 20 per cent of the native whites said they did not know whether or not there was any difference. However, over half of them (53 per cent) were convinced that there was none.

'No — both sides import them and land the country with paying for them.'

'I haven't noticed any. They must all look to coloured people otherwise they wouldn't keep bringing them in.'

'Only in theory. Both say they'll deal with the problems of immigration when they're in opposition but continue to let them into the country when they're in power.'

The replies from the immigrant respondents to the question were fairly similar to those given by the whites. A quarter said that they did not know if there was any difference between the parties. A further 34 per cent said that they were sure that there was none. For example:

'No difference at all. No one is concerned about us.'

'The watch and the clock keep the same time — only their faces are different.'

'Before they got into power Labour was acting as if they favoured the coloured people but they've done nothing — I don't know if their hands are tied or what — but they're no different from the Conservatives.'

'Both their attitudes is to forget everything and sweep it under the carpet. In their basic thinking they are both the same.'

The general picture which emerged from these and other questions was that of two disadvantaged and apprehensive groups of people who felt their interests were not being well served by either of the major parties. Such an impression was anticipated in the case of the immigrants given the circumstances surrounding their short stay in Britain. The extent of disillusionment amongst the native whites, however, was not so expected. And, whilst some of the dissatisfaction expressed with the Labour Government may have been a direct result of the unpopular economic measures it was taking at the time, the widespread belief in the essential similarity of the two parties did appear to be more deeply rooted. Unfortunately, there is no way of demonstrating how firmly held were the beliefs expressed in the interviews. All that can be said is that the impression gained in the course of the study was that, in very many cases, they were deeply held and had developed over a period of years. And certainly when the long-standing insecurity and relative poverty of most of those interviewed is taken into account it is not at all difficult to imagine how such views could have developed. No doubt many of the disillusioned in the sample still voted Labour when the 1970 Election came round. Whether they did so with enthusiasm or conviction is another matter. It may well be that they, and others like them, did so not because they had changed their views in any fundamental way but because no other acceptable alternative had presented itself.

The pattern of voting in both of the 1974 General Elections makes it plain that the complete ascendancy of the Labour and Conservative parties at Westminster is no longer assured. Given the current political situation and serious economic difficulties facing the country, minor parties could well capture many more votes in future elections. In deteriorating central city areas, similar to that in which the research was conducted, where the population is hardest hit by runaway inflation and cut-backs in public spending, groups like the National Front which have established positions on those issues (like immigration) which have contributed to the present disenchantment might make gains. It is certainly unlikely that the comparative consensus which has emerged amongst the major parties on race relations would survive any such period of political change, and the scene could then be set for a much more open exploitation of the race issue than has so far occurred.

The lack of confidence in both parties shown by the immigrant respondents leads to speculation about how they too might behave in the future. It has sometimes been assumed that since coloured immigrants are concentrated at the lower end of the occupational ladder (and since the Labour Party has been slightly less hostile to their presence in Britain than the Conservatives) they will become incorporated in British politics in the same way as members of the white working class: a view reinforced by the now fairly substantial evidence that most immigrant voters have supported Labour candidates in past elections. However, there is other more compelling evidence which suggests that neither coloured immigrants themselves nor their children will establish a significant foothold in our existing party political structure. Furthermore, should it become more unstable it is even less likely that this will happen. Odd individuals have succeeded and no doubt will continue to succeed in constituency parties, and even emerge occasionally at a national level, but those capable of representing the grass roots have little chance of becoming established in any major party. As Deakin has noted, the Labour party has made no serious effort to recruit coloured members, still less adopt them as candidates.[41] Moreover, the evidence which I presented above suggests that it may even find it difficult to hold onto its immigrant votes.

It could be argued that, with the passage of time, increased acculturation will lead working-class immigrants and their children to identify with the Labour Party in the same way as the native whites. However, there are several reasons why this does not seem very likely — at least for those interviewed in Nottingham. Some of them already share the same dissatisfaction with the Labour Party as members of the indigenous population. A further and perhaps more crucial factor is that most still seem to see themselves primarily as Jamaicans, Indians and Pakistanis, rather than simply non-white citizens of the United Kingdom. Even amongst those Jamaicans who identified strongly with Britain on their arrival, as many as 90 per cent continued to identify more strongly with Jamaica — often after many years in this country. The corresponding level of identification with their homeland was even higher amongst the Indians and Pakistanis (96 per cent).[42] Whilst this pattern of identification does not in any way rule out the possibility of increased class consciousness amongst coloured people it (along with the other factors mentioned) does make it more likely that it will find an ethnocentric expression rather than cut across racial and ethnic lines as some anticipate.

Political organisation along ethnic group lines seems to be the most likely way in which coloured people will seek to improve their position in British society. Indeed there have already been many developments in this direction in Nottingham and elsewhere. However, at least amongst those immigrants interviewed in Nottingham, such moves do not appear to enjoy widespread or unqualified support. Respondents were asked: 'Some people have suggested it would help West Indian immigrants (or Pakistanis, etc. as appropriate) if they got together and decided to vote for the same party. What do you think of this view?' Amongst the West Indians only 18 per cent were in favour and as many as 52 per cent were opposed. In the case of the Indian respondents, somewhat more were in favour (37 per cent) but a clear majority were still opposed (59 per cent). Only in the case of the Pakistanis were more in favour of the suggestion than opposed to it (45 per cent as against 41 per cent) but even here less than half expressed approval.

The two main kinds of objections were that immigrants should vote as individuals (e.g. 'This is absolutely wrong. We should not be tied to one party. We should look after our own interests as individuals. We are not sheep to be guided or pushed about by any one shepherd') and that such a move would only make things worse (e.g. 'I don't think that's right — I don't think we should vote together. If we did it would just make them discriminate more'). A second question put to respondents was: 'Other people have suggested that Indian immigrants (or Pakistanis, etc. as appropriate) should try to get other Indian immigrants (or Pakistani, etc. as appropriate) elected as councillors and MPs. What do you think about this view?' In this instance, majorities of Indians and Pakistanis voiced their approval (59 per cent and 61 per cent respectively) as did almost half of the West Indians (48 per cent), and only a handful of respondents actually expressed disapproval (11 per cent, 5 per cent and 7 per cent). However, some respondents did qualify their support for the proposal — either on the grounds that it would depend very much on the personal qualities of the candidate (16 per cent) or on condition that he was also prepared to represent his English constituents (8 per cent). Furthermore, whilst very few respondents were opposed to the suggestion, some 40 per cent of the West Indians and 20 per cent of the Indians and Pakistanis did doubt if it would do any good. And, it must be added, that since these qualifications were offered spontaneously, and not in response to follow-up questions, the figures could very well underestimate the extent of such feelings. In other words, whilst there may be considerable support for the principle of electing immigrant councillors and MPs, there can be no doubt that many of those in favour might choose not to support immigrant candidates in particular elections. The third question put to respondents in this sequence was: 'I have also heard some people suggest that Indian immigrants (or Pakistani, etc. as appropriate) should form their own political party in this country. What do you think about this view?' As many as two-thirds of the Indians and half of the West Indians and Pakistanis were aginst such a development. The proportions in favour were no more than 26 per cent, 28 per cent, and 32 per cent respectively.

So despite the fact that most of the immigrant respondents did not feel that either of the two main parties represented their views or were favourably disposed towards them, they were still not at all enthusiastic about the particular political initiatives on which they were asked to comment. Only just over a quarter were in favour of bloc voting and the formation of separate political parties, and not even the half who favoured the election of immigrant MPs and councillors did so without qualification. On the whole, the West Indians were less likely to support the suggested initiatives than the Indians and Pakistanis. This probably reflects not only the greater cultural autonomy of the Indians and Pakistanis but also the extent and character of immigrant organisa-

tion which already exists in Nottingham (and elsewhere). Since the
Asians are much better organised and more prepared to think in communal terms, one would expect them to be more prepared to consider
undertaking ethnically specific political initiatives. The relative commercial success of some Asian immigrants could also lend weight to
any such intitiatives which are taken. The West Indians, despite their
greater disillusionment with their lot in Britain, often still cling to their
links with British people and, despite having been in Britain rather
longer on average, are not nearly as well organised.

What seems most unlikely in the immediate future is that all three
ethnic groups in Nottingham will organise under the common badge of
colour. In addition to being asked for their views on the suggested
political initiatives with respect to their own ethnic group, all respondents were asked about them as possible initiatives for coloured people
as a whole. In none of the three ethnic groups was there a consistently
greater proportion in favour of this kind of combination. Indeed, more
often than not there was a fall in support for or an increase in the proportion positively against them. Combining in this way would obviously increase the chances of success for any such initiatives but,
whatever some might want to say about the 'real interests of coloured
people' *vis-à-vis* the white British, there is no doubt that most simply
do not see themselves as belonging to a homogenous group with
genuinely common interests. Indians and Pakistanis do, of course, have
a great deal in common, but the gap between them and West Indians is
still very large.

In the course of the interviews in Nottingham, Indian and Pakistani
respondents were asked: 'What do you think of West Indians in
general?' The converse of the question was put to the West Indians.
One of the most striking features of the answers was how many respondents were unable to offer any relevant comments because they had
had no contact with members of the other group. This was the case for
33 per cent of the West Indians and 37 per cent of the Indians and
Pakistanis. The most frequent comment made by the West Indians
about the Asians, was the extent to which they were different and kept
to themselves. As many as 42 per cent made remarks of this sort.

> 'Got no time for them — you can't speak to them at all — if you
> want them to do something at work you got to swear at them to
> get them to understand.'

> 'I don't think I like them very much. They speak their own language
> and I can't understand what they say. They're different — they
> don't try to mix so we don't try.'

More explicitly critical comments were made by 22 per cent and no
more than 11 per cent made what could be classified as friendly or not
unfavourable remarks. Those Indians and Pakistanis who had experi-

enced sufficient contact with West Indians to answer the question also made more critical remarks than friendly. By far the most common complaint was that West Indians were rough, aggressive and generally uncultivated. For example:

'He gets the money and spends — just like English people. Don't bother about the children or anything. I think he is crack-minded. He don't bother about anything. He says if I knock somebody and get trouble I don't care. He is very rough.'

'This is a very serious question. 75 per cent of Jamaicans do not work — all they do is go to the races and go out with prostitutes. They are tarnishing the name of the whole immigrant community. They do not use their brains — perhaps God willed it that way — I do not know. But they spoil things for all of us.'

Even more striking support for the contention that Nottingham's Indians, Pakistanis and West Indians do not see themselves as members of a single group with common interests comes from the answers to another question. West Indians respondents were asked: 'Do you think you have more in common with Indians and Pakistanis than you have with English people?' and a corresponding question was put to the Indians and Pakistanis. As many as 83 per cent of the West Indians and 43 per cent of the Indians and Pakistanis said that they had more in common with the English. Moreover, a further 31 per cent of the Indians and Pakistanis said that as far as they were concerned they had nothing in common with either. No more than 8 per cent of the West Indians and 20 per cent of the Indians and Pakistanis felt they had more in common with each other than with the English. This pattern of identification helps to explain not only the lack of enthusiasm for political action organised on the basis of colour but also why organisations which represent all coloured people in Nottingham have had so little success to date. Continuing prejudice and discrimination on the part of English people may well help to bring members of the three ethnic groups together — especially in the case of the 'second generation.' Moreover, political organisations based on colour, like other political groupings, do not necessarily need massive grass roots support before they can be influential. Nevertheless, on this evidence there does not seem to be much immediate prospect of an effective and widely supported political organisation based upon colour as such.

In this chapter I have explored the relationship between race, elections and politics which has existed to date and speculated on the directions in which it might go in the future. I have argued that in interaction with other issues and factors the race issue has probably had a significant indirect impact on voting behaviour and on attitudes toward our existing party political structure. In particular, I have suggested that the race issue has made an important contribution to the now prevalent disillusionment with the two major parties. Despite their attempts to respond to public opinion on the subject of immigration control, it seems that the particular decisions which have been taken by both major parties have not endeared them to either coloured immigrants or native whites. Indeed the main effect of them has probably been to create further disenchantment all round. The fundamental and historic shift in policy represented by the 1962 Commonwealth Immigration Act did not please those British subjects whose traditional freedom was now curtailed. Neither, however, did it do very much to satisfy those native whites who wanted control. By the time the Act came into force there were already about one million coloured people in Britain and many felt that the legislation had come too late to be of very much value. The further restrictions introduced in 1965, 1968 and 1971 can also be seen as responses by politicians to the apparent wishes of the electorate. Yet they will often have been interpreted (especially by those more generally weary with politics and politicians) as clear indications that the situation had been repeatedly allowed to get out of control. The publicity given to 'illegal' immigrants and to Powell's charges of a 'cover-up' on the extent of coloured immigration no doubt served to reinforce such fears — as did his representation of himself as one of the few politicians responsible enough to speak out on behalf of the common man against those evidently irresponsible people in authority who had allowed the 'crisis' to arise in the first place.

These policies and developments have looked very different when seen through the eyes of Britain's coloured immigrants. The increasingly tight immigration controls and, with the 1968 and 1971 measures, openly racial character of the restrictions could not but have increased the disillusionment and cynicism amongst them. The more positive measures intoduced by the Labour Government in 1965 and 1968 may even have exacerbated such feelings. Certainly those in Nottingham who were politically conscious enough to be familiar with them were not ignorant of the fact that the NCCI and Race Relations Board were set up in the same year that the Labour Government, far from repealing the 1962 Act which it had vigorously opposed when out of office, introduced far tougher immigration controls. Neither did the glaring weaknesses of the 1965 and 1968 Race Relations Acts escape the notice of politically conscious immigrants. They were (not unreasonably) seen as further evidence of the Labour Party's vacillations. On the other hand, the same Acts were seen by some native whites as clear evidence that coloured immigrants were being put in a privileged position.

The extent to which race remains an important factor in British politics depends not only on the sum of individual relationships which develop between immigrants and natives (and their children) and the level of prejudice and discrimination in the white population. No less crucial will be the general economic, social and political climate in which race relations develop. At a time of deepening crisis and growing uncertainty about the competence of politicians to deal with our problems, the scope for open exploitation of the race issue whether for its own sake or as part of a larger scenario is very much greater. Whether the potential of the race issue will be utilised in this way is impossible to predict. What is certain is that race is so much a part of British history, culture and social and economic structure that it will be very difficult to erase it from our political life.

NOTES

1.   I am grateful to M.D. King, M. McDougall and Ivor Crewe for their advice and comments.
2.   '. . . the 1964 General Election, and in particular the result in Smethwick, made colour and race major factors in British politics for the first time.' E.J.B. Rose, the then Director of the Survey of Race Relations in Britain in his Foreword to Nicholas Deakin (ed.), *Colour and the British Electorate 1964*, Pall Mall Press, London, 1965.
3.   Edward Scobie, *Black Britannia. A History of Blacks in Britain*, Johnson, Chicago, 1972, p. 8.
4.   *Ibid.*, pp. 62-75.
5.   A.H. Richmond, *The Colour Problem*, Pelican, London, 1955, p. 238.
6.   Scobie, *op. cit.*, pp. 160-3.
7.   Nicholas Deakin, 'The British Nationality Act of 1948: A Brief Study in the Political Mythology of Race Relations,' *Race*, vol. XI, no. 1, pp. 77-83.
8.   Nicholas Deakin and Jenny Bourne, 'Powell, The Minorities, and the 1970 Election,' *Political Quarterly*, Oct.-Dec. 1970, pp. 402-3.
9.   D.E. Butler and A. King, *The British General Election of 1964*, Macmillan, London, 1965, pp. 296 and 354.
10.   Nicholas Deakin, 'Colour and the 1966 General Election,' *Race*, vol. VIII, no. 1, p. 17.
11.   In a highly emotional reply to Powell's speech Benn had declared: 'The flag of racialism which has been hoisted in Wolverhampton is beginning to look like the one that fluttered twenty-five years ago over Dachau and Belsen.'
12.   Deakin and Bourne, *op. cit.*, pp. 405 and 407.
13.   D.E. Butler and Michael Pinto-Duschinsky, *The British General Election of 1970*, Macmillan, London, 1971, pp. 327-8 and 408.
14.   D.E. Butler and D. Stokes, *Political Change in Britain. Forces Shaping Electoral Choice*, Pelican, London, 1971, pp. 411-2.
15.   *Ibid.*, p. 422.
16.   *Ibid.*, pp. 420-5.
17.   For example, see Deakin and Bourne's discussion of the 1970 election, *Ibid.*, pp. 401-2.
18.   Butler and Stokes, *op. cit.*, p. 220.
19.   It is true that Butler and Stokes found that more electors distinguished between the parties in areas of high immigrant concentration. However, they emphasise that even in such areas the position was not markedly different from elsewhere. 'Too much ought not to be made of these differences. Even in areas of high immigrant concentration, voters were much less likely to have a clear per-

ception of party difference on this issue than on, for example, nationalisation.'
Butler and Stokes, *Ibid.*, p. 424.
20.   Deakin, 'Colour and the 1966 General Election,' *op. cit.*, p. 17.
21.   In his discussion of the 1970 campaign (with Jenny Bourne) Deakin again
made use of the swing but drew particular attention to the fact that 'the swing
towards the Conservatives slowed up considerably in areas of substantial immigrant settlement.' Deakin and Bourne, *op. cit.*
22.   Deakin, 'Colour and the 1966 General Election,' *op. cit.*, pp. 17-8.
23.   Deakin and Bourne, *op. cit.*, p. 402.
24.   I am grateful to R.J. Wybrow of the Gallup Poll who supplied me with
the figures on which the diagram is based.
25.   Indeed, at one point in 1969 as many as 57 per cent judged the parties to
be 'much the same.' Those periods where clear majorities held that important
differences did exist coincided with phases of electoral activity. The peaks of
1951, 1955, 1959 and 1964, for example, coincided with general elections. However, the 1966 Election did not seem to result in the usual temporary reversal of
the trend and by 1969 only 39 per cent of those interviewed believed there to be
an important difference between the parties.
26.   National Opinion Polls have obtained similar results. For example, in 1968,
49 per cent of their respondents agreed with the view that: 'Nowadays there's
no real difference between the parties.' In 1972, when asked: 'How much
difference do you think there really is between the Conservative and Labour
parties?' 43 per cent said 'not very much' and 8 per cent said 'none at all'; and
56 per cent also asserted that there was not as much difference between the
parties as there used to be. National Opinion Polls, *Political Bulletin*, February
1968 and June 1972. For other similar findings see Butler and Stokes, *op. cit.*,
p. 558.
27.   Polls, 11, no. 4. Quoted by J. Dennis, L. Lindberg and D. McCrone,
'Support for Nation and Government among English Children,' *British Journal of
Political Science*, vol. 1, pp. 25-48.
28.   NOP *Bulletin*, February 1968. It is not clear how recently such cynicism
has developed. It certainly seems to have existed thirty years ago. In 1944 a
sample of Gallup respondents were asked: 'Do you think that British politicians
are merely out for themselves, for their party, or to do their best for the
country?' Thirty-five per cent said they were out for themselves, twenty-two per
cent said they were out for their party and only thirty-six per cent said that they
were out to do their best for the country. Quoted by Dennis *et al.*, *ibid.*, p. 43.
29.   Both the 1951 and 1966 Elections were held in October with registers
about one year old. Moreover, both followed relatively indecisive elections a
short time before. The respective turnout rates were 82.5 per cent for 1951 and
75.8 per cent for 1966.
30.   Some 2,611,000 more votes were cast in February 1974 (as compared
with 1970). Despite this the Conservative vote fell by over 1,253,000 and that for
Labour by 592,000. The Liberal vote, however, increased by 3,878,000 and that
for the other minor parties by 576,000.
31.   Another possible indication of disillusionment is the increasing volatility
of the electorate in by-elections. Falls in support for the governing party of more
than 20 per cent occurred in only 2 or 3 per cent of by-elections in the periods
1945-55, but the respective figures for the period 1955-9, 1959-64 and 1966-8
were 10 per cent, 18 per cent and 48 per cent.
32.   It is true that the parties reflect clear class differences in their origins and
in their sources of finance and electoral support, but in other crucial respects
class differences are no longer very evident. In the interwar years 72 per cent of
Labour MPs were rank and file workers and only 15 per cent were university
educated. By 1966, the proportion of workers amongst Labour MPs had fallen to
30 per cent. This change is even more dramatically reflected at the top of the

party. At the beginning of 1969 only one member of the Labour Cabinet had been previously employed as a manual worker. See Butler and Stokes, *op. cit.*, pp. 153-4.

33.   That many Labour MPs may be socially mobile scholarship boys is not without relevance, but the different life experiences and consequent social gulf between the ordinary working-class elector and many of those purporting to represent him is still very real.

34.   This is not to say that no significant or ideological differences remain. But, despite 'Clause 4,' Labour governments have not vigorously sought to bring about the public ownership of the means of production and, despite the Conservatives' emphasis on individualism and their apparent belief in the virtues of the market economy, they have not made any attempt to dismantle the major features of the welfare state or pursue widespread *de*nationalisation. During its period of office in the 1960s, the Labour government adopted economic policies which entailed both a marked rise in unemployment and a lowering of the real incomes of ordinary people in order to defend the pound and Britain's international balance of payments. Perhaps even more conspicuously, although the Conservatives came to power in 1970 promising to restore a greater degree of market freedom, they were defeated in 1974 defending a statutory prices and incomes policy.

35.   For evidence on the public's attitudes on permissiveness see National Opinion Polls, *Political Bulletin*, September 1972.

36.   53 per cent of a recent NOP sample went so far as to agree that: 'Britain is a third-class power nowadays.' Quoted by Dennis *et al., op. cit.*, p. 31.

37.   Butler and Stokes, *op. cit.*, p. 421.

38.   *Ibid.*, pp. 90-1.

39.   Details of the study can be found in Daniel Lawrence, *Black Migrants: White Natives. A Study of Race Relations in Nottingham*, Cambridge University Press, 1974, Appendix 1.

40.   K. Coates and R. Silburn, *Poverty: The Forgotten Englishmen*, Penguin, 1970.

41.   N. Deakin, 'Political Rights of Minority Groups,' *New Community*, vol. 1, no., 3, p. 191. However, Schaefer does suggest that those who make financial contributions to the Labour Party are less likely to be strongly prejudiced than members of the Conservative or Liberal Parties. See R.T. Schaefer, 'Party Affiliations and Prejudice in Britain,' *New Community*, vol. 1, no. 3, pp. 296-9.

42.   Lawrence, *op. cit.*, pp. 35-8. A study of West Indians between the ages of sixteen and twenty-four in London found that two-thirds identified more strongly with the West Indies than with Britain. See D. Stevenson, 'Second Generation West Indians: A Study in Alienation,' *Race Today*, vol. 2, no. 8 (August 1970).

EMPIRICAL STUDIES: THE POLITICS OF RACIAL MINORITIES

4. PARTICIPATION IN ELECTIONS BY ASIANS IN BRADFORD

M. J. Le Lohé

Introduction

This is a rather limited study of one of many effects which a particular group of immigrants have had upon politics in a particular city. Although they will be mentioned as an influence upon participation the issues which have arisen as a consequence of the presence of this group are largely ignored. Again, other groups of immigrants, and other towns and cities, are mentioned only incidentally and the conclusions of this study do not necessarily have wider application.

The way in which participation is considered is also narrow, being limited to the electoral processes of voting and standing as candidates. There is a large area of participation, particularly pressure-group activity, which is important but also ignored. The largest audiences in St George's Hall are common to 'pop stars' and meetings organised by the Pakistan People's Party and the largest protest march in Bradford in 1973, estimated at 2,000, concerned the shooting of two youths at India House.

The field covered by this study is, then, rather narrow and the terms used in it are rather narrowly defined. There are problems when one uses, for example, the term coloured population,[1] but, in this particular instance it is both possible, and necessary to use certain working terms which are capable of being related, with some precision, to electoral data, and thus it is unnecessary to consider other definitions.

The term Asian will be used, and unless otherwise defined, this will mean persons whose full names are commonly found in South Asia. Typical of these are Muslim, Sikh or Hindu names such as Mohammed Hussain, Malkit Singh or Balwant Mistry. This definition will exclude a tiny minority of persons who are genuinely Asian, but not South Asian, such as Wai Kwok Pau[2] and it will also exclude women married to Asians such as Maureen Khan. It will, however, include East African Asians or West Indian Asians. This working use of the term Asian is adhered to because it has been used consistently and precisely in studies of Bradford over a number of years and it makes possible certain comparisons which demonstrate growing influence and political socialisation.

It should be stressed that the term Asian does not give a measure of the total coloured population for, apart from the few orientals, there are also West Indian and African residents. Nor can the term be equated with immigrants, for, apart from West Indians, Irish or other Europeans,[3] a considerable proportion of younger Asians were born in Bradford or at least in Britain. Admittedly one can speak of immigrant origin, or first generation descendants, or of persons born in the coloured New Commonwealth countries (with its attendant problems of white immigrants), but this working use of the term Asian avoids some of these problems of definition and it has one outstanding advantage in studies of electoral participation. This is that one can produce data about electors and voters with a high degree of accuracy. The electoral register is the definitive document of the electorate and uncertainties about under-enumeration in the Census or even about under-registration of potential electors can be set aside. Furthermore when it comes to observing who actually voted, one can ask for electoral numbers and check that those whose appearance was Asian actually had fully Asian names.

In so far as the electorate is concerned one then has two categories: Asian and a residual category of non-Asian. The term non-Asian also is a working term which covers a very mixed group. There will be an insignificant number of persons who are truly Asians, whites born in Asia or orientals, but the non-Asians really cover the rest of the world. The overwhelming mass of them have names such as John Smith or Betty Robinson, but a few, such as Jan Rudalski[4] will betray non-British origin and a number of others, such as Cecil Price, will not betray their non-British origin.

There is, in fact, an elector called Cecil Price who is coloured and who was born in the West Indies, and no doubt there is also a similar elector somewhere called John Smith. One might guess that, say, Beresford Hamilton or Hesketh Philip are West Indians but guesses of this kind lack accuracy and, with the working term non-Asian, become unnecessary. When one comes to observe voters at polling stations one can have two sub-categories within the non-Asian group. The West Indian John Smith can easily be distinguished, by an observer taking numbers, from a white John Smith. Thus insofar as voters are concerned we may have three categories: Asian, Afro-West Indian and European, but these last two sub-categories cannot be accurately related to the electorate to give precise statements about the level of turnout.

Yet limited statements about West Indian turnout can be made. These depend upon assumptions about the size of the West Indian electorate, but, based upon random samples of the electorate and the evidence which comes from Census material, these assumptions must be reasonably accurate. In 1970, for example, a random sample of the electors of the Manningham Ward in Bradford generated 155 names, of these 32 were Asian and three of the 123 non-Asians were found, on the doorstep, to be West Indian. This suggests that about two per cent of that electorate were West Indian and about 77 per cent were white, thus the non-Asian electorate in Manningham, allowing for some sampling error, would be at least 95 per cent white. The electoral register is, of course, definitive for our purpose but the Census provides useful supporting evidence. The 1971 Census Small Area Statistics for the Manningham Ward enumerates 655 persons born in *New Commonwealth America* whereas 12,809 were born in Great Britain and 454 were born in other parts of Europe. Admitting that there are persons born in Britain of West Indian origin on the one hand, and that there is possibly some under-registration of potential West Indian electors on the other hand, the assumption that up to five per cent of the non-Asian electors in Manningham are West Indian would appear reasonable. Knowing the number of West Indians who voted one can then use that assumption to suggest the approximate level of West Indian turnout and the possible range of error associated with that figure.

The fact that West Indians form such a small minority of the New Commonwealth Immigrants resident in Bradford needs some emphasis. The picture shown in one ward, Manningham, is not quite typical, as the 1971 Census for the County Borough enumerates 2,010 persons born in the *New Commonwealth America*, 5,965 in India and 11,080 in Pakistan within the total of 294,175. This fact, or state of affairs, is also very helpful for it means that the bulk of the New Commonwealth immigrants, being Asian, are easily identified on the electoral register and that those non-whites who cannot be so identified are only a small minority of the non-Asian total. This situation is peculiar to Bradford, as an analysis of the 1966 Sample Census showed that this city had a higher proportion of Asian born amongst its Commonwealth born residents than any other major urban area in the United Kingdom.[5] Such a situation makes Bradford particularly suitable for study, especially for a study in participation.

The Asian Electorate, Its Location and Political Significance

1 The Old Boundaries

Fortunately one can usually find copies of electoral registers for previous years and in Bradford these can be used to chart the growth of the Asian electorate. In 1954 only 341 Asian names could be found on the city's electoral register, but by 1959 there were three wards each of which included about that number. Two of these wards, Exchange and Listerhills, thereafter had substantial increases in their Asian electorates and by 1962 both had totals of over a thousand. At the same time the demolition of housing was reducing the total electorate, thus the percentage who were Asian tended to grow more rapidly than their actual numbers. By 1962 Asians formed 25.9 per cent of the electorate in Exchange which was then the smallest ward in the city.

At Listerhills the Asian level was lower at 19.7 per cent but their total of 1604 gave a subjective impression, particularly in certain polling districts, that Asians were in the majority.

By 1967, when the ward boundaries were altered, Asians accounted for 28.2 per cent of the electorate in Exchange and 27.5 per cent of that at Listerhills. Two other wards, Manningham and South, had about 10 per cent and a further three, Bolton, Little Horton and North East had over 5 per cent. Before proceeding to consider the importance of these figures it should be noted that the degree of geographical concentration of Asians is not shown by these figures. In each of these wards certain polling districts which were close to the commercial centre of the city had high proportions of Asians, whereas other, more suburban, polling districts within the same ward had few, if any, Asians. Thus, for example in the Bolton Ward in 1967 Asians accounted for 5.6 per cent of its total electorate, but 84 per cent of these 539 Asians were in one down-town polling district where they formed 46.4 per cent of the electorate.

One might conclude from these figures that Asians formed an important element in the electorate in two wards, were a substantial element in two others and were significant in a further three. We are, however, considering not statistical significance but political significance and must look for some measure which will relate potential political influence to the particular electoral bloc. One possible method of assessing political significance would be to relate the Asian electorate to the majority year by year. Majorities are not constant things, but the average majority in a ward is easily calculated and may be used to suggest the number of votes normally needed to reverse a result. To be realistic one should not compare the average majority with the Asian electorate since that assumes that they will all turn out to vote. If one expected, say, a third of the Asians to turn out to vote this would be more realistic, although, of course, for this purpose of assessing potential political significance we are still being unrealistic in assuming that all Asians are going to vote for the same party.

Nevertheless this kind of situation could occur if there was a substantial bloc vote which could be delivered by its leaders. To the extent that these leaders were apolitical, in a British party sense, they could deliver to any candidate who happened to please them, or, conversely, switch from any candidate who happened to displease them. To some degree it will be shown that this has happened in Bradford where a substantial Pakistani vote has gone to the Conservatives, and one might also note that in Rochdale a similar bloc appears to have supported the Liberals.[6] One should, however, emphasise that this has happened only to varying degrees and that it is still unrealistic to regard any Asian group simply as a switchable solid bloc.

Whilst it is admittedly unrealistic it does suggest a guiding limit and whenever that limit is passed, if not sooner, candidates will need to take Asians into account in their electoral calculations. Indeed Asian leaders, or putative leaders, may move into the electoral market place and attempt some local vote bargaining before that limit is reached. Again it is accepted that any such bargaining is considerably weakened if the votes have previously gone to the loser and switching them will do no more than increase the winner's majority. But, for our purpose here we need some simple measure of this kind of significant electoral influence and our guideline may remain as that where a substantial Asian electorate is more than three times the average majority. This situation obtained in two relatively safe Labour wards, Exchange, from 1959 onwards, and Listerhills, from 1960 onwards, and also in the marginal ward of Bradford Moor after 1961. Since the City Council was highly marginal (it changed control three times in this period) the Asian electorate could have considerable political significance.

This significance was mainly, in those years, at the council level for the Asian electorate did not really have the same potential in the Parliamentary constituencies. The wards with the highest numbers of Asian electors were mainly grouped within the Bradford East constituency. Their numbers there were considerable with 4,110 Asians on the register for the 1964 General Election, 4,231 for that of 1966 and 5,454 for that of 1970 when Asians formed 13.6 per cent of the total. The Labour majorities in Bradford East were much larger than these figures and this concentration in a very safe seat meant their influence as potential swing voters was non-existent. In the marginal seats of Bradford North and Bradford West much smaller numbers of Asians were potentially more important, for example in 1964 at Bradford North there were 1,150 Asians and Labour gained the seat with a majority of 1,398. Yet the Asian electorate, at that time, was never seen as the key to Parliamentary success.

2 The New Boundaries

The 1970 General Election was the last to be fought on the old boundaries and after it three completely new constituencies were created although three of the old names were retained. The name Bradford East was abolished and, although it over-simplifies, one can think of that constituency being divided between the other three which retained their names. The part of Bradford East which contained the concentration of Asian settlement was transferred to enlarge the new Bradford West. This change, however, not only enlarged that constituency but also made it the most marginal of the three new seats.

Bradford West was now a marginal with a substantial Asian electorate whose votes might be decisive. If the General Election of 1974 had taken place early in February the Asian electorate would have been 10,991. As it was the direct and indirect consequences of the Pakistan Act[7] considerably reduced that electorate and when the election was fought, on the new register, the figure was reduced to 6,976. This was still roughly three times Mr Lyons majority of 2,219.

Asians then were regarded, in 1974, as being one of the keys to electoral success in Bradford West. In the other constituencies they were not in such a critical position even on the electoral register in force before mid-February 1974. The number of Asians in Bradford North on that register was 4,520 but, considerable though that number was, the Labour majority at the actual election was 6,617. At Bradford South with a majority of 7,653 the 132 Asians could hardly suggest that the weight of their voting power was of much consequence.

The change in constituency boundaries had taken account of the new ward boundaries introduced for the local elections of 1968. These changes also had consequences for the size and significance of the Asian electorate. It will be recalled that, immediately before the redistribution, in 1967, two wards named Exchange and Listerhills had a level of Asian electors which exceeded a quarter of the total electorate. These two small city centre wards were incorporated in new wards of about twice their size which extended further out into the suburbs and neither of these possessed, at that time, an electorate with quite such high proportions of Asians. The newly created University Ward, however, included most of Listerhills and parts of Exchange. The other parts of Exchange had been amalgamated with the Asian polling district of Bolton and most of the old Manningham Ward to produce a new ward still called Manningham. Thus the two new wards – Manningham and University – had substantial numbers of Asian electors.

These numbers were to grow, largely through the arrival of dependants, and this growth may be seen in the Census data. The 1966 Sample Census of 10 per cent rounded up to a hundred, enumerated 10,630 Bradford residents who were born in India or Pakistan. The 1971 Census enumerates 17,045 and a majority of these, 9,289, resided in either the Manningham or University Wards. As Asians moved in whites moved out so that within an approximately stable total electorate, the proportion who were Asian increased quite quickly. The level of one quarter Asian was passed first in the University Ward when, in 1970, it reached 26.5 per cent, but that at Manningham was close behind with 23.7 per cent. The growth in the proportion who were Asian continued and in the final election for Bradford City Council in 1972 the level reached 32.6 per cent at University and 28.2 per cent at Manningham.

There were also at that time three other wards with just over ten per cent who were Asian but there was still to come the final crescendo in the elections for the new metropolitan authorities in 1973. After this the numbers dropped considerably with the consequences of the Pakistan Act. The wards were unchanged for the elections to the new Bradford Metropolitan District Council and on the 1973 Register Asians formed 44.1 per cent of the electorate in University and 35.1 per cent of that at Manningham. For the West Yorkshire Metropolitan County a new electoral division was created by amalgamating the Manningham, University and Little Horton Wards. Since Little Horton was one of the three wards with over 10 per cent of electors who were Asian, this accident of amalgamation produced an electoral division with 9,887 Asians in a total of 32,814 (30.7 per cent) to elect two county councillors.

One cannot produce average majorities for these new county electoral divisions, but since there were only 647 votes between the lowest winner and the highest loser in this division, the electoral significance of this number was clearly considerable. There was also another county division created by combining Bradford Moor and Undercliffe with a substantial Asian electorate. The number there, however, was 2,172 which is not quite three times the winner's majority of 842.

The new district divisions were exactly the same as the wards of the county borough, thus average majorities can be calculated. Taking three times the average majority between 1970 and 1973 and comparing this with numbers of Asian electors it cannot be doubted that the Asians were significant at University and Manningham throughout the period. From 1971 onwards Asians also numbered three times the average majority of 375 at Bradford Moor but in the other wards, even where there were more than a thousand Asians, they did not achieve this level of significance.

To recapitulate, the number of Asians on the electoral registers at Bradford grew, year by year, until the Pakistan Act took effect in 1974. They concentrated their residence in certain areas and, using a working guideline, they could be regarded as electorally significant from 1959 onwards. Under the old boundary arrangements this was confined to city elections and happened first at Exchange, then at Listerhills and then at Bradford Moor. Under the new boundary arrangements Asians became significant for Parliamentary elections in the Bradford West constituency. Although at first, in 1968 the proportion who were Asian in the new enlarged wards dropped below a quarter even then they were significant at Manningham and University. Subsequently Asians also became significant at Bradford Moor and thus when the new metropolitan district council was elected they could be regarded as significant in three divisions. As to the new metropolitan county divisions in Bradford they were clearly significant on one two-member seat and almost significant in a single-member one.

It must be concluded that in some part of Bradford the Asian electorate counts as an important political factor. It is, however, a potential which has to be realised by turning electors into voters.

Mobilising the Asian Vote

1 The Early Period

The first known attempts to mobilise the Asian electoral potential
coincided with the achievement of our significance guideline at Exchange Ward in 1959. The candidate concerned was the late Mr Norman
Bishop, a solicitor who stood as the Conservative and qualified through
his business premises in the ward. Mr Bishop, serving as an officer in
the Indian Army, had learned to speak some Urdu and, when interviewed about this time, he stated that he saw as many as forty Asians
in a day. Mr Bishop was very helpful to his Asian clients who needed
legal assistance to purchase houses and businesses or in dealing with
passports and nationality problems but, business apart, he also appeared
to have the affairs of the Asians very much at heart. At election times
he was very active calling at the houses occupied by Asians and personally contacting Asian electors to gain their support.

Mr Bishop did not win Exchange in 1959 which was not surprising
for it was regarded as one of the safest Labour seats. The surprise,
however, came in 1960 when he fought again and won to become the
first Conservative to do so since it was created in 1937. The question
now arises as to whether Mr Bishop's efforts to mobilise the Asian vote
were responsible for his apparently spectacular success, as Mr Bishop
himself believed.

Looking at the situation rather more objectively, looking for example for evidence of swing or of increased Conservative votes, there is
no indication that this did actually happen. In all comparable centre
city wards the boost in the Conservative vote was actually greater than
that at Exchange when Mr Bishop first became a candidate in 1959. In
1960 the swing in Exchange to the Conservatives was greater than that
in neighbouring central wards, but the Conservative vote actually fell
most at Exchange. Nor was the remarkable Conservative gain at Exchange an isolated affair for there were four other wards where they
won their first post-war victories. The conclusion, in this instance, is
that there is really no evidence that mobilising Asian voters was the
key to Councillor Bishop's success, but in politics myth can be more
important than reality and there is clear evidence that the parties began
to act upon the myth.

At the next election in Exchange the Labour candidate attempted
to mobilise Asian voters. Not speaking Urdu or having numerous contacts he could not adopt the technique of personal approach used by
Councillor Bishop, and had to adopt a leaflet approach. The leaflet,
translated from Urdu, stated that the Conservatives wanted to send
back the immigrants to the place from which they came and exhorted
them to vote Labour. Councillor Bishop, working for the Conservative
candidate, strongly denied this and promised that he would personally

visit Indian and Pakistani residents to assure them of their future in Britain.[8] Labour won the election, and the swing was just about the same at Exchange (7.2 per cent) as it was in the city as a whole (6.2 per cent), a fact which can be interpreted in a variety of ways. It could be alleged, for example, that leaflets can counter a personal approach, or, alternatively, it might be suggested that Asian voters were having no effect whatsoever upon the results. Whether they were having any effect or not, the point is that the two main parties were making efforts to get that vote.

The two main parties were not the only seekers of the Asian vote, for the Liberals won a by-election in 1959 at Listerhills and their winner held his seat at the May election in 1960. The Liberal did not then rely upon the Asian vote, for he had the much greater bonus of an unofficial anti-Socialist alliance which gave him Conservative votes in a straight fight. In 1963, however, when he came to try and hold the seat he did face a Conservative opponent, and needed to try for every vote. He had helped Asian electors and he had spoken very sympathetically about their problems, but his problem, of getting their support, was suddenly made much more difficult by a further bid for the Asian vote.

This further bid came from an Independent, an Independent who had the considerable advantage of being an Asian himself. Mr Aslam was a local shopkeeper and businessman who was apparently well known and well liked among the Asians in the neighbourhood. He was also well organised with more than a score of workers taking numbers, marking off registers and driving cars to bring in the voters. He gained 446 votes which was only a hundred less than the Conservative, and clearly demonstrated that it was possible to mobilise a substantial Asian vote. His efforts, plus the Labour and Liberal efforts to activate the Asians were very effective, for a study of the Liberal teller's returns showed that 60.9 per cent of the 246 Asians registered at polling station KB had voted. The level of turnout of the non-Asians was 43.1 per cent.

Mr Aslam was not the only Independent for two others joined the Labour candidate in opposing Councillor Bishop in Exchange. They were neither as well known nor as well organised as Mr Aslam in Listerhills but their efforts, plus the Labour efforts, plus Councillor Bishop's very effective Asian organisation also produced a high level of Asian turnout. From surveys conducted at the time[9] it appeared that 595 (43.1 per cent) of the registered 1,423 Asians voted whereas the non-Asian turnout was only 40.3 per cent.

Thus in 1963 we have a situation in which Conservatives, Independent Asians, Labour and Liberals were all attempting, in one or both wards, to stimulate Asian electors into going out to vote. It is clear that these efforts were very successful and the Asians actually turned out in greater numbers than the non-Asians who lived in the same area. The lesson was plain that, if candidates put in the effort, the vote could be mobilised, but there was also another lesson for their votes had not affected the anticipated result. Labour candidates had been returned for both Exchange and Listerhills at every election since their disaster of 1960 and Mr Bishop lost his seat at Exchange just as surely as the Liberal at Listerhills, and all the other Liberals and Conservatives who had unexpected victories in 1960.

It seemed as if the Asian vote, substantial though it was, could not work wonders for either Conservatives or the Liberals. As far as the Independent candidates were concerned they had demonstrated that there was no clearway to the council outside the established system and no Asian ever attempted this again for eight years. Labour councillors appeared to be confident of holding these seats without devoting much effort to the Asians and thus, all round, the 1963 experience appeared to lead to questions about the value of diverting relatively scarce resources to the activation of the Asian electors.

2 The Period of Apathy 1963-9

Other factors also encouraged the parties to become disinterested in the Asian vote. The Liberals who were on the wane at this time began to drop out of contests in central Bradford, but, more important, there was a major change in the Conservative approach. Mr Bishop went off to contest elections in the Urban District where he resided instead of the place where his business premises provided a candidate's qualification. Although Mr Bishop did not withdraw entirely from political activity in Bradford the principal agent in mobilising the Asian voters was now largely lost to the Conservatives. Furthermore, when he had been on the Council, Mr Bishop had advocated a moderate policy in the Council Group and had successfully resisted hard-liners with all his authority as the expert on immigrant matters. We are not considering attitudes or issues here, but in earlier years the Conservatives had appeared as a pro-immigrant party. As soon as Councillor Bishop was gone they began to move steadily in the opposite direction and views, regarded by Asians as hostile, were expressed which made it not only hypocritical but also rather dangerous to mobilise the Asian vote.

The Conservatives appear to have decided at this time to pursue the anti-immigrant vote rather than that of immigrants. At the General Election of 1966 the appeal to the anti-immigrant whites was muted but they still did not make serious efforts to mobilise the Asians. During that campaign their Chief Agent stated: 'We are making no special effort this time. No pleas in Urdu or Bengali. I do not believe that more than twenty per cent of the 7,000 coloured people entitled to vote in Bradford will go to the polls.'[10] This policy of not making serious efforts to pick up Asian votes continued after this, even in wards where it was becoming a significant factor. In 1969 at Manningham the Conservative candidate is reported as saying 'I wouldn't go out of my way to attract their vote.'[11] It might be noted that he won without it, indeed, at the end of the decade the Conservatives seemed to be winning everything in Bradford, filling no less than 96 per cent of the seats in the Council Chamber when the new boundaries came into effect in 1968.

The Conservatives, then, did not need and did not openly appeal for the Asian vote at this time. Labour candidates, on the other hand, needed every vote they could get, but fearful of a net loss of support which was expected if they lost white supporters, were equally disinclined openly to go after Asian votes. Locally the Labour Party had tended to be silent on the immigration issue, those few statements which were made either equivocated or struck a balance between the anti-immigrant and pro-immigrant views. Labour candidates could not then claim the immigrant vote as the price of support, but they still needed it. This point appeared to be made by a story which circulated in May 1967. According to this, Labour workers found two car loads of Pakistanis and rushed them in just as the poll closed. Labour just managed to hold the ward — Exchange — by twelve votes.

The problem for major party candidates at this time, particularly for Labour candidates, was how to get the Asian vote. There were no more candidates who spoke Urdu, which would permit the kind of direct personal approach which Mr Bishop had made. The leaflet approach was not greatly favoured because it was expensive and of doubtful effect, and as we have seen the Conservatives had actually announced that they had given it up. Nevertheless, some Labour candidates still made the effort. There was, however, a third approach — the technique of working through agents.

This third technique had the advantage that it could be employed, as it were, quietly. As long as it was undertaken on a small scale there was no associated publicity and the danger of white backlash was avoided. Asians who were said to be leaders could develop a separate organisation which would get out the Asian vote on the day. There were disadvantages; for example, the Asian leader who had delivered the votes might have misguided notions about the favours which a councillor could arrange in order to show his appreciation, but it is clear that candidates did work in this way. It was effective and it made open appeals unnecessary, but it was only on a very small scale.

Thus between 1963 and 1969, apart from some small-scale operations through Asians acting as agents or brokers, there appeared to be nobody with either the will or the ability to mobilise the Asians and this period is remarkable for its apathy. This can be seen first in a study of the 1964 elections which did not distinguish between West Indians and Asians but reports that 164 'immigrants' voted in Listerhills and 227 'immigrants' in Exchange.[12] Using the sample interviewed in that study as a guide to the proportion who were Asians it would appear that Asian turnout had fallen to about 8.5 per cent in Listerhills and

13.0 per cent in Exchange.

The study in 1966 [13] was designed specifically to measure the level of Asian turnout. For the local elections in May it covered six polling stations in five wards. Table 1 indicates that the Asian vote in Exchange and Listerhills had shrunk to very low levels, and the 0.7 per cent level at the Manningham station appears to be a record in apathy. It is worth noting that the highest level observed here is in South where the Conservative candidate was campaigning with statements which were tough on immigrants.

Table 1 Asian and Non-Asian Turnout in May 1966

Ward	Polling Station	Electors		Voters		Turnout as a percentage	
		Asian	Non-Asian	Asian	Non-Asian	Asian	Non-Asian
Bolton	BH	453	570	10	116	2.2	20.4
Exchange	GF	406	401	25	79	6.2	19.7
Listerhills	KB	808	1470	56	397	6.9	27.0
Listerhills	KD	575	788	21	191	3.7	24.2
Manningham	LA	270	976	2	232	0.7	23.8
South	NF	183	1454	23	383	12.6	26.3

3 The Period of Political Awakening 1969-74

The Conservative candidate's campaign in South Ward in 1966 (which was associated with relatively higher Asian turnout) is possibly one clue to the later development of a pronounced change in the propensity of Asians to go to the polls. It is possible that Asians felt menaced by local pronouncements about restricting their rights to social security payments or to sending money to Pakistan. Mr Powell made his first speech on the dangers which would arise with a substantial immigrant population in April 1968 and, in 1969, a local Conservative councillor, Mr Merrick, alarmed many Bradfordians with statements associating immigrants with crime and disease.

The growing feeling that sections of the host population were hostile to immigrants was strengthened when Mr Merrick contested a by-election in November 1970 gaining almost as many votes as the Conservative and founding the Yorkshire Campaign to Stop Immigration. The association between these events and an observed increase in Asian turnout is not, however, proven as causal and one other event in 1969 appears to have been at least as stimulating for Asian electors as any feelings of alarm about hostile statements and campaigns. This event was the nomination of Dr Qureshi as the Liberal candidate for Manningham.

A study was made of Central Ward, Rochdale, in 1968 when the Liberals also nominated a Pakistani as their candidate.[14] This election took place just after Mr Powell's speech and again there is uncertainty about the importance of the twin stimuli of host hostility and a kinsman candidate. There is, however, no uncertainty about the consequences. It may be immaterial whether the Liberals selected these Asians out of a desire to make some noble gesture of principle or whether it was a more mundane matter of electoral tactics, but the results were very material in that Pakistanis became both diligent voters and, apparently, devoted Liberals.

On polling day, in Bradford, it soon became obvious that Dr Qureshi's supporters were exceedingly well organised and that they were making considerable efforts, with considerable resources of cars and workers, to get the Pakistanis out to vote. In addition to this, Mr Khan, the Secretary of the Pakistani Immigrant Welfare Association, and a member of the Labour Party, was working hard to get out those Asians who had promised to vote Labour. Their efforts combined to produce the remarkable result of an Asian turnout which was almost twice that of the non-Asians. This is shown in Table 2 which records our observations.

Table 2 Asian and Non-Asian Turnout, Manningham 1969

Polling Station	Electors		Voters		Turnout as a %	
	Asian	Non-Asian	Asian	Non-Asian	Asian	Non-Asian
LA	349	823	210	219	60.2	26.6
LB	253	2784	134	802	53.0	28.8
LC	6	824	nil	357	nil	43.2
LD	431	1096	257	341	59.6	31.1
LE	29	2612	22	893	75.9	34.2
LF	309	690	182	212	58.9	30.7
LG	577	603	336	173	58.2	28.7
LH	583	284	225	49	38.6	17.3
Total	2537	9716	1366	3046	53.8	31.4

The two polling districts, LC and LE, which were 99 per cent white deviate from the consistent pattern, but since these turnout figures relate to so few Asians they cannot be regarded as significant. Disregard these two *white* districts and the pattern is consistent, for the Asian turnout rate is about double that of the non-Asian rate in all of them.

It will be noted that one of the polling districts, the first one, LA, also appears in Table 1, which relates to 1966. Although there had been boundary changes this particular polling station had not been affected and thus these figures are comparable, for LA covered exactly the same area at both elections. The contrast between the turnout rate of 0.7 per cent in 1966 and 60.2 per cent in 1969 could hardly be more dramatic. It might be erratic, an isolated result of no proven significance, but there is other evidence to indicate that this was not so. Polling stations LG and LH as observed in 1969 correspond very closely to the area covered by polling stations BH and GF in 1966. In 1966 the average Asian turnout in the amalgamated area BH/GF was 4.1 per cent (35 voters in an electorate of 859) whereas in 1969 the average, for almost the same area is 48.8 per cent. Henceforth the Asian vote was to be a factor of considerable significance in the electoral calculus of candidates in the Manningham Ward.

This phenomenon of electoral awakening cannot then be questioned, but one still must question its cause. Put simply, was the cause Dr Qureshi or Mr Powell? An approach to the answer to this question is suggested by noting that Dr Qureshi was a local phenomenon whereas we would expect the impact of Mr Powell to be nationwide. If there is no evidence of an electoral awakening of Asians outside Manningham then there is a clear suggestion that the principal cause was Dr Qureshi's candidature.

The University Ward is adjacent to and similar to Manningham with about the same proportion of Asian electors, but different in that it had no Asian as a candidate. University can therefore be regarded as a suitable control, particularly the three polling stations where Asians formed between a third and a half of the electorate. Whilst it is agreed that the proportion of Indians is greater in the University Ward for this purpose it makes no difference since Indians and Pakistanis would equally feel the hostility. Turnout in the University Ward fell in 1969 to just over four-fifths of the level recorded in 1968 and in the three Asian polling districts it fell to just under four-fifths of the level in the previous year. In Bradford as a whole turnout fell by about one-tenth and so one must conclude that the spectacular rise at Manningham was deviant from the norm in the city as well as in University. The principal cause of Asian activation must have been Dr Qureshi.

A careful study of turnout in Manningham reveals that in the two districts which had few Asians the pattern there conformed to that in the city as a whole since it also fell by about one-tenth. Table 3 shows that turnout changes were directly related to the proportion of the electorate who were Asian. The final column of the Table expresses the change in 1969 compared with 1968 but takes into account changes in the number of electors.

Table 3 Ballot Box Returns 1968 and 1969

Polling Stations	Percentage of Asian Electors	1968	1969	Percentage Change
G and H	55	427	803	+ 99.8
A, D and F	30	975	1391	+ 49.7
B	8	861	934	+ 9.9
C and E	1	1411	1267	− 10.2

This association between fuller ballot boxes and Asian electors, and between more empty ballot boxes and white electors clearly denies the possibility that the increased turnout could be explained in terms of white backlash. The conclusion at this stage is simply that a good Asian candidate could activate Asians so that they would proportionately outvote their non-Asian neighbours, and that it was the organisational effort of that candidate which produced this phenomenon.

However, events in 1970 cast some doubt upon this conclusion and suggest it is too simple. The Social Science Research Council sponsored research into Asian voting behaviour for both the local and the general elections and this suggests that the effect of Dr Qureshi was really no more than to give an advanced boost to a growing tendency for Asians to participate in the electoral process.

By 1970 the membership of the Labour Party in Manningham had become predominantly Asian. Originally the party adopted one of its Asian members as its candidate but when Mr Khan died suddenly his place was taken by Mr Brogden, a white man. Mr Brogden, who has also since died, was able to take advantage of a good Asian organisation and certainly this Asian support helped him to gain the seat back from the Conservatives.

The Labour Party was not alone in its efforts to mobilise Asian voters in 1970, for Mr Nawaz contested the seat as the candidate of the Pakistan People's Party. His organisation was also good, by the standards of the mid-sixties, but it did not compare with that of Dr Qureshi. It is only a subjective impression, but, from observations at the time, it seemed as if the combined efforts of the Labour Party and Mr Nawaz in 1970 were not really up to the organisational input of the Liberal Party and Dr Qureshi in 1969. These impressions appear to be confirmed by the results for Mr Nawaz only gained 11.2 per cent of the total votes cast, and, if all his 488 votes came exclusively from Asians, he only gained 41.0 per cent of the Asian vote, a calculation based on our observations which are given in Table 4.

Table 4 Asian and Non-Asian Turnout, Manningham 1970

Polling Station	Electors Asian	Electors Non-Asian	Voters Asian	Voters Non-Asian	Turnout as a % Asian	Turnout as a % Non-Asian
LA	373	791	152	198	40.8	25.0
LB	310	2865	188	865	60.6	30.2
LC	16	852	4	417	25.0	48.9
LD	598	929	280	303	46.8	32.6
LE	65	2688	37	1011	56.9	37.6
LF	355	657	136	189	38.3	28.8
LG	624	539	193	123	30.9	22.9
LH	633	270	199	61	31.4	22.5
Total	2974	9591	1189	3167	40.0	33.0

Table 4 shows that Asian turnout actually fell when compared with 1969 as recorded in Table 2, but it still remained clearly above the level of the non-Asians. On this occasion, then, without a really well organised Asian candidate, the evidence suggests that the phenomenon associated with Dr Qureshi was not simply a nine-day wonder and Asians were becoming diligent voters. The local election study, however, produced further evidence that this was so, for, as a control, we had covered a polling station in the University Ward where 41.0 per cent of the electors were Asian but there was no Asian candidate. Here we found that the Asian turnout level was 37.1 per cent which exceeded the 34.1 per cent level of the non-Asians.

Comparing the ballot box returns of 1969 and 1970 it is possible to pick out the observed polling station in the University Ward as one of those where there was an unusual increase in turnout. This particular station, KD, was one of the three which were mentioned earlier as having between a half and a third of the electorate who were Asian. The turnout pattern in the other two was the same with an increase of about a half in the proportion of persons voting. This impressive boost in turnout was confined to the three stations with high proportions of immigrants and one must presume that the high level of Asian turnout actually observed at the station KD also explains the boost at the other two similar stations.

The 1970 study also covered the General Election in June and polling stations which had been observed at the General Election of March 1966 were again observed. The Social Science Research Council also sponsored research for the General Election of 1974 when the same were again observed and all these General Election findings are given in Table 5.

Table 5 Asian and Non-Asian Percentage Turnout in General Elections

Polling Station	Asian			Non-Asian		
	1966	1970	1974	1966	1970	1974
KB	29.5	69.7	71.1	62.0	55.9	71.6
KD	37.4	71.9	83.2	45.8	48.0	61.5
LF	-	66.8	76.4	-	57.4	61.7
LG (BH)	35.8	67.2	75.3	55.1	46.3	53.8
LH (GF)	22.4	60.1	82.1	42.9	46.7	37.6
LD	-	-	70.5	-	-	60.7
KC	-	-	72.9	-	-	67.6

The increased level of Asian electoral activity in 1970 as compared with 1966 is plain from these figures, but, at the time, white party workers in the field were well aware of it through their own experiences. The Labour agent in Bradford East was approached by so many Asians offering help that he may have thought he had more Asian helpers than whites. It seemed as if there had been a spontaneous and largely un-solicited movement amongst Asians in the interests of the Labour Party. There is other outside evidence that this was so in so far as constituencies 'with substantial numbers of immigrants' in the West Midlands were distinguished by unusually small swings against Labour, similar to that noted in Bradford East.[15]

The third column in Table 5 shows that the high level of Asian turnout observed in 1970 was not merely maintained but improved upon in 1974. Two points which should be made here are, first, that higher turnout was a national phenomenon and it was also observable, at four out of five stations, with the non-Asians. The second point is that it is suspected that one effect of the Pakistan Act had been to delete from the Register not only those who were now genuinely aliens, but also Asians disinterested in either political activity or form-filling, consequently the register had lost a high proportion of those who were apathetic, non-voters.

Taking these two points into account it would not seem necessarily true to assert that by 1974 the Asians had become even more diligent as voters than they were in 1970, but it is quite clear that they had sustained their diligence. The SSRC sponsored study of the local elections in 1971, and small unsponsored studies in 1972 and 1973 show that Asians consistently maintained their relative diligence throughout these years.

The special feature of the local elections in 1971 was that for the first time in Bradford a major party contested a council seat with an Asian candidate. Mr Manawar Hussain fought Manningham as the Labour Party candidate and this was also the occasion for the first major trial of strength by candidates from the Yorkshire Campaign to Stop Immigration. In addition to observing all the polling stations in Manningham Ward two other stations were observed where Asians did not have the opportunity to vote for one of their kinsmen. One of these was station HE in the Heaton Ward where 29.1 per cent of the electors were Asian and the other was, once again, KD where the percentage of electors who were Asian had now risen to 43.

In Manningham the Asian level of turnout was 36.2 per cent compared with the non-Asian level 28.4. At the one station observed in University the Asian level was 28.8 per cent as against 21.2 for the non-Asians, and at the station in Heaton the comparison is between 28.3 and 24.7 per cent again in favour of the Asians. One cannot claim that this is a statistically sound sample which could be used to infer the behaviour of all Asians in Bradford but it does clearly suggest that Asians are nowadays generally more diligent voters than non-Asians who live in the same area.

So far as Manningham is concerned one can express the importance of the Asian vote in another way which is more impressive. In 1971 Asians formed 26.3 per cent of the electorate but since they were responsible for 1,273 of the 3,924 votes cast at polling stations they are best regarded as one third (32.4 per cent) of the voters. A vote of these proportions is comparable not simply with the proportions of the winning candidate but directly with the total vote of the winner. If all these Asian votes were for the same candidate then, on the evidence of recent Manningham results, that candidate would need only about three hundred non-Asian votes to become the winner.

The contemporary situation would appear to be that the Asian electorate is readily mobilised and that the participation of Asians as voters is of considerable significance in Bradford's politics. A number of questions, however, remain to be considered. First, there is the question of the extent to which participation is observable in terms of Asians standing as candidates. Secondly, there is the question of what this political awakening, particularly the diligence in voting, indicates in terms of political socialisation.

Asians as Candidates

Six Asians stood as candidates — two of them twice — in elections to Bradford County Borough Council. Despite the power of the Asian vote none of them were successful. The only Asian to sit in that Council Chamber had to get in, as it were by the back door, for Manawar Hussain, failed councillor, was elected an alderman in 1972.

In addition to these eight contests with Asian candidates there was an Asian contestant in the General Election of 1970 and there were four contests with Asians on the ballot papers for the new metropolitan authorities in 1973. In the 1973 contests two candidates once again failed in Manningham but Alderman Hussain won the county seat and a month later was also elected to the Metropolitan District Council as a member for the University Ward.

1 The First Independents

There is nothing remarkable about the early failures of Asian candidates to get themselves elected for they had the disadvantages of standing as Independents and of standing in 1963 when they could only appeal to a relatively small Asian electorate. There were three Asian candidates at the election, one of whom, Mr Aslam, has already been mentioned.

Mr Aslam first appeared in Bradford politics in 1958 when he spoke at a Conservative election meeting in Exchange. The newspaper stated that he was a graduate of Punjab University, and a bus conductor, who spoke as the Secretary of the Pakistan National Society in Bradford to announce that he would support the Conservatives and expected all the members of his Society to do likewise. When interviewed in 1963 he revealed that he owned shops, houses, an export-import business and private-hire cars, and he gave the impression that he was an important member of the Kashmir National Muslim Association. He regarded the Labour Party as an ally of the Communist Party and a danger to a free society.

It would seem reasonable that a successful businessman with right wing views might be approached as a potential Conservative candidate. The principal figure in Listerhills Ward Conservative Association, however, had strong views on immigration and if Mr Aslam wanted to be approached, he waited in vain. Possibly he was more content to demonstrate that a highly organised candidate could mobilise a substantial Asian vote, but he also demonstrated that there was no hope of election outside the major parties. The two other Independents, Mr Razul and Mr Qureshi fought Exchange and made it even more obvious that no Asian had a hope of reaching the Council Chamber by standing as an Independent.

These two candidates are interesting because they gave the first indication that the Asian vote might be split on issues which were not understandable in contemporary Bradford politics, but which related to the politics of the 'old country.' Their reasons for opposing one another were not at first obvious. They were rather non-commital when interviewed, although each was confident of winning. Mr Razul was the most confident and had no fear that Mr Qureshi would win, for he claimed an army of election workers who guaranteed him 2,500 votes, whereas Mr Qureshi would only get ten. In fact, Mr Razul got 52 and Mr Qureshi got 88.

The real rivalry between them, almost certainly, arose through Mr Razul's patriotism and his strong feelings about Kashmir. Mr Razul was a Mirpuri who had fought against the Indians in Kashmir. Mr Qureshi was born in India, had been in the Indian Civil Service and had fled to Pakistan. A *Guardian* reporter quoted Mr Razul as saying that Mr Qureshi was not a true Pakistani.[16] Later, in an interview, he insisted that he had been misrepresented but, nevertheless, made it clear that anyone who had not fought for free Kashmir was quite unworthy of support. This kind of argument, with the suitability of candidates in Bradford local elections depending on politics in another continent, was to arise again, with another candidate called Qureshi who was the next Asian to fight an election in Bradford.

2 The Liberal Experiment

In 1969, Dr Qureshi became the first Asian to achieve a really substantial proportion of the vote, gaining 26.7 per cent (1,194) of the votes at Manningham. His candidacy, as a Liberal, was the principal cause of the high Asian activation which marks the beginning of what I have called the period of political awakening. After Dr Qureshi, politics in Manningham were never going to be the same again. It was, however, not the impact of his Liberal colours but the impact of the colour of his skin that was important.

The Liberal candidacy was somewhat surprising since the Liberals had not recently contested Manningham and they were not thought to possess any organisation in the ward. Nevertheless, white Liberals from other wards, even from other cities, came in to help and, combining with personal friends of Dr Qureshi, produced an impressive organisation and an impressive result. The result in Manningham was in many respects the best Liberal performance in Bradford at that election.

The Liberals, however, have not contested Manningham since that occasion. It was a 'one-off' affair and one is inclined to conclude that adopting Dr Qureshi, who, allegedly, had helped the Labour Party in previous elections, was something of an experiment. It was perhaps an experiment with the forthcoming General Election in mind, for in June 1970 the Liberals contested Bradford East Parliamentary Constituency, which includes Manningham, for the first time since the constituency was formed. Their candidate, Mr Musa, a Pakistani journalist, was brought up from London to fight the constituency in which 5,454 of the 40,720 electors had Asian names, and a good Liberal performance looked likely.

The Liberal performance was not good, for Mr Musa gained only 660 votes which compares very unfavourably with Dr Qureshi's 1,194 in a local election in what was only a part of the constituency. There are several possible reasons for this, one of which is that Mr Musa was seemingly imposed from outside the local Asian communities and lacking any firm base there got little support. Some Asians actually indicated that they resented his intrusion.

A second reason might be found in the fact that the Labour Party, at that time, had become the recipient of Pakistani electoral support. This has already been referred to and further evidence of this allegiance is given below. In particular the Manningham Ward Labour Party was predominantly Asian and had developed a good organisation to get out the Asian vote for the Labour candidate. On the other hand there could be a third reason, that Asians, like the native whites, might allow themselves the luxury of voting for a third party in local elections but regarded General Elections as, essentially, a more important contest to decide which of two parties should form the government.

Whatever the explanation the General Election in Bradford East was very discouraging for the Liberals and Mr Musa. If one makes the unlikely assumption that no white man voted Liberal, so that all Mr Musa's votes came from Asians, we can make certain calculations. Observers noted that 1,666 Asians voted at four polling stations where 2,480 Asian electors were entitled to vote. If this 67.2 per cent turnout rate also applied to the other 2,974 Asian electors in the constituency the total number of Asians who voted in Bradford East would be 3,665. Thus, assuming every Liberal vote was an Asian vote, over three thousand Asians denied their vote to Mr Musa and he received, at most, only 18.0 per cent of that Asian vote. If, say, only 330 white electors in the whole constituency voted Liberal, so that half Mr Musa's votes came from whites, his share of the Asian vote would be reduced to a mere nine per cent and the Liberal experiment must be regarded as a failure. In the sense that he did not win Dr Qureshi also failed as a Liberal candidate, yet, in terms of the size of his vote he had made a considerable breakthrough. Nevertheless, the Liberals never tried again with an Asian nor any other candidate in Manningham. On the other hand there was, never again, an election in Manningham without an Asian candidate.

In November 1969, the Labour Party in Manningham chose Saleem Khan, their Secretary, as the Labour candidate. Mr Khan, who was the full-time secretary of the Pakistan Immigrants' Welfare Association, had been active within the Labour Party for several years, and actually held office as the vice-chairman of Bradford North Constituency Labour Party. Mr Khan, who was the first Asian chosen as a Labour candidate, died suddenly at the end of February. Several Asians offered to take Mr Khan's place as Labour candidate, but none of them was on the Labour Party's approved list of endorsed candidates. The new candidate adopted was Mr Brogden, the official of the Transport and General Workers Union who was responsible for passenger transport.

3 The Pakistan People's Party

Mr Khan's place as the Pakistani fighting the election in Manningham was taken by Mr Nawaz. Mr Nawaz had previously been a member of Mr Brogden's union and apparently considered that the union, and Mr Brogden personally, had failed him when his employment by Bradford Corporation Transport Department came to an end. According to Mr Nawaz the Bradford Branch of the Pakistan People's Party (UK) had been formed in October 1969, but there was no indication of its existence or of the intention to contest local elections before nomination day.

Other Pakistani groups made statements of disapproval at Mr Nawaz's action. The Chairman of the Islamic Institute wrote to the *Telegraph and Argus* to say that 'to stand on the ticket of a party which has no concern with problems in this country is pure farce.' Mr Shahid, secretary of the Pakistan Association condemned his action in similar words and was joined by Mr Patel of the Coloured People's Union, both these organisations calling upon coloured people to boycott the elections. Mr Manawar Hussain, Chairman of the Pakistani Progressive People's League in Great Britain also asked his countrymen not to support Mr Nawaz. Mr Hussain's organisation, which had been established for three years, was inclined to support the Labour Party, and Mr Hussain was to be nominated as the Labour Party candidate for Manningham in 1971.

Mr Nawaz, however, refused to stand down and an article appeared in the *Telegraph and Argus* in which the municipal reporter quoted him as insisting that he would 'represent the interests of the whole ward.' The report went on to say that Mr Nawaz was reluctant to define his party's political position, and that it was not the policy of the party to disclose its membership figures. Mr Nawaz's agent, Mr M.M.U. Siddiqui, also had an ambiguous political position for he had previously assisted the Labour Party, but he also had contacts with the Conservative Party.

Two documents issued by the Pakistan People's Party (UK) Bradford Branch were studied. One of these was a duplicated document on three sheets of foolscap which will be termed the manifesto. The foreword included the statement that 'The political realities evaluated analytically after agonising reappraisal, make inevitable the formation of a new Party with a new programme and a fresh approach.' A series of ten statements on policy points followed on education, housing, health, welfare, immigration, religious holidays and industrial relations. The section on industrial relations included the passage, 'In the past, the Unions in collaboration with the employers, have completely neglected the interests of the Textile Workers.' A later passage on unionism said that the unions had failed all workers and would continue to do so.

The election address gave no indication of the party policy, in fact it looked very much like a copy of that used by the Social Credit candidates in Manningham from 1967 onwards. In many passages the words used were identical with those in the Social Credit address, even to the extent of claiming that the party was different from other political parties.

If one looks again at Table 4 it can be seen that two polling districts (LG and LH) are predominantly Asian. These two districts in the east of Manningham give an inaccurate impression to anybody visiting or residing in that area that Asians are in the majority in the ward. A spokesman for the Pakistan People's Party justified putting up Mr Nawaz as their candidate on precisely these grounds. Mr Nawaz, although he must have known from the electoral registers that there were almost ten thousand whites in the ward also seemed confident of success. He certainly had a good organisation getting in the Asian vote in the eastern districts, but it still did not appear as good as Dr Qureshi's in 1969 and he could hardly expect the kind of white support a Liberal candidate might attract.

Mr Nawaz got more votes than the Social Credit candidate, but that was his only consolation. He gained 11.2 per cent of the vote which was much worse than Dr Qureshi and he had the extra disappointment of watching Mr Brogden returned as the councillor. Immediately after the election he wrote to the Town Clerk to ask him to arrange a fresh election. To the press he stated, 'the whole thing was a farce. I did a lot of work in the ward and I expected to get more than 488 votes. I should have had 1,500.'

4 Labour's Misfortunes

It is worth noting that although the Liberals never tried again with an Asian candidate after Dr Qureshi, the Labour Party began each subsequent election in Manningham by adopting an Asian as their candidate. This should not be taken to mean that the Labour Party was consciously demonstrating its altruism, nor does it mean that the Labour Party was deliberately indulging in calculated opportunism. The subsequent history of adopting Asians as candidates was an accident of the membership of Manningham Ward Labour Party which had become predominantly Asian. It was also a matter of a series of accidents that none of them ever got elected.

The first accident was the death of Saleem Khan in 1970. The second accident, or series of accidents, came in 1971. Councillor Brogden won Manningham for Labour, in 1970, with 55 per cent of the two-party vote and the ward was the fifth safest Labour seat in the city. Thus when Manawar Hussain was adopted by Labour for the next election his prospects of success seemed good. No doubt some white voters who traditionally voted Labour might desert him, but if he could pick up Mr Nawaz's 488 and add this to the majority of 376, he should survive. Quite simply he had to gain the Asian vote as Dr Qureshi had done and avoid losing too much of the white vote, which Councillor Brogden had gained. A strong swing to Labour in the opinion polls made the task of Manawar Hussain look easy.

My Hussain did not win. The Manningham Ward went completely against the swing in Bradford. In the other wards there was a swing of 13.0 per cent to Labour and many supposed Conservative strongholds acquired a Labour councillor. At Manningham alone the swing was to the Conservatives (8.3 per cent) and a ward, accepted as Labour, returned a Conservative councillor. A number of events which occurred before the election may have contributed to this remarkable defeat. They appear almost as a further series of accidents which prevented an Asian from being elected to the Council.

The first event was the entry of a new political party, the Yorkshire Campaign to Stop Immigration. This party, although it might claim otherwise, was not designed to discourage racial prejudice and its possible influence on Mr Hussain's prospects was difficult to predict. If there was a substantial white backlash vote Mr Hussain could anticipate a substantial number of Labour desertions.

The second event did not occur in Bradford for it was the troubles in Bangladesh, which was Mr Hussain's original homeland. In February there was actually some doubt about whether or not Mr Hussain was going to be able to contest the election for he had disappeared inside what was then East Pakistan. He managed to return in good time but only to face attacks from the Pakistani community in Bradford, whose origins are predominantly in West Pakistan. His sympathy with the movement for Independence for Bangladesh soon appeared as a distinct disadvantage.

The reaction at first seemed to be led by Mr Nawaz as a Pakistan People's Party spokesman. At the end of March and in early April he wrote to Mr Hussain asking him to withdraw because a man '. . . from East Pakistan should not stand in an area which is predominantly a West Pakistan community.'[17] Mr Nawaz was quoted as saying that it would be suicide for Mr Hussain to stand and said that, if he did not withdraw, the Pakistan People's Party would mount a vigorous campaign against him.

Mr Nawaz himself soon became the centre of controversy for other persons claiming to be officials of the Pakistan People's Party asserted that Mr Nawaz was no longer an official of the party and that he had no authority to make statements on behalf of the party. Mr Nawaz disputed this and insisted, in April, that he would contest the election. He did in fact do this but he stood as an Independent and not as the official Pakistan People's candidate. Nevertheless, Mr Nawaz was clearly going to cause Mr Hussain some trouble.

More serious trouble was to come because of Mr Hussain's association with the Bangladesh movement. An article in the *Telegraph and Argus*[18] had the headline, 'Immigrants switch polls backing from Labour to Tory.' The article was a report of a meeting called by Mr

Darr who was an executive member of the Bradford Islamic Mission. Mr Darr said that immigrants in the Manningham and University Wards had long been staunch supporters of the Labour Party, but that some Labour MPs' recent distorting statements on the disturbances in Pakistan had caused them to decide to support the Conservatives. Mr Suleman, vice-president of the Pakistan Immigrant Welfare Association stated that he had come to the meeting to announce full support for the Conservatives. These men claimed to speak on behalf of the immigrant community, and although there is no way of testing the validity of these statements, things were clearly getting worse for Mr Hussain. The bodies involved in this meeting, which was attended by the Conservative candidates, were definitely important, indeed the Pakistan Immigrant Welfare Association had been Saleem Khan's, and Labour's, main source of support.

The Labour Party took the matter seriously and their Whip, Councillor Smith, attacked these Pakistani leaders in the press. He did not deny that they were leaders but questioned their logic and insisted that, 'Elections in Bradford are not about the problems of Pakistan.'[19] The Labour Party had, however, become clearly associated with the Bangladesh movement and the Conservatives had become associated with the interests of West Pakistan.

This association actually became clearer after the election. In June the cricket match between Yorkshire and Pakistan took place at Bradford and the leader of the Bangladesh demonstration was Mr Hussain, officially described as Yorkshire spokesman of the Action Committee. The West Pakistanis attacked Labour MPs for espousing the Bangladesh cause and the local Conservative MP argued the case of President Yahya Khan and spoke of the 'Holy War' which he was fighting.

It was quite clear that a proportion of the Pakistanis would not be prepared to vote for a Bangladesh (Labour) candidate. On the other hand Mr Hussain could be confident of the support of the Bengalis and of the Indians. Unfortunately for Mr Hussain the Indians are very few in numbers in this part of Bradford and it was believed that at least 70 per cent of the Pakistanis originated in the West. If the majority of the Asians in the ward intended either to abstain, to even vote against him, whilst on the other hand a substantial number of non-Asian Labour voters proposed to do the same then Labour had the misfortune of having their candidate, Mr Hussain, in the wrong place at the wrong time.

5 Mr Hussain's Defeat

There is fairly strong evidence that if Mr Hussain had taken the majority of the Asian votes he would have won, for surveys, taken at the time, indicate that he was very close to the Conservative in the non-Asian sector. There were two surveys — a random sample on the non-Asian electorate was interviewed immediately before the election and a random sample of known non-Asian voters was interviewed after the election, and they both suggested that it was close between the two main parties.

The survey before the election actually gave the advantage to Mr Hissain, even amongst those 59.3 per cent of the respondents who knew that the Labour candidate was a Pakistani. This knowledge that the Labour candidate was coloured was, of course, a matter of critical importance. It was well brought out by the 77 interviewees who expressed an opinion about which party was likely to win. One anticipated victory for a non-existent Liberal. Without this last answer, the majority of the remainder (52.0 per cent) anticipated victory for Labour. Conservative victory was predicted by 41.3 per cent and 6.7 per cent thought the Yorkshire Campaign candidate would win. There was, however, a highly significant difference between the answers given by those who knew the Labour candidate was a Pakistani and those who did not have that knowledge. Amongst those who knew about Mr Hussain, 27 predicted a Conservative victory as against 22 who thought Mr Hussain would win. Amongst those who did not know that the Labour candidate was a Pakistani only 5 anticipated a Conservative victory whereas 17 were confident that Labour would win. Thus the majority predicted for Labour depended upon those who did not know the Labour candidate was a Pakistani.

The post-election survey was also confined to non-Asians, all of whom were known to have voted. When asked how they had voted, 97 non-Asian voters divided as follows:

Conservative	32	(33.0 per cent)
Labour	29	(29.9 per cent)
Social Credit	1	(1.0 per cent)
Yorkshire Campaign	17	(17.5 per cent)
Refused	18	(18.6 per cent)

It was strongly suspected that many of those who refused, which included those who said they could not remember, had actually voted for the anti-immigrant candidate but were reticent to say so. With these numbers one cannot be confident, statistically, in asserting that the majority of the two-party vote of the non-Asians went to the Conservatives, but it is clear that for Mr Hussain to be the winner he would need a majority of the Asian vote.

We know, of course, that he did not win. Indeed we know precisely how many votes each candidate received (Table 6), and Table 7 gives the observed sizes of the Asian and non-Asian votes. Many other details are known with accuracy, for example there were only 43 West Indians in the total non-Asian vote of 2,651 and there were 87 postal voters, none of whom was Asian because there were no Asians registered as postal voters. The voting behaviour in other wards in Bradford is also known and one can begin to build up a picture of what happened in this election.

109

Table 6 The Results in Manningham 1971

			%
Mrs M. Wood	(Conservative)	1531	38.8
M. Hussain	(Labour)	1343	34.0
J. Abbott	(Yorkshire Campaign)	802	20.3
M.M. Nawaz	(Independent)	163	4.1
J.E. Jennings	(Social Credit)	109	2.8
Total Valid Vote		3948	
Majority		188	

Table 7 Asian and Non-Asian Turnout, Manningham 1971

Polling Station	Electors		Voters		Turnout as %	
	Asian	Non-Asian	Asian	Non-Asian	Asian	Non-Asian
LA	485	818	163	160	33.6	19.6
LB	329	2750	146	764	44.4	28.7
LC	12	837	6	341	50.0	40.7
LD	678	851	210	218	31.0	25.6
LE	72	2674	50	860	63.9	32.2
LF	419	665	125	152	29.8	22.9
LG	719	505	353	114	49.1	22.6
LH	623	250	220	42	35.3	16.8
Total	3337	9350	1273	2651	36.2	28.4

The first point which should be made is that turnout at Manningham, compared with 1970, was down by 3.3 per cent. This was contrary to the general movement in the city where turnout rose, on average, by 3.0 per cent. The fall in Manningham is, however, more fairly compared with a rise of 4.2 per cent since the average for the whole city tends to minimise the influence of the additional anti-immigrant candidates. Voters at Manningham had the additional voting option of an anti-immigrant candidate who, of course, provided an additional input of effort to turn out the vote. Anti-immigrant candidates also stood in twelve other wards against Conservative and Labour candidates and there turnout rose by 4.2 per cent, whereas in the five wards with a straight fight (the eighteenth ward had a Liberal) it rose, on average, by only 2.4 per cent.

This is an analysis of turnout based upon official returns, but comparing Table 4 and Table 7 it is possible to analyse the movement of turnout in terms of Asian and non-Asian electors. One might first note that there were 84 more Asian voters in 1971 and that there were 516 fewer non-Asian voters. This, however, does not take into account changes in the electorate for one can also see that the non-Asian turnout rate dropped from 33.0 per cent to 28.4 per cent and that the Asian rate also fell (the 84 more votes came from a bigger electorate) from 40.0 per cent to 36.2 per cent. Taking 1970 as 100 the index of non-Asian voting in 1971 would be 86 and of Asian 90.5.

Looking at the individual polling districts in these Tables it will be seen that the non-Asian rate fell, more or less consistently, in each of them. The non-Asian electors in Manningham had clearly behaved very differently from those elsewhere in Bradford for they had stayed at home in greater numbers, whereas in the other wards (the comparable index is 113) they had shown an increased propensity to go to the poll. It would seen reasonable to assume that many of these, some of whom were located in the surveys, stayed at home because the Labour candidate was coloured.

Some comparisons between the Asian turnout rates in 1970 and 1971 can also be made using these Tables. The two polling districts (LC and LE) in the western sector of the ward have too few Asian electors to justify significant conclusions, but in the remaining stations the pattern is clear. The Asian vote declined in four stations, as it was also observed to decline in the control station in the University Ward, but it rose considerably in LG and slightly in LH. Mr Hussain lived in LG where the Bengalis were concentrated and one can still see a slogan attacking Yahya Khan's regime daubed on the walls. The Bengali area overlaps this district and extends into an adjacent part of LH district which had the moderate increase. The pattern appears to be one of increased activity by Bengalis but of increased abstention by West Pakistanis possibly because they could not bring themselves to vote for a protagonist of Bangladesh. Mr Hussain therefore lost out in both the Asian and the non-Asian sectors.

Known facts about turnout levels and about the votes which candidates received can be augmented by observation. The student observers at the polling stations noted everything of interest besides the electoral numbers and the ethnic origin of the voters. At LG the observer noted

Mr Hussain's organisation was exceptionally good with a fleet of cars and a large van bringing in immigrants clutching Hussain leaflets and being marshalled by Mr Hussain himself or one of his helpers. The observer noted that he omitted '3 van loads' but still counted 152 Asians who came in vehicles bearing Mr Hussain's name. It would seem that between a third and a half of the Asian voters came to vote in transport provided by Mr Hussain, even though the polling district is a small one and they had only short distances to walk. By contrast there were no Conservative cars until one appeared with a single Asian just before 9.00 p.m., and the occupant then found that it was the wrong place.

At LH the Bengali (Labour) dominance was much weaker for while the observer noted seven different Hussain cars operating there were four operating for the Conservatives. The proportion of Asians, judged by the colour of leaflets held in their hands, who voted Conservative was about half the number voting for Labour. This station was also different in that some Asians were observed carrying leaflets of Mr Nawaz.

At the other stations there was visible evidence that Asians were supporting the Conservatives in quite substantial numbers. At LA the observer saw as many Asians carrying Conservative leaflets as there were Asians carrying Labour and at the other stations Asians were frequently brought to the poll in Asian-driven Conservative cars. It was thus quite clear, simply from standing outside the polling stations, that Mr Hussain may have solid support in the Bengali area, but elsewhere he had failed to gain the Asian vote, in fact many observers doubted whether he had gained the majority of it.

Observers had noted non-Asian voters carrying Hussain leaflets and they had noted non-Asians coming in to vote in Labour cars. At station LB, however, it was clear that most whites coming in cars had been brought by the Conservatives, the count there being 69 in Conservative cars compared with 15 in Labour cars. The districts in the far west of the ward (LC and LE), which are over 97 per cent non-Asian, seemed to be showing very strong Conservative leanings and it looked to the observer as if, overall, Mr Hussain was not gaining a clear majority of either the non-Asian or Asian vote.

To all these observations the evidence of the surveys, the data on turnout and results we can add an analysis of what happened to the party vote elsewhere in Bradford. In the twelve comparable wards in Conservative vote fell by 21.9 per cent and the Labour vote was increased by 6.7 per cent. In Manningham the Labour vote fell by 34.8 per cent whereas the Conservative vote fell by only 9.0 per cent and one cannot resist the view that in addition to Labour's very poor performance the Conservatives had done positively well. Compared with other wards the Conservatives had picked up a considerable number of votes from somewhere and these almost balanced their losses from national unpopularity and the arrival of an anti-immigrant candidate. One can actually calculate that the Conservatives in Manningham had gained about 470 more votes (their majority was 188) than one would anticipate from their record in similar wards.

It is possible to play around with the figures in many ways. It is possible to take into account various assumptions such as no Asian would vote for the anti-immigrant candidate or that no white man would vote for Mian Mohammed Nawaz, the Independent Pakistani. The interesting point is that the only acceptable conclusion is the same as that which the student observers found by simply standing outside the polling stations all day long. The Asians in Manningham who voted either Conservative or Labour were split about equally between those two parties. As the Indians and Bengalis had presumably stayed local to Labour a substantial proportion of Pakistanis had switched to the Conservatives as their leaders said they would. There cannot really be any doubt that the loss of Manningham by Mr Hussain to the Conservatives was less a matter of white backlash and more a matter of Pakistani politics. Those who might be described as backlash voters tended to support the anti-immigrant candidate, a process which, not infrequently, meant a loss of support to the Conservatives. The explanation of the positive advance of the Conservatives was symbolised by the observation, on polling days, of brown hands clutching blue leaflets. Every known fact and every observation at the time, and the evidence of later research, particularly a survey of Asian voters in February 1974, makes it clear that Labour's loss of Manningham was primarily a consequence of the 1971 troubles in Bangladesh.

6 The Aftermath, Subsequent Local Elections

The loss of Manningham was a serious blow to the Labour Party and some of its members believed that it was bad tactics to permit Mr Hussain to fight Manningham again. In June a dispute broke out in the Labour Party with one councillor publicly alleging that his party was discriminating against Mr Hussain in its selection procedures. Mr Hussain, however, was strongly placed in his own ward party and was again selected to fight Manningham in 1972, leaving some Labour Party members outside that ward highly concerned that a vital ward in a marginal constituency was being thrown away.

Their concern was justified for Mr Hussain lost again in 1972. Admittedly Labour was generally less successful that year than they had been in 1971 with a swing to the Conservatives in Bradford of 6.2 per cent,[20] thus the swing of 6.6 per cent to the Conservatives in Manningham was not out of line. Yet it did prove that Mr Hussain's defeat was no flash in the pan and his presence had apparently turned Labour's fifth safest, of the nineteen seats, into the second safest Conservative seat.

In October 1972 Mr Hussain was kicked upstairs and became an alderman. This would, previously, have been a most ingenious tactic, but, the Local Government Act took the 'upstairs' away and Alderman Hussain was back on the ground floor as an aspiring councillor in the new authorities. It must be admitted that the Labour Party knew full well that the office of alderman was to be abolished. In a sense the title may have strengthened Manawar Hussain's position, for by voting for him the Labour Group showed their confidence in him and he was again endorsed as an official Labour Party candidate.

Nevertheless, some members of the Labour Party were dismayed that he was to fight again; the new metropolitan district council would be highly marginal. Alderman Hussain, however, still had a strong base in Manningham and he also had many contacts, including fellow councillors, with the University Ward Labour Party. It was not surprising therefore that he was adopted to fight the new combined Manningham, University and Little Horton county electoral division. What did surprise some outsiders was that he was adopted for the University Ward rather than Manningham for the district elections in May.

The county seat returned two members and Manawar Hussain, who came second to his Labour running mate, had his first taste of electoral success. He might succeed again in May, but how and why had he managed to switch from Manningham to University? A newspaper report[21] of the University Ward Labour Party selection meeting explains that 'Embarassment was felt within the party because (25) new members were recruited just before a meeting to choose prospective candidates for the metropolitan district elections, among whom Alderman Hussain had been short-listed.' The newspaper indicated that whilst the treasurer of that party, Mr John Godward, was pleased to see new recruits, who could outnumber the regulars by two to one, speaking personally, he felt it right to adjourn the meeting when many of the selectors could not understand anything that the English candidates had to say.

At the adjourned selection meeting two sitting white councillors were chosen along with Alderman Hussain to be the Labour trio in May. It proved a wise choice, for Manawar Hussain, who now lives in the ward, came top of the poll with over 500 more votes than the most successful Conservative and almost 100 more than the average of the other two Labour candidates.

It was also a wise choice personally for Manawar Hussain since in the same district election Asians again failed in Manningham where three Conservatives, Mrs Curtis, Mrs Smith and Mrs Wood were returned. Mr Hussain's place as the Asian candidate of the Labour Party was taken by C.M. Khan, but he and his two white colleagues gained only 44.6 per cent of the two-party vote. It is interesting to note, however, that Mr Khan kept up well with his two running mates for Mr Khan's 863 is equivalent to 93.8 per cent of their average of 920.

The candidates at Manningham were not confined to three Conservative and three Labour for there were also three from the British Campaign to Stop Immigration (the successor to the Yorkshire Campaign mentioned above) the persistent Mr Jennings of the Social Credit party and an important newcomer, Mr Riaz Shahid, who stood as an Independent. Mr Shahid was important because with 1,033 votes he almost won and because he was at the centre of two subsequent matters which received wide publicity.

The first of these two matters related to the election for Mr Shahid alleged that the count had been rigged. He lost by 61 votes to Mrs Smith and claimed at a press conference[22] that four summary sheets carrying 153 votes in his favour disappeared whilst he and his agent went out of the room for ten minutes to get a cup of coffee. His demand for a recount was refused and Mr Shahid told the press conference 'I don't think the local authority wants to see a coloured Independent candidate in the council, just in case he may be a nuisance.' The Town Clerk put the complaint in the hands of the police, a neighbouring police force then investigated the complaint that a sheet was deliberately destroyed by counting officials to favour Mr Shahid's opponents and a file was sent to the Director of Public Prosecutions. The charge was rejected and Mr Shahid commented 'I am far from satisfied. They have hushed it up completely.'[23]

The second of the two matters is interesting because, although it does not arise from the election, it may give some idea of what Mr Shahid stood for as an Independent. In December Mr Shahid was reported as giving up his £3,500 per annum position as a leader of the Pakistani community and returning to Pakistan for the sake of his daughters. As an orthodox Moslem he said 'I cannot allow my little girl, who has reached the age of puberty to mix with boys freely.'[24] The local authority had placed her in a co-educational secondary school and refused to arrange education for Muslim girls in a single-sex school. Whilst Mr Shahid's views could be appreciated, many observers were perplexed when he took his family to Pakistan since his wife was Glasgow-born and like his daughter, Anne, had never been to Pakistan and spoke only a few words of Urdu.

Apart from the intriguing Mr Shahid there is still an intriguing question about the May elections. This concerns the success of Manawar Hussain in University on the one hand, and, on the other, his earlier failures, and Mr Khan's failure in Manningham. It is intriguing, not only because it may explain why Manawar Hussain switched, but also because in so many respects the two wards are very much alike. According to the 1971 Census 25.7 per cent of Manningham residents were born in Asia compared with 28.9 per cent of those in University. At Manningham 88.4 per cent of the economically active males were manual workers with 58.7 per cent semi-skilled or unskilled, with the comparable figures of 88.9 per cent and 55.1 per cent at University.

Pulzer stated 'class is the basis of British party politics; all else is embellishment and detail.'[25] One wonders what detail or embellishment explains the divergent behaviour of these twin wards.

The research project for the General Election of February 1974 involved an examination of the electoral registers and a count of the number of electors with Muslim, Hindu or Sikh names. This was not the register used in the 1973 elections and the Pakistan Act, in theory ought to have reduced the proportion of Moslems on the register, although it is also true that not all the Moslems were Pakistani, but this information still gives a clear guide to a fundamental difference between the wards. The research showed that whereas 87.4 per cent of the Asian names in Manningham were Muslim the level in University was only 51.3 per cent. The 1971 Census also gave a similar picture, although residents are not the same as electors, for the ratio of Pakistan birthplaces to Indian birthplaces in Manningham is approximately 4:1 whereas in University it is 3:2.

The General Election of February 1974

It has laready been noted that the Asian vote was regarded as crucial in the new marginal seat of Bradford West. The adherence of the Pakistanis to the Conservatives had produced repeated elections of Conservative female councillors in Manningham since 1971, and, if it could be sustained, John Wilkinson, the MP for the old Bradford West would improve his chances of winning the new seat. Mr Wilkinson made considerable efforts to retain this loyalty; for example, he defied the Conservative Whip and voted for a Labour amendment to the Pakistan Bill on the 28th June 1973. Equally, Mr Edward Lyons, then MP for Bradford East, who was to contest the new West constituency, made considerable efforts to regain Pakistani support. Research after the election suggests that they had to settle roughly for a draw.

It is appropriate to speak of Mr Lyons regaining Pakistani support because all the evidence is that in 1970, when most of the Asians were in Bradford East, he had their overwhleming support. This too was referred to above but one must add another piece of evidence which is the survey conducted by National Opinion Polls in April 1971.

This survey[26] included 286 'coloured' respondents in Bradford East Constituency, but there is a clear indication that by 'coloured' was meant Indians and Pakistanis, for on several occasions the survey referred to the Indian and Pakistani communities in Bradford, and at one point contrasted them with the West Indians in Brent. The answers to the various questions are shown as percentages, but since the number of respondents is known it is possible to calculate the original raw scores when appropriate.

In Bradford East it was found that 20 per cent of respondents were not registered. The remaining 80 per cent included 9 per cent who did not vote and 7 per cent who didn't know or refused to answer. Recalculating the 9 per cent non-voters on the 80 per cent who were registered suggests a turnout rate of 88.75 per cent. This is considerably higher than the average rate of 67.1 per cent actually observed, and shown in Table 5, but it has often been shown that respondents are inclined to exaggerate in this matter.[27] The percentage of those who indicated a party preference is the residual 64, comprising 59 per cent who said they voted Labour, 3 per cent who voted Liberal and 2 per cent who voted Conservative.

It would appear from this that 183 respondents gave a partisan answer. The NOP percentages were rounded off and in recalculating there is a discrepancy of one respondent, but the distribution appears to be, Labour 169 (91.8 per cent), Liberal 9 (4.9 per cent) and Conservative 6 (3.3 per cent). In terms of the two-party vote, Labour, according to this, had a 96.6 per cent share leaving the Conservatives with a mere 3.4 per cent. In the light of this evidence one can only speak in terms of Mr Lyons trying to regain the Asian vote in 1974. Before proceeding to that election one might reflect how this distribution relates to the observed Asian vote and what it means in absolute numbers. It was calculated above that, in 1970, there were 3,665 Asian voters in Bradford East, thus Mr Lyons should have received 3,364 whereas his Conservative opponent had 121. The Liberal, Mr Musa, then received 180 Asian votes and his other 480 must have come from non-Asians.[28]

The research programme in February 1974 included a post-election survey of Asians which was conducted by Asians. Student observers had produced an accurate list of Asian voters in seven polling districts and two per cent of these known voters were sampled at random. In addition to this, a slightly larger random sample was taken of the electorate in the other polling stations so that the whole of Bradford West Constituency was covered, and an adjustment was made so that both samples were consistent in terms of voters.

In this survey it was possible to distinguish between the nationalities of the Asians, and Table 8 breaks down the 117 respondents by nationality. There is a marked contrast between the Indians and the Pakistanis, for in terms of the two-party vote the Conservatives had a narrow advantage (53.4 per cent) amongst the Pakistanis but Labour had overwhelming support (93.9 per cent) amongst the Indians. In one sense, the true figure of Labour support is even higher for one of the two Indians who voted Conservative said that he did so for luck, he wanted Labour to win but since whoever he voted for always seemed to lose, he voted Conservative. Furthermore, the Indian, a Gujarati woman, who voted for the Independent Democratic Alliance, also wanted to vote Labour but had become confused by the five names on the list.

Table 8 Asian Voting in February 1974

Voted	Country of Origin			Total Asian
	Pakistan	India	Bangladesh	
Conservative	31	2	1	34
Labour	27	31	3	61
Liberal	3	nil	nil	3
Ind. Dem. Alliance	1	1	nil	2
Refused or 'Don't Know'	11	5	1	17
Total	73	39	5	117

It is possible to use our observations of Asian turnout and translate these figures into votes, although, of course, they should be treated with caution to allow for sampling error in relation to the main parties, and it is quite unwarranted for any statistician to infer conclusions from the small numbers supporting the minor parties. At seven polling stations where 3,700 Asians were on the register, 2,774 were observed to vote. The total Asian electorate in Bradford West was 6,976 and provided that the 47 per cent of the electorate which was not observed also had a turnout rate of 75 per cent the number of Asians who voted was 5,230. Taking Table 8 as our guide, this suggests that 3,190 of Mr Lyon's votes came from Asians compared with 1,778 of Mr Wilkinson's.

Although it is quite unwarranted statistically, I cannot resist the point that 105 Asian votes appear to have been given to the Independent Democratic Alliance candidate, who tended to take an anti-immigrant line. Since his actual vote was 200 it is ironic that he may have gained more than half his votes from immigrants.

One point which came out in the survey was that a large proportion of the Pakistanis who voted for Mr Wilkinson were not really Conservative supporters. Amongst the questions put to respondents was one which asked whether they thought the result of the election was good or bad. It was surprising how many Conservative voters colunteered the view that a Labour government was good for the country but that Mr Wilkinson's defeat was bad for Bradford. It is possible that Mr Wilkinson had one of the largest personal votes in the country, for, applying the kind of distribution found by NOP in 1971, he had attracted something like 1,600 more Asian votes by 1974.

Conclusions

Participation by Asians in elections has now become a matter of some significance in Bradford. Asians are important as electors, as voters and as candidates, and an Asian now sits as a councillor at both levels of the metropolitan area.

It may have seemed a long time with many setbacks before the first Asian reached the Council Chamber, but this should be seen in perspective. Compared with other immigrant groups in Bradford they were quick to participate as candidates and relatively quickly achieved success. The time schedule being roughly ten years for the first candidate, 1963, and another ten for the first councillor. The two immigrant groups who have a much slower record are the nineteenth-century Irish and the twentieth-century Europeans. In some respects they are not strictly comparable as electoral qualifications are involved but a comparison does help a balanced view.

Richardson[29] points out that by 1851 Bradford had attracted more Irish than any other West Riding town. The Irish born at that Census numbered 8,687, but there were in addition an estimated 12,000 second generation Irish and the total inhabiting the original township was equivalent to approximately 20 per cent of the total population. Their patterns of residence and employment closely resemble those of the twentieth-century Asians but the rapidity of the political assimilation does not. As far as one can discover the first Catholic of Irish descent to enter the Council was Mr Duggan in 1872.

Tannahill[30] states, 'The West Riding of Yorkshire shows the highest proportion of European Voluntary Workers to the population, and Bradford is the most popular city.' The 1951 Census enumerates 5,409 persons as being born in Poland and the USSR, although many of these would not be eligible to vote since they were originally aliens. Nevertheless, it is remarkable that it was not until 1972 that a name like Wyszecki first appeared on a ballot paper in Bradford. This unsuccessful Conservative stood again in 1973 and was one of those defeated by Mr Hussain.

The road to the Council Chamber may, then, have seemed long and rough to Asians but, compared with other immigrant groups, it was not too difficult. Certainly, Asians are still disproportionately represented on the council but then the political system is not organised for sectional representation, and other groups, the young, the women, and the working class, are also under-represented. So far as Catholics are concerned it was not until 1965 that the proportion of Catholic councillors rose to equal the proportion of Catholic electors. If Asians were to follow the Catholic pattern there would still be another century to wait.

The speed with which Asians have learned to go out and vote suggests that this will not be the case. What I have chosen to call a political awakening is really quite a remarkable development, for Asians are much more inclined to go to the poll than their non-Asian neighbours and consequently the Asian vote is much more significant than their numbers on the register would suggest. Yet how is this to be explained and does it really mean that the political socialisation of these immigrant communities is at an advanced stage?

Anwar[31] suggests that the high degree of participation by the Pakistanis in Rochdale was a consequence of an anti-immigration candidate (Bradford's Mr Merrick) in the by-election of 1972. Certainly, feelings of conflict with out-groups could stimulate participation but it is also known that there was a high degree of participation in Rochdale four years before.[32] It is conceded that Mr Powell's speech may have been a stimulant in 1968, but it is certainly equally important that the Liberal candidate was an Asian who organised the vote.

This input of organisation appears to be the important factor and it seems as if it is best when it comes from within the community. In Manningham one can say that Dr Qureshi stimulated voting in 1969 but it would be more appropriate to say that he mobilised it. When Dr Qureshi did not stand again in 1970 the level of Asian participation subsided. I would suggest that the level of Asian participation in the General Election of 1966 at Bradford was low because nobody put in the effort to organise it. In that same election Lawrence indicates that at Nottingham various prominent Asians gave some leadership and a good immigrant organisation produced a remarkably high turnout rate of 87.9 per cent.[33]

This emphasis upon organisation does not mean that the stimulation of hostility is denied. What is suggested is that this may be one catalyst which will start the process. The process appears to be that leaders and community organisations become involved in supporting a particular candidate and it is they who mobilise the vote. I do not mean to imply that the masses then follow like a flock of stupid sheep, for interviews frequently show that Asians are well informed about British politics, but various factors help these Asian groups to maintain a high degree of cohesion. The fact that they may vote for opposing candidates does not contradict this, it merely underlines the point that we should think of Asian communities, in the plural.

This has some implications if one takes the view that a high level of voting participation indicates an advanced level of political socialisation. In Bradford it has been shown that Pakistanis in the Exchange-Manningham area voted first Conservative, then Liberal, then Independent, then Labour and then Conservative again. One can find evidence that a majority of Pakistanis in Bradford, Nottingham and Rochdale supported different parties all at the same time. This does not suggest that Pakistanis have internalised or even identified with, to use Kelman's[34] terms, the political attitudes which are typical of British politics. The situation is much nearer a very early stage, what Kelman might describe as compliance, with a biddable vote easily transferred because the norms of behaviour, the political attitudes, have not been adopted with any deep conviction. The political socialisation shown by the strong propensity to go out and vote is, in this sense, very superficial.

Further evidence of this is to be seen, in Bradford, when the politics of the old country seem more important than those of the new. The red and green rosettes of the Pakistan People's Party looked rather alien in Green Lane, Manningham. The man who had not fought in Kashmir deserved no votes in Bradford and the misfortunes in Bangladesh ruined a Labour candidate's chances. What one observes here is, clearly, participation in politics by Asians in Bradford, but this is not always the same as participation in Bradford's politics.

NOTES

1.   G.B. Gillian Lomas, *The Coloured Population of Great Britain*, London, 1974, pp. 20-1, considers definitions.
2.   In 1974 there were 36 electors in Bradford West with Chinese names.
3.   The 1971 Census enumerates 3,100 Irish born, and 4,605 European born in Bradford County Borough.
4.   In 1974 there were 1,044 electors in Bradford West with Eastern European names.
5.   *Report of the Race Relations Board for 1967-68*, HMSO, London, 1968, pp. 42-5.
6.   M. Anwar, 'Pakistani participation in the 1973 Rochdale local elections,' *New Community*, vol. III, nos. 1-2, Winter/Spring 1974, p. 69.
7.   The Pakistan Act 1973 was a consequence of Pakistan's withdrawal from the Commonwealth in January 1972. The most important provision for our purposes is that Pakistanis became aliens, losing their Commonwealth citizenship, and the right to vote in Britain. Disenfranchised Pakistanis remained on the electoral register from 25 July 1973 until the new register came into force on 16 February 1974.
8.   *Telegraph and Argus*, Bradford, 9 May 1961.
9.   Spiers, M. and Le Lohé, M.J., 'Pakistanis in the Bradford Municipal Elections of 1963,' *Political Studies*, vol. 12, no. 1, 1964.
10.   'Are the Immigrant Electors Interested?' *Yorkshire Post*, 18 March 1966.
11.   Stuart Bentley, 'Local Elections in Bradford May 1969,' *Race Today*, vol. 1, no. 1, May 1969, p. iv.
12.   M. Spiers in N.D. Deakin, *Colour and the British Electorate*, Pall Mall, London, 1965.
13.   M.J. Le Lohé *et al.*, 'Colour and the 1966 General Election,' *Race*, vol. VIII, no. 1, 1966.
14.   M.J. Le Lohé and A. Goldman, 'Race in Local Politics,' *Race*, vol. X, no. 4, 1969.
15.   Nicholas Deakin and Jenny Bourne, 'The Minorities and the General Election, 1970,' *Race Today*, vol. 2, no. 7, July 1970, p. 205.
16.   *The Guardian*, 1 May 1963.
17.   *Telegraph and Argus*, Bradford, 26 March 1971.
18.   *Ibid.*, 8 May 1971.

19. *Ibid.*, 12 May 1971.
20. *The Economist*, 13 May 1972.
21. *Telegraph and Argus*, Bradford, 23 December 1972.
22. *Ibid.*, 16 May 1973.
23. *The Guardian*, 6 September 1973.
24. *Ibid.*, 10 December 1973.
25. P.G.J. Pulzer, *Political Representation and Elections*, London, 1967, p. 98.
26. National Opinion Polls, *Political Bulletin*, No. 98, May 1971.
27. A.H. Birch, *Small Town Politics*, London, 1969, is an early study, with an example of this on p. 59.
28. It should, however, be noted that since the number of respondents is so small there is no statistical validity for this inference.
29. C. Richardson, 'Irish Settlement in Mid-Nineteenth Century Bradford,' *Yorkshire Bulletin of Economic and Social Research*, Vol. 20, No. 1, May 1968.
30. J.A. Tannahill, *European Voluntary Workers in Britain*, Manchester, 1958, p. 141.
31. M. Anwar, 'Pakistani participation in the 1973 Rochdale local elections,' *New Community*. vol. III, nos. 1-2, Winter/Spring 1974.
32. M.J. Le Lohé and A. Goldman, 'Race in Local Politics,' *Race*, vol. X, no. 4, 1969.
33. Daniel Lawrence, *Black Migrants: White Natives*, Cambridge University Press, 1974, p. 135.
34. H.C. Kelman in M. Jahoda and N. Warren, *Attitudes*, London, 1966, pp. 151-2.

5. A SENSE OF POLITICAL EFFICACY: A COMPARISON OF BLACK AND WHITE ADOLESCENTS

Anne-Marie Phizakalea

As unemployment and homelessness among young West Indians rise, so do official fears that the prevalent feelings of passive hostility and frustration must find their expression in increasing support for militant black organisations.[1] Most Indians in the sixteen to twenty-four year old age range indicate disenchantment with the political system and the majority claim they are prepared to fight for their rights as black men.[2]

The central concern of this paper is to determine whether black adolescents of school-leaving age have already developed and internalised the belief that government is unresponsive to the needs and demands of people like themselves. In turn, the extent to which they believe that influence can be exerted, in a conventional way, over the decision making process by those who do not share in formal institutionalised power will also be examined. The nature of these adolescent beliefs relate to an individual's sense of political efficacy. While they should be viewed merely as predispositions to certain forms of political behaviour, they will influence later reactions to political events and experiences. In addition, they provide an indicator of the reservoir of support which exists for different types of political activity.

The Concept of Political Efficacy

There is a vast amount of literature on sense of political efficacy, which is known to correlate with voting and positive attitudes toward the legitimacy of the political system.[3] There is, in addition, some conceptual confusion over the meaning of the term. The concept has traditionally been viewed as a norm of democratic society, encompassing a reciprocal belief about how the system is meant to work; that government should be a responsive agent of the people and in turn, that the citizenry can affect the decision making process.[4]

In practice, the items used to measure a sense of political efficacy amongst children and adolescents tap an individual's *perception* of government responsiveness to people like themselves and the extent to which they believe that influence can be exerted over the decision making process. The conceptual leap from how the system *should* work to the individual's perception of how it *does* work, is large. At the same time, the latter emphasis gives us an actual measure of the individual's feelings about government responsiveness and personal political efficacy.

The individual who believes that political authority is responsive to the needs and demands of people like himself and who also feels causally important in the political world, is considered to be politically efficacious.

The conceptual leap from *ought* to *is* requires some reconsideration of the reciprocal nature of the two components in the concept. Until now research has not explored the possibility that while an adolescent may not believe that government is responsive to the needs and demands of people like himself, he may believe nonetheless that influence can be exerted over the decision making process or vice-versa. There is no reason why the two components should be reciprocals of each other.

This draws attention to the fact that measuring an individual's sense of political efficacy is a far more complex task than asking an individual whether he or she intends voting. In this paper there is no *a priori* assumption that young blacks, many of whom are immigrants to Britain, actually have a coherent attitude structure in this area.[5]

The aims of this paper are, therefore, twofold. Firstly to locate which factors act as accelerators to the rate at which a coherent attitude structure relating to a sense of political efficacy is acquired by black adolescents in Britain. Secondly, to document and account for whatever differences exist between the level of political efficacy demonstrated by black adolescents in comparison with their white working-class counterparts of supposedly low ability in English secondary schools.

None out of eleven recent studies in the United States report that, controlling for socioeconomic status black adolescents are less politically efficacious than their white counterparts.[6] Explanation of these differences is limited and mainly speculative. For various reasons which will be outlined in the next section, it is hypothesised at a general level that (a) black adolescents in Britain will have a less developed attitude structure relating to a sense of political efficacy than their white counterparts, and (b) that black adolescents will feel less politically efficacious than their white counterparts.

In testing the second hypothesis it is hoped that a more than speculative attempt can be made to locate the origin of whatever differences might exist between the two ethnic groupings. To this end, the validity of two explanations which have been posited as providing some theoretical guidance for researchers of ethnic differences in political efficacy will be assessed.

Factors Relating to the Rate and Level of Acquisition of a Sense of Political Efficacy

The nature of the dependent variable being examined and the social and ethnic composition of the sample upon which this study is based dictates to a large extent the rationale upon which these hypotheses are formulated. A sense of political efficacy is known to be a product of family socialisation and an individual's societal position.[7] Thus the approach adopted in examining both the rate and the level at which a sense of political efficacy is acquired, is a simple sociostructural view of the political socialisation process. This view draws together a large number of *vicious* or *benign* circles of socialising influences. It assumes that those individuals most likely to benefit from current political arrangements are also more likely to feel politically efficacious. For example, various studies indicate that the combination of socialisation within a manual working-class home and attendance at a non-selective school is likely to result in an adolescent internalising a politically passive role.[8]

This view takes into account the double handicap of being both lower class and lower caste. It draws out attention to the fact that however similar social conditions and experiences may appear to be, they remain ethnically specific. Thus, we cannot assume that over time black adolescents become facsimiles of their white counterparts. Nor can we assume studies in the United States are comparable such that their findings and conclusions are equally applicable to British conditions.

Within this framework, certain facts of West Indian adolescent life will be considered as likely to have a debilitating effect on the rate and level of acquisition of a sense of political efficacy. At the most fundamental level it should be emphasised that West Indian adolescents are barred from full social acceptance in British society because of the colour of their skin.[9] At school they remain the out group, so that a pattern of formal acceptance and informal segregation between black and white adolescents has become a norm.[10]

The consequences of this rejection are already clear. The social adjustment of children and adolescents born in Britain of West Indian descent is no better then those who emigrated to this country.[11] In adolescence this is manifested by a continuing identification with the West Indies and a growing dissatisfaction with their lot in British society.[12] These conditions are unlikely to promote culturally relevant political learning or elicit high levels of political efficacy.

In addition, parent-child relationships tend to be characterised by persistent conflict. It is suggested that this leads to alienation and rebelliousness against parents and authority in general among black adolescents.[13] This also means that West Indian adolescents stand in an unfavourable position to receive relevant information contributing to a sense of political efficacy from the home environment. Discounting the fact that parents will have a very real difficulty in presenting themselves as models for imitation and subsequently, as agents of political socialisation, apathy is the prevalent attitude towards participation in the adult black community.[14]

Finally, the educational deficiencies suffered by the majority of West

Indian adolescents must be taken into consideration. The extent to which social maladjustment and emotional problems effect a West Indian adolescent's real academic potential cannot be assessed. But of all the children of ethnic minorities who have received all their education in Britain, those of West Indian parentage are likely to perform at lower levels than others.[15] The problem is intensified by substantive educational handicaps. Most West Indian families settle in twilight zones which means that there is a high probability that the child will attend a school in an educationally underprivileged area.[16] Secondly, West Indian pupils are classified as English speaking, which is quite inaccurate. Their strong dialect is not wrong English, but completely unsuited to achieving educational success in British schools.[17]

The triple handicap of psychiatric disturbance, linguistic deficiencies and culturally biased tests of attainment, means that the majority of West Indian adolescents find their way into the lowest or remedial streams of secondary schools.[18] The result is thousands of black adolescents entering the job market each year with the dubious benefit of an education in the lowest streams of English secondary schools.

At this point the more critical reader will argue that most of these disadvantages of home background, attendance at a school in an educationally underprivileged area and culturally biased tests of attainment are equally applicable to the white working-class adolescents who share these conditions with their black counterparts. This is not denied, but white working-class adolescents are less likely to feel uncertain about their role in British society. They do not suffer the double alienation from home and the wider society of which they are part, but which remains rejecting. They are not exposed to pressure from parents to seek high status jobs, while being given daily reminders at school through low teacher expectations, that such aspirations are inappropriate for people like themselves. Finally, they are not judged socially unacceptable because of the colour of their skin.

At the sociopsychological level alone there exists this complex of disabilities which are likely to retard the acquisition of political attitudes. Perhaps more important, these conditions cannot provide the secure psychological base upon which feelings of political efficacy might develop.

Last, but not least, are the hard political facts with which a black individual in Britain is faced. Black people in Britain have no formal political power of their own to bring influence to bear on a white dominated political system. Their minority status prevents any of the major parties regarding their vote as worthy of serious attention for some time to come.[19] At the same time, support gathers for individuals and parties who exploit racialist issues.

Finally, the timing of this study should be taken into consideration. The incumbent governing party of the time was the Conservative Party and there is evidence to show that young West Indians identify the party with racial prejudice.[20]

The cumulative impact of all these factors is likely to have a debilitating effect on both the rate and level of acquisition of a sense of political efficacy. At the same time each individual is an active participant in the political socialisation process. Individuals may accept, reject or modify various interpretations of political reality to which they are exposed. It is, therefore, only reasonable to assume that black adolescents may demonstrate a variety of political learning patterns. At one extreme, they may view white dominated political institutions as simply irrelevant to their own life situation and fail to acquire any attitudes in this area at all. Alternatively, they may adopt the most expedient coping strategy, demonstrating an increasing familiarity with politically relevant information and attitudes in conformity with the social and political beliefs of their white working-class counterparts. Finally, at the other end of the spectrum, black adolescents may indicate increasing familiarity with culturally relevant knowledge, juxtaposed by a set of beliefs which reflect an accurate appraisal of black political reality in Britain.

All of these reactions are feasible in circumstances where the social conditions and experiences of two social groups are very similar, but remain ethnically specific.

General Hypotheses Concerning the Rate at which a Coherent Attitude Structure Relating to a Sense of Political Efficacy Develops

The development of a coherent attitude structure relating to a sense of political efficacy should not be confused with the measurement of an individual's sense of political efficacy. The latter relates to the distribution of a sense of political efficacy demonstrated by an individual. It is normal practice to categorise individuals into low, medium and high levels of political efficacy on the basis of their responses to an index of items. Before this can be done, an individual must demonstrate that he or she has actually developed attitudes in this area. Again it is normal practice to set an arbitrary cutting line of 'don't know' responses in an index, if an individual is to be given an overall efficacy score. Respondents who fall below that line are deemed not to have developed a coherent sense of political efficacy.

There is some evidence to show that those factors which produce variation in the level of an individual's sense of political efficacy are the same as those which affect the development of a coherent attitude structure in this area.[21] All of the following have been examined in the past as correlates of a sense of political efficacy: age, family and peer group politicisation, self-expressed interest in politics, positive party identification, sex, and the relationship between social class and school type.[22]

The accumulation model of political attitude acquisition assumes that a steady growth in information and opinions about the political system will be apparent with age.[23] Applying this rationale to the present sample, a steady growth in attitude acquisition should be apparent among black adolescents with increasing length of residence in Britain. Expressed in a concrete form it is hypothesised:

H_1: Length of residence:
That a quantitative increase in response patterns relating to a sense of political efficacy will be apparent among black adolescents over time.

The hypothesis that, as an undifferentiated group, West Indians will have a lower level of attitude acquisition than whites. At the same time, it is not assumed that length of residence will explain all the variation in the rate at which attitudes will be acquired. The model takes no account of individual differences which may accelerate or retard this process, nor the impact that differential exposure to certain personal and impersonal agencies of political socialisation may make.

Face-to-face groups such as the family and peer group have a pronounced influence on political learning.[24] It is, therefore, reasonable to assume that black adolescents who discuss politics fairly frequently with either their friends or their parents, are more likely to develop a coherent attitude structure in this area, than adolescents who rarely or never discuss politics with these groups. It is, therefore, hypothesised:

H_2: Discussion of politics:
That frequent discussion of politics with primary groups will promote attitude acquisition.

Furthermore, it is hypothesised:

H_3: Political knowledge and interest:
That the higher the level of political knowledge and interest demonstrated by an adolescent, the greater the likelihood that an attitude structure will have developed.[25]

Two studies at least have indicated that a positive party allegiance acts as an accelerator of political attitude acquisition.[26] It would seem that party allegiance acts as a sort of filter through which political events and experiences, otherwise too complex or of little interest, can be made relevant and directed.[27] Thus it is hypothesised:

H_4: Party allegiance:
That adolescents with a positive party allegiance will be more likely to have acquired attitudes in this area, than those who lack a party label.

Politics has traditionally been regarded as male territory. Easton's study indicates that fewer girls than boys at each grade level have developed a coherent attitude structure relating to a sense of political efficacy.[28]

These findings may be culture-bound, for according to one study carried out in Appalachia, supposedly a matriarchal subculture, girls are more politically orientated than boys.[29] In only limited respects can the West Indian community in Britain continue to be categorised as matriarchal.[30] At the same time, the West Indian mother retains a strong role within the family. It is, therefore, quite reasonable to hypothesise:

H_5: Sex:
That black girls will demonstrate the same level of attitude acquisition as boys.

In Tapper's systematic study of the interaction between social class, school type and streaming, the acquisition of political attitudes is depressed to a very low level among working-class adolescents in the lowest streams of secondary modern schools.[31] Streaming, therefore, accentuates the traditional distinctions relating to passive versus active political role socialisation, which has in the past differentiated non-selective school pupils from their academic grammar school counterparts. One recent study suggests that the fully comprehensive school blurs these rigid distinctions.[32] It is, therefore reasonable to hypothesise:

H_6: School type:
That black adolescents attending comprehensive schools will have a more fully developed attitude structure relating to a sense of political efficacy than their secondary modern school counterparts.

Finally, certain dispositions may affect an adolescent's receptivity to internalising political information. With evidence to show that many black adolescents express uncertainty and dissatisfaction with their lot in British society, it is reasonable to hypothesise:

H_7: Evaluation of Britain:
That black adolescents who are dissatisfied with British society and who hold a negative evaluation of the country will be less likely to acquire attitudes about British political institutions, than adolescents who are more positively orientated towards Britain.[33]

Hypotheses Relating to the Level of Political Efficacy Demonstrated by Black and White Adolescents in Britain

Earlier in this paper it was reported that out of eleven recent studies in the United States, nine indicated that with socioeconomic status held constant, black adolescents are less politically efficacious than their white counterparts. It has been emphasised that inferences should not be made in the expectation that these findings are equally applicable to British conditions. Nevertheless, various culturally specific factors have been enumerated which are likely to have a debilitating effect on a black adolescent's sense of political efficacy in Britain.

It should be reiterated that many of these factors are shared by the white adolescents in this sample, whose expressed attitudes form the basis of comparison. Furthermore, recent evidence indicates that white adolescents of varied socioeconomic status demonstrate a restrained sense of political efficacy.[34] This is paralleled by a declining belief among the adult white population in the responsiveness of government.[35] The balance of evidence would suggest:

H_8: Political efficacy among whites:
That white working-class adolescents of supposedly low ability will demonstrate a restrained sense of political efficacy.

The extent to which ethnicity acts as an additional restraint on a sense of political efficacy is an open empirical question.

The central concern of this paper is not to explain why feelings of political efficacy are apparently being eroded among British youth. The aim is limited to an examination of whatever differences might exist between black and white adolescents in this area and to an explanation of the origin of these differences. To this end the validity of two explanations which have been proposed by Paul Abramson as theoretical guidelines for researchers in this field will be assessed.[36] The first is called the social deprivation explanation. It suggests that blacks' experience of restricted social opportunity engenders low levels of self-competence. In turn, self-competence provides a psychological base upon which a sense of political efficacy develops. Thus ethnic differences in political efficacy result from sociostructural conditions that contribute to low feelings of self-competence among blacks.

The explanation is intuitively appealing given evidence that lower-class black children in the United States reveal a weaker sense of self-competence than their white counterparts.[37] Additional factors which may contribute to low levels of self-competence, other than the perception of restricted social opportunity have been specified earlier in the paper. This is important because information on the extent to which black adolescents accurately perceive or are willing to admit the existence of restricted social opportunity in Britain is at best ambivalent.

Bhatnagar concludes from his findings that the discrepancy between vocational aspiration and expectation could well be the major cause of the higher rate of maladjustment amongst West Indian schoolchildren. He concludes that the child has already anticipated the discrimination he is likely to meet in the world of work and develops a sense of resentment. This reasoning is difficult to validate. School leavers rarely refer to racial discrimination as a possible obstacle to their job aspirations. Furthermore, they are reluctant to attribute a failure to obtain the job that they want to racial discrimination.[38]

The implications are clear, if black adolescents do not perceive or will not admit to restricted social opportunity, then this factor alone cannot engender low levels of self-competence. In addition, the evidence produced by Abramson to test this relationship is conceptually confusing. Measures of self-competence and self-esteem are referred to in such a way that the reader is given the impression that they refer to the same personality component. This is misleading because self-esteem relates to subjective self-assessment. In contrast, self-competence refers to the individual's feelings of mastery over the environment, in particular to his chances of success in life. The difference is subtle, but important.

Two empirical studies in Britain indicate that black adolescents demonstrate a more positive self-assessment than their white working-class counterparts.[39] The balance of evidence suggests that a reformulation of the social deprivation explanation is appropriate along the following lines:

H_9 :   Self-competence and political efficacy:
That self-competence will prove to be a weak predictor in accounting for ethnic differences in feelings of political efficacy.

And it is also hypothesised:

H_{10} :   Self-esteem and political efficacy:
That black adolescents will demonstrate higher levels of self-esteem than their white counterparts, but this will not engender higher levels of political efficacy among black adolescents.

The second explanation proposed by Abramson is called the political reality explanation. It suggests that young blacks are less politically efficacious than whites because they know that blacks have less institutionalised power than whites and are, therefore, less able to influence the decision making process.[40] This reasoning is equally applicable to British conditions. The basic problem with this explanation is that blacks are assumed to know these facts. Only one study in the United States has actually tested the relationship between political knowledge and political efficacy. It was found that increasing political knowledge had no effect on black adolescents' feelings of political efficacy.[41] The explanation remains intuitively reasonable despite the dearth of evidence. At the same time it should be verified whether increased levels of political knowledge among blacks are in fact related to a more accurate appraisal of political reality. In order to do this, it is necessary to examine the reasoning which lies behind an individual's belief concerning his or her ability to influence the decision making process. It is therefore hypothesised:

H_{11} :   Political knowledge and political efficacy:
That black adolescents with high levels of political knowledge, will

be less politically efficacious than their white counterparts with correspondingly high levels of political knowledge.

And it is also hypothesised:

H_{12}: Political knowledge and political reality:
That black adolescents with high levels of political knowledge will be most likely to indicate a perception that political reality differs for blacks and whites in Britain.

The Data

The main data source used in this study consists of responses to a self-adminstered pencil and paper questionnaire completed by all the fourth year pupils in six secondary schools, five in London and one in Birmingham. Two months later the schools were revisited and a subsample of randomly selected pupils were asked to participate in personal, semi-structured interviews. The interview data forms an important part of the findings reported in this paper.

The sample does not claim to be representative for various reasons. No sampling frame existed from which a random sample could be drawn. Moreover, in order to minimise the number of attenuating influences on the relationship between race of respondent and the particular dependent variables under examination, it was necessary to bias the sample in certain respects. It was decided to draw the sample from schools whose ratio of black to white pupils was approximately equal in the lower ability groups, and whose social class composition as a whole was comparable, that is, schools which drew predominantly on working-class catchment areas. A large number of schools in certain areas were contacted and head teachers were asked if they were willing to supply a written estimate of the *actual*, rather than offical, social and ethnic composition of the school.

As official approval for this research was not forthcoming from the educational authorities involved, it was not possible to go further in selecting schools randomly from this comprehensive listing. Given this limitation, it was necessary to gain approval of the research from individual head teachers of schools which represented the desired racial and socioeconomic characteristics.

After collecting the data, questionnaires completed by adolescents in the higher ability groupings were omitted, being disproportionately white and middle class. In addition, all questionnaires completed by adolescents of any other ethnic grouping except those of British and West Indian descent were excluded. Appendix 1 sets out the socioeconomic and ethnic composition of the sample by type of school. The questionnaire data were collected from 349 white and 381 black adolescents in three types of school:

(i)   Three secondary modern schools, two in inner-city London and one in inner-city Birmingham.

(ii)   Two mixed comprehensive schools located in a Greater London Borough which is fully comprehensive. While mixed ability teaching is practised up until the fourth year in these schools, they both draw on predominantly working-class catchment areas which severely circumscribes the extent to which they can be classified as fully comprehensive.

(iii)   One boys' comprehensive school in South London which draws on a socially heterogeneous catchment area and has a low ratio of black to white pupils. The school was included in the sample in order to assess the impact that variation in the social and ethnic composition of a school has on the political orientations of its pupils.

After the follow-up interviews had been carried out, black and white adolescents were matched by socioeconomic status. Only those West Indians who had completed a full English education were included in the sample. This left forty-three white adolescents and thirty-five black adolescents. The interview data collected from this small subsample should be viewed merely as indicating important trends in areas for which the questionnaire technique was unsuitable.

Findings

The first general hypothesis of this study was that black adolescents in Britain will have a less coherent attitude structure relating to a sense of political efficacy than their white counterparts. The adolescents in this sample were unable to cope with a large battery of questions, so that it was necessary to find a small number of questions which were relevant, that is which elicited the least number of 'don't know' responses and which also produced a satisfactory degree of reproducibility. The three items finally selected for inclusion in the questionnaire index were:

(1)   'The government usually takes notice of what people like me and my family think.'

(2)   'The government always wants to help people like me and my family.'

(3)   'People like me and my family cannot get the government to take notice of what we think.'

Response format was agree/disagree/don't know for all three items. Respondents who gave more than one 'don't know' response were deemed not to have developed a coherent attitude structure relating to

133

a sense of political efficacy.

The first general hypothesis of the study is borne out by the finding that 34 per cent of the West Indian adolescents in the sample against 17 per cent of the white adolescents have not, using this criterion, developed a coherent attitude structure relating to a sense of political efficacy. This difference was anticipated due to a large number of black adolescents being immigrants to Britain, thus providing the rationale for H_1 : Length of residence.

The findings reported in Table 1 indicate that the relationship between length of residence and the development of a coherent attitude structure is only moderate to weak in strength. At the same time only 23 per cent of the black adolescents who have received a full English education fail to demonstrate a coherent attitude structure.

Table 1 Length of Residence by Non-Coherent/Coherent Attitude Structure among Black Adolescents

	Non-coherent N = 130 %	Coherent N = 251 %
0 - 3.5 yrs	37.7	21.1
3.6 - 9.5 yrs	37.7	35.1
9.6 yrs	24.6	43.8

gamma. 35, $x^2 p < .001$

Given the number of other factors which may accelerate or retard the process of attitude acquisition, it is not altogether surprising that only a moderately strong relationship exists between length of residence and attitude acquisition.

The findings reported in Table 2 suggest that H_2 : Discussion of politics, is borne out in relation to frequency of discussion with parents, indicating that adolescents who discuss politics with their parents fairly frequently are more likely to have developed a coherent attitude structure than adolescents who do not. While the peer group is obviously the more salient reference group for black adolescents it does not supersede the impact of the parental model. The peer group may compensate for or replace parents as models for imitation and identification during adolescence, but it does not promote higher levels of politicisation. It should also be noted that the predominantly infrequent rate of discussion with either parents or friends is testimony to the very low level of salience attributed to politics among these adolescents.

Table 2 Frequency of discussion by Non-Coherent/Coherent Attitude Structure among Black Adolescents

	PARENTS		FRIENDS	
	Non-coherent N = 130 %	Coherent N = 251 %	Non-coherent N = 130 %	Coherent N = 251 %
Often	0	4.4	1.5	6
Sometimes	13.8	25.9	18.5	24.3
Rarely	12.3	21.1	17.7	19.5
Never	73.8	48.6	62.3	50.2

gamma. 46, $x^2 p < .001$ gamma. 23, $x^2 p < .05$

Table 3 Political interest and Political knowledge by Non-Coherent/ Coherent Attitude Acquisition among Black Adolescents

	Political Interest		Political Knowledge		
	Non-coherent N = 130 %	Coherent N = 251 %	Non-coherent N = 130 %	Coherent N = 251 %	
Very	1.5	12.7	26.9	33.1	High
Somewhat	10.8	12.4	20.0	16.7	Medium
A little	30.8	34.3	53.1	50.2	Low
Not at all	56.9	40.6			

gamma. 32, $x^2 p < .001$ gamma. 08, not significant

The findings reported in Table 3 indicate that H_3: Political knowledge and political interest, is only partially valid. Self-expressed interest in politics does act as an accelerator to attitude acquisition, but political knowledge does not. This is probably explained by Easton's conclussions concerned the development of an attitude structure relating to a sense of political efficacy. He suggests that this development is not dependent on the child's ability to understand how the system is meant to work, nor upon the child's level of information. It appears to be simply an outgrowth of a general understanding of the individual's particular social environment.[42]

The findings reported in Table 4 indicate that H_4: Party allegiance, is valid in a very limited respect. Unless an adolescent is an Independent, the benefits of having a positive party allegiance in promoting attitude acquisition are negligible. This finding relating to Independents bears out evidence produced by Hess and Torney, who found that children who were Independent of either of the two major parties were the most politicised group of children in their sample.[43]

Table 4 Party Allegiance by Non-Coherent/Coherent Attitude Structure among Black Adolescents

	I don't know N = 65	I won't vote N = 95	Cons N = 8	Labour N = 200	Other N = 13
	%	%	%	%	%
Non-coherent	40.0	31.6	34.5	35.5	0
Coherent	60.0	68.4	62.5	64.5	100

Table 5 Sex of Respondent by Non-Coherent/Coherent Attitude Structure among Black Adolescents

	Boys N = 255	Girls N = 126
	%	%
Non-coherent	33.7	34.9
Coherent	66.3	65.1

No relationship.

The findings reported in Table 5 indicate the validity of H_5: Sex. The sex of the respondent has no effect on the extent to which the adolescent has or has not acquired an attitude structure in this area. The findings reported in Table 6 suggest that there is little supportive evidence to uphold H_6: School type.

Table 6 School type by Non-Coherent/Coherent Attitude Structure among Black Adolescents

	Sec. Mods N = 167 %	Comps N = 160 %	Boys Comp N = 54 %
Non-coherent	34.1	36.3	27.8
Coherent	65.9	63.8	72.2

No significant difference.

The type of school a black adolescent attends has very little impact on attitude acquisition. Boys in the socially heterogeneous comprehensive school demonstrate a slightly higher level of attitude acquisition, but the difference is so small that this advantage cannot be attributed to the impact of variation in the social and ethnic composition of the school or to the school type itself.

Table 7 Evaluation of and Satisfaction with Life in Britain by Non-Coherent/Coherent Attitude Structure among Black Adolescents

Evaluation of Britain	Non-coherent N = 130 %	Coherent N = 251 %	Satisfaction with Life	Non-coherent N = 130 %	Coherent N = 251 %
Negative	21.5	31.7	Very unhappy	4.6	9.6
Positive	26.2	26.3	Fairly unhappy	58.5	61.8
Highly positive	52.3	43.0	Happy	29.2	23.1
			Completely happy	7.7	5.6

gamma. 18, not sig. at .05   gamma. 18, not sig. at .05

Finally, the findings reported in Table 7 suggest that an inverse relationship to that which was predicted in H_7: Evaluation of Britain, is apparent. Although the relationship is very weak and fails to reach statistical significance, there is a tendency for adolescents with coherent

137

attitude structures ro be less satisfied with life in Britain and to evaluate the country less positively than their counterparts who fail to demonstrate a coherent attitude structure.

This difference might well be accounted for by factors very similar to those which form the basis of the political reality explanation. A more accurate appraisal of British society seen through the spectacles of a black adolescent, stimulates rather than retards attitude development.

Assessing the influence of those selected predictors, in promoting attitude acquisition, it might be inferred that coming from a politicised home and being interested in politics are added advantages to having a full English education for a black adolescent.

Finally, the extent to which the factors which promote attitude acquisition among black adolescents are also ethnically specific will be assessed. Examining the effect of these predictors in promoting attitude acquisition among white adolescents, it is evident that both similarities and differences characterise the political learning patterns of the two ethnic groupings.

Frequency of discussion with parents bears a weak relationship to attitude acquisition among white adolescents compared to their black counterparts, gamma. 23, $x^2 p < .05$. The influence of the peer group is weaker. But at the level of the individual, both self-expressed interest in politics, gamma. 37, $< .05$ and increasing levels of political knowledge, gamma. 30, $x^2 p < .05$, act to promote attitude acquisition, though weakly, among white adolescents. The effects of sex and school type bear no relationship to attitude acquisition among whites, however, the differential effects of positive party allegiance are remarkably similar between the two ethnic groupings. One hundred per cent of the white adolescents who opt for allegiance to a minor party and 95 per cent of the Conservative supporters indicate a coherent attitude structure.

On balance the similarities outweigh the differences. If those factors which affect the development of a coherent attitude structure are the same as those which produce variation in the level of an individual's sense of political afficacy, then the impact of ethnicity on the latter is likely to be slight in producing variation. The validity of this assumption must now be assessed.

A Sense of Political Efficacy, Black and White Adolescents Compared

Excluding all those respondents who failed to answer two or more items of the questionnaire political efficacy index, Table 8 stratifies the two ethnic groupings by a sense of political efficacy. In terms of percentage differences, black and white adolescents' feelings of political efficacy are very similar to those reported in studies conducted in the United States. At the same time, H_8 : Political efficacy among whites,

Table 8 Political Efficacy by Ethnic Group Membership

	White N = 290 %	Black N = 251 %
Low	73.9	91.2
Medium	14.6	7.2
High	11.5	1.6

gamma. 56, x^2 p $<$ .001

Only respondents answering two or more items of the questionnaire index are included. High efficacy response set = Agree/Agree/Disagree, score of 2 for each efficacious response.

High political efficacy score = 6
Medium = 4.5
Low = 2.3
Excluded = 0.1

is borne out by the finding that both ethnic groupings demonstrate a predominantly low sense of political efficacy. Statistical significance should, therefore, not blind us to the substantive significance of these findings; ethnic differences in a sense of political efficacy are not large.

The extent to which the actual difference can be attributed to ethnicity alone will be assessed by examining the two explanations proposed by Abramson. Data necessary to test the first type of explanation posited as accounting for ethnic differences in feelings of political efficacy were collected during the course of personal interviews with the small subsample.[44] Due to the sample size, N − 78, these findings must be accepted as indicators of trends only.

A simple two item index of political efficacy was used in the interviews which shifts the emphasis of the sentiments being tapped to the second component of the concept of political efficacy; that is, to the individual's perception of personal political efficacy. The questions were:

(1) 'Do you think that politics is so complicated that most of the time ordinary people don't understand what is going on?'

(2) 'Do you think that voting is the only way that people like you and your family can have any say about how the government runs things?'[45]

H_9 : Self-competence and political efficacy, is borne out by a weak relationship in the predicted direction between personal competence and political efficacy amongst white adolescents, gamma. 28, x^2 p < .01 and an even weaker relationship among black adolescents, gamma. 28, x^2 p < .05. The more important findings are peripheral to the relationship being tested. Firstly black adolescents are not significantly less self-competent than their white counterparts. Secondly, using this alternative political efficacy index, while the percentage difference between the two ethnic groupings is comparable to that in the questionnaire data, the actual level of political efficacy is higher. Forty-four per cent of the white adolescents score medium to high, against 26 per cent of the black adolescents. It is suggested that this difference can be explained by the shift of emphasis in the sentiments which are tapped by the two indexes. An adolescent may have perfectly rational reasons for believing that the government is not responsive to people like themselves, while maintaining the belief that he or she is personally politically efficacious and can, if necessary, exert influence over the decision making process. The difference suggests that there is some validity in the notion that the two components involved in a sense of political efficacy are not necessarily reciprocals of each other.

Table 9 Self-Esteem: Black and White Adolescents Compared

	White N = 43 %	Black N = 35 %
High	58.0	69.0
Medium	37.0	31.0
Low	5.0	0

gamma. 24, not sig. at .05

H_{10}: Self-esteem and political efficacy, is a departure from the Abramson thesis. The findings in Table 9 indicate that as predicted black adolescents demonstrate a slightly higher level of self-esteem than their white counterparts. However, the predicted inverse relationship between self-esteem and political efficacy among black adolescents is not borne out. Seventy-eight per cent of the black adolescents with medium to high political efficacy scores have correspondingly high levels of self-esteem, against 65 per cent of the adolescents with low levels of political efficacy. The finding is not altogether surprising if we accept that the items used in the interview schedule shift the emphasis of this attitude structure to the individual's belief in personal political efficacy. This speculation is given further empirical support if the relationship between self-esteem and political trust is examined. The measure used for tapping feelings of political trust relates to the honesty, competence and fairness of government.[46] A strong inverse relationship exists between self-esteem and political trust in the black subsample, gamma. 66, x^2 p < .001. The higher the self-esteem of a black adolescent, the less trusting he or she is of British politicians and government. Neither a positive nor inverse relationship exists in the white sample between self-esteem and political trust, gamma. 02.

The validity of the special deprivation explanation is limited to the extent that self-competence cannot be seen as providing a psychological base upon which feelings of political efficacy develop among adolescents of school age at least. Studies from the United States would support this conclusion.[47] According to Abramson's thesis an adolescent must at least perceive a situation of restricted social opportunity if it is to engender low levels of self-competence. The findings of this study and others would indicate that information on this perception among black adolescents is minimal.

At the same time the testing of this explanation has drawn attention to three important points. Firstly, that political scientists should be fully aware of the nature of the psychological variables they introduce as intervening variables. Secondly, that caution should be shown in assuming that the two components involved in a sense of political efficacy are reciprocals of each other. Finally, that the high levels of self-esteem and low levels of political trust demonstrated by black adolescents repudiate the old racial stereotype and emphasise the danger of assuming that blacks in Britain will continue to passively adapt to the role of second-class citizens.

Abramson's second explanation of how ethnic differences in a sense of political efficacy are engendered is far less complex. It suggests that young blacks are less politically efficacious than whites because they know that blacks have less institutionalised political power than whites and are, therefore, less able to influence the decision making process.

It is suggested that the basic problem with this explanation is that black adolescents are assumed to know these facts. Thus H_{11} : Political knowledge and political efficacy, will be tested by returning to the questionnaire data and examining the responses of only those adolescents in the sample with a high level of political knowledge. Forty-five per cent (fifteen) of the white adolescents with high political efficacy scores have correspondingly high levels of political knowledge. None of the black adolescents indicating a high level of political knowledge demonstrate a high level of political efficacy. Thus at face value H_{11} seems to have some validity. However, an item analysis of the political efficacy index reveals a good deal more about the relationship between political knowledge and political efficacy between the two ethnic groupings. If H_{11} : Political knowledge and political efficacy, was tested by examining the responses to the third item of the political efficacy index, the hypothesis would be rejected. The index is composed of three items: the first two relate to an individual's belief in the responsiveness of government and the third to an individual's belief that people like themselves can influence the decision making process. Responses to this third item reveal that 20 per cent (fifteen) of black and 26 per cent (thirty-three) of white adolescents with high levels of political knowledge give an efficacious response to the question. Ethnic differences in a sense of political efficacy are attenuated once the nature of the sentiments being tapped in the index shift to the individual's assessment of his or her capacity to influence the decision making process.

Even at this superficial level it is evident that a small number of black adolescents with high levels of political knowledge differentiate between the two components in the concept of political efficacy. In order to test the validity of H_{12} : Political knowledge and political reality, it is necessary to look at the explanations respondents give for their response to the third question. Fifty-four per cent of the black adolescents who answer the question efficaciously and who have a high level of political knowledge, suggest unconventional methods of exerting influence over the decision making process, such as demonstrations and strikes. In contrast 72 per cent of the white adolescents uphold the belief that influence can be exerted by conventional methods, such as writing to an MP or simply by voting. Black adolescents obviously believe that they will not get a fair hearing unless they act outside of conventional channels. This could be interpreted as supportive evidence of the assertion that black adolescents with a high level of political knowledge will be more likely to indicate a perception that political reality differs for blacks and whites in Britain. This assertion can only be truly verified by comparing the written answers given by all the respondents in the sample to the third item, to those given by adolescents with high levels of political knowledge. An edited description of these answers is given in Table 10.

The percentage of responses which refer to powerlessness, being working class or black, gives some credence to the notion that groups whose societal position is one of minimal power either by race or class, will indicate a restrained sense of political efficacy. At the same time, black adolescents as a whole give very little indication that their lower levels of political efficacy can be explained by a perception of the double handicap they experience as a neglected minority grouping.

Higher levels of political knowledge increase the likelihood that an adolescent will have developed attitudes in this area and be capable of giving a rational reason for their expressed beliefs. But these increased levels of political knowledge have only a marginal effect on their perception of political reality in comparison with their less knowledgeable

Table 10 Reasons given by the two Ethnic Groupings for their answers to the question: 'People like me and my family cannot get the government to take notice of what we think.'

Response	Explanation for this response	Total sample		Respondents with high knowledge scores	
		Black N = 381 %	White N = 349 %	Black N = 118 %	White N = 162 %
Disagree	A belief in conventional methods of exerting influence	3.9	13.4	5.9	16.5
Disagree and agree	The use of unconventional methods of political action (Respondents differ in the extent to which they feel these methods will be effective)	6.8	8.8	11.0	10.6
Agree	Description of powerlessness, inaccessibility of government	16.0	18.1	22.9	20.5
Agree	Because we are working class	9.4	15.1	11.9	21.3
Agree	Because we are black	8.1	0	5.9	0
Agree	Reference to a macro-level issue seen as detrimental to the interests of the working class	4.1	10.5	5.1	8.1
	DON'T KNOW. 64% of the black adolescents and 63% of the whites in this category give a 'don't know' response to the question itself	51.4	34.1	37.3	23.0

counterparts.

Length of residence in Britain then becomes an important intervening factor. Dropping the control for political knowledge, 65 per cent of the black adolescents who suggest unconventional methods of political activity in order to exert influence over the decision making process, have had a full English education. Life experience as a black within a white society does not necessarily mean a higher level of political knowledge. But if the two combine, there is a high probability that the adolescent will indicate a perception that political reality does differ for blacks and whites in Britain. Adolescents in the intermediary grouping (those who have lived in Britain for between 3.6 and 9.5 years directly preceding the study) indicate the highest level of dissatisfaction with life in Britain and they evaluate the country least positively. As political knowledge increases amongst this group, so does the tendency to view political reality in the same way as their more knowledgeable, fully English educated counterparts. Lacking a positive attachment for the political community itself, it is likely that these nascent political attitudes will crystallise with experience in the world of work.

Of the two explanations posited as accounting for ethnic differences in a sense of political efficacy, the political reality explanation is definitely the most valid. At the same time it has limitation. The explanation does not attempt to explore the possibility that predictors other than political knowledge might have a significant impact on the shaping of an adolescent's sense of political efficacy. Predictors which may promote or retard the type of political awareness is characteristic of only a small group of black adolescents in the sample.

Keeping in mind that high levels of personal political efficacy indicate a qualitatively different orientation among black adolescents in comparison with their white counterparts, the influence that various predictors, which are known to promote high levels of efficacy, will be examined.

At the face-to-face level, frequent discussion with friends and parents is positively, though not significantly, related to promoting higher levels of political efficacy among blacks. In contrast, there is no such trend apparent in the white sample. Self-expressed interest and knowledge in politics are both related to increased levels of political efficacy among blacks, gamma. 53, $x^2 p < .05$ and gamma. 41, $x^2 p < .001$ respectively. The more interested and informed a black adolescent is about politics, the greater the likelihood that he or she maintains a belief in personal political efficacy. Surprisingly, neither of these predictors have a marked influence on the level of political efficacy demonstrated by a white adolescent.

Party allegiance bears no relationship to a sense of political efficacy in the black sample but its impact on the white sample is marked. Fifty-five per cent of the adolescents who express allegiance to the Conservative Party demonstrate a high level of political efficacy. This finding backs up Tapper's conclusion that adolescents of supposedly low ability express satisfaction with the responsiveness of government as long as the party they favour is in power.[48] As the majority of adolescents with a positive party allegiance support Labour, the timing of this study possibly acts as an attentuating influence on the real extent of ethnic differences in a sense of political efficacy.

Girls in both ethnic groupings demonstrate higher levels of political efficacy than boys, although the difference is not statistically significant. Attendance at a comprehensive school also acts as a slight advantage. The shortfall of girls in the sample attending secondary modern schools does not account for this difference. Pupils of both sexes and ethnic origin attending secondary modern schools are less likely to have a sense of political efficacy than their comprehensive school counterparts.

Finally, the more positively a white adolescent evaluates Britain, the higher the probability that he or she will demonstrate a high level of political efficacy. The finding is in accord with Easton's thesis, that a positive attachment for the political community itself provides the cognitive base upon which supportive feelings develop for the political system itself.[49] That base is lacking for the majority of black adolescents, manifested by a weak inverse relationship between satisfaction with life in Britain and political efficacy. The less satisfied an adolescent is with life in Britain, the greater the likelihood that he or she will view the government as unresponsive, but maintain a belief in personal political efficacy.

Drawing these findings together, they lend support to, rather than detract from, the political reality explanation. Political interest and knowledge remain the best predictors of whether or not a black adolescent crosses the threshold and develops a sense of political efficacy which reflects black political reality in Britain. Furthermore, a belief in personal political efficacy, as distinct from a belief in government responsiveness has different roots for black and white adolescents.

Conclusions

This paper has focused attention on the development of a sense of political efficacy among black and white adolescents. It is now widely accepted that political differences among adults have their origin in childhood and adolescent conceptions of the political world. These conceptions will, to a large extent, determine whether an individual adopts an essentially passive or active political role in adulthood.

The aims of this paper were, therefore, twofold: firstly, to establish the extent to which these conceptions have crystallised among black adolescents, many of whom are immigrants to Britain and, secondly, to document and account for whatever differences exist between the conceptions held by black adolescents in comparison with their white counterparts. It has been emphasised that these adolescent conceptions must be viewed merely as predispositions to certain forms of political behaviour. But the nature of those conceptions provide an excellent indicator of the reservoir of support which exists for different types of political activity.

Accepting the validity of findings from existing research relating to the correlates of a sense of political efficacy, it was hypothesised that black adolescents would have a less developed sense of political efficacy and demonstrate lower levels of efficacy than their white counterparts. These hypotheses were formulated in the knowledge that the white adolescents in this sample are exposed to the same social conditions and experiences which have a debilitating effect on a sense of political efficacy. At the same time, it was anticipated that ethnicity could act as an additional restraint.

In relation to the rate at which attitudes are acquired it was suggested that factors other than length of residence would retard the process among black adolescents. In particular, it was anticipated that a number of black adolescents would withdraw completely from 'playing the game.' These assumptions were shown to be erroneous. The level of attitude acquisition among black adolescents who have received a full English education compares favourably with their white counterparts. Secondly, dissatisfaction with life in Britain slightly promotes rather than retards attitude acquisition. The supposedly debilitating factors that had been earmarked as ethnically specific, do not act in the way that had been anticipated.

There is in fact every indication that most of the factors which promote or retard acquisition among black adolescent correspond with those in the white sample.

These findings pointed to the possibility that ethnicity in itself would produce only slight variation in feelings of political efficacy. This was borne out by the finding of small, though significant, ethnic differences in a sense of political efficacy. Taken at face value this finding might have led to the conclusion that the political socialisation process is the same for blacks and whites in England.

But because ethnic differences were apparent, Abramson's two explanations were assessed in order to measure the extent to which these differences could be attributed to ethnicity alone. The testing of these explanations must lead to a partial reassessment of the conclusion that political socialisation and political reality are the same for the two ethnic groupings.

Abramson's first explanation contributes little to our understanding of ethnic differences in a sense of political efficacy. But it drew attention to two important factors. Firstly, that black adolescents in Britain do not fit the old racial stereotype of the self-hating black. Their self-esteem is higher than that of whites and juxtaposed by a strong distrust of politicians and government. Secondly, the efficacy items used to test this explanation gave some indication that political efficacy is not a unidimensional sentiment.

This speculation was given empirical support in the testing of the political reality explanation. The more politically aware black adolescents in the sample differentiated between the two components involved in the concept of political efficacy and tapped by the items in the questionnaire index. These adolescents, along with the majority of their black counterparts have internalised the belief that government is unresponsive to the needs and demands of people like themselves. But in contrast to the prevalent reaction among blacks, they uphold a belief in personal political efficacy. A belief that influence can be exerted over the decision making process by those who do not share in formal political power. In addition, it is among this small articulate group of blacks that some indication is given that political reality differs for blacks in comparison with their politically efficacious white counterparts. Efficacious black adolescents are more likely to suggest the use of unconventional methods of political activity in exerting influence over the decision making process. It is inferred from this finding that black adolescents realise that they will not get a fair hearing unless they act outside of conventional channels.

The political reality explanation is given further empirical support by the finding that predictors other than political interest and knowledge, which are normally associated with increased levels of political efficacy, contribute little to a further explanation of variation in a sense of political efficacy among black adolescents. A belief in personal political efficacy also springs from different roots for black and white adolescents.

Drawings these findings together it is evident that various social forces combine and result in a broad differentiation of the black sample into three groupings. At one extreme, there is a large group of adolescents whose attitudes towards government responsiveness and personal effectiveness have not as yet crystallised into a coherent attitude structure. Controlling for length of residence, their low level of political interest, discussion and knowledge, suggests that they will in adult life join the ranks of the politically apathetic.

At the next level there is a large grouping of adolescents who demonstrate a very similar pattern of political learning to their inefficacious white counterparts. This grouping can be subdivided into those who appear to have perfectly rational reasons for holding these views and a group whose sense of political efficacy is backed up by a shaky cognitive base.

At the other extreme there is a small group of politically aware, predominantly English educated adolescents who indicate an ethnically specific conceptualisation of political reality. It is likely that these adolescents will be politically active and be prepared to secure social change by using methods viewed by established authorities as illegitimate. Their numbers are small, but they form a definite reservoir of support for militant black organisations.

It is the large group of black adolescents who form the middle ground between the two extremes whose adult political behaviour is the most difficult to predict. Experience in the world of work could change their fairly passive view of political reality, promoting a higher level of political awareness and a reassessment of adolescent conceptions of the political world. The realisation of this transformation is increased as long as white society continues to deny young blacks their right to treatment as full and equal citizens.

On the theoretical side, the major findings of this study might be accepted as cautionary guidelines for other researchers in three respects. Firstly, that black adolescents did not react at a psychological level to their minority status in the way that had been anticipated. Their high levels of self-esteem juxtaposed by low levels of political efficacy and trust indicate the need for a more cautious and exploratory approach in our work when introducing psychological dispositions as intervening variables. Our assumptions in this area are possibly culture-bound and in need of reassessment.

Secondly, the researcher may need to pay more attention to an item analysis of a political efficacy index. This would ensure that important differences in the way in which an individual responds to the two components in the concept are not overlooked. An item analysis in this study prevented the erroneous conclusion from being drawn that ethnic differences in a sense of political efficacy are not worthy of serious attention.

Finally, it is suggested that adopting a theoretical approach along the lines of the political reality explanation may be the most rewarding for further research in this area. At the same time attention should focus on locating which factors promote higher levels of political knowledge and interest among black adolescents.

Appendix 1

Details of Sample

The Social Composition of the Sample Stratified by School Type. The White Middle-Class Component was Given a Weight of 15/29

	Secondary Moderns		Comprehensives		Boys Comprehensive	
	White N = 116 %	Black N = 167 %	White N = 128 %	Black N = 160 %	White N = 105 %	Black N = 54 %
Middle class*	11	15	14	15	25	15
Skilled manual	39	30	45	26	48	41
Semi- and unskilled manual and unemployed	50	55	41	59	27	44

*   Middle class includes all occupations which are non-manual.

The Ethnic Composition of the Lower Ability Groupings in the Sample Prior to Weighting by School Type

Secondary moderns
N = 296

White %	Black %
44	56

Comprehensives
N = 304

White %	Black %
47	53

Boys Comprehensive
N = 184

White %	Black %
71	29

The Sample Stratified by Sex and School Type

	Secondary moderns N = 234 %	Comprehensives N = 131 %
Girls	21	57
Boys	79	43

The shortfall in girls makes the sample unrepresentative of the population as a whole. But all analyses of data were stratified by sex and if large differences were apparent these were reported

NOTES

1.   The most recent official fears are expressed in *Unemployment and Homelessness: A Report*, Home Office, HMSO, 1974. The one year study was prepared for the Home Office by the Community Relations Commission. These fears are quite explicitly stated as far back as 1968, see par. 11, chapter 1 of the *Report From the Select Committee on Race Relations and Immigration. The problems of coloured school leavers, Session 1968-1969*, HMSO, London, 1969.

2.   Survey conducted for *The Times* by Peter Evans, *The Times*, Tuesday 23 February 1971 and 26 February 1971. See also the widely published survey conducted by Peter Wallis and Dennis Stevenson, a brief account of which can be found in *Race Today*, August 1970, pp. 278-80. 'Second Generation West Indians; A Study in Alienation.' The full unpublished report is available from the authors, c/o Conrad Jamieson Associates, London, W.1.

3.   See in particular, G.A. Almond and Sidney Verba, *The Civic Culture: Political Attitudes in Five Nations*, Princeton, University Press, New Jersey, 1963, pp. 230-57. For a systematic discussion of the concept of political efficacy within the context of political socialisation research, see David Easton and Jack Dennis, 'The child's acquisition of regime norms: Political efficacy,' *The American Political Science Review*, no. 61, 1967, pp. 25-38. Footnote 4 on p. 27 gives a full bibliography of studies in the United States relating the the concept and its correlates. British studies include R.E. Dowse and J. Hughes, 'The Family, the school and the political socialisation process,' *Sociology*, vol. 5, no. 1, 1971, pp. 21-49; Paul Abramson, 'The differential political socialisation of English

secondary school students,' *Sociology of Education*, Summer 1967, pp. 146-69; Ted Tapper, *Young People and Society*, Faber and Faber, London, 1971; Geoff Mercer, 'Political Learning and Political Education,' (University of Strathclyde, unpublished Ph.D. thesis, 1971) also Geoff Mercer, 'The impact of formal political education in adolescent political learning; the case of Modern Studies and political efficacy among Scottish schoolchildren,' (paper presented to the University of Exeter Conference on Political Socialisation, September 1971); Richard Rose, *Politics in England*, Faber and Faber, London, 1974, chapter on political socialisation; Paul Abramson and Tim Hennessey, 'Social class, social structure and political competence,' (mimeo, Michigan State University, 1967). For a more general view of English adolescents' affect for government, see Jack Dennis, Leon Lindberg and Donald McCrone, 'Support for Nation and Government among English children,' *British Journal of Political Science*, vol. 1, part 1, January 1971, pp. 25-48, and also R.A. Butler, 'English Secondary School Adolescents: An analysis of political discontent,' (University of Sussex, M.A. dissertation, August 1969).

4.   Robert E. Lane, *Political Life: Why and How People get involved in Politics*, The Free Press, Glencoe, 1959, pp. 147-55.

5.   In January 1972, there were 280,000 immigrant children in British schools, 36 per cent of whom are of West Indian descent, according to DES statistics. According to the DES criteria 'immigrants' are 1) children born outside the British Isles who have come to this country with their parents or to join parents, other relatives or guardians whose country of origin was abroad; 2) children born in the United Kingdom to parents whose country of origin was abroad and whose parents, to the best of the head teacher's knowledge, have not been in this country more than ten years (the date being moved up each year). For this reason, when the term immigrant is used in this paper it refers to adolescents who have lived in Britain for less than two years. DES statistics do not take into account adolescents of immigrant parents who have lived in Britain for more than ten years, but who still may need extra attention or language teaching, which obviously underestimates the problems some schools face. For example in February 1973, the school roll of Newfoundland Road School, Bristol was 269. Under the DES formula there were 6 per cent immigrant pupils. The actual number of children of overseas parents was 74 per cent, see p. 44 and the whole of Chapter 9 of *The Select Committee on Race Relations and Immigration, Session 1972-3, Education, Report*, HMSO, 1973. The chapter indicates and condemns the deficiencies of this definition.

6.   A summary of the findings of all these studies except Anthony M. Orum and Roberto S. Cohen's 'The development of political orientations among black and white children,' *American Political Science Review, 1973*, vol. 38, (Feb.), pp. 62-74, are documented in the Appendix of Paul R. Abramson's article, 'Political efficacy and Political trust among Black Schoolchildren: Two Explanations,' *The Journal of Politics*, vol. 34, 1972, pp. 1243-75. The other eight studies which report ethnic differences in political efficacy are as follows: Kenneth P. Langton and M. Kent Jennings, 'Political Socialisation and the High School Civics Curriculum in the United States,' *American Political Science Review*, 62, September 1968, pp. 852-67; Sandra Kenyon, 'The Development of Political Cynicism among Negro and White Adolescents,' (paper presented at the 65th annual meeting of the American Political Science Association, New York, 2-6 September 1969); Jack Dennis, 'Political learning in Childhood and Adolescence: A study of Fifth, Eighth and Eleventh graders in Milwaukee, Wisconsin,' (Madison: Wisconsin Research and Development Centre for Cognitive Learning, 1969); Joan E. Laurence, 'White Socialisation: Black Reality,' *Psychiatry*, no. 33. (May 1970), pp. 174-94; Schley R. Lyons, 'The Political Socialisation of Ghetto Children: Efficacy and Cynicisms,' *Journal of Politics*, vol. 32 (May 1970), pp. 288-304; Pauline Vaillancourt, 'The Political Socialisation of Young People: A

panel survey of youngsters in the San Francisco Bay area,' (University of California at Berkeley, 1972, unpublished Ph.D. dissertation); Jerald G. Bachman, *Youth in Transition, 11: The Impact of Family and Intelligence on Tenth Grade Boys* (Ann Arbor, Michigan: Institute for Social Research, 1970); Edward S. Greenberg, 'Black children and the Political system,' *Public Opinion Quarterly*, vol. 34, 1970, pp. 333-45.

7.   Robert E. Lane, *op. cit.*, p. 151.

8.   The conclusion of Ted Tapper, *op. cit.*, Richard Rose, *op. cit.*, and Paul Abramson in 'The differential political socialisation of English secondary school students,' *loc. cit.*

9.   J.K. Bhatnagar, 'A study of adjustment of immigrants in a London school,' (University of London, 1969, Ph.D. thesis), pp. 177-8.

10.   Stuart Hall, 'Black Britons: Some Teenage Problems,' *Community*, no. 3, July 1970.

11.   Bhatnagar, *op. cit.*, p. 277.

12.   See Peter Wallis and Dennis Stevenson, *op. cit.*, Peter Evans, *op. cit.*, and Gus John, *Race in the Inner City – A Report from Handsworth, Birmingham*, Runneymede Trust, London, 1970.

13.   Gus John's impressionistic work provides an extremely sensitive understanding of the nature of the generational conflict in West Indian homes. *Ibid.*

14.   J. Rex and R. Moore, *Race, Community and Conflict: A Study of Sparkbrook*, Oxford University Press, London, 1967, p. 114.

15.   Alan Little, Christine Mabey and Graham Whitaker, 'The education of immigrant pupils in Inner London Primary Schools,' *Race*, vol. IX, no. 4, pp. 449-50.

16.   Evidence by the Community Relations Commission to the *Select Committee on Race Relations and Immigration: The Problems of Coloured School Leavers*, Report, p. 20.

17.   Evidence given by the National Foundation for Educational Research, *Select Committee on Race Relations and Immigration' Education*, Report, p. 13.

18.   *Select Committee on Race Relations and Immigration, Session 1973-4, Education*, Report, p. 13 and vol. 2, Evidence, p. 253. Also p. 41, par. 153. See also Bernard Coard, *How the West Indian child is made educationally subnormal in the British school system*, New Beacon Books, London, 1973, also 'The education of immigrant pupils in Primary schools,' report of a working party of the inspectorate and the school psychological service, *Inner London Education Authority*, London, 1967, also pp. 183-6 of Nicholas Deakin *et al.*, *Colour, Citizenship and British Society*, Panther Books, London, 1970.

19.   Derek Humphry, 'Organising the Black Vote,' *Race Today*, May 1970, pp. 150-2.

20.   Peter Wallis and Dennis Stevenson, full unpublished report, *loc. cit.*, p. 17.

21.   David Easton, *loc. cit.*, pp. 34-8, examines the effects of IQ, social class and sex on the rate of attitude acquisition; R. Hess and J. Torney's study, *The Development of Political Attitudes in Children*, Aldine Pub. Co., Chicago, 1967, is more comprehensive in examining the effects of a large number of variables throughout the text. Ted Tapper's study indicates that the lowest level of attitude acquisition in this area is found among working-class students in the bottom streams of secondary modern schools, *op. cit.*, pp. 11, 118, 130. All of these studies indicate that the factors which retard attitude acquisition itself are also the factors which are related to low levels of political efficacy.

22.   For a discussion of family and peer group politicisation see K.P. Langton, *Political Socialisation*, Oxford University Press, New York, 1969, pp. 142-60 and Geoff Mercer's paper presented to the University of Exeter Conference on Political Socialisation, *loc. cit.*, pp. 9-10. Mercer's findings suggest that self-expressed interest along with age dominate variation in feelings of political efficacy (p. 18). For the influence of party identification and attitude acquisition

see the whole chapter devoted to this area in Hess and Torney, *op. cit.*, pp. 198-211. See also Tapper, *op. cit.*, p. 115. For discussions of social class and school type see R.E. Dowse and J. Hughes, *loc. cit.*, p. 19, Paul Abramson, 'The differential political socialisation of English secondary schoolchildren,' *loc. cit.*, Ted Tapper, *op. cit.*, and K.P. Langton, *op. cit.*, pp. 154-60.

23.   As described in R.D. Hess and Judith Torney, *op. cit.*, p. 19.

24.   Both Langton and Mercer suggest that family politicisation is related to a sense of political efficacy. The measuring instrument used in this study was 'Do you ever talk to your parents/friends about politics?' Often/sometimes/rarely/ never.

25.   Political interest was measured by the following question, 'How interested would you say you were in politics?' Very interested/somewhat interested/a little interested/not at all. Political knowledge was measured by the number of correct responses to the following questions: (1) 'Name three British men or women in politics' (a respondent was given a score of 1 for each correct response); (2) 'What is an election?' (the respondent was given a score of 1 for answering correctly). Total scores of 1, 1 or 2 were scored as low, 3 as medium and 4 as a high level of political knowledge.

26.   See footnote 22 for reference to Hess and Torney and Tapper's findings. Respondents were asked in the questionnaire: 'If you were 18 now, who would you vote for?' (I don't know/I wouldn't vote/Conservative/Labour/another party).

27.   See Fred Greenstein, *Children and Politics*, Yale University Press, 1965, p. 82.

28.   David Easton, *loc. cit.*, pp. 36-7. See also Fred Greenstein, 'Sex related political differences in childhood,' *Journal of Politics*, 23, 2 May 1971, pp. 353-71. Also, *Children and Politics*, *op. cit.*, pp. 115-7. Hess and Torney, *op. cit.*, pp. 173-94. R.E. Dowse and John Hughes, 'Girls, Boys and Politics,' *British Journal of Sociology*, March 1971, pp. 53-67.

29.   Herbert Hirsch, *Poverty and Politicisation*, The Free Press, Collier-MacMillan, 1971.

30.   R.R. Bell, 'The lower-class Negro family in US and Great Britain: Some comparisons,' *Race*, vol. XI, October 1969, no. 2, pp. 173-81.

31.   Ted Tapper, *op. cit.*, pp. 130-41.

32.   Geoff Mercer, 'The impact of formal political education in adolescent political learning; the case of Modern Studies and political efficacy among Scottish schoolchildren,' *loc. cit.*, pp. 10-2. The school in Scotland produced as many adolescents with high levels of political efficacy as the grammar schools.

33.   Satisfaction with life in Britain was measured by a scale used in various studies of the assimilation of immigrants; 'How happy do you feel about your life in Britain?' (Very unhappy/fairly unhappy/happy/completely happy). Evaluation of Britain was tested with a modified form of the Osgood semantic differential test, using only evaluative factors. The respondent was given a set of ten scales defined by opposing adjectives. The subject's rating on these scales is taken and summed to obtain a measure of the respondent's general attitude towards the concept.

34.   R.A. Butler, *op. cit.*, p. 78 and Jack Dennis, Lindberg and McCrone, *loc. cit.*, pp. 39-48.

35.   *Gallup Poll Index*, No. 98, March 1968, pp. 67-8.

36.   Paul Abramson, 'Political Efficacy and Political Trust among black schoolchildren; Two explanations,' *loc. cit.*, pp. 1249-58.

37.   Esther Batle and Julian Rotter, 'Children's feelings of personal control as related to social class and ethnic group,' *Journal of Personality*, no. 31, 1963, pp. 482-90, see also M. Brewster-Smith, 'Competence and Socialisation,' in J.A. Clausen (ed.), *Socialisation and Society*, Littlebrown, Boston, 1968, pp. 312-13.

38.   Bhatnagar, *op. cit.*, p. 260. In Beetham's study of school leavers only two West Indian respondents in his sample mentioned racial discrimination as a pos-

sible obstacle to their attaining the job they wanted; see David Beetham, *Immigrant school leavers and the Youth Employment Service in Birmingham,* Institute of Race Relations, 1968, p. 22. Ken Sillitoe reports the extreme reluctance that West Indian interviewees in his sample show to attributing their failure to getting the job they wanted to racial discrimination, see 'The West Indian school leaver' (Paper presented at the seminar on research on the field of Race Relations, University of Aston, 22 May 1973, p. 14).

39.   David Hill, 'The attitudes of West Indian and English adolescents in Britain,' *Race*, vol. XI, January 1971, no. 3, pp. 313-9, Beetham, *op. cit.*, also reports that West Indian adolescents have a more positive self-image than whites.

40.   Paul Abramson, 'Political efficacy and political trust among black children; Two explanations,' *loc. cit.*, pp. 1258-65.

41.   Harrell R. Rodgers, 'Toward explanation of the political efficacy and political trust of black schoolchildren' (paper presented at the annual meeting of the Southwestern Social Science Association, San Antonio, Texas, 29 March-1 April, 1972).

42.   David Easton, *loc. cit.*, p. 31.

43.   R.D. Hess and J. Torney, *op. cit.*, pp. 198-211.

44.   During the pre-test period the J.B. Rotter Internal versus External control of reinforcement scale was used for testing self-competence. The pre-test sample included adolescents up to the age of seventeen, some of whom handled the instrument successfully (the younger respondents had difficulty). It was, therefore, decided to adopt a simple measure which had relevance for all adolescents. A single question was asked, 'Being completely honest with yourself, how good do you think your chances are of getting ahead in life?' Respondents were asked first to assess whether they thought their chances of success were excellent/good/fair/not much chance (scored 1, 2, 3, 4), and secondly the probe was used to extract more information relating to the respondent's answer. Self-esteem was measured by the following scale: 'Thinking about yourself, tell me whether you agree or disagree with the following sentences: (1) "On the whole I am happy with myself as I am"; (2) "I certainly feel good for nothing at times"; (3) "I am able to do things as well as most other people." ' High self-esteem was scored as agree/disagree/agree, total score 6.

45.   High political efficacy set is disagree/disagree for both questions; score total of 4. The two items are extracted from the most commonly used political efficacy index used in research, see David Easton, *loc. cit.*, p. 28.

46.   The scale used for measuring political cynicism or trust has been widely used in political socialisation research. Cynicism appears to be a manifestation of a deep-seated suspicion of other's motives and actions, see M. Kent Jennings and Richard Niemi, 'The transmission of political values from parent to child,' *The American Political Science Review*, 62, March 1968. The questions were: 1) 'Do you think that people in the government waste a lot of money in taxes, waste some of it, or don't waste very much of it?' (Responses were scored: a lot = 1, some = 2, not very much = 3); 2) 'Do you think that quite a few people in the government are a bit crooked, not very many are, or do you think hardly any of them are?' (Responses were scored: a bit = 1, not many = 2, hardly any = 3); 3) 'Would you say that the government is run by a few big interests looking out for themselves or that it is run for the good of the people?' (Responses were scored: first option = 1, alternative = 2); high trust = 8, medium = 5, 6 and 7, low = 3 and 4.

47.   Sandra Kenyon, *loc. cit.*, p. 82; Jack Dennis, 'Political learning in childhood and adolescence,' *loc. cit.*, p. 83; and Harrell Rodgers, *loc. cit.*, p. 11, all found very weak though positive relationships between personal competence and political effectiveness.

48.   Ted Tapper, *op. cit.*, p. 118.

49.   See David Easton, *A systems analysis of political life*, Wiley, New York, 1965, pp. 320-42.

6. PROTESTANT 'IDEOLOGY' CONSIDERED: THE CASE OF 'DISCRIMINATION'

Sarah Nelson

After over one thousand deaths in Northern Ireland, a protracted IRA bombing campaign, Protestant retaliatory violence, and continued conflict over appropriate constitutional structures for the province, the precipitating factor of the present conflict — allegations of discrimination against Catholics — might almost be forgotten. Yet, as the 'catchword' of the civil rights movement, 'discrimination' formed the central issue of Northern Ireland politics during at least the first two years of civil unrest. Arguments about it filled the literature of all parties to the conflict during this time. They revolved largely round two basic questions: first, did discrimination against Catholics exist in Northern Ireland? Secondly, if it did, what were the reasons for it?

The allegations made by various groups concerned with civil rights suggested the denial of equal opportunity to Catholics in a number of spheres — the political, the social, the economic. They included the allocation of jobs in state and in private employment; allocation of council houses and other resources by local authorities; the drawing of ward and electoral boundaries; and the voting system for Stormont elections. (Some protesters even claimed that the Northern Ireland border was itself a 'gerrymander.') The discrepancy between Protestant and Catholic emigration was also pointed out.[1] The substance at least of the allegations was broadly accepted by all parties to the conflict, including the Eire and British governments, with the exception of parts of the accused community itself — the Ulster Protestant majority. The publication of the Cameron Report,[2] which concluded that anti-Catholic discrimination had existed in Northern Ireland since Partition and sought to give evidence for this, could leave Protestants in no doubt that the British government had now joined with Northern and Southern Irish Catholics in regarding 'discrimination against Catholics' as a major cause of 'the Northern Ireland problem,' and in assuming that its eradication was a prerequisite to a 'solution.'

That many Protestants refused to acknowledge the *facts* of discrimination had already been made clear by the findings of Richard Rose's 1968 opinion survey, which formed the basis of his book *Governing Without Consensus*.[3] In reply to the question 'do you think Catholics in Northern Ireland are treated unfairly,' 74 per cent of Protestants answered 'no' while an equal percentage of Catholics replied 'yes.' This was in fact the question which produced the highest degree of polarisation in response between the two religious groups. Paisleyite opposition to reforms passed by the O'Neill and Chichester-Clark governments also showed that substantial numbers of Protestants fiercely opposed any measures designed to give increased power, oportunities or rights to their Catholic fellow countrymen.

Protestants who would not admit to the existence of discrimination or the need for reform thus found themselves isolated in a fundamental way from all other parties to the conflict: similarly the latter shared some basic premises and definitions which provided a common framework of perceptions and hence a means of communication, despite important differences in long term aims and policy. In the same way, the great mushroom cloud of debate on the society and politics of Northern Ireland which developed in Parliament, in the Press, in academic journals and elsewhere was 'unreal' to many Protestants because it overwhelmingly accepted basic premises which they would not, and revolved around questions like: 'why is there anti-Catholic discrimination in Northern Ireland? What has gone wrong with the society which practises it?' Everyone else could join in the debate and find it meaningful because they shared beliefs in the salience of the questions, even if their answers often differed. The result was that large numbers of Protestants were excluded from a range of discussions which were substantially about themselves — their 'ideology,' beliefs, 'fears,' the motivations leading them to behave in a 'discriminatory' way towards Catholics and to react to both the allegations and the reforms in an intransigent manner.

'Racial' Theories of Behaviour

A number of theories were postulated about the reasons for Protestant behaviour, most of them suggesting the existence of some kind of 'racist' or 'supremacist' anti-Catholic ideology which provided rationalisations for discriminatory activity.[4] Pronouncements were made about the kind of situation the 'Northern Ireland problem' constituted; as it is hard for many present day observers to believe that people can fight over 'something like religion,' there has been a tendency to try and simplify the Ulster bog by pigeonholing it neatly as a 'colonial' or 'race relations' or 'economic conflict ' or other situation of a type familiar to social scientists. Very few researchers have seemed to feel that looking in detail at the perceptions of Protestants themselves about the conflict will aid their understanding of the situation substantially. Catholics too have suffered an 'excess of theorising,' but less so, because at least in the first years on the conflict, research students appeared to find Catholics more sympathetic, more fashionable and more interesting subjects of study, hence they were better able to get a word in edgeways.[5]

There has been a tendency amongst those who analyse the politics of Northern Ireland to see Protestant behaviour and attitudes as linked to a desire for superior political power and economic wealth in themselves. This has been a long-held and much publicised viewpoint of most left wing and republican groups in both Ireland and Britain,[6] and its adoption tends to encourage perhaps hasty comparisons of Northern Ireland with countries as diverse as Algeria, Rhodesia or the southern states of the United States, especially among those who consider that Northern Ireland to constitute a 'race relations situation.'

For example, in a rather confused paper,[7] Robert Moore seeks to demonstrate that post-colonial Northern Ireland constitutes a 'race relations situation' which will not be solved by the mere removal of economic causes of conflict, because 'the prime role of the majority is . . . to dominate the minority . . . their privileges . . . are based on racial considerations which are more salient than the economic . . . the basis of the order lies in . . . beliefs about others . . . the parties to a race relations situation believe certain behaviour by others is inevitable.'

The major problem confronting anyone trying to decide if a situation is one of 'race relations' stems from contradictions and uncertainties in the literature of 'race' itself: his decision may depend upon which author he follows. In the literature, there are differences of opinion about the very definitions of 'race' and 'racism,'[8] and of 'caste';[9] of terms like 'pluralism' or 'assimilation.' Nor is there agreement on what the 'specific implications for sociology and social policy' of race relations situations actually are.

If Moore's analysis was consistent or proved his contentions in terms of his own definitions of race issues (which follow those of John Rex)[10] it might have value as one useful approach to the subject, but this is not the case. If his contention that economic factors are not at the heart of the social order or the conflict[11] is to hold weight, the statement that 'power and privilege do not seem (sic) to be so exclusively based on social class as in other European capitalist societies will hardly be sufficient. He would not only have to make a detailed examination of Northern Ireland's economic system and its relation to the British one, but also concern himself with Protestant-Catholic ratios in different types of employment, and attitudes to cooperation with Catholics among various Protestant socioeconomic groups. (These areas would also have to be examined by anyone who wished to show the paramountcy of economic factors.)

Using one of Rex's criteria for a 'race relations situation,' Moore has to establish the existence of 'some kind of deterministic theory' justifying ascriptive allocation of roles and rights to the minority group. Though he admits that 'it is not easy to find explicit and recognisably racist justifications of the ascriptions of roles' and can only provide as 'evidence' three quotations from late nineteenth century writers, one from *Le Nouvel Observateur* and one from 'a Catholic recently interviewed by the *Sunday Times*,' he nevertheless concludes that racism has an active role which has taken on a life of its own and cannot now be eliminated by the elite. By 'racism' he seems to imply 'the existence of a considerable body of deterministic theory about Catholics' which includes the theory that '99 per cent of Catholics are disloyal' and a religious theology that 'ascribes unchanging characteristics to Roman Catholicism and Roman Catholics.' However, this body of theory is nowhere explored in any kind of systematic or detailed way.

If we, like Moore, adopt Rex's citerion in preference to, for example, Banton's narrower ones [12] we shall have to ask a range of questions and answer them better than he does. The concerns will have to be both 'objective' and 'subjective.' We will need to know in detail the extent and the type of discrimination which Catholics suffered, and consider how far, at different historical periods, they contributed to their own exclusion in certain fields through deliberate choice. We will have to discover the numbers and the types of theories about Catholics used by Protestants, how 'deterministic' and systematic they are, which groups use them and on what occasions (and with what result).[13] This will involve actually talking to Protestants, as well as historical study. Both these things will also encourage us to ask how far the theories can be described as mere myth or rationalisation, and how far they have reflected social reality. For example, some Ulster Catholics are 'disloyal,' anti-British and intent on undermining the existence of Northern Ireland, and are proud to admit it. Unless we take the position that 'feelings of nationality' are quite unimportant or a mere mask for other feelings,[14] we have to face an issue which has always loomed large in Ulster politics but is not significant in some 'race relations situations' in some other countries. From Moore's paper (and several other writings on the politics of Northern Ireland)[15] one would hardly guess that the 'national question' and the problem of conflicting national aspirations existed historically at all, except as a 'bogey' or 'delusion' in the minds of certain Protestants. Moore avoids discussion of this question, and of the whole basis of the 'state' in Northern Ireland by declaring that 'the details of [Partition] and the political background do not considerably concern us here.' But they do, very much; for there is considerable dispute about the motives of Protestants in opposing home rule at this time; were they 'undemocratic,' 'racist,' based on a lust for power or wealth, or did they first of all reflect a sound perception of the economic interests of the North of Ireland at this time?[16] (The only real benefits Moore ascribes to Protestant workers in a Northern Ireland linked to the United Kingdom are those which result from discrimination against Catholics.) Yet he hints at one point that important differences in the land system and the industrial development of the northeast corner distinguished it from the rest of Ireland but then goes on to deny the significance of these. In view of the north's distinctive history, anyone concerned with 'race relations situations' must also ask how far it could ever be described as a 'colonial' or 'post-colonial' society; it is certainly not the same type as the south of Ireland.[17]

I have suggested, then, that awareness of the *fact* of discrimination in Northern Ireland must be supplanted by historical and structural study, and investigation into the content of 'ideologies,' before any decision can be made about 'the kind of social situation' which exists in Northern Ireland.[18] The nature of the 'ideologies' must be of particular concern to anyone wishing to demonstrate that it is a 'race relations situation.' Very little systematic research has been done on 'Protestant ideologies'[19] and in this paper I am more concerned with asking questions about these rather than answering them, because my investigation is not wide ranging enough to be able to do this. It is concerned with the ways in which Protestants talk about 'discrimination,' and what these reveal about their attitudes to politics in general, and to Catholics in particular. As a 'subjective' study of perceptions, and a restricted one at that, it can only make a partial contribution to the variety of types of study I indicated above to be necessary for those concerned with 'race relations situations.' It can also only make tentative conclusions, because the number involved in the open ended interviews was small (about fifty people) and not distributed rigorously amongst, for example, different socioeconomic or political groups. Some comments are drawn from informal conversations held with Protestants, held over the last three years.

I chose this area of study for several reasons: first, because of the key position the issue held in the politics of the province; secondly, to try and find out exactly why many Protestants could not accept basic premises about the political situation which other parties to it shared; thirdly, to discover if conventional academic or pseudo-academic explanations of their behaviour, and their intransigent response to the civil rights campaign and subsequent reforms, provided either accurate or adequate understanding. How much evidence could be produced of 'racist' or 'supremacist' theories among Protestants?

Findings

There were several major findings of the research which this paper will seek to show and elucidate. First of all, though discrimination is thought of as an issue of greatest concern and interest to Catholics, Protestants in Northern Ireland show considerable concern with it and talk and think about it a great deal. Secondly, it is something about which many of them hold confused, ambiguous or contradictory opinions — both about its existence, and about whether it is right or wrong. This in itself is not surprising: social scientists have long established the fact that people can hold contradictory opinions.[20] It is something, however, which the opinion poll cannot clearly demonstrate on all occasions, and which will have implications for political behaviour. Thirdly, specifically 'racist' ideologies could only be said to have been employed by a minority: it would be more accurate to say that

159

many Protestants hold ideological beliefs which justify discrimination, and others which condemn it, and that this fact is one important source of the confusion some demonstrate. Fourthly, it became obvious that the intransigent response given to the civil rights movement and to the reforms was caused by a variety of factors, only some of which could be related to 'ideology.' Lastly, accurate analysis of the findings seemed to call for a keen awareness of the differences in political culture between at least Anglo-American and Northern Irish society. Northern Ireland presents many problems to the research student in this respect, for in many outward ways it appears similar to our own society, while some of the differences are not readily apparent until one has lived there for some time.

'Denial' Responses

I opened my discussion of 'discrimination' with respondents with the question: 'there's been a lot of talk in Northern Ireland about 'discrimination' against Catholics. Do you think this existed or not?'

Two facts quickly became clear from the ensuing responses. First of all, the reaction of the majority was denial, thus apparently confirming the findings of Rose's survey. But the denial was almost without exception qualified during the discussion that followed, so that virtually all respondents had admitted to some forms of anti-Catholic discrimination at least by the conclusion of the interview. Thus we have already found that the opinion poll results on the subject are misleading, and are faced with the problem of why most respondents felt bound to deny the question initially.

Secondly, it became obvious that 'discrimination' was an issue of considerable importance to respondents. Everyone was anxious to express opinions about it, and some were preoccupied with it to an almost obsessive degree. Talking about it made many respondents both angry and defensive: they protested that they had been unjustly accused, portrayed as villains in the eyes of the world while the 'real' troublemakers had escaped criticism, and had been the victims of a false and widespread propaganda campaign. Everyone felt the necessity of vindicating their own community to some degree at least, and some went to considerable lengths to do so. That is, they did not know in advance what questions I was going to ask so could not have prepared a ready answer: yet their response almost resembled a long impassioned closing speech for the defence at a murder trial!

This kind of reaction might be regarded superficially as the expected response of a 'guilty party' who tries to conceal or rationalise his complicity in injustice, and whose conscience makes him uncomfortable. The fairness of this assessment may be more accurately gauged when the content of their further discussions on 'discrimination' is examined. Some considerations, however, might be made at this stage which suggest other contributory factors to this kind of reaction.

First of all, we must consider the likely effect of the Civil Rights campaign on Protestants given the circumstances in which it took place. World attention did not come gradually to Ulster: rather it burst upon it like a force ten gale, which blew against the Protestant community with general hostility and condemnation even after the first killings of British soldiers by Catholics.[21] There was widespread acceptance of the analysis of the civil rights movement, in which 'discrimination' was the central theme, coupled with a general ignorance of Northern Ireland and its historic conflicts: an ignorance traditionally encouraged by the Unionist establishment where the 'outside world' was concerned, which many Protestants may since have had cause to regret. The civil rights movement made demands in the name of a cause widely accepted as 'just'; they did not feel that they had to offer anything in return (such as abandoning republican activity). In those early days, the impression that Irish Catholics were in any way to blame for the existing situation was hardly conveyed at all, and in the prevailing climate of opinion, any protests or complaints at Catholic behaviour by Protestants were likely to be construed as attempts to conceal or rationalise injustice. If there was certainly a degree of truth in their protests that certain clergy and politicians had always discouraged acceptance of or participation in the institutions of Northern Ireland,[22] and that some Catholics had always tried to undermine Northern Ireland's very existence, nobody wanted to hear it. Protestants also realised that several of those calling most vociferously for 'British rights' and 'British standards' had previously expressed clearly republican and anti-British sentiments, and were angered by their apparent hypocrisy.

In this kind of situation where even if you have valid points to make no-one listens to you, a feeling of powerlessness results (something not normally associated with Protestants) which produces anger and frustration. Denied the opportunity of a rational response, Protestants hit back in other ways, so that a vicious circle of expectations and images was created. After Burntollet they were branded as barbaric; the inarticulate literature they produced reinforced the image of a bigoted and even vicious people; and the response of distaste further antagonised and frustrated Protestants. They could count on no articulate left wing intellectuals to put their case or write their pamphlets, and exposition of their viewpoint was harder for them anyway, as a dominant group which had never had to justify their position in this way. One Democratic Unionist activist explained:

'I first decided I must go into politics when I saw a TV programme in 1969. A camera crew went up the Falls and talked to a man beside a barricade about what was happening. He gave this great long speech and suddenly I realised from his accent, "hang on he's not local at all and he's putting their case." We had nobody like that, we just felt so helpless.'

During this period a resentment and anger against the media's presentation of the situation in Northern Ireland built up in the loyalist community and is only now beginning to diminish. As a result they shunned the media for years and failed to use it to their advantage. It is in the context of their perception of it as a hostile force that incidents like the smashing of TV cameras must be understood.

One particular source of annoyance was the impression given of the 'one man one vote' issue (the property qualification actually disenfranchised more Protestants than Catholics, as some civil rights supporters themselves emphasised).

'The impression was of a totalitarian state which completely disenfranchised the Catholics. This was what all my friends in England seemed to think. I spent hours trying to explain to them but we never got the chance to do this over the media.'

(middle-class Unionist respondent)

The impression that comes across strongly in conversations with Protestants is that the swift-moving events of this civil rights period had traumatic effects, to which they are still reacting and from which many have not recovered. The fact that the bulk of criticism came from the country of which they thought they were the most loyal citizens was a shock in itself, and the feelings of inferiority and resentment towards certain left wing and Catholic intellectuals which developed at this time are often still in evidence.

What has also been suggested is that the way the campaign was conducted and developed, and the way it was interpreted outside Northern Ireland, contributed to intransigent reaction apart from the demands themselves. We might discuss possible contradictions in the civil rights movement in connection with this point. Without doubt most of its campaigners, and the Catholic community in general, saw its purpose as improving the position of Catholics. The movement's literature, however, often suggested a concern for all sections of the community who suffered injustice under the Unionist system. Open appeals for Protestant working-class support were made in People's Democracy literature. Protestant lack of support, however, or even violent opposition, did not lead to intensification of efforts to increase that support but rather to a 'giving up' on the Protestants, which could not fail to be obvious to everyone. This was nowhere more conspicuous than in People's Democracy circles.[23] As time progressed virtually every left wing group[24] with the exception of the Official Republican movement appeared to abandon hope for Protestant salvation, at least until the dialectics of the struggle had fully worked themselves out. It was this tendency, rather than the initial noises of goodwill, which thus grew to be the reality for Protestants and which exerted an important influence on their perceptions of the campaign.

We must also consider the likely effect of the accusations themselves,

and the kind of reaction they would tend to produce in the 'accused.'
In the name of a cause widely accepted as just, all parties outside
Loyalist ranks were demanding concessions that were not merely
material. The first necessity was an admission of past misconduct. Thus,
although the material demands were straightforward, they involved
something more profound – an examination of fundamental beliefs
and personal integrity. No Protestant was able to ignore the implications of the accusations; in a sense all were personally accused and
threatened as supporters of a state whose integrity was cast into doubt.
Whatever their position, whatever their personal knowledge of discriminatory practices, they were liable to feel the weight of righteous
condemnation:

> 'I went over to England just after it started. People began talking
> about the troubles and then someone asked what religion I was.
> When I said Protestant their whole attitude changed and they said
> we were all bigots.'
>
> *(This social worker did not hold a high*
> *opinion of Unionist politics)*

It is likely that in a situation which constitutes a serious threat to an
individual's self-respect and his integrity as a person, the retrieving of
this integrity will be the thing of primary importance to him. The first
need may be to wipe out doubts in his own mind by whatever methods
he can seize on. The angry and defensive reactions of many of my
respondents showed that these particular accusations did indeed often
come across as a profound personal threat. Admission of unjust practices in the society is also felt as an admission of personal complicity,
so for personal reasons people will try not to make such an admission
to themselves as well as to me, for as long as possible. This increases
the likelihood of an intransigent response and prevents people facing
up to the possibly painful reality of the situation, especially if this involves re-examining cherished beliefs, or questioning the integrity of
those one has been brought up to respect most highly. One Unionist
with a long and irreproachable record of public service was unable even
to discuss the issue of 'discrimination' without losing his temper
though he did not react like this to other issues. It was obvious that he
saw the accusations as a profound threat to his own 'honour' and that
he could not bring himself to contemplate the possibility of his colleagues' less honourable behaviour. He needed to deliver a long exoner-
ating tirade every time the subject was discussed. On other occasions I
was faced with intelligent and educated respondents who made a range
of hardly credible statements and accusations. One's natural reaction
was 'he can't really believe that.' Yet it was clear that they did: so
strong was the need to vindicate themselves personally. Some people
would also grasp eagerly at a 'line of defence' they heard or read,[25]
however implausible it was; this then became a 'catch phrase' or

'community myth.' (For example, the burning of Bombay Street in August 1969 evoked shame and guilt in the Protestant community which has proved hard to cope with. A 'community myth' has grown up that 'they burned Bombay Street down themselves.' The alternative is painful to many people, especially in view of their perceptions of 'the kind of people Protestants are,' which I shall discuss later.)

I am not suggesting here that Ulster Protestants are somehow unique in making this kind of response to threat. It is likely that many groups who have come under challenge in other societies react in similar ways, and that part of their intransigence may be explained by such consider-ations as the above. But these kinds of effects at a personal level tend to be little discussed or realised by those who analyse their behaviour.

Another point which should be borne in mind is that the accusers were implicitly expecting, even demanding, that all Protestants accepted both the need for reform, and the reforms themselves. If they did not instantly do so, they were considered intolerant, or bigots trying to maintain the 'Protestant ascendancy.' But if we consider Northern Ireland's history, it becomes clear that this is both a consider-able and an unrealistic demand. One of the province's greatest prob-lems has always been the high degree of segregation existing in all spheres of life between religious groups, with high levels of hostility, suspicion and fear. Many people come into direct contact with those of the other religion only rarely, are relatively unaware of the condi-tions under which the 'other side' lives and draw what knowledge they have from what they are told by their own community leaders.[26] Patterns of discrimination varied, in any case, amongst different types of employment and in different regions, and it is quite likely that many Protestants were generally ignorant about it, whilst not making any particular efforts to investigate the rumours. However, what the accusers were asking was that Protestants accept on trust what their traditional enemies claimed to be true. Given the historical circum-stances of a divided society, there are so many reasons why they would tend not to do so that it is perhaps only surprising that so many Pro-testants did support the reform measures.

We have therefore discussed a number of reasons distinct from 'ideology' or 'desire to perserve privileges' which may have increased Protestant intransigence towards the civil rights demands: the existence of some valid grievances against Catholic behaviour or individual Catholic public figures; the nature of the campaign, its presentation and wider reaction to it; psychological difficulties in accepting the allega-tions; and 'communication' barriers in a divided and segregated society.

The 'no' response which so many gave to the initial question may be interpreted as a kind of shorthand for a more complex reply, which might run as follows : 'no there wasn't as much as was claimed, and what there was can be explained by their own faults or behaviour or the peculiar circumstances of Northern Ireland which you (the researcher) don't understand.' It reflects a deep rooted feeling that their community has been unjustly criticised and signifies the intention to make some defence of it. It also became obvious, however, that there were differences in the way 'discrimination' was defined, so that some people did not see the injustices complained of as 'discrimination' at all, but something else, and hence were able to deny its existence.

When people made the initial denial I then asked: 'why do you think some people said there was discrimination?'

During the civil rights campaign conscious efforts were made by prominent figures in the Unionist and loyalist camp to identify the movement with republican or 'extreme socialist' agitation and to imply that the demands were a 'front' for a well planned IRA campaign. The 'Belfast Newsletter' revealed its skill at hunting down the lone tri-colour flag in a civil rights march and printing photographs of it. Belief in a 'troublemakers' theory is still widely found throughout the Protestant community. It serves the function of enabling people to identify a ready scapegoat and once again to avoid facing up to the possible truth of the allegations. There are three particular reasons why such a view is likely to fall on fertile soil. First of all, community relations during the late 1960s were widely recognised to be the best that had obtained in Northern Ireland's history — superficially at least, the two groups seemed to be losing their hostility and cooperating freely. Many people, therefore, could only interpret divisive activty as coming from 'troublemakers' bent on destroying the new spirit. Secondly, as these interviews were conducted during 1972-3, after the downfall of Stormont, when the persistance of a devastating IRA bombing campaign and of Catholic alienation despite reforms made it appear to many Protestants that their worst doubts about the civil rights movement had materialised. They began to say 'we gave them all they asked for and look what happens' so that even former O'Neill supporters were beginning to redefine the past. Thirdly, ideological predispositions about Catholic sympathies towards Republicanism, strengthened by experience of actual previous anti-partitionist campaigns[27] among many Protestants make them highly receptive to this kind of 'IRA front' theory. It is interesting that most working-class Protestant activists who were beginning to talk during 1973 and 1974 of 'fifty years of misrule' and the 'fur coat brigade' nevertheless hold to the belief that a small group of IRA members organised the 'civil rights' after a long and careful period of preparation. They will admit that discrimination existed against both sections of the working class, but not that it was disproportionately anti-Catholic:

> 'The Catholics got it wrong. It was the Unionist party discriminating against everyone else. Jobs for the boys and plenty of backhanders, I saw them myself.'
>
> *(ex-Unionist party worker)*

165

While the high degree of suspicion about and hostility towards Catholic intentions in many Protestant working-class areas might encourage acceptance of the 'IRA plot' view [28] and of the notion that Catholics were largely responsible for their own exclusion, there are other reasons why poorer Protestants would find the Catholic-oriented civil rights demands particularly hard to support. People living in slum houses found themselves identified with the 'Protestant ascendancy,' the civil rights movement seemed to be presenting to the world injustices they too had to accept as things purely inflicted on Catholics:

'I had worked with them all my life, I used to visit this RC friend and she lived in exactly the same kind of kitchen house [29] as me. Therefore I couldn't see the civil rights case and blamed it on the students. They had their grants which is more than I had, I brought up a family on a widow's pension. But things just seem to keep getting worse whatever we do, which is what makes you think there must be some foreigners behind it all.'

(working-class housewife, Alliance Party)

Unless and until numbers of Protestant working-class people acknowledge that the pre-1968 political system did discriminate disproportionately against Catholics, it is doubtful how successfully they can develop common understanding and policy with Catholic working-class groups in future; because they do not share basic beliefs about what was wrong with that society, nor the same understanding of its structure.

Whether or not respondents put forward the 'troublemakers' view in answer to my second question, a large section put forward the notion that the complaints were 'misguided' in that everyone had a fair chance, but Catholics could not or would not take it. How did they support these positions?

When comparisons are made between Northern Ireland and places like Rhodesia, Algeria or the southern states of the United States, the reader may easily assume that 'Protestant ideology' shares some of the assumptions found among whites in these countries to the effect that the oppressed group is somehow inherently inferior, less intelligent or civilised, dirty, feckless breeders and so on. But findings which seem to verify this need to be treated with great caution. At a 'folk' level a widespread Protestant belief may be found that Catholics do not keep their houses, or streets, or farms, as neat or clean as do Protestants, and this is sometimes related to the fact that Scots immigrants placed more emphasis on such virtues as 'neatness,' unlike the native Irish. But Protestants do not fight Catholics, or refuse to share power with them, because they are 'dirty' or 'untidy'; if this is a 'racist' belief, it hardly has important political consequences! [30] The beliefs which do are not, for the vast majority, based on the notion that Catholics are inherently endowed with unfavourable characteristics, but on the view that the malignant influence of other forces (notably the Catholic Church) works to produce these:

'It's not surprising that they couldn't get on in life. How can a woman in Ballymurphy keep her house clean or get a good education for her children when the Church says she must have ten or twelve of them? She's bound to be poor. It's the Church's fault.'
(Unionist respondent)

'Instead of fighting for a better deal for their people the politicians were always carping on about a united Ireland. Same with the priests and the schools, they spend their time teaching their children to be rebels, that's more important than a good education.'
(UDA respondent)

'They always encourage them not to take part. When I worked in the post office there was this lad of seventeen who had to tie string round bundles of letters, I noticed he was tying a whole ball of string round each bundle. I said, "Patrick, what are you doing?" He was muttering "break the state break the state." It's criminal the notions they put into them at that age.'
(Unionist respondent)

'Their own people get them – e.g. the IRA. There was a third of places reserved for Catholics in the police force. The Church always discouraged them from joining and if they did they might be shot by the IRA – look what happens in the UDR now.'
(DUP respondent)

It is most important to recognise, in particular, that the widespread Protestant view that Catholics 'don't work' or 'don't want to work,' which has anguished many a trade union activist in the past, is not based on the notion that Catholics are inherently lazy or workshy.[31] It is based on the belief that they do not wish to work for that particular state; that they would rather milk it of social security and make use of it without contributing anything to it. Witness this discussion, held at a UDA club in January 1973:

First man: 'I employed them on a building site, well half of them didn't turn up and I discovered most of them were drawing assistance at the same time. They just didn't want to put anything in. After that I felt reluctant to employ any of them again.'
Second man: 'But RCs in Scotland don't behave like that do they? [to me] I'm from Dundee and I've worked with them. They support the state, they don't bring it down.'
First Man: 'That's right. But you people don't understand what they're like here.'

These quoted statements all show how it is possible for Protestants who believe these things to mantain a belief that 'everyone has a fair chance' when confronted with statistics showing Catholic under-representation or disproportionate unemployment in certain fields. They allocate the blame elsewhere. It is difficult to describe these beliefs as 'racist' in any accepted sense, though they do become 'deterministic' if and when people believe that Catholics cannot escape the influence of their Church nor act independently from it. Frank Wright[32] discusses this question at length, but exaggerates the extent to which Protestants believe Catholics are 'tied' to their Church. Most so-called 'extreme' Protestants I met had clearly ambiguous feelings about this. On the one hand their upbringing influenced them to believe in the tremendous power of the Catholic Church and its 'hold' over its flock. On the other, they usually believed in the existence of a large, if vague and indeterminate body of 'good Catholics,' as it were, who could be won away from subversive activities, leaving a small group of IRA whom they (the loyalists) could 'deal with no bother.'

What can be said is that the prime objection made against Catholics today does not concern their 'racial difference' but rather their 'disloyalty' and anti-British hostility. This is not to deny that one of the major reasons many Protestants oppose a united Ireland is because they feel it would be culturally alien: that the southern Irish are 'different.' But several research students including myself have heard northern Catholics express the same feelings about southerners, and Rose found that more Protestants felt the English were 'much different' to themselves than felt northern Catholics were.[33] As many republicans believe Protestants have been 'artificially' separated from themselves by a scheming imperialist power, so many Protestants believe Catholics have been 'made' different by a scheming Church.

Though numbers of the majority community tend to see themselves as more industrious, well-organised and self-reliant than other Irishmen, in a vague kind of way, the respondents who introduced specifically 'racial' concepts into their discussion of the causes of the conflict were so few that they stood out clearly as 'deviant.' They belonged almost entirely to the right wing Vanguard movement, a group which has developed 'Ulster nationalism' to a more systematic and elaborate level than any other party and whose views on the subject appear to have won little support.[34] These people often talked at length about the 'racial' characteristics of the Scots Irish — their thrift, industry, dignity and so on — and gave often implausible accounts of their historic origins. They incorporated their beliefs into their political policies, which suggest the desire for an authoritarian and puritanical type of society. (Most members had a low opinion of the 'permissive' or 'dissolute' nature of modern British society.) It should be borne in mind, however, that the same people who criticised the characteristics of Catholics (and even they were often unsure what 'racial group' *northern* Irish Catholics now belonged to) frequently displayed distaste for the political pretensions of working-class Protestants, and some scepticism about their political ability; although they had just eulogised them for their admirable 'Protestant' characteristics.

What kinds of beliefs about their own society did people demonstrate when they expressed the view that discrimination was 'wrong' and that their community was not guilty of it? Why did some people seem to have such a high regard for the integrity of their own group and its leaders that they were unable to believe the allegations?

Much is said about Protestant ideology about Catholics; less about Protestant ideology about Protestants. What kind of people are they? They are the law-abiding, constitutional people; not the rebels. They abide by democratic procedures, supporting the state rather than bringing it down with bomb and bullet: 'I think Protestants are more – well, dignified – we exhaust all constitutional means before taking to the gun.' (*Vanguard respondent.*) A Protestant woman stood watching a blaze started by Protestants in Sandy Row, during which a fireman was shot dead. Shots were ringing out a short distance away, but she was unable to believe the evidence of her own eyes. She remarked: 'it can't be Protestants. We don't do things like that.'

An observer might sceptically point out that it was easy for Protestants to be law-abiding in a state which benefited them; they had little reason or need to oppose it. This is quite true, but Protestants are unlikely to see the situation in this way, because 'Protestant law and order' was their only model of 'law and order' itself. It does not diminish their belief in themselves as law-abiding people, as the great difficulty and confusion some respondents showed in discussing or admitting to Protestant violence demonstrated.[35]

As they are constitutional 'democrats,' so they are a just and tolerant people who believe in 'fair play for all.' There are several contributory factors to this notion. The first influence springs from the 'official version' of what Northern Ireland 'is.' It always had all the trappings, constitutional and electoral procedures and forms of a Western democracy on the British model. If British children could be socialised into beliefs about British democracy like 'fair play' and 'integrity,' so could the children of Northern Ireland's majority community; indeed, their schools probably placed greater emphasis on the virtues of the 'mother of Parliaments' than British ones.

A second factor almost makes it compulsory for Protestants to believe these things about themselves simply because they claimed British identity, but also because for them 'Home Rule' was synonymous with tyranny and clerical dominated government. If they were fighting to escape injustice and preserve freedom, they could hardly be guilty of the very malpractices they claimed to oppose, after that freedom was granted.

On my first point, it might be claimed that the United States and Britain also have official 'ideologies' which condemn discrimination,

169

yet 'racist' and discriminatory behaviour continues. This is true, although I not feel that 'racism' in these countries should be cynically dismissed as similar to that of countries in which it is sanctioned by law (like South Africa). The disparity between 'theory' and 'practice' in the former leads to mental conflicts among those who indulge in 'racist' behaviour and influences their rationalisations of it. But even in Britain and the United States, there is no similar pervasive 'folk myth' about the historic role of one group in preserving liberty and freedoms against another who wishes to destroy these and substitute a clerical tyranny, as one finds in Northern Ireland.

The third contributory factor, which has links with the second, is the influence of Protestant religious principles. The Calvinist view of the relationship between religion and politics does make justifiable, on occasions, the denial of free speech and other political rights, and these arguments were used by Paisley and the anti-ecumenical and anti-O'-Neill movements of the late 1960s. I shall discuss some influences this view may have had on Protestants who believe discrimination is 'right' later. This question is again looked at in detail in Wright's paper. Nevertheless two points about it may be considered here. First of all, given the uneasy balance of forces and the tensions inherent in Northern Ireland, it was very likely that some kind of opposition movement to O'Neill's apparently liberalising policies would emerge; in its stance – that the ruling class was betraying the principles of 'true' Protestantism[36] – it followed the tradition of earlier anti-establishment Protestant movements. But because Paisley, with his exceptionally powerful personality, became the beacon round which most opposition to the new trends gathered, it does not follow that all his knowledge of, or commitment to, the principles of 'Bible Protestantism' which shaped the way his opposition to change was framed. We simply have very little knowledge of the perceptions and motivations of his supporters at this time. It is likely that Wright has exaggerated the importance of the 'religio-political' interpretation of events among Protestants because his interviews were largely conducted with members of Paisley's own party (the D.U.P).

Historically it has always been difficult for working-class Protestants to criticise the ruling class in terms other than those which claim a 'betrayal of Protestantism' without laying themselves open to smears about 'communism' or 'undermining Protestant unity,' and to the embarassingly eager attentions of would-be reformers on the 'other side.' Paisley's campaigns against O'Neill, and the kinds of criticisms made of the latter by many working-class Protestants suggest Boulton[37] is wrong in saying that loyalists opposed O'Neill 'because he was soft on Catholics, not because he left Protestants in slum houses.' They opposed him on both; their position prevented them from making open class demands.

Secondly, the tenets of fundamentalist Protestantism may give rise to contradictory beliefs in those who hold them. On the one hand, Calvin himself subordinated the exercise of political liberty to the defence of a certain conception of religion; so evangelical Protestants have demanded that politicians be vigilant to defend the socialising institutions and practices of Protestant society from the encroachments of Popery. Though this is justified on the grounds that complete freedom will lead to the undermining of freedom itself by Catholicism (thus Orange author S.E. Long: 'a strong Protestant stand is not the contradiction of equality but rather a guarantee that justice for all is protected') nevertheless the practice of the principle — as in the Paisleyite street demonstrations — caused disquiet among Protestants themselves. In 1967 the Methodist Church was prompted to issue a statement that 'exercising pressure and intimidation to curtail freedom is to be disloyal to essential Protestantism.' What is meant here by 'essential Protestantism?'

'Where Protestantism flourishes liberty flames . . . Protestantism is the torchbearer of liberty.'[38] The number of my respondents who justified their belief that discrimination was 'wrong' from Protestant *religious* principles was far greater than the number who drew on these to rationalise it. Even among Protestants who are not regular churchgoers or even believers,[39] the idea that Protestants are somehow 'free men' of independent mind, who do not oppress nor behave unjustly, unlike those in the hold of the Catholic Church, still exerts a powerful influence. What should be understood is that despite the hierarchical and authoritarian elements of the Unionist system which Protestants accepted, and despite the evidence of such as Rose's survey[40] which indicated a high degree of deference to authority in both communities, many Protestants still tend to perceive themselves as 'free men' who neither allow themselves to be 'bossed around' nor to treat others unfairly:

'You know I think one reason why we can't get unity and have all these independent candidates standing is, people think they know their own mind and won't be told what to do . . . this is a traditional Protestant idea . . . sometimes I feel it can be our undoing . . . '
(DUP respondent)

'Discrimination is against our beliefs . . . the Protestant ethic is equal rights for all, special privileges for none.'
(Vanguard respondent)

(This 'catch phrase' about equal rights was repeated by several respondents in discussion and has figured in arguments about discrimination in the loyalist press.)

Self-perceptions like this, if they persist or are deliberately maintained, may work actively to hinder understanding of a political situation or to prevent redefinitions of it. As beliefs about 'individual freedom' may have acted as a barrier to the realisation of lack of freedom in traditional Protestant society, so beliefs about the 'just behaviour' of Protestants may make it harder for them to believe or to examine seriously criticisms made of their society's conduct towards Catholics.

'Admission' Responses

Insofar as there was a pattern to people's responses — and what I describe is by no means universal — denial with 'proofs of integrity' would come first, and commonly counteraccusations about Catholic discrimination would follow. In doing this the respondent implicitly admitted that it did exist, and that he was familiar with it.

Discrimination 'Inevitable'   The kinds of remarks which followed these counteraccusations suggested that in fact there was widespread acceptance among perhaps all sections of Northern Ireland, before reform, that forms of discrimination were somehow inevitable and 'natural,' as were certain corrupt electoral practices. (This does not mean they felt they were 'right.') The responses provide both valuable and interesting information about the expectations about politics that tended to be fostered in the population. In the grim and often tragic circumstances of day-to-day life in Northern Ireland, discussions on this subject could also provide some light relief. In most ways, the province is now a sad and hate-filled place. In a few ways, it is — or was — quite refreshingly corrupt.

The commonest types of counteraccusation are exemplified by these comments, the substance of which at least I have had repeatedly transmitted to me.

'They did it too. In fact, they were worse. We let them work in our factories, but did you ever hear of a Protestant getting a job in the Falls? Or living in the Falls!' (Names of discriminatory employers are given.)

(Unionist respondent)

'What about the nationalist councils? You never hear about Newry do you. Let a Protestant try to get a house in Newry!'

(Unionist respondent)

'The South are the biggest discriminators of all. My relations lived in Monaghan and they couldn't get a job. Also just look at the Protestant population — down from 24 per cent to 4 per cent.'

(DUP respondent)

Accusations were also frequently made about British society:

'They're hypocrites with their race relations problems. And all the politicians do it too you know. Harold Wilson is in the Masons — how do you think he got where he did?'

(UVF respondent)

172

I then asked respondents why people in Northern Ireland seemed to give preference to their own 'side' in this way. Most of them had by now admitted, at least, that there were 'Protestant firms' and 'Catholic firms' well known to be such.

'Well — fear, partly. People liked to be with their own, you just felt more at ease, obviously.'

(Vanguard respondent)

'I guess it was just accepted that people looked after their own.'

(UVF respondent)

'Look, it was just people's way of doing things here till outsiders started interfering. Given time, it would have died out naturally — in fact, it was doing so.'

(Vanguard respondent)

Now why did respondents simply not admit this at the beginning? This extract from a group interview with D.U.P. activists suggests a reason:

'We were all getting along just great before the troubles — all the working-class people. How could we be "discriminating" when we let them live and go shopping in our area? [the Shankill] They used to come to our houses . . . look, we knew we couldn't get a job in (*X*) bakery but we didn't complain, we just accepted it. Then they started complaining about "discrimination!" '

The answer is that many Protestants simply did not look upon certain practices as 'discrimination' at all — for example, in private employment. (Virtually everyone admitted, however, that the gerrymandering of Derry was wrong.) They just accepted them as an inevitable and natural part of life. Thus they had never thought of 'complaining' about Catholic discrimination until Catholics started lamenting Protestant discrimination! (The weight of this they felt would, of course, have been considerably less than that which Catholics felt; there were many more 'Protestant firms.') The responses also give information about expectations regarding 'proper' Catholic-Protestant relations. The precept 'each looks after his own' is not seen as shameful, even if it is regrettable. It is merely natural, given the historic segregation and conflict of Northern Ireland. Also, it is a sad reflection on the province's history that to some respondents, 'discrimination' obviously implied gross oppression or injustice, or activities like the burning of Catholic houses or their eviction from the shipyard. To them the years before 1968, when the Catholics were getting both a better 'deal' than previously and friendly response from Protestants in their daily contact, seemed to hold the highest degree of accord that could be hoped for in a divided community, and perhaps the greatest degree of justice. Hence they were particularly unable to understand why Catholics protested at that time: were they not doing better than anyone had expected or indeed than many of them had deserved?

Why is it that we find a high degree of acceptance of some forms of discrimination as 'inevitable' in Northern Ireland? How was it that a respondent could discuss at length his belief 'as a socialist' that all men should get jobs on merit, and later appeal to me that it was surely natural for people to give jobs to their friends; and was obviously confused and upset when I pointed out the contradiction? It seems likely that many in Northern Ireland were simply not *aware* of the extent to which they unconsciously accepted values. On the one hand, Protestants were given to believe their government, modelled on the British 'democratic ideal' and Protestant egalitarian principles, represented values which would make the practice of discrimination impossible. On the other hand, political realities often diverged sharply from the ideal, so that people developed more than one set of expectations of 'what politics is about.' For fifty years Unionists and Nationalists played the same sterile game: 'cutting up the sectarian cake,' 'looking after your own,' the use of patronage, the great 'numbers' obsession with resultant electoral and local government corruption, including the practice of 'vote early and vote often.' This was the essence of politics to many people who witnessed it. Comments about Britain 'doing the same' do raise embarassing questions about her fitness to appear in Northern Ireland in the role of 'angel,' especially in view of findings about racial discrimination there,[41] but they also demonstrate something else at times. Some people obviously could not believe that other countries did not indulge in many of the practices apparent in Northern Ireland, because they seemed a 'natural' part of politics. (In this they may be more in line with feeling in other countries throughout the world than British people are.)

It was remarked before the 1973 (P.R.) election that many people would be incapable of abandoning their personation activities even if it no longer benefited them to continue: it was just a lifelong habit. I met several activists from all parties who condemned corrupt practices, including personation, at elections and then explained confidentially 'of course it's shocking but if they do it you have to do it too.' Some were experts at personation spotting: 'they never change their earrings or shoes' one remarked. Someone asked me if Britain had 'that kind of thing.' I replied 'not in the same way.' He commented wistfully, 'isn't it rather boring then?' I think he was right.

'Everyone did it'; or, if they didn't, they were liable to lose out. Catholics had first and foremost a practical reason for rejecting and condemning electoral practices and gerrymandering, or discrimination in private employment: their gains were small, and overall they could never 'win.' I am not suggesting here that civil rights leaders were merely making cynical use of arguments about 'British standards' or 'human rights'; but, as an oppressed minority group, they were easily able to call on arguments with widespread emotional appeal outside

Northern Ireland. It just seems naive to assume that most Catholics have 'shaken off' the kinds of expectations about politics my respondents demonstrated here, or were free of them in the first place. To put it at its crudest, Protestants could best secure 'Protestant power' through discrimination and other practices. Catholics could best secure 'Catholic power' through demanding an 'open society.' They had the advantage of being able to present their demands in the name of noble ideals like 'non-sectarianism' and 'equality,' but this does not mean all Catholic politicians have been able to abandon socialised assumptions about politics or that all Catholics are honest in their proclaimed desire for a 'non-sectarian society.' Indeed there is nothing more natural for a people who daily felt themselves oppressed and humiliated, in a province where the image of politics as a game where one side's gain must surely be the other's loss has always been widespread, to wish to 'put the others down' if the controlling power was theirs. This is what many Protestants fear. The difference is that their attitudes on this were recognised and condemned: on the whole, similar Catholic attitudes were neither. It is unrealistic and dishonest, in this situation, for Catholic politicians to describe all Protestant fears or resentments as 'unfair' or the mere product of indoctrination.

We have discussed the view that discrimination was wrong and did not exist; that it was inevitable and did exist. As respondents became more heated and confused under the gimlet eye of a Strathclyde sociologist, a number of them betrayed the fact that they believed discrimination was necessary, or justifiable, or even right, in certain circumstances.

Discrimination 'right'   I have only met one respondent who declared openly that he thought discrimination was 'right.' He went further than this in suggesting that it was built into the British constitution, and that those who wished to abolish it were acting 'unconstitutionally.' To prove his point he read to me the whole of the 1707 Act of Union between Scotland and England, which he appeared to have standing by for emergencies such as this. (The Act barred Catholics from holding certain public offices, and some of these laws remain on the statute book today.) He suggested Protestants had a positive duty to ensure the maintenance and supremacy of the Protestant religion from the encroaches of Catholicism. Where that duty necessitated the practice of discrimination on occasions, he had no objection to make.

It might be thought that enough respectable precedents existed in Protestant and Orange 'theology' to give Protestants the confidence to assert that discrimination against Catholics was almost a duty,[42] yet throughout my time there I have found very few people who were willing to do so, or to use the kind of argument of my respondent above. Yet in countries like South Africa, Rhodesia or Algeria, people have openly made use of pseudo-scientific or biblical arguments to

175

justify their treatment of the native population. Some reasons why Protestants do not like to think of themselves as 'people who discriminate' have already been suggested. Where they feel it is justified or permissible, they tend to redefine the situation in which they act so as to attach the minimum of 'blame' to themselves.

Discrimination 'Justified'   Some people obviously thought, even if they did not express it, that there was really nothing wrong with giving Protestants first choice of jobs, because they believed Catholics did not have the motivation to work well for Northern Ireland anyway. If they made themselves objectionable in employment despite the chances they were given, and lost trust as a result, their decreased opportunities could not fairly be described as 'discrimination,' for 'equal rights means equal responsibilities.' Thus, if they heard Catholic complaints, they were not going to fall over backwards to rectify them. Their attitude might be summarised in these lines from a loyalist song:

'And when their babies learn to talk
They shout "discrimination."
Their dad just lies in bed all day
And lives upon the nation.'[43]

(This was a particularly common view among Protestants in depressed areas of the city. Many of them were also unemployed but they did not complain about it; they 'went and looked for work.' Hence, they felt, if Catholics failed to obtain work, it must be because they did not really want it; yet they always seemed to be blaming Protestants for working at all.)

Another reason why some Protestants were unable to feel actively aggrieved about the 'injustices' stems from a feeling that 'this country is ours anyway' which persists in some circles even though people may feel it is 'unworthy' or feel guilty about it. It is not something they say openly, unless they have reached an extreme state of exasperation. Put crudely, what some Protestants feel is that 'They' have the South and have persistently tried to 'take' the North too, which has only been preserved as a safe place for Protestants and Protestantism through constant struggle. 'They' have caused the southern Protestant population to dwindle to a small percentage, and refuse to respect the democratic wishes of the northern majority for separation. Hemmed into a mere six counties Protestants may be,[44] but in these they are going to run their state in the interests of their own people, and if the minority cannot respect majority wishes, they are quite free to leave it. How Catholics are treated rests on Protestant decision; as they have been treated far better than southern Protestants despite their treasonable behaviour, they have no right to start complaining to the world.

This kind of 'gut feeling' can coexist with other different or even contradictory feelings about 'discrimination' in a section of Protestants.

176

It can be made respectable to themselves by being dressed as an essentially 'democratic' feeling. The association of the word 'democracy' with 'majority rule' has been strongly entrenched in the political culture of Northern Ireland among both loyalists and republicans.[45] When the civil rights movement used arguments about it to mean in fact another aspect of 'democracy' — protection and respect of minorities — they were stressing a facet of the term which was familiar in Britain and the United States, but decidedly unfamiliar in Ireland.

Discrimination 'Necessary'   Despite Lord Brookeborough's famous utterances,[46] the number of people who claimed the employment of Catholics constituted an actual security risk was small, and they tended to work in the shipyard or large factories: 'You can't trust them, I'm not surprised they don't want to employ them. They sabotage the factories, etc., look what they did to the Goliath crane.'[47] (*UDA respondent.*) On the other hand, nothing becomes more quickly obvious to the outsider than the fact that very many Protestants are deeply afraid of being 'taken over' or 'outbred' by Catholics and of being physically oppressed by them, and feel nervous about entrusting them with any kind of power. The most striking characteristic of a community historically dominant, well organised and successful in so many walks of life is its singular *lack* of confidence in its own efficacy and power. In all my conversations on the subject of Irish unity I have only encountered a small minority who do not talk in terms of being 'taken over' or 'absorbed' by the South; they cannot conceive of unity in any other way. This kind of situation makes it likely that even if Protestants feel discrimination is 'wrong,' they will hold back from fighting any unjust measures which prevent the dreaded 'takeover' of Northern Ireland; such as the gerrymandering of electoral boundaries. This is likely to be particularly true of Protestants living in Derry and other border areas. If gerrymandering is a form of 'discrimination,' it becomes a 'necessary' one, even if Protestants cannot openly admit it to be such. The importance for political attitudes of the fact that Protestants form a minority in the whole of Ireland, and perceive themselves first and foremost as such, cannot be overstressed, and is often forgotten.

Why are many Protestants so afraid of a 'takeover?' Why did several respondents see Catholics as fundamentally aggressive people continually plotting to subvert their territory?

'Look at this map of Belfast. I'll show you all the areas they've taken over since the troubles started.'[48]

(Vanguard respondent)

'They are so aggressive, we live and let live but they come into an area slowly at first, then gradually they take all of it.'

(Unionist respondent)

'We opposed mixed housing because what they do is this. First they get enough votes to elect a nationalist councillor, then enough to put out a loyalist if not elect a nationalist MP. Then gradually they will take over all of Northern Ireland.'

(DUP respondent)

Religious ratios in Northern Ireland have always meant that the 'numbers game' has assumed continuous importance for Protestants who fear the consequences of Catholic power. It is unlikely that these fears can be substantially overcome by reassuring words (a favourite activity of Catholic politicians) or even by structural or economic change, or 'education'; because their roots lie only partially in an 'ideology' about Catholics which can be changed. (For example, Wright[47] discusses one image of the Catholic Church as a monolithic and aggrandising force which subverts freedom and destroys independence of mind.) However, what many Protestants fear is simple physical oppression of their group by the other religious group, of being literally 'driven into the sea.' (One respondent, on hearing I came from Scotland, asked anxiously: 'are you ready to take us when [*sic*] we come?') Thus, if 'myths' about the Catholic Church can be changed, it is unlikely that memories of past atrocities by one group on another, carefully handed down through generations, can be easily eradicated. 'Ideology' may have contributed to these events, but what is relevant is that they are historical facts, which themselves increase intergroup hostility. History provides several sound reasons why one community should not trust to the goodwill of the other: the present conflict has provided many more, and an infinite number of bitter memories. In my discussions with people of both religions about childhood recollections I asked what they were told about 'the other side.' Far fewer respondents talked about 'character stereotypes' than about particular historic incidents — the twenties troubles, the burning of relatives' houses or the shooting of friends. Protestants and Catholics were people who fought each other.

The Concept of 'Discrimination'

I suggested at the beginning that though debates about 'discrimination' are often thought to have largely involved the Catholic community, many Protestants have appeared much absorbed with the subject. It is almost as though they had 'absorbed' the onslaught of criticism about discrimination which took place in the early years of the conflict, and become themselves obsessed with it; while Catholics were simultaneously moving away from immediate preoccupation with the issue. A striking feature of much of the Unionist and loyalist literature of recent years has been the frequency with which the word 'discrimination' appears in a wide variety of contexts, where policies of other parties are being criticised. Respondents also attached several different meanings to the word: some, for instance, implied by it violence perpetrated by one side on another, or intimidation, or unfriendly face to face behaviour. One man described the movement of Catholics into a Protestant area as 'discrimination.' How have these situations come about, and why have we now got to the stage where the word 'discrimination' (like 'fascism') has become almost meaningless?

There may be two contributory factors. First, it is likely that many Protestants and probably Catholics too may still not be very clear exactly what 'discrimination' is at all, or hold different sets of notions about it, and may be unsure exactly what the civil rights movement meant by the term. People tend to identify all the civil rights demands, in a sort of 'package,' as complaints about 'discrimination'; but can and should we group together protests about employment ratios, gerrymandering or corrupt electoral practice? We have seen in this paper that some Protestants have different attitudes to different parts of the 'package,' and it seems that closer definitions of 'discrimination' are now called for both in discussion and in academic analyses of the issue.

Secondly, there was one thing which no-one could have doubts about: its negative connotation and consequent emotional appeal. It was a truly 'Bad Word.'[50] So, Protestants not unnaturally felt, if Catholics could gain widespread sympathy by using it perhaps they could too: if Paisley described British refusal to increase Ulster representation at Westminster as 'discrimination,' tying it in with that well-worn Catholic phrase 'second class citizens,' surely anyone of consistent beliefs would sympathise with their position. Those who thought this were probably disappointed, but judging again from literature and politicians' public utterances, many Protestants still appear to believe that shouting 'discrimination' as often as possible will strengthen their position in the eyes of others.

Possible social scientists have not studied with enough interest the way people use of manipulate language and concepts for their own defence, often with great skill. Some loyalists have become adept at taking over the arguments of their opponents and 'throwing them back in their faces,' and their adversaries have been slower to counter this. Witness one respondent, protesting at 'imposed' British appointments in government or public service:

> 'You can't have built-in sectarian appointment in government and the rest. It's wrong that you should get a job on the basis of religion . . . it shouldn't matter what religion you are.'

His opponents might feel they were in fact less 'sectarian' than he was; but they would have to admit: they had it coming to them.

Party Differences

I have said little throughout about differences in attitude towards 'discrimination' among members of different parties, being more concerned with discussing complexities and ambiguities in the thinking of many Protestants to whom I talked; and what these might tell us of the nature of society and politics in Northern Ireland. Some false impressions may be gained without at least a few observations about such differences. It would be broadly true to say that most people supporting parties to the 'loyalist' side of those now known as Faulkner Unionists have at best ambiguous feelings towards the civil rights movement and its demands, and show some of the often contradictory responses explored here. Most of the quotations are drawn from people on this part of the spectrum. It should hardly need to be said, however, that many Protestants openly admit to the justice of the civil rights demands and the necessity for reform; far fewer, probably, than did so in 1969, before the anti-partitionist campaign with its embittering consequences disillusioned many people causing them to redefine the situation past and present.

General differences in emphasis exist among 'loyalist' parties as well as 'moderate.' Vanguard are the keenest proponents of 'reds under the bed' communist conspiracy theories (their term for the IRA — the 'Provoffs' — is illuminating) which may reflect their middle-class and petit bourgeois supporters' fears of the working classes in general. As hinted earlier, Unionists of all shades tend to feel particularly threatened at a party and personal level by the accusations, and this may cause them to take a more intransigent position than they would otherwise; besides, some of them have lost power and prestigious positions as a result of the political developments. The Democratic Unionists are shackled by no such considerations, for Paisley like his predecessors in the tradition of independent Unionism has never spared the Unionist Party criticism. This party has tended to attract two distinct types of support: first, members of Paisley's church and his close personal followers, drawn substantially from rural areas (especially Antrim) holding strongly to fundamentalist religious ideas and in their social conservatism probably not much different from right wing Unionists and Vanguard members; secondly, working-class people from Belfast whose attitudes on social questions do not differ substantially from NILP members, and who were disillusioned with the elitism, undemocratic structure and upper-class interests of the Unionist Party. For these people, and for members of other working-class political or paramilitary groups, increasing disillusionment with their traditional representatives has brought about some changes in attitude to the civil rights campaign and a feeling that social reform is needed for both sections of the working class.[51] But as I have pointed out, they will not yet admit that discrimination worked disproportionately against the Catholic population.

180

The Northern Ireland Labour Party made representations to the British government about discrimination several years before the start of the conflict, and the lack of notice taken by the Labour government has left a residue of bitterness among members still very noticeable today. Why then did the majority of their activists I interviewed seem uncomfortable talking about 'discrimination' and frequently try to play down the extent of its existence? The reason may be traced to the party's own serious problems in winning support. To be successful, it needed a large Protestant vote: much of its time was spent trying desperately to convince Protestant workers that it was sound on the Border issue, without a great deal of success.[52] It faced the problem which confronts and often wrecks all socialist groups seeking joint Protestant-Catholic support: do we sit on the fence or maintain discreet silence on contentious issues; or do we take a stand traditionally associated with one community? On the constitution its stand made sense, in that far more Catholics would vote for a pro-Union party than Protestants for a nationalist one. On discrimination, the risks involved in suggesting it was disproportionately anti-Catholic appeared too great, and their pamphlets called discreetly for 'British standards' for 'all citizens.'[53] The civil rights movement made them feel both embarassed and resentful; the first, because it said what they had not, the second because a motley bunch of liberals, republicans and others, some of whose motives might be disputed, received all the credit for making points they too had made long ago, when no-one had listened. Talking about discrimination is embarassing, because it brings back memories of prevarication and raises questions about both the accuracy of their judgement and the morality of their position. Nevertheless, it is the easiest thing in the world to condemn people in this kind of dilemma: NILP baiting is a favourite pastime in Northern Ireland, especially in left wing intellectual circles. Intellectuals are not always so good at suggesting feasible alternatives, though they are good at opting out or emigrating in times of difficulty.

The Alliance Party, which draws large support from former O'Neill supporters, is quite open about the existence of discrimination, and with its predecessors has an honourable record in pressing for reform. Many members are people who took no interest in politics — or at least in reform — till recent years, and it is likely that some of these feel guilty about their former complacency, or even complicity in the old system. Thus some of my respondents would spend much of the interview stressing their sterling efforts to liberalise the local Unionist Party and so on. But I think that Alliance has effectively reduced the number of painful questions its members need to ask themselves by virtue of the ideology it has developed — one which makes perfectly good sense considering the kind of support it seeks to attract. Its line has been that both communities are to blame for the present situation through their traditional pursuit of 'sectarian politics.'[54] Thus, people on either 'side' who may feel guilty can spread the load on to the other! Also, it is unashamedly the 'never too late' party — no tardy conversions scorned. The situation is far too desperate for any time to be spent in recriminations, and the slate is wiped clean. This allows members to surge onwards into a new era knowing that, if they are guilty, 'so are we all.' But there is a price to be paid for joining a party of this kind, which the educated middle class who form a large part of its membership may find easier to pay than other groups. The price demanded is that one forgets the past rather than tries to understand it, and denigrates as 'tribal' many of the heroic values symbolised by such as '1690' and '1916' which so many Ulster people have been brought up to revere. Many Alliance and NILP members show they have broken out of traditional ways of thinking; that they have competence and imagination and genuinely desire a system with high standards of justice and tolerance for everyone. Yet so often they seem so afraid of the dangers of 'emotionalism' that they appear to other Ulstermen to lack gut feelings or emotions or local pride; or at least seem afraid to show them. In a province which already mourned over 800 dead it was inappropriate to model the 1973 Alliance election leaflet on a supermarket 'special offer' coupon. O'Neill was very anxious that his people should be pleasant to each other and that Ulster should look respectable to the world outside; but, aside from any other failings, 'he didn't even talk like an Ulsterman.'[55]

People on the 'outside' often tend to assume that if all Ulster people thought like the 'moderates,' problems of prejudice and discrimination would disappear. This is very much open to dispute, but the situation will not arise in any case because most Ulstermen do not think like them, nor do they vote for them. In Northern Ireland the political values which encouraged bigotry and discrimination have also been the cause of great selflessness and heroism. In the kind of political culture Ulster has, where so much value is placed on emotive symbols and heroic principles, it is unlikely that many people will be persuaded to change their behaviour through admonitions that they are children — in the grip of 'tribalism,' 'myths' or 'shibboleths,' or in danger of rejection by Britain through bad behaviour. (A patronising approach, in any case.) A group which manages to harness some of these 'heroic' values to the cause of change or reconciliation, and to accept that not all 'extreme' beliefs or traditional manifestations of culture (which seem to embarass many liberals[56]) necessarily impede these goals is more likely to win support for its policies from those sections which show the greatest communal hostility.[57]

APPENDIX

Abbreviations Used

DUP   Democratic Unionist Party
CRA   Civil Rights Association
IRA   Irish Republican Army
NILP   Northern Ireland Labour Party
PD   People's Democracy
UDA   Ulster Defence Association
UVF   Ulster Volunteer Force (proscribed 1966, de-proscribed 1974)
VUPP   Vanguard Unionist Progressive Party

NOTES

1.   The literature on these points is substantial: but see e.g. Campaign for Social Justice, *The Plain Truth*, 1969; Fermanagh C.R.A., *Fermanagh Facts*, 1969; Aidan Corrigan, *Eye Witness in Northern Ireland*, Voice of Ulster Publications, 1969.
2.   Cameron Commission, *Disturbances in N. Ireland*, Belfast, HMSO, Cmd. 532, 1969.
3.   Richard Rose, *Governing Without Consensus, an Irish Perspective*, Faber 1971, p. 497, Question 43.
4.   See e.g. Robert Moore, 'Race Relations in the Six Counties,' *Race*, XIV, 1972, pp. 21-42. Michael Farrell reflected the feelings of many nationalist and left-wing observers of Northern Irish politics in his view that 'Religious hysteria and Protestant "fears" in the North were quite deliberately whipped up . . . the ruling class . . . cannot wish away the Protestant supremacist ideology they've spent so long inculcating' (Northern Star, issue 5).
5.   Social workers in Ballymurphy used to tell me of the numerous research students, psychologists, etc. who flocked there during 1970-1. The bias towards Catholics was partly the fault of loyalists themselves, however, who until 1972-3 were suspicious and uncooperative towards pressmen and researchers. Max Hastings, *Ulster 1969*, London, Gollancz, 1970.
6.   See the Farrell quote above. In similar vein Anthony Coughlan writes: 'Partition is the basis of Ulster Unionism whose raison d'être is Unionist ascendancy and the privileges that have gone with that.' Cf. Liam de Paor, *Divided Ulster*, Penguin, 1970; Rosite Sweetman, *On Our Knees*, Pan, 1972. There has been some debate among people of this viewpoint about the Protestant working class: are they misguided dupes, or an integral part of the 'ascendancy' which must be overthrown before socialism can flourish?
7.   Moore, *op. cit.*
8.   Again, the literature is substantial. But cf. articles by Zubaida, Banton and Rex in Zubaida (ed.), *Race and Racialism*, Tavistock, 1970; Ciba Foundation, *Caste and Race*, Churchill, 1967; P.S. Cohen, 'Need there be sociology of race relations?', *Sociology*, VI, 1972, pp. 101-8: theoretical papers in the journal *Race* including H. Dickie Clarke, 'Some issues in the sociology of race relations, *Race*, XV, Oct. 1973.
9. Cf. Ciba Foundation, *op. cit.*, especially Chapters 1, 2, 3, 6; Andre Beteille

Caste Class and Power, University of California, 1965; C.C. Cox, *Caste Class and Race*, Doubleday, 1948. See also Patrick McNabb, 'A people under pressure,' *Lancaster Conference in Northern Ireland, 1971*, mimeo ('Catholics are not simply a minority of a particular religious persuasion; they are a conquered and colonised people. The conquest was made concrete and continually stressed in the establishment of a rigid caste system').

10.　'We shall speak of race relations structure or problem, insofar as the inequalities and differentiation inherent in a social structure are related to phsyical and cultural criteria of an ascriptive kind and are rationalised in terms of deterministic belief systems' (Zubaida [ed.], *op. cit.*, p. 39). Moore cites two other criteria that Rex has drawn up elsewhere: the existence of two or more identifiable groups, and a high degree of conflict.

11.　Yet Moore himself seems uncertain about this throughout, often drawing on Marxist or pseudo-Marxist analyses of historical events in the North.

12.　Cf. Michael Banton, 'The Concept of Racism' in Zubaida (ed.), *op. cit.*, pp. 17-33, and Rex's criticism of his approach, p. 38.

13.　Cf. Frank Wright, 'Protestant Ideology and Politics in Ulster,' *European Journal of Sociology*, vol. XIV, 1973, pp. 213-80. He also challenges some conventional views, suggesting that 'extreme' Protestant ideology has sometimes functioned to regulate conflict and facilitate cooperation; and that the greatest hostility to Catholics is not necessarily found among Protestants most threatened by economic competition.

14.　Republicans often appear inconsistent on this point. The nature and the destiny of the 'one Irish nation' plays a central role in both left and right wing republican ideology. The 'socialism' of the Communist Party of Ireland has been criticised by the Offical Republican movement for underplaying the importance of Irish nationalist articles of faith. On the other hand they rarely acknowledge the legitimacy of Protestant feelings of British identity, which are seen either as fundamentally 'mistaken' or as a cloak for more material motives.

15.　Cf. David Boulton, *The UVF 1966-73*, Torc Books, 1973: the writings of Andrew Boyd; Rosita Sweetman, *op. cit*,; Liam de Paor, *op. cit.*, underplays this issue, a fact which cannot obscure the general merit of this book.

16.　In recent years the British and Irish Communist Organisation has seriously challenged republican one-nation theory and nationalist interpretations of Irish history through the argument that two nations developed historically in Ireland, due to the uneven development of capitalism. Cf. *The Two Irish Nations*, 1971; *The Home Rule Crisis*, 1972. all published by B. & I.C.O., 10 Athol Street, Belfast.

17.　Cf. paper by Schutz and Scott (pp. 26-54) in this issue.

18.　'Discrimination' is a concept readily identified with 'race relations' situations. The tremendous publicity over 'discrimination' in Northern Ireland is likely to have encouraged hasty conclusions about the character of the conflict as a result, when detailed research was what was needed.

19.　Cf. Frank Wright, *op. cit.*, and the excellent and undervalued work by Rosemary Harris, *Prejudice and Tolerance in Ulster*, Manchester University Press, 1972.

20.　See, for example, Robert E. Lane and Donald O. Sears, *Public Opinion*, Prentice Hall, Englewood Cliffs, 1964, and Philip Converse, 'The Nature of Belief Systems of Mass Publics,' in David Apter (ed.), *Ideology and Discontent*, Free Press, Glencoe, Ill., 1964.

21.　In talking to many British people about Ulster one notices a considerable 'time lag' effect. Until recently, and despite the Provisional campaign, one noticed little sympathy for Protestants and a tendency to see the situation in simplistic 'civil rights' terms. Now, more and more British people seem to be saying 'a plague on both your houses,' which is of little assistance to either faction.

22.   Generally speaking, the reverse of the position taken by American Negroes and most immigrants to Britain: they sought acceptance, and were refused it. It was only *after* the perceived failure of 'constitutional' civil rights campaigns that groups like Black Power began large-scale advocacy of alternatives to participation in 'white' institutions.

23.   Cf. People's Democracy Newspaper *Unfree Citizen* and their post-internment literature in general. However, possible the majority of its original members have now left the movement. Cf. Paul Arthur, *The Peoples Democracy*, Blackstaff, 1974; J. Comerford, 'The Dynamics of a radical movement in Northern Ireland politics: the P.D.,' unpublished Strathclyde University thesis, Sept., 1972.

24.   Apart from the B. & I.C.O. (*op. cit.*) who have become more and more uncritically pro-Protestant in recent months.

25.   The function both of politicians and localised newspapers, which have proliferated in Ulster since 1969, in providing and disseminating these 'community myths' deserves serious study.

26.   Frank Wright, *op. cit.*; D.P. Barritt and C.F. Carter, *The N. Ireland Problem*, Oxford University Press, 1962; D.P. Barritt and A. Booth, *Orange and Green*, Northern Friends Peace Board, 1972.

27.   Cf. Tim Pat Coogan, *The IRA*, Fontana, 1970; J. Bowyer Bell, *The Secret Army*, Sphere, 1970; D. Williams (ed.), *The Irish Struggle 1916-26*, Routledge & Kegan Paul, 1966.

28.   Experience strengthened this view in those who sought evidence; a UVF leader recounted how a UVF group had gone to an early civil rights meeting in Derry. 'All the offices were filled, there was a tricolour in one corner and a starry plough in the other — why no Union Jack?' Civil rights leaders did make conscious efforts to restrain their supporters' enthusiasms though. Professor Rose tells of asking Mike Farrell why Irish marchers were singing American songs, and was told that at least this prevented them singing republican ones.

29.   Kitchen House: the cramped two-up two-down house standard in working-class areas of Belfast.

30.   But complaints about cleanliness and 'disease' played an important part in British respondents' rejection of coloured immigrants. Cf. E.J.B. Rose *et al.*, *Colour and Citizenship*, Oxford University Press, 1969, Part VII, especially Tables 28. 9-12.

31.   In black-white situations, a traditional belief about 'natives' among 'settlers.' The view of coloured immigrants in Britain as a 'workshy' people (cf. Rose, *op. cit.*; W.W. Daniel, *Racial Discrimination in England*, Penguin, 1968) may demonstrate the lingering influence of colonialist mythology. In this context cf L.P. Curtis, *Anglo Saxons & Celts*, Bridgeport University Press, 1968.

32.   Frank Wright, *op. cit.*, especially pp. 223-32.

33.   Richard Rose, *op. cit.* Questions 18d & 18e.

34.   See the NOP poll of April 1974 for BBC Ulster (especially An. 4A) and various polls on the subject commissioned by the *Belfast Telegraph*.

35.   People often found difficulty in believing atrocities attributed to Protestants were not 'really' the work of the IRA. Where the evidence was indisputable, they rationalised the violence by talking of the extreme provocation suffered for years by incredibly patient and law-abiding Protestants. One reason why most Protestants feel more dilemmas about firing on British troops than they did in 1912-14 — a period remembered with pride rather than shame on the whole — may be that then, prominent elements in British society supported their stand and legitimised it in moral terms. In Ulster too, as one Unionist explained, 'all the *best* people in society were in the gunrunning, my grandfather took part, not like today with these criminal elements in the UDA, etc. running about.' The 'best people,' of course, stood for noble ideals, 'law abidingness' and constitutionalism, and were understood to act for the greater good of all these things.

36.   Frank Wright, *op. cit.*, especially pp. 214-6: Rosemary Harris, *op. cit.*

37.   David Boulton, *op. cit.*
38.   Quoted from the *Protestant Telegraph* by Wright, p. 224.
39.   Not a contradiction, as anyone familiar with Ulster politics will know, and the subject of numerous anecdotes. Cf. 'Wanted, reliable cook general, Protestant (Christian preferred)' cited in Barritt and Booth, *op. cit.* Some Ulster people will describe themselves as 'Protestant' or 'Catholic' atheists; church attendance on the militant Shankill has been estimated to be as low as 15-20 per cent. The religious 'label' subsumes a variety of political, social, religious, cultural and nationalistic beliefs.
40.   Richard Rose, *op. cit.*, Questions 6a-6a, 59a-59c.
41.   Cf. W.W. Daniel, *op. cit.*
42.   Cf. Wright, *op. cit.*
43.   *Orange Cross Book of Songs and Verse*, 2nd ed. Obtainable from Orange Cross, 10 Upper Charleville St, Belfast 13. Contains more interesting material on attitudes to 'Ulster' and to 'civil rights.'
44.   In view of the popular nationalist view that Unionists skilfully calculated how many northern counties they could hold and sacrificed their southern brethren, it is interesting that several respondents remarked to me angrily: 'They even took three counties *away from us*.'
45.   The principal argument used by nationalists against Partition has been that it thwarted 'the democratic wishes of the majority.' Cf. the utterances of the Nationalist Party as reported in the Northern Ireland Hansard; a good example of the thinking of Southern politicians can be found in *Irish Unity. Northern Ireland. Anglo-Irish Relations*, Irish government publicity bureau, 1971, Protestants continue to echo the kind of protest made by this Unionist pamphleteer in 1886, a protest which Catholics might well have made in another context: 'Are the minority bound to submit to the will of the majority? A good friend of mine tells me of the kindness and forbearance with which we should be treated . . . we don't want to depend on anyone's forbearance, like Daniel in the lion's den.' (Northern Ireland Public Records Office, 64 Balmoral Avenue, section 989C.)
46.   'Many in my audience employ Catholics, but I have not one about my place. Catholics are out to destroy Ulster with all their might and power' (1933). 'I recommend those people who are loyalists not to employ Roman Catholics, 99 per cent of whom are disloyal.' (1934) Quoted in Martin Wallace, *Northern Ireland, 50 years of self-government*, David & Charles, 1971.
47.   The immense crane dominating the Harland and Wolff shipyard, and the object of several sabotage attempts in recent years.
48.   Cf. Community Relations Commission Research Unit, *Flight, a Report on Population movement in Belfast during August 1971*. This shows how Catholics tended to crowd into inner city areas while Protestants evacuated to the suburbs. Hence the latter tended to interpret Catholic movement as 'proof' that they were 'taking over' the city.
49.   Frank Wright, *op. cit.*
50.   In its dictionary definition, it has neither a negative nor a positive connotation; it merely means to 'differentiate' or 'distinguish.' Several respondents tried to engage me in arguments about semantics.
51.   As the rich members contributed both finance, and cars for elections, working-class demands rended to play but a small part in D.U.P. policy statements. It is likely that the party's working-class support in Belfast will drift into the UVF's new political party should this survive and achieve successes.
52.   NILP reached its peak of parliamentary representation in 1958, when four members were returned to Stormont. One of these told me: 'I reckon it took from '49 to '58 to convince working-class Prods we were sound on the Border. They knew the Unionists were Tories but they'd say to me, "I agree with your views, but the devil you know . . ." etc.'
53.   Cf. *Ulster Labour in the Sixties*, NILP, 1962; election literature, 1969

(published by Sigma Services Belfast) Paddy Devlin's face beams from his election address above the alogans: 'Full British Rights – full British standards.'

54.   Alliance Party of Northern Ireland, 6 Cromwell Rd, Belfast 7. Cf. *Statement of Principles; Alliance Solution for Northern Ireland*, March 1972; many other policy documents are available. The Alliance concept of 'tribalism' is discussed in the article by Anthony Cowdy, 'The Alliance Party' in *Crossbow*, Jan-Mar. 1971.

55.   I have rarely heard a good word spoken of O'Neill from anyone other than his personal followers: his aloofness and inability to communicate caused much resentment, especially among his associates. One Unionist MP told me: 'All this opposition within the party, it wasn't just the idea of "civil rights." They were just delighted to seize an issue that would bring him down.' Peter Gibbon, in 'The dialectics of religion and class in Ulster,' *New Left Review*, 55, 1969, lucidly analyses the structural tensions in Northern Ireland society so as to suggest that conflict over reforms was inevitable. (The paper is also worth reading for its discussion of the fifty-year Unionist/Nationalist 'game.') The volume of adverse comment on O'Neill from political activists in Northern Ireland does raise this question, however: Had the personality and the tactics of the reformer been different, could the reform measures have been passed without all the consequences that followed?

56.   One prominent member of Alliance had an exactly equal number of 'Orange' and 'Green' gramophone records; but at least he allowed them in his house. The 'loyalist' wife of another member I interviewed slipped into the room when he went out and nervously but proudly played me a sentimental 'Orange' record. His reaction on returning proved that her nervousness was justified.

57.   An NILP activist remarked recently to a UVF leader: 'If I said what you said to your people I'd be called a Fenian-lover, but you can get away with it.' Another UVF leader of some perceptiveness told me how he had addressed the crowds at the Ulster Workers Council strike 'victory' march on the evils of sectarianism. I asked him if this was well received. He laughed and replied 'It didn't matter, they just took one look at my uniform and roared.' Neither the UVF nor a group like Sinn Fein may be equipped at present to break down the divisive or 'mythological' elements in the ideologies of many Ulster people; for they themselves share some of these. Nevertheless, people from this background, who can most fully understand the 'world views' of their supporters, their inspiring as well as their corrupting elements and the factors giving rise to them and who are not afraid to appeal to emotion in the effort to make conciliatory policies acceptable, may ultimately be those who can achieve what the 'moderates' have failed to do.

I should like to thank Professor Richard Rose, Dr J.R.S. Wilson, Professor J.P. Cornford and Mr Frank Wright for their observations and comment on the draft and final stages of this paper.

7. NOT QUITE BRITISH: THE POLITICAL ATTITUDES OF ANGLO-JEWRY

Geoffrey Alderman

It is a curious and noteworthy reflection on Jewish idiosyncracies that most research which has been carried out into the structure and characteristics of the Jewish community in Great Britain has been carried out by Jews, and that very little of what they have written concerns itself with the political aspirations of the community. Jewish historians have, of course, investigated the battle for Jewish emancipation in the nineteenth century.[1] In recent years, too, there has been much interest in the immigration controversy before 1914, not least because of the striking similarity of views between those who opposed Jewish immigration then, and those who oppose coloured immigration now.[2] But these avenues of research are, after all, concerned with the dim and distant past, and with a framework of party politics which has long since disappeared. Since the Great War, the Anglo-Jewish community *per se* has not been the subject of party political controversy, and the distinct political attitudes of that community appear to have been studiously avoided by those who have written about British Jews. Dr Lipman's *Social History of the Jews in England 1850-1950* contains some information on the spread of socialism among Jewish immigrants at the end of the nineteenth century, but nothing at all on twentieth-century trends.[3] *A Minority in Britain*, edited by Maurice Freedman in 1955, dealt with almost every aspect of Jewish life except politics.[4] Even Chaim Bermant's witty and penetrating examination of Anglo-Jewry in the 1960s made no attempt to deal with Jewish involvement in politics.[5] It is almost as if the subject were taboo.

And so in a sense it always has been. The ambition of those who led the small Jewish community (about 50,000 strong) in Britain a century ago, having been relieved of discriminatory legislation and being politically emancipated, was to be allowed to merge, chameleon-like, into their British background, to be accepted as Jewish by religion but British by nature. This was especially true of the political arena. It was well known that only a few very rich Jews could contemplate a life in politics. Perhaps for this reason the mass of Anglo-Jewry had displayed a surprising indifference during the emancipation struggle.[6] Yet there were other political rights which Jews had not been slow to exercise. Pre-eminent among these was the right to vote. An Act of 1835 had relieved Jewish voters from the necessity of taking a Christian form of oath at parliamentary elections. In fact, returning officers had seldom exercised the power to demand such an oath.[7] At the Liverpool election of January 1835, for instance, Asher Ansell (who voted Liberal) had no hesitation in describing himself as a 'Jewish rabbi'; the same gentleman had, however, voted in the December 1832 election, though on that occasion he had prudently given his profession as 'reader.'[8] For this Jewish minister of religion, being able to vote at all was more important than being able to vote as a Jew — though the ability to do so was doubtless welcomed. Similarly, the epic struggle of Baron Lionel de Rothschild to gain admission to the House of Commons as MP for the City of London, culminating in the passing of the Emancipation Act in 1858, was not in any sense a movement to obtain special representation of the Jewish community in the legislature, even though this was an obvious by-product. Rather it was simply a movement to establish the right of individual Jews to sit in Parliament on terms of absolute equality with non-Jews.[9] That having been achieved, the assumption was that Jewish citizens would henceforth be able to play a full part in the life of the country: with distinction, certainly, but not in any sense distinctive.

This is the hope that has been cherished by the leaders of Anglo-Jewry throughout the turbulent and often harrowing experiences through which the community has passed over the last hundred years. The *Jewish Chronicle*, for instance, which, with a circulation now in the region of 70,000 in a community of around 400,000-450,000 often accurately reflects the accepted views of the Jewish 'establishment,' loses no time in telling its readers with pride how many Jewish MPs have been elected to Parliament.[10] It has never, however, sought to promote a specifically Jewish vote, and indeed has on occasion deprecated attempts by others to do so. 'The whole idea of Jewish political emancipation was based on equality between Jews and other citizens,' a *Chronicle* correspondent wrote in 1951; 'to establish a Jewish vote would mean to reverse that principle, to the service of which the first generation of Jewish MPs devoted all their talents.'[11] In like manner the Board of Deputies of British Jews, founded in 1760, the representative body of the Anglo-Jewish community, has always discouraged talk of a Jewish vote. The corollary to this attitude is that the political opinions of British Jews are in substance no different from those of the gentile majority, that for that reason alone they are not worth investigating, and that (according to opinions expressed by prominent Jews to the present author) even if an academic investigation of the validity of this theory were to be undertaken, it would nonetheless be imprudent, even dangerous. The vision is still of an Anglo-Jewish community totally integrated with the existing political structure. But the vision remains stubbornly unfulfilled.

In the beginning most Jews were Liberal. The Tory party was, after all, the party of the Established Church; the High Tory majority in the House of Lords had acted as a barrier to the advancement of Jewish emancipation for more than a decade; and some of the arguments put forward against the Jews, both in and out of Parliament, reflected the traditional Tory view that Church and State were part of an inseparable entity, in the promotion of which Jews ought to play no part.[12] Liberals and Whigs opposed these views from a variety of motives, most of them sincere though some of them frankly opportunist. In 1847, for instance, Liberal candidates were asked to publicise their support of the admission of Jews to Parliament as a way of obtaining Jewish votes.[13] So it was natural that the first professing Jews to enter Parliament should have done so on a Liberal ticket. Jewish Tories there certainly were; Sir Moses Montefiore (1784-1885), doyen of the nineteenth-century Anglo-Jewish community, counted himself among them. But the first Jewish Conservative MP, the coalmine-owner Saul Isaac, did not enter Parliament until 1874. What broke the Liberal hold on Jewish political opinions had little to do with the Jews. Those who led the Jewish community in the late Victorian period were financiers, merchants and industrialists. They shared the fears of their much more numerous gentile counterparts that the Liberal Party was moving too far towards the radical camp; so they turned for comfort to the Conservatives. Sir Julian Goldsmid and Baron Ferdinand de Rothschild deserted Gladstone and became Liberal Unionists. More significant, however, was the career of Lionel Louis Cohen, a founder of the Jewish Board of Guardians and of the United Synagogue, who was also a Vice-President of the National Union of Conservative Associations, and Conservative MP for Paddington North, 1885-7. Attacked in 1885 by the Jewish publicist Lucien Wolf for daring to stand on a non-Liberal platform, Cohen retorted that it was in the interests of the Anglo-Jewry that they should be seen to support more than one party.[14] In 1880, seven of the ten Jewish parliamentary candidates were Liberals and four Jewish Liberal MPs were elected, as against one Conservative. In 1900 twenty of the twenty-two Jewish candidates were Unionists, of whom seven were elected as against two Liberals.

Whether this swing to the right in the Anglo-Jewish establishment was mirrored by a similar swing among the Jewish electorate is, however, much less certain. The absence of pollbooks, of course, and of opinion surveys, makes any theory difficult to test. But if the career of Lionel Cohen reflects the change in attitude of the Jewish establishment, the political campaigns of Sir Samuel Montagu (Lord Swaythling), banker, philanthropist and Liberal MP for Whitechapel, 1885-1900, surely attest to the endurance of Liberal loyalties amongst a sizeable section of the working-class Jewish community of London. And the strong probability is that the mass of Jewish voters remained Liberal whilst the leadership became, in general, Conservative. At all events, Jewish political inclinations were less unevenly divided between the major parties in 1900 than they had been in 1850. To that extent the community looked as if it had achieved some sort of political assimilation.

All this was to be changed by the great wave of pogroms which spread across Russia and eastern Europe after 1881. Persecuted Jews searched desperately for places of refuge. Most of those who could emigrate went to America. But between 1880 and 1914 alone, 150,000 of them settled in the British Isles.[15] The political repercussions which this mass migration had upon Anglo-Jewry were momentous. The immigrants posed a grave and most unwelcome problem for the Jewish leadership. They were the means by which an entirely new political philosophy made its way into Anglo-Jewish thinking. More unsettling still, their condition was symptomatic of the basic insecurity of world Jewry in an age of nationalism; the answer — Jewish nationalism — made and continues to make deep inroads into the conventional pattern of British party politics as Jews in this country perceive it.

This is not the place to examine the phenomenon of Jewish immigration into Britain at the end of the last century, or the reaction to it of the gentile community, except to point out that that reaction was far from favourable. The so-called problem of aliens from eastern Europe became a political football. Successive Trade Union Congresses in the early 1890s passed resolutions calling for restrictive measures.[16] 'Rich-Jew anti-semitism,' encouraged by the outbreak of the Boer War, and preached by some British socialists, added fuel to the fire.[17] In 1900 Major William Evans-Gordon, newly elected Unionist MP for Stepney, formed the British Brothers League to press the case for restriction.[18] The League was run by Unionist MPs, and it was not long before the Unionist government responded to it by appointing a Royal Commission on Alien Immigration (1903) and by passing an Aliens Immigration Act two years later. On that occasion A.J. Balfour, the Prime Minister, spoke in Parliament of the need to protect British civilisation from having in its midst 'an immense body of persons who . . . by their own action, remained a people apart.'[19] The Liberal Party seized upon the semi-offical anti-semitism of the Unionist government as a potential vote-winner. In the general election of 1906 Liberal candidates pressed the message home to their Jewish voters.[20] The Liberal administrations in and after 1906 administered the Immigration Act as humanely as possible. But they did not repeal what was, in fact, a popular measure.[21] Anti-semitism remained deep-rooted, able to surface again (as in South Wales in 1911) whenever the country was faced with hard times.[22]

All these developments, stretching over a period of twenty-five years, dismayed and terrified the Anglo-Jewish leadership. They were naturally worried about the effects which the influx of thousands of Jewish pauper refugees was having upon the standing and safety of the community already here. Beyond that, however, it is possible to detect snobbery pure and simple. The refugees were stark reminders of the humble origins of the Jewish establishment, and for that reason alone they were not welcome. The Jewish Board of Guardians advertised in the Jewish press in Russia and Roumania that Jews who sought to escape persecution by coming to Britain would face many hardships, and would not obtain relief from the Board during the first six months of residence — when they needed it most. Those refugees who did reach Britain were encouraged to continue their journey to America or South Africa, and some were persuaded to return whence they had come.[23] Sir Benjamin Cohen (Lionel Louis' brother), President of the Board of Guardians 1887-1900 and Conservative MP for East Islington 1892-1906, actually voted for the Aliens Immigration Act; in so doing he was merely giving practical expression to the feelings of many of the leading Anglo-Jewish families.

The liking of the refugees for the leadership was also open to doubt. They showed little enthusiasm for the established institutions of the Anglo-Jewry. They shunned the cathedral-like structures in which Anglo-Jewry was accustomed to worship, and set up instead their own small, noisy, informal synagogues by the dozen in London's East End and in the provinces. Those who were religious, moreover, had little regard for Chief Rabbi Hermann Adler, whose orthodoxy they doubted.[24] Those who were not religious or who, at any rate, did not see in religious devotion a universal panacea, saw little merit in adherence to the Liberal or Conservative parties. They brought with them from eastern Europe a buoyant socialist tradition, set up Jewish trade unions, and generally showed acute impatience 'with the slow methods of English trade unionism.'[25] If, in the short run, this led to further friction between working-class Jews and the British trade union movement, in the longer term, when the Labour Party espoused socialism in 1918, it helped pave the way for the entry of thousands of Jewish voters into the Labour camp. In the general election of 1918 three Jews stood, unsuccessfully, as Labour Party candidates.

The spread of socialism amongst the mass of poor Jews in Britain was bound to intensify the suspicion and animosity with which the newcomers viewed their older-established middle-class brethren. But the rift was widened beyond repair by the growth of the Zionist movement. Theodor Herzl had hoped to find support for his movement from among the Anglo-Jewish leaders whom he visited in the 1890s, but he was sadly disappointed. Samuel Montagu gave him a warm reception, to be sure. 'He confessed to me,' Herzl wrote in his diary, ' — in confidence — that he felt himself to be more an Israelite than an Englishman.'[26] Montagu, however, was very much the exception to the rule. Most of the leadership regarded being Jewish simply as a religious connotation. The possibility of Jewish *nationhood* was not merely foreign to their ears; it struck at the heart of the process of political, social and cultural assimilation of which they were so proud. Without a Jewish State they were well bred British Jews. With it, they automatically became exiles in the land of their birth, and their loyalty to Great Britain could be questioned. The recently arrived immigrants from eastern Europe were already exiles. Zionism offered a permanent solution to their problems of persecution and wandering, and they gave it their support.

To Herzl the plight of European Jewry was a severely practical one, and he did not care particularly whether the Jewish State was set up in Palestine, El Arish, Cyprus or East Africa. With his death, in 1904, leadership of the movement passed to younger men, like Chaim Weizmann, for whom a Jewish State elsewhere than in Palestine was unthinkable. 'Return to the Promised Land' was a concept with which the Jewish masses of London, Leeds, Glasgow and Manchester could easily identify. Hermann Adler, addressing the Anglo-Jewish Association in July 1897, had condemned the forthcoming First Zionist Congress (to be held in Basle) as 'an egregious blunder,' and had denounced the idea of a Jewish State as 'contrary to Jewish principles.'[27] Aba Werner, the extremely orthodox and much respected Rabbi of the *Machzike Hadass* (Upholders of the Religion) synagogue in London's East End, was a fervent Zionist, who actually attended the Second Zionist Congress in Basle in 1898, and the Eighth at the Hague in 1907.[28] The Rabbi of the same synagogue from 1916 to 1919 was Abraham Isaac Kook, later to become Chief Rabbi of the Holy Land during the Mandate period. Religious leaders of this calibre commanded instant loyalty from orthodox Jews recently arrived in Britain from eastern Europe, and among these people, therefore, Zionism was bound to find a large following. Zionist views filtered through to the universities, and fired the imaginations of the children of immigrants. In time, therefore, Zionism became a more middle class movement.[24]

The more assimilated Jews and the older-established Jewish families did not give up without a struggle. Edwin Montagu, second son of Samuel Montagu, became Secretary of State for India in July 1917, and tried as best he could to sabotage the proposed Balfour Declaration. 'All my life,' he told Lloyd George, 'I have been trying to get out of the Ghetto. You want to force me back there!'[30] David Lindo Alexander, President of the Board of Deputies, and Claude Montefiore, President of the Anglo-Jewish Association, had already denounced Zionism in the correspondence columns of the London *Times*. 'Emancipated Jews in this country,' they pleaded, '. . . have no separate aspirations in a political sense.'[31] The bluff almost succeeded. In the event, the Board of Deputies repudiated the letter, as did Chief Rabbi J.H. Hertz and Lord Rothschild. With help from gentile Zionists, such as Sir Mark Sykes and Lord Milner, the Balfour Declaration was promulgated. The Anglo-Jewish establishment tried to make the best of a bad job. They formed a League of British Jews and launched the *Jewish Guardian* as platforms from which to voice their anti-zionism.[32] Claude Montefiore, the 'prophet' of Liberal Judaism, continued to preach against Zionism, even to the extent of blaming the Zionist movement for the rise of Nazi Germany.[34] As late as 1943 the social worker Basil Henriques, together with Sir Jack Brunel Cohen, formed the Jewish Fellowship to make a last-ditch stand against the fulfilment of the Balfour Declaration in post-war Palestine. Henriques had 'found Zionism well entrenched in the East End with flourishing Zionist youth groups and he feared that they must somehow undermine the British loyalties of the Jewish youngster.'[35] The impact of the Fellowship was minimal; its importance lay rather in the very fact of its existence, for it reflected the obsessive patriotism with which the Anglo-Jewish establishment was then attempting to conceal its lack of identity with British Jewry as a whole.[36]

Zionism had become a practical possibility in 1917. The Labour party adopted a socialist constitution in 1918. Thenceforward the political views of British Jews took to new and unfamiliar directions.

Whatever hopes Disraeli might have had of winning over Anglo-Jewry for the Conservative cause had been posthumously shattered when the party, under Balfour, had thrown in its lot with the anti-semitic lobby.[37] But Jewish suspicion of Conservatives (as distinct from Conservatism) continued long after the immigration issue had died down. The Conservative Party had replaced the Liberal Party as the party of the bosses, the party of industrial as well as landed money. It was not, therefore, a party which commended itself to poor immigrants and their children. Jewish suspicions of the party were intensi-fied when a number of Conservative MPs lent their support – even if only temporarily – to the British Union of Fascists in its early days. Although the fascist campaign against British Jewry did not become formal policy until the autumn of 1934, Jews suspected its existence from the start. When Lord Rothermere swung the *Daily Mail* behind the BUF, Jewish advertisers threatened economic sanctions unless he relented. He did so, in magnificent style, by devoting two leading articles in praise of the Jewish contribution to British life.[38] Above and beyond this, however, Jews became exasperated with the policy of appeasement towards Nazi Germany in Europe and towards Palestinian Arab violence in the Middle East. The Munich agreement of 1938 and the 1939 White Paper on Palestine (signalling the abandonment of the Balfour Declaration) were interpreted by most British Jews as proof positive that the Conservative Party – albeit with some notable excep-tions – was prepared to turn a blind eye to the plight of German Jewry whilst depriving it of an escape route.

Qualitative evidence[39] suggests that Jewish support for the Liberal party persisted long after the party's post-1924 decline, and that many Jews who moved into the outer suburbs of London just before and after the Second World War were careful to take their Liberal politics with them. Being out of office gave the Liberal Party a distinct advan-tage in this respect, for on the subjects of Nazism and Palestine it came to the Jewish community with fairly clean hands. The Liberal leader Herbert Samuel, one of the few top ranking Jewish politicians of the interwar period, had championed the idea of a Jewish National Home in Palestine as early as 1914. As first High Commissioner for Palestine Samuel tried to steer a middle course which did not always please Zionists, but which did at least allow the *Yishuv* (the Jewish community in the Holy Land) to take firm root. Later, as Viscount Samuel, he supported Chamberlain's Munich policy but at the same time used his influence to speed the rescue of German Jewish refugees, especially the children.[40] Many Jewish Liberals felt that under such circumstances they could hardly desert the party which had emancipated them.

But the very fact that the Liberal Party was no longer credible as a party of government made it unattractive to Jews (as to gentiles), especially to those Jews who grew up in the 1920s and 1930s, who had been born in this country, and who therefore inherited none of the submissiveness of their parents. Their parents, weary with the flight from persecution, were only too glad to find a country which would allow them to live in peace; the poverty and the squalor, which they were accustomed to anyway, were easily bearable. The children of the immigrants, educated in the ways of British democracy, were determined to build a better life. Entry into the Conservative Party was unthinkable, entry into the Liberal Party seemed pointless. There was already a strong socialist tradition among certain sections of the Jewish immigrant population. Its failure to make headway at the turn of the century was partly due to its hostility to religious observance. But the orthodoxy of the fathers and mothers was giving way to the religious laxity, even outright atheism, of the sons and daughters. Then came the rise of fascism abroad and at home. In addition, many young Jews who remained orthodox believed that they saw in the socialist creed echoes of the economic and social paternalism prescribed by Jewish law. And were not the institutions of the *Yishuv*, such as the kibbutz, based upon socialist principles? Socialism, in short, seemed to provide the answers to the problems of Jews the world over. Many Jews joined the Labour and Communist parties, and many more supported these movements through the ballot box. In 1935, sixteen Jews were elected to Parliament, but only four were socialists. In 1945, twenty-eight Jews were elected. Of these, only one was a Conservative — and an Independent Conservative at that; twenty-six were members of the Labour party, and one was a Communist. In 1950 all twenty-two Jewish MPs were Labour party members, as were the seventeen Jews elected in 1951.

In 1945 it looked, therefore, as if the Labour Party was set to capture Jewish political loyalties — not completely, of course, but to a very great extent. That it failed to do so can be explained in two words: affluence and Israel.

Estimates of the Jewish population of Great Britain are notoriously approximate, but certain trends are beyond dispute. The first is that total Jewish population rose steadily to a peak of around 450,000 in

1950.[41] Since then it has been declining, through emigration (mainly but not only to Israel) and complete assimilation, and in the mid-1960s stood at about 410,000.[42] Today the total is probably lower still. At the same time over half Anglo-Jewry has always lived in the London area. In 1850 the proportion was 60 per cent; in 1970 it was about 68 per cent, or 280,000.[43] Of the 32 per cent of Anglo-Jewry who do not now live in London, nearly three-quarters (over 94,000) live in Manchester, Leeds, Glasgow, Liverpool, Brighton, Birmingham and Southend.[44] In short, in Britain the Jews have always been town dwellers, and this is truer today than it has ever been.

Secondly, within these urban centres, and pre-eminently within the Greater London area, Jews have moved out of the original semi-ghetto areas of settlement, into the suburbs. Thus the East End of London, which at one time accounted for two-thirds of London Jewry, now contains less than a quarter, while the outer London area accounts for 58 per cent. More specifically, the four northwestern London boroughs of Barnet, Brent, Camden and Harrow account for an estimated Jewish population of 110,000, with another 19,000 living in Redbridge, in the northeast.[45] The pattern has been repated, on a lesser scale, in other towns; in Leeds, for instance, Jews have moved out of the Leylands and Chapeltown into the newer suburban districts of Moortown and Alwoodley, and even further afield.[46]

The Second World War of course played its part in this process. But wartime destruction of city centres merely hastened a trend which was already under way. Jews became more prosperous, and as they did so they wished to climb further up the social ladder and escape their ghetto origins. Krausz, in his investigation of the Jewish community of Edgware (now part of the London borough of Barnet), has given some fascinating insights into this process. Edgware Jewry is thoroughly working class in origin, and 53 per cent of Professor Krausz's sample had been born in the East End of London. Yet over 80 per cent regarded themselves as belonging to the middle class, and only just over 8 per cent said they belonged to the working class.[47] From the point of view of occupation, moreover, Jewish men in Edgware are to be found predominantly in the professional, managerial, skilled and self-employed groups of workers, which is the exact opposite of the picture for the general population of the district.[48]

The political implications of this trend are not hard to discover. The relentless drive of Anglo-Jewry into a middle-class property-owning suburban existence has as its corollary the tendency to part company with socialism and the Labour Party, and to espouse instead the cause of Conservatism or (a convenient halfway house) return to the Liberal fold. Some electoral effects of these developments, as revealed in a survey undertaken during the February 1974 general election campaign, will be discussed later on. Here it is worth noting that the Labour Party has lost its monopoly of Jewish MPs. The phenomenon of the Jewish

Conservative MP reappeared (in the person of Sir Henry d'Avigdor Goldsmid) in 1955. Two Jewish Conservatives were returned in the elections of 1959, 1964 and 1966. In 1970 the number jumped to nine, and in February 1974 to twelve. This rise has therefore been maintained independently of the relative party strengths nationally at each general election. Possibly just as significant has been the reappearance of Jews as Liberal Party candidates. In February 1974, out of a total of one hundred Jewish parliamentary candidates, thirty were Liberals. Though only one (Clement Freud) was actually elected, there does seem to be evidence here of a partial return of Jews to their original political home.

The influence of greater material prosperity and of social expectation upon the erosion of Labour Party loyalties is, of course, not confined to the Jews, though the overwhelming concentration of Anglo-Jewry in a few large urban centres has made the process in their case particularly impressive. With the Jews, however, a further and unique factor contributed towards the swing away from socialism. This was the creation of the State of Israel in May 1948, and the Middle East policy of the Attlee government. There is no need here to recount the events leading to the breakdown of the Mandate. During the Second World War the Labour Party had made many pro-Zionist pronouncements and, once the full horror of the Nazi Holocaust has been revealed British Jews hoped that Foreign Secretary Ernest Bevin would lose no time in bringing the Jewish State into being. Instead came delay and (to Jewish eyes at least) pro-Arabism. In particular, Bevin's policy towards Jewish refugees and illegal immigrants in Palestine seemed nothing short of barbaric. The vast majority of British Jews regarded — and still regard — Bevin as an anti-semite.[49] During the late 1940s British Jews were asked to finance illegal activities in Palestine, to help purchase and smuggle arms, to smuggle refugees into the Holy Land, even to finance Jewish underground armies fighting against British troops. Many Jews gave generously to these causes without asking too many questions; solidarity with their brethren in Palestine proved stronger than loyalty to the country of which they were citizens.[50] The Labour Party, so friendly to Zionism when out of office, now seemed bent on frustrating the fulfilment of Zionist aspirations. Whilst leading Jewish members of the Labour Party tried to repair the damage, there was much unrest among the rank and file, and the party lost Jewish votes as a result.

Then came the Suez campaign of 1956 which (at least as far as it involved Israel) many Jews supported though it was condemned by the Labour Party in opposition, and the sponsorship, by Harold Wilson's government, of United Nations' Resolution 242, calling upon Israel to withdraw from 'territories' occupied in the 1967 war. Since then, Jewish Labour MPs have had a hard time of it explaining the vagaries of Labour's Middle East policy to their co-religionists.[51] It is true, of course, that pro-Arabists are to be found in the Conservative as well as in the Labour party, and that the Liberal party suffers in Jewish eyes because of the anti-Israeli sentiments of many Young Liberals, and may suffer even more now that the noted Arab apologist, Christopher Mayhew, has left Labour and joined the Liberal Party.[52] The fact is that British Jews expected a more committed attitude towards the Jewish State from Labour. The Labour Party in Britain has official contacts with its counterpart in Israel (*Poalei Zion*), and in the Parliament elected in February 1974, fourteen of the Jewish Labour MPs returned were members of it — making *Poalei Zion*, as some Jews wryly observed, one of the largest parties in the House of Commons. Yet Jews have been puzzled over the past couple of decades as the negative impact which they allege Jewish Labour MPs as a whole have had on the party.

The net effect of affluence and Israel has been that since the mid-1950s Jewish support has been spread more evenly between the major political parties in Great Britain. There are Jewish Tories, Jewish Liberals, Jewish Socialists, even Jewish members of Plaid Cymru and the Scottish National party. In that sense, meaning simply how Jews vote and what are their political affiliations, the outstanding characteristic of the Jewish vote is, broadly speaking, one of political assimilation. On a few special occasions (Israel apart) — such as when *Shechita* (Jewish ritual slaughter) was under attack in Parliament in 1968 — Jews, often irrespective of their degree of religious devotion, will come together in defence of cherished principles. And British Jews are openly hostile to parties of the extreme right, such as the National Front. Parties which have as their aim the repatriation of coloured immigrants are regarded by the Jews as racialist parties, with whom there can be no truck.[53] But British Jews differ widely on a vast range of everyday social and political issues. There is not, and never has been, a separate Jewish political party in Britain, though at various times Jews have, from a variety of motives, found it convenient to favour one of the major parties rather than another.

Yet it is equally true that in certain constituencies British Jews possess considerable voting strength, should they choose to exercise it *en bloc*. This is particularly so in the Greater London area, in parts of which, as has already been shown, Jews represent sizeable proportions of the total population: 19 per cent in the boroughs of Barnet and Hackney, for instance.[54] In a situation in which 'safe' parliamentary seats are getting scarcer, their votes could easily affect the outcome of an election. The Jewish vote, in this sense, is something about which Jewish leaders have in the past been noticeably reticent.

The *Jewish Chronicle*, widely read 'Organ of British Jewry,' takes pains at each general election to inform its readers exactly how many Jewish candidates stand, and how many are elected, as if this in itself were of some tangible benefit to the community as a whole. In fact, impressive though the list of Jewish MPs may look on paper, and impressive though the steady increase in the total number of Jewish MPs — to a record forty-six in February 1974 — may be, the Jewish lobby in Parliament is much less monolithic in reality. Even among Jewish Labour MPs in recent years are to be found some who take little or no part in promoting Israel's cause at Westminster, others who are contemptuous of the Jewish establishment in Britain, especially the Board of Deputies, yet others who are openly critical of Jewish religious orthodoxy, and one (Robert Sheldon) who voted in favour of the Bill to interfere with *Shechita*.[55] Most Jewish Labour MPs backed Hugh Gaitskell's condemnation of the British invasion of Egypt in 1956, just as two of the nine Jewish Conservatives (Robert Adley and Keith Joseph) voted in favour of Foreign Secretary Alex Douglas-Home's embargo of arms shipments to Israel on 18 October 1973. That forty-six Jewish MPs *were* returned in February 1974 is of course noteworthy, for they account for over 7 per cent of the total number of MPs in the House, whereas Jews nationally amount to less than 1 per cent of the total population of the United Kingdom.[56] It is certainly possible to theorise about situations in which (particularly in times of a minority government) a danger might arise to world Jewry, or to British Jewry, on such a scale as to provoke the use of Jewish voting strength to the full in Parliament. Such extreme situations apart, and if past practice is anything to go by, Jewish power in Parliament, though real, is not nearly as substantial as the figures might suggest.

But the power of the Jewish vote at elections is another matter. At the turn of the century, fear of the anti-alien agitation and its implications did give rise to a movement to organise the Jewish vote, on behalf of the Liberals. Even the *Jewish Chronicle* felt constrained to descend from its politically non-partisan pedestal on this issue.[57] Nowadays the Board of Deputies discourages talk of a Jewish vote, and advises members of the community to tell enquirers that it does not exist. Religious leaders used to take a similar line, refusing to use the pulpit to speak on matters affecting domestic politics. The view commonly held by both lay and religious leaders is that at the moment Anglo-Jewry is not under attack and that, for instance, to urge Jewish voters to use the power of the ballot box on behalf of Israel would be counterproductive, and only 'make trouble' for the community here. In any case, they add, foreign affairs never figure prominently in election campaigns.

But all but the most assimilated Jews feel that their fate is somehow bound up with that of the Jewish State, which they helped to build and which they continue to support. In consequence, renewed conflict in the Middle East in October 1973 gave to Anglo-Jewry a new political awareness. Angry at the policy of the Conservative Government towards Israel, but remembering too the ambivalent attitude of the previous Labour administration, Jewish voters were quick to ask MPs and candidates blunt questions about their attitude to the Middle East conflict. The first signs of this movement were evident at the Hove by-election, held on 8 November 1973. Hove was held by the Conservatives in 1970 with a majority of over 18,000. The Jewish electorate is said to be around 4,000, mostly Conservative. Normally, therefore, the Jewish vote in Hove would not be crucial for a Conservative candidate. But in the autumn of 1973 Conservative fortunes were at a low ebb, and the Liberals were in the ascendant. It was evident that the Liberal challenge at Hove was going to be a strong one. Local Conservatives attempted to attack the Liberal candidate by referring to the pro-Arab sympathies of some sections of the Young Liberals. Jewish Liberals retaliated by producing statements in support of Israel made by Liberal leader Jeremy Thorpe. The local Jewish leadership, apparently in an attempt to 'defuse' the situation, and play down the Jewish vote aspect of the campaign, sent a deputation to the main candidates to find out just what they thought about the Middle East. On polling day the Conservative candidates, Tim Sainsbury, scraped home with a majority of 4,846 over the Liberal, Des Wilson, in second place. No one can be sure what part the Jewish vote actually played in this drama. Chaim Raphael, of Sussex University, believes that the Jews, convinced by the assurances of support for Israel from Tim Sainsbury, returned to the Conservative fold.[58] Perhaps they did. The importance of Hove, however, lay in the fact that it demonstrated that there was a Jewish vote to be fought for, and that political pressure by Jewish voters on behalf of Israel was a force to be reckoned with.

The Zionist Federation of Great Britain had, meanwhile, been preparing a list (*Why did they ignore Israel?*) of every MP who abstained or voted with the government on 18 October. The list was given wide publicity and a covering letter, from Public Relations Committee Chairman Eric Moonman (now a Labour MP once more), urged that MPs whose names were on the list be contacted to account for their behaviour. 'If your MP voted for the Alec Douglas-Home line,' Moonman advised, 'you should also add that his action has considerably distressed a number of his constituents . . . a so-called even-handed policy will always harm Israel.' 'We are,' the letter ended, 'maintaining a precise record of parliamentary voting and attitudes.' The Commons debate on the arms embargo had in fact provided Jewish voters with a critical yardstick by which they were able to measure the degree of support their MPs were prepared to give the Jewish State. Memories of the Yom Kippur War had not dimmed in the minds of British Jews. When a general electiom was announced for the end of February 1974, Anglo-Jewry remembered Israel, just as parliamentary candidates remembered Anglo-Jewry.

This was not perhaps so obvious in constituencies such as Hackney Central, Hackney North and Tower Hamlets (Bethnal Green and Bow), where the victorious Labour candidates (Stanley Clinton Davis, David Weitzman and Ian Mikardo) clearly owed their success to the solidly working class composition of their electorates rather than to the fact that they are Jewish, known to be Jewish, and are strong supporters of Israel — though this certainly helped. More revealing were marginal constituencies, held before the election by Conservatives, where the Labour challengers were Jewish. This happened in two of the Redbridge constituencies, Ilford North and Ilford South. In Ilford South, A.E. Cooper lost his seat to the Labour candidate, Arnold Shaw, by 1,143 votes. But Tom Iremonger, in Ilford North, retained his seat by the narrow margin of 285 votes. One factor contributing to such different results, in adjacent areas was that Iremonger had defied the Conservative whips and voted against his own governing party in October. Cooper merely abstained. Iremonger, moreover, wooed his Jewish voters in a vigorous campaign, both on the issue of Israel and on that of Soviet Jewry, and had indulged in some forthright advertising in the *Redbridge Extra*, a locally distributed supplement of the *Jewish Chronicle*.[59] Cooper has, it would seem, learned the lesson, and since his defeat has publicly taken a more positive pro-Israel stand.[60]

In Middleton and Prestwich, the Jewish area of north Manchester, Labour captured the seat from the Conservatives by a majority of 517 votes. In this case neither candidate was Jewish, but the Conservative candidate and previous MP, A.G.B. Haselhurst, had also had his name included on the Zionist Federation's list. Had he voted against the government the previous October, instead of abstaining, he might have picked up enough Jewish support to have held his seat. This may be contrasted with the result in Hampstead (in Camden), where Geoffrey Finsberg (Conservative) retained his seat with a substantially increased majority. Finsberg, who is Jewish, had also voted against the government in October 1973.

In one London marginal constituency I was able to organise a systematic survey of Jewish voting intentions during the February 1974 election campaign. The constituency was Hendon North, in Barnet, and includes such thickly populated Jewish areas as Edgware and Mill Hill. The total electorate is slightly over 50,000 of which about 15,000 are Jews. This high proportion alone made Hendon North an ideal setting for a case study, for John Gorst, the Conservative MP, elected in 1970, had then had a majority of 3,179. John Gorst is not Jewish, but has kept in close touch with his Jewish constituents, and voted against the government on 18 October 1973. By his unswerving support for Israel he was able to win the admiration of the Rev. Saul Amias, minister of the 5,000 strong Edgware United Synagogue. Rev. Amias, outspoken and extrovert, grew up in the East End of London, where the sordid living conditions of Jew and non-Jew alike instilled in him a passion for social justice, and made him a socialist. But Israel's situation in October 1973, and John Gorst's action in the Commons at that time, made a deep impression on him. Though a socialist, Rev. Amias announced in the local press that he was not merely going to vote for Gorst on 28

February 1974; he had agreed to sign Gorst's nomination papers.

So the Middle East (not without some embarassment to Jewish members of the Labour and Liberal parties in the constituency, and to local Zionist leaders) became an issue in the Hendon North campaign. A sample of 150 Jews were asked about their voting intentions.[61] Nearly 16 per cent of those who had not voted Conservative in 1970 indicated that they would now do so because of John Gorst's anti-government stand on the Middle East. A further 6.4 per cent, who voted Labour or Conservative in 1970, said they would now vote for the Liberal candidate, who had also come out in strong support of Israel in 1973; the replies of these people (and of a further 1.6 per cent Jewish Labour voters who said they would now abstain) stressed disillusion with the Middle East policies of both major parties when in power.

When the votes were counted, John Gorst retained his seat with his majority only slightly reduced to 2,612 (he had predicted for himself a majority of only 1,350). The Liberal candidate emerged with over 21 per cent of the vote, as compared with 10 per cent in 1970. In the adjacent constituency of Hendon South, where Peter Thomas, then Secretary of State for Wales, was returned, the Liberal candidate displaced Lavour as runner-up. And in nearby Finchley, Margaret Thatcher, the Conservative Education Minister, saw her majority almost halved while the Liberal share of the vote increased by 11 per cent. As ministers, of course, both Thomas and Thatcher had been obliged to vote with the government in October 1973, but local Jewish criticism of them had been, and continues to be, no less intense for all that. It is noteworthy, too, that Thomas and Thatcher faced Liberal opponents who were Jewish, and this factor also seems to have played a part in the results.[62]

The conscious wooing of Jewish voters in the general election of February 1974 went largely unnoticed by the national news media, but its significance was not ignored by politicians or Jewish leaders. Tom Iremonger's appeal to the Jewish voters of Ilford North in the *Redbridge Extra*, and the hostile reaction to it of Martin Savitt, the Board of Deputies Defence Committee Chairman, was the subject of heated exchanges at a subsequent Board meeting.[63] The impact of the Jewish vote in Hendon North, which certainly helped and probably enabled John Gorst to retain his seat, was the subject of much local criticism, particularly from Labour and Liberal party members (including Jews).[64] At the same time some orthodox Jewish Zionists made no secret of their delight at the turn of events there. Elsewhere, specific appeals to Jewish voters, especially by Jewish candidates, came in for a fair amount of adverse comment from prominent members of the community.[65]

The truth is that many leading British Jews are intimately connected with the major political parties, and are now embarassed by the revelation that Jewish voters no longer regard themselves as bound by

the conventional criteria of party loyalties in this country, but are prepared to vote in a specifically 'Jewish' way. The *Jewish Chronicle*, for
instance, was strangely silent about the action of Rev. Amias in Hendon
North, but went out of its way in February 1974 to stress that Jews
were apparently voting on domestic issues; it came to this conclusion
after publishing interviews with forty-four Jews, fourteen of whom,
however, had indicated that the policies of the major parties towards
Israel *would* be a factor in their decision which way to vote. Even the
Zionist Federation, which did so much to bring Jewish pressure to bear
on MPs at the time of the Yom Kippur War, remained mute during the
general election period; a spokesman remarked that they did not think
it 'proper' to intervene in the election. On a more personal note, the
present author (who is Jewish) can reveal that unofficial disapproval
was communicated to him from various quarters (and is still being
communicated to him) once it became known that the study of the
Jewish vote in Hendon North was under way.

But there are signs that attitudes are changing. The Board of Deputies, meeting on 17 February 1974, was told by its president, Sir
Samuel (now Lord) Fisher, that Jewish voters had the right to question
candidates about attitudes to Israel, Soviet Jewry and Arab oil policies,
and that it was perfectly proper for them to do so. The minister of one
Hendon synagogue, having previously confessed that he would be 'torn
to pieces' by his lay leadership if he tried to use the pulpit to speak on
behalf of John Gorst (whom he supported), later on felt able to state
publicly, with reference to Hendon South, that Peter Thomas would
have to be 'taught a lesson.' Rabbis of synagogues in or adjacent to
Hendon North were not too happy about Rev. Amias' *démarche*; some
feared it might provoke an anti-Jewish backlash, others that it was not
'the right thing' for a Jewish religious leader to do. But most of them
thought that the use of the Jewish vote to support the parliamentary
friends of Israel was perfectly in order, even desirable, and one rabbi
went further, declaring that though he would not at that time use the
pulpit to urge support for any political party, he was prepared to admit
that circumstances (which he did not specify) could arise in which he
might have to change his view. By officially endorsing Gorst's nomination in Hendon North, therefore, Rev. Amias was able to sidestep the
difficulty other religious leaders were clearly experiencing in their relations with lay heads of their congregations.

One thing is clear. The Jewish vote is a minor but not insignificant
fact of political life, more especially now that such a fluid political
situation exists in Great Britain. With so much uncertainty surrounding
the future development of Israel's relations with her Arab neighbours,
MPs with large blocks of Jewish voters want to be sure of their support.
They may well be accused of pandering to sectarian interests. But they
know, as they have always known, that a Jewish vote exists; to offend
it is a chance they can ill afford to take.[66]

What exactly is the party political breakdown of that vote today? The subject arose publicly in the summer of 1974, when there was much speculation in the press about a September election. It was pointed out that Thursday 26 September, one of the dates mentioned, would also be Yom Kippur, the Jewish Day of Atonement, which even non-religious Jews attempt to observe, and upon which all work – including the marking of a ballot paper – is forbidden. A *Sunday Times* columnist, estimating the total Jewish vote as 'something over 300,000' (a not unreasonable figure) pointed out that the virtual disenfranchising of Jews if an election were held on 26 September could have a significant effect in constituencies where Jews were concentrated.[67] An article in the *Jewish Chronicle* reported that one of Harold Wilson's Jewish colleagues was alleged to have advised that this hardly mattered from the Labour point of view, since most Jews vote Conservative anyway.[68] The fact is that, in spite of its importance, no-one knows for certain what exactly are the political affiliations of Anglo-Jewry today. As suggested earlier, however, the Labour Party in spite of the large number of Jewish MPs in its ranks, can no longer claim to occupy a special place of affection as far as British Jews are concerned. And the drift into a middle class existence has accelerated the move of Anglo-Jewry towards centre and right-of-centre political attitudes.

The Hendon North sample gives some supporting evidence. The voting pattern, as revealed by the sample, is set out in Table 1. Twenty-four people declined to state how they had voted in 1970, or which way they intended to vote on 28 February 1974. Of the remainder, column 1a tabulates, by percentages, the voting behaviour in 1970, and column 2a tabulates the intended voting behaviour in 1974. Columns 1b and 2b give the percentages as proportions only of those who *actually* voted in 1970 and of those who were *already decided* as to their 1974 intention. For the purposes of comparison, the London and Southeast regional pattern of party preferences for social classes AB and C1 (that is, the non-manual occupations), as given by Butler and Stokes,[69] is reproduced.

Some features of the results deserve comment. The high proportion of Jews in the sample who did not vote in 1970 would seem to be explained partly by the fact that the election was held in June, when some were on holiday. The high proportion who were undecided as to their 1974 voting intention reflected genuine perplexity, both about domestic issues and about the Middle East question. Support for the Liberal Party in 1970 and 1974 was higher than the London and Southeast regional pattern, support for the Conservatives was lower. The drop in Jewish support for the Labour Party was very marked. In 1970 Jewish support for Labour was higher than the regional pattern, or almost as high; it now approaches that pattern much more closely, and may even be lower. Over half the respondents in the sample voted Conservative in 1970. If the 1974 votes of those who were undecided at the time of the survey are shared out among the three major parties on the basis of the 1970 proportions, the Conservative Party emerges with 58 per cent of the Jewish vote, the Labour Party with 19 per cent, and the Liberal Party with 23 per cent.

Table 1 Party Preferences of a Sample of Hendon North Jewry

| | Vote in 1970 | | Intended vote in 1974 | | London and southeast | |
	All	Those who voted only	All	Those declaring definite intention only	Class AB	Class C1
	%	%	%	%	%	%
Conservative	42.9	55.1	41.3	59.1	74.1	58.5
Labour	20.6	26.5	11.1	15.9	13.0	28.8
Liberal	14.3	18.4	17.5	25.0	12.7	12.5
Other	-	-	-	-	0.2	0.2
Did not vote (1970)	17.6					
Could not vote (1970)	4.4					
Undecided (1974)			27.0			
Will abstain (1974)			3.1			
	100	100	100	100	100	100

It may be objected that these figures are only to be expected from such a constituency. Of the five wards in Hendon North, only two return Labour councillors to Barnet borough council — Colindale and Burnt Oak; the other three — Edgware, Mill Hill and Hale — all return Conservative councillors. Yet it is precisely in Edgware, Mill Hill and Hale that the Jews of Hendon North are to be found and where all the synagogues of the constituency are situated. Hendon North is Conservative partly because so many Jews (around 5 per cent of the total Jewish vote of Great Britain) live there.

Local election results provide further evidence of the trend. There are at present four inner London boroughs where Jews form over 5 per cent of the population, and four outer boroughs. In Table 2, the number of 'Jewish' wards in each of these boroughs has been estimated (from personal knowledge and the siting of synagogues), and the number of Labour and Conservative councillors returned for these wards in the borough elections of May 1974 is shown in the right hand columns (no Liberal or other candidates were returned in the wards concerned); the overall state of the parties in the boroughs (excluding vacant seats) is shown if the left hand columns.

Table 2 Results in the Jewish Wards of Eight London Boroughs

	All Wards				Jewish Wards		
	No. of coun- cillors	Lab	Con	Other	No. of coun- cillors	Lab	Con
Inner London							
Camden	65	53	12	0	15	3	12
Hackney	65	65	0	0	28	28	0
Tower Hamlets	65	65	0	0	19	19	0
Westminster	65	26	39	0	24	5	19
	78	209	51	0	26	55	31
Outer London							
Barnet	65	18	46	1	33	2	31
Brent	65	40	25	0	35	16	19
Harrow	56	14	39	3	12	3	9
Redbridge	65	16	49	0	44	6	38
	83	88	159	4	45	27	97

It will be seen that in the four inner London boroughs, the Jewish wards account for only a third of the total number of wards, and return just over one-quarter of the total number of Labour councillors in these boroughs, but nearly two-thirds of the Conservative councillors. In the four outer boroughs the Jewish wards form over half the total; they return less than a third of the total number of Labour councillors, but over half the Conservative councillors. It must be conceded at once that these figures are far from conclusive. It is always dangerous to engage in 'cross-level reference' — to infer the partisanship of a group of voters from the election results in a much larger aggregate (constituency, ward, etc.) of which they form only a small part. Thus, in many of the Hackney wards, Jews and coloured immigrants live side by side, so that much of the Labour vote could conceivably have come from the latter rather than from the former. Nor do the figures (especially in view of poor turnout at local elections) reveal anything about attitudes of Jewish voters to the Liberal Party. These factors, however, would tend to under- rather than over-exaggerate Jewish support for the Conservative and Liberal parties.

It is no part of the author's intention to predict what may happen to the Jewish vote. But the London borough statistics, taken together with the Hendon North survey, and with qualitative evidence, suggest that Jewish Labour voters (at least in London) are becoming fewer in relation to Jewish Liberals and Conservatives. The old Jewish East End areas, now absorbed into Hackney, Newham and Tower Hamlets, are areas of declining Jewish population. The young Jews have moved away, leaving their parents and grandparents to maintain the institutions of Jewish communal life as best they can. These are areas of Jewish Labour voters but they are, by and large, middle-aged and old voters, with no children living nearby to whom they can transmit their own political culture. Over half London Jewry (158,000) now lives in the outer London boroughs, and the four cited in Table 2 account for over 70 per cent of this total. Even in Labour strongholds in inner London there are to be found pockets of Conservatism which turn out, from personal observation, to be Jewish: amongst the ultra-orthodox communities of Stoke Newington and Stanford Hill, in Hackney, for instance. Whether this trend will continue is quite a different matter. Events in the Middle East, and the postures of the British political parties in this respect, could be crucial. So too could the growth of extremist parties.

Writing in 1959, Brotz characterised the position of the Jews in English society thus:

'Jews are neither a political bloc nor one of a number of minority blocs with whom they are roughly equated in the public eye . . . Both the small size of the community and the centralised party structure make it impossible for Jews to control strategic levers in the electoral machine.'[70]

This is no longer the case. There are some anti-Zionist Jews. There are Jews of the 'New Left' who, whilst opposing racist policies and politics root and branch, claim that they do so on humanistic grounds, not because they are Jews. These people form a vocal but very small fraction of the Anglo-Jewish community. Most British Jews are deeply concerned about Israel's safety and survival. They are worried by the growth of the National Front and other parties of the extreme right.[71] They are tending to find themselves more at home in the Liberal and Conservative parties rather than in the Labour Party. But the psephologists and the political pundits have taught them all about electoral swings and marginal constituencies. They now appreciate how much political influence they can exert, and they are prepared to exert it unashamedly.

British Jews know, moreover, that as an ethnic rather than a racial minority, the criteria by which they make political judgments are not quite those of the non-Jewish majority amongst whom they live. There always was a 'Jewish' dimension to these criteria; now there is an Israeli dimension too. What is needed is much more information about Jewish political views. Nothing has been said in this paper, for instance about the spread of political views, or the extent of Zionist commitment, *as between* the various levels of religious orthodoxy in the Anglo-Jewish community. What can be said at present about the political attitudes of the community as a whole must perforce be based more on qualitative than on quantitative evidence, more on the experience of London than of provincial Jewry. The necessary fieldwork has simply not yet been done, though, if the author's experiences are anything to go by, the Jewish masses of Great Britain will be far less diffident about cooperating in such research than the pronouncements of some of the leadership might suggest.

NOTES

1.   See especially U.R.Q. Henriques, 'The Jewish Emancipation Controversy in Nineteenth-Century Britain,' *Past and Present*, no. 40 (July 1968); I. Finestein, 'Anglo-Jewish Opinion During the Struggle for Emancipation,' *Transactions of the Jewish Historical Society of England*, XX (1959-61), 113-43.
2.   I. Finestein, 'Jewish Immigration in British Party Politics in the 1890s,' in *Migration and Settlement Proceedings of the Anglo-American Jewish Historical Conference . . . July 1970*, Jewish Historical Society of England, London, 1971, pp. 128-44; B. Gainer, *The Alien Invasion*, Heinemann, London, 1972; J.A. Garrard, *The English and Immigration: A Comparative Study of the Jewish Influx 1880-1910*, Institute of Race Relations, London, 1971; L.P. Gartner, *The Jewish Immigrant in England 1870-1914*, Allen & Unwin, London, 1960.
3.   V.D. Lipman, *Social History of the Jews in England 1850-1950*, Watts & Co., London, 1954.
4.   M. Freedman (ed.), *A Minority in Britain: Social Studies of the Anglo-Jewish Community*, Vallentine, Mitchell, London, 1955. The same might be said of J. Gould and S. Esh (eds.), *Jewish Life in Modern Britain*, Routledge & Kegan Paul, London, 1964.
5.   C. Bermant, *Troubled Eden: An Anatomy of British Jewry*, Vallentine, Mitchell, London, 1969.
6.   Henriques, *loc. cit.*, 127-9.
7.   C. Roth, *A History of the Jews in England*, Oxford University Press, 2nd edn., Oxford, 1949, pp. 246, 253.
8.   Liverpool Pollbooks of 1832 and 1835, in the Institute of Historical Research, London.
9.   Lionel de Rothschild must certainly have had such Jewish voters in his constituency; his co-protagonists, such as David Salomons at Greenwich or

Francis Henry Goldsmid at Great Yarmouth, almost certainly did not. The aim was never to obtain the special representation in Parliament of the Jewish Vote.

10.   Bermant, *Troubled Eden*, p. 165, reckons that the readership of the *Jewish Chronicle* is around 250,000.

11.   *Jewish Chronicle*, 19 October 1951, 15.

12.   Henriques, *loc. cit.*, 131-4.

13.   *Ibid.*, 130.

14.   I. Finestein, 'The New Community 1880-1918,' in V.D. Lipman (ed.), *Three Centuries of Anglo-Jewish History*, Jewish Historical Society of England, London, 1961, p. 111.

15.   L. Kochan, 'Jews on the Move,' *Listener*, 27 May 1971, 677.

16.   Gainer, *op. cit.*, p. 96.

17.   Garrard, *op. cit.*, pp. 189-96.

18.   Gainer, *op. cit.*, pp. 67-73.

19.   *Parliamentary Debates*, 4th series, cxlix, 154, 10 July 1905.

20.   Garrard, *op. cit.*, pp. 143-7.

21.   *Ibid.*, pp. 132-3.

22.   See my article, 'The Anti-Jewish Riots of August 1911 in South Wales,' *Welsh History Review*, VI (1972), pp. 190-200.

23.   Bermant, *Troubled Eden*, pp. 22-7; Kochan, *loc. cit.*, p. 678.

24.   B. Homa, *A Fortress in Anglo-Jewry*, Shapiro, Vallentine, London, 1953.

25.   Garrard, *op. cit.*, p. 171; see also Lipman, *Social History of the Jews in England*, pp. 131-3; Gartner, *op. cit.*, pp. 100-41; Finestein, 'The New Community 1880-1918,' in Lipman, *Three Centuries of Anglo-Jewish History*, pp. 120-1.

26.   Quoted in C. Bermant, *The Cousinhood* (Eyre and Spottiswoode, London, 1971), p. 242.

27.   Finestein, *op. cit.*

28.   Homa, *op. cit.*, p. 112.

29.   Bermant, *op. cit.*, p. 112.

30.   F. Owen, *Tempestuous Journey*, Hutchinson, London, 1954, p. 427; Bermant, *The Cousinhood*, pp. 258-61.

31.   *Ibid.*, p. 260.

32.   *Ibid.*, pp. 260-3.

33.   'Liberal' is used here in the religious sense.

34.   Bermant, *The Cousinhood*, p. 319.

35.   *Ibid.*, pp. 381-2.

36.   The threat of an 'establishment' backlash against Zionism during the Second World War was taken seriously; Zionists took avoiding action by 'packing' the Board of Deputies with their own supporters: Bermant, *Troubled Eden*, p. 102.

37.   For evidence of some Jewish support for the Conservative Party, and of the erosion of that support as a result of the anti-alien agitation, see Garrard, *op. cit.*, pp. 117-31.

38.   Sir Oswald Mosley, *My Life*, Thomas Nelson & Sons, London, 1970, p. 343; C. Cross, *The Fascists in Britain*, Barrie & Rockliff, London, 1961, p. 118. See also, W.F. Mandle, *Anti-semitism and the British Union of Fascists*, Longmans, Green, London, 1968.

39.   Based on personal interviews.

40.   Bermant, *The Cousinhood*, pp. 341-53.

41.   H. Neustatter, 'Demographic and Other Statistical Aspects of Anglo-Jewry,' in Freedman, *A Minority in Britain*, p. 76.

42.   S.J. Prais and M. Schmool, 'The Size and Structure of the Anglo-Jewish Population, 1960-65,' *Jewish Journal of Sociology*, X (1968), 7.

43.   Lipman, *Social History of the Jews in England*, p. 168; S.J. Prais,

'Synagogue Statistics and the Jewish Population of Great Britain, 1900-1970.' *Jewish Journal of Sociology*, XIV (1972), 217.

44. Prais, *loc. cit.*
45. *Ibid.*, pp. 221-2; the Redbridge figure could well be an underestimate.
46. E. Krausz, *Leeds Jewry* (Jewish Historical Society of England, Cambridge, 1964), pp. 24-5.
47. E. Krausz, 'A Sociological Field Study of Jewish Suburban Life in Edgware 1962-62 with special reference to Minority Identification' (unpublished University of London Ph.D. thesis, 1965), pp. 93, 103.
48. *Ibid.*, p. 67.
49. J. Parkes, *Whose Land?*, Revised edn., Penguin Books, Harmondsworth, 1970, pp. 290-1.
50. E. Samuel, 'Changing Attitude of British Jews to Israel,' *Jewish Chronicle*, 2 February 1951, p. 13.
51. Ian Mikardo, the Labour Party chairman and a Jewish MP, addressing a Zionist Federation forum in June 1974, admitted that between thirty and fifty Labour MPs were pro-Arab, and added that this group included 'a few nut cases': *Jewish Chronicle*, 14 June 1974, p. 7.
52. *Hendon Times*, 7 June 1974, p. 4: letter from (Jewish) Liberal Party member H.I. Lightstone, on the subject of the Young Liberals; private information.
53. Board of Deputies of British Jews, *Annual Report*, 1968, pp. 24-6, 29.
54. Based on the 1970 estimates of Jewish population in Prais, *loc. cit*, p. 222, and the annual estimates of the population of local authority areas in England and Wales, at mid-1973, given by the Registrar-General.
55. Paul Rose, MP, 'The So-Called Jewish Lobby in Parliament,' *Jewish Chronicle*, 29 May 1970, p. 7.
56. The size of Jewish representation in the House of Commons is itself a source of embarassment and worry in some Jewish quarters. A speaker in a Jewish 'Brains Trust' organised on the eve of the 1964 general election 'thought that there were too many Jewish candidates' (there were eighty-six in all): *Jewish Chronicle*, 23 October 1964, p. 16.
57. See Garrard, *op. cit.*, pp. 120-31, especially his examination of the Jewish Vote in the Northwest Manchester by-election of 1908.
58. *Jewish Chronicle Colour Magazine*, 24 May 1974, pp. 34-5.
59. *Jewish Chronicle*, 22 March 1974, p. 7.
60. *Daily Telegraph*, 25 May 1974, p. 14.
61. The survey was carried out between 12 and 17 February 1974. It was decided at the outset to interview only in those wards – Mill Hill, Hale and Edgware – where Jews were known to live in large numbers. No attempt was made to interview on a quota basis, or to include questions relating to the background of the respondents. Streets were chosen at random, and within them Jewish households were selected haphazardly. Respondents were asked which way they had voted in 1970, and what their voting intention was in 1974. If their party preference had changed in anyway, they were invited to give reasons for their new choice. Of the 150 Jews interviewed, only 24 refused to answer the questions at all. It is possible to identify a Jewish household by the *mezuzah* fixed to the upper right hand front doorpost of the dwelling. A *mezuzah* (literally 'doorpost') is a piece of parchment on which are written verses from Deutoronomy; Jewish law requires the fixing of such pieces of parchment (usually in a wooden or metal case) on the doorposts of every dwelling place; Krausz, in his Edgware study (see no. 47), p. 119, found that 88 per cent of his respondents displayed a *mezuzah* on the front door.
62. The interesting question raised here – whether Jewish voters show any preference for Jewish candidates – is one about which very little concrete evidence exists. But some has recently come to light concerning polling in the

Hackney Borough Council elections of May 1974. In the Northfield Ward only three of the ten contestants were Jewish. Of the 412 votes cast for the Jewish Liberal candidate, Maurice Owen, 310 were cast on the party line; many of Owen's other votes were linked with those for the Communist candidate (Monty Goldman, a Jew) or, to a lesser extent, with those of R.B. Coleman, a Conservative candidate, also Jewish. Maurice Owen, fighting in a ward thickly populated with orthodox Jews, personally polled more votes than any other Liberal candidate in the borough. In the Springfield Ward (another orthodox Jewish area) Harry Goldstein, a strictly orthodox Jew, was one of the three Jewish Liberal candidates; he polled 89 and 101 votes in excess of his fellow Liberals. And in the New River Ward, which also contains many orthodox Jews, H. Lobenstein, a strictly orthodox Jew himself and a former Alderman of the borough, polled 901 votes, as against 677 and 636 votes for his fellow Conservative candidates. These instances suggest that being Jewish, and particularly being orthodox in an orthodox Jewish area, may have a limited but distinct advantage, at least at the local election level, where Jewish electorates are concerned.

63. *Jewish Chronicle*, 22 March 1874, p. 7.
64. *Hendon Times*, 8 March 1974, p. 4; 15 March, pp. 4, 8; 22 March, p. 4; 7 June, p. 4.
65. See, for example, *Jewish Chronicle*, 1 March 1974, p. 22; comment by 'Ben Azai'; 15 March, p. 23: letter from Labour MP Maurice Orbach and Councillor John Bull; 29 March, p. 29: reply from B. Silver, Liberal parliamentary candidate for St Marylebone (Westminster); 5 April, p. 25: letter from Councillor Donald du Parc Braham.
66. For some evidence of the canvassing of the Jewish vote in the late nineteenth century, see Garrard, *op. cit.*, pp. 113-17.
67. *Sunday Times*, 30 June 1974, p. 32.
68. *Jewish Chronicle*, 5 July 1974, p. 21; see also Philip Kleinman, 'Day of judgment,' *op. cit.*, p. 22, and G. Alderman, 'How Jews Vote,' *op. cit.*, 19 July 1974, p. 10.
69. D. Butler and D. Stokes, *Political Change in Britain*, Macmillam, London, 1969, p. 140.
70. H. Brotz, 'The Position of the Jews in English Society,' in R. Bendix and S.M. Lipset (eds.), *Class, Status and Power*, 2nd edn., Routledge & Kegan Paul, London, 1967, p. 348; Dr. Brotz's article originally appeared in the *Jewish Journal of Sociology*, V (1959).
71. Much consternation was caused in the spring of 1974 by the appearance of an article in *Spearhead*, the journal of the National Front, attacking *Shechita* (see *Jewish Chronicle*, 31 May 1974, p. 6), and by a bizarre appeal by Michael Coney, a National Independence Party candidate in the South Tottenham Ward of Haringey; Coney appealed to his Jewish voters (of whom there are no great number) 'not to vote only on religious lines' — an apparent reference to the fact that Labour councillor Aaron Weichselbaum was Jewish. Local Jewish leaders interpreted Coney's action as actually an attempt to deprive Weichselbaum of non-Jewish support by playing on local hostility to Jews. Coney was elected and Weichselbaum defeated, even though another Labour candidate was victorious.

EMPIRICAL STUDIES: THE WHITE BACKLASH

8.   THE NATIONAL FRONT IN LOCAL POLITICS: SOME INTERPRETATIONS

Duncan Scott

The material in this chapter was largely obtained during a period of
participant observation for a wider study [1] of the impact of ethnic
minorities on local politics. For over six months the researcher was
involved in establishing relationships across the political spectrum,
during which time the National Front made its first major incursion
into Fettlerbridge [2] politics. It was hoped at that point to be able to
'. . . sympathetically study the racist's "problem" of how to check
desegregation and increase racial discrimination.' [3]

A central concern in this paper is to demonstrate that the methods
of traditional political science are not able to produce sufficiently useful insights into the nature of deviant political organisations. It is hoped
that some of the ethnographic material that follows will demonstrate
more clearly the dynamics of a young social movement. Evidence will
be presented to suggest that much of what appears to be 'political'
activity is in fact an outlet for other social needs, that the processes of
becoming a member of a 'deviant' political movement precede ideological rationalisation, and that the rules of membership, at various levels,
are 'learned' in the cause of political activity.

The National Front is usually labelled a 'deviant' — a process initiated by both mainstream and fringe political opponents and often
embraced as a tactical move by Nationa Front activists themselves. One
fundamental assertion of this paper concerns the nature of this deviance. Whatever the merits of references to 'fascism' and 'conspiracy' a
large proportion of National Front political activity and beliefs can be
closely compared with the informal norms and activities of sections of
the working class. As part of this argument it will be necessary to
demonstrate that traditional definitions of deviance derive from a
framework of narrow *formal* politics. But much social behaviour is
located outside these arenas and yet still warrants the label 'political':
it is this *informal* political activity which is compared with that of the
National Front. In view of the dearth of material in this area tolerance
is sought for the tentative lines of comparison which are drawn.
Finally it will be emphasised that deviance is not a state but a process
and an intermittent and irregular process at that. The pragmatic responses of the actors involved will preclude any simple ideological
explanations.

Some Perspectives on Traditional Approaches to the Study of 'fringe' Political Activity

A good illustration of one of the focal concerns of contemporary political science is that provided by Butler and Stokes.[4] In a three year period they interviewed over 2,000 people in three waves. Both authors were clearly aware that their particular methods could have been supplemented by other approaches, in order to avoid those overemphases of quantitative measurement which often neglect '. . . both the relationship between local and national behaviour and the place of the election in a historic context, as well as the working of the political system.'[5]

Butler has written elsewhere about the particular problems involved in the study of politics.[6] In essence the politicians will grant him access to '. . . the people who are making decisions, and [permit him to] listen to them discussing ideas still in embryo, only if he is willing to accept a remarkable degree of self-censorship.' The 'insiders' will tolerate the 'outsider' only if the latter plays by the traditional rules.

All human behaviour is difficult to study because of the concealment of motives, the rationalisation of activity, and the combined ignorance of both actors and observers in the face of the complexity of motives and actions. Nevertheless, the political scientist seems to have capitulated to a process of professionalisation which reifies the statistic and the dissection of political memoirs. Even recent text books on political sociology exemplify this tendency.[7]

When attempts are made, therefore, to understand political behaviour which is conceptualised as 'deviant,' there are few established works upon which to base one's own research. Hobsbawm thought historians '. . . being mainly educated and townsmen, have until recently simply not made sufficient effort to understand people who are unlike themselves.'[8] Similarly it has been argued that political scientists have not been involved as much as sociologists in current protest activities because '. . . perhaps they were self selected for a certain pragmatic realism; or perhaps the current of political teaching runs that way and cools hot tempers.'[9] Both self-selection and the influence of the traditional subject matter seem to have been critical elements in the socialisation of political scientists. Richard Rose's observation of civil servants and political elites may also apply to political scientists: 'their only experience of England north of Oxford and Cambridge may be confined to short business trips or holidays in the most rural, and most atypical parts of the UK.'[10]

Thus political behaviour outside the traditional party framework has been covered by Rose in a single paragraph on Parkin's study of the Campaign for Nuclear Disarmament.[11] CND could be studied because it had '. . . persisted long enough to permit analyses of its recruits.' Because of the *ad hoc* pre-political nature of so many protest movements

215

'. . . they are difficult to document. *New Society* often carries comments about these groups.' In spite of this inadequate 'documentation,' the same author felt able to conclude that anti-immigrant groups at constituency level were of little significance in 1974[12] – a conclusion based on a ten year old study by Deakin,[13] and on an article in a popular weekly magazine. This slender basis for judgement is replicated in the major work on the 1970 General Election, where the reader is urged to use the monthly magazine *Race Today* as a source of regular information about race and politics.[14] In view of the fact that Enoch Powell gained more column inches in national newspapers than the entire Liberal Party [15] it is remarkable that knowledge of race and racism seems dependent on a popular journal and an increasingly unpredictable monthly. At least these ubiquitous professorial monitors of our electoral life might encourage their *students* to dig deeper into the workings of the political system.

In a criticism of Runciman's study of relative deprivation,[16] Edmund Leach argued in favour of a particular kind of 'digging' viz. 'If you want to know how manual workers feel about white-collar workers, go and stand on a shop floor and watch and listen.'[17] The usefulness of this advice is underlined in a study of car workers which convincingly warns against simplistic talk of the 'political apathy' of workers, ' . . . a lot of them care about not caring . . . *In spite of himself* the assembly-line worker is made apathetic by being a number.'[18] This insistence on the need to locate measurement of behaviour within the appropriate contexts of meaning is also underlined in a suggestion that both middle and lower classes ' . . . have values which could be turned in the direction of political authoritarianism *under certain conditions*.'[19]

Information on the behaviour of anti-immigrant organisations is regularly available from a range of observers who might be characterised as 'ornithologists.' From journals as diverse as the *Guardian, Morning Star* and *New Community* it is possible to assemble a 'bird-watcher's eye-view' of the latest marches, manifestoes and conspiratorial realignments. Typical comments label one branch of the National Front as 'quite strong' whereas a personal observation of this, definitions of 'strength' aside, suggest 'intermittent, localised and ineffective' might be more appropriate. More common are the geographies of right wing migrations, such as an article covering two-thirds of a page where the air is filled with the whirrings of at least seventeen overlapping groups and fifteen equally overlapping 'key figures.'[20] This is not to decry such material but merely to add that it must be used with caution.

That such information remains a central source of data was underlined in an indirect way by the report in a recent internal bulletin of the British Sociological Association on the failure of members to form groups on immigration and social movements because of a lack of response.[21] In the United States the study of political deviance has recently received much greater attention, partly due to the importance of McCarthyism in the 1950s and to the import of the Wallace and Black Power groups in the 1960s. A central tendency in such studies[22] has been the implicit acceptance of how 'unreasonable' the extremist politics have been. But the student needs to discover how such people interpret their objective situation in what to them may be a thoroughly 'reasonable' way. Such a perspective begs a re-examination of the values which are part of the labelling perspectives of deviancy theory — an exercise championed in recent years by members of the National Deviancy Symposium. Walton's study of the Weatherman[23] asks the question 'deviant from what?', but then only seems to take the argument in a 'radical-left' direction. We do not seem to be presented with the possibility of radicals of another persuasion.

No doubt the Weathermen provided material with which to make more general points. There remains, however, the nagging concern as to how far members of the Deviancy Symposium are also caught up in particular ideological stances which direct their enthusiasms. A simple headcount of their Research Register for 1974 reveals considerable interest in drugs, sexual identity and policing whereas only ten entries out of 262 mentioned political delinquency or deviance. At the twelve symposia between November 1968 and January 1973 over seventy papers were presented and only the Walton paper and one by a 'Comrade X' discussed aspects of what could be termed formal political deviance, assuming 'political' is not an open-ended definition.[24] The present paper cannot, however, undertake a separate study of the 'differential treatment of political deviance.' Suffice it to say that traditional political science tends to engage in historical studies[25] or urges reliance on journals, whilst ethnomethodology has yet to make a positive contribution in this area.

The Research Process — Some Central Problems

In the case of quasi-secret movements the researcher has often assumed a complete participant role, but in this instance the advice of Polsky was taken as a guiding principle '. . . you damned well better not pretend to be "one of them" . . . either you will . . . get sucked into "participant" observation of the sort you would rather not undertake, or you will be exposed, with still greater negative consequences. You must let the criminals know who you are, and if it is done properly it does not sabotage the research.'[26]

I tried to assemble information by a series of interviews with National Front activists, and then concentrated on two of these for more detailed comment on the internal workings of the branch. My role was never clearly understood, although I took the precaution of obtaining means of academic identification. Even when it was established that I might be a teacher or a student, that still did not remove the possibility of my links with 'Moscow,' 'the New Left,' 'Transport

217

House' or 'the Special Branch.'

At the end of 1970, when the major period of fieldwork was at an end, the local National Front branch activists numbered between twenty and twenty-five. This core of regular attenders, distributors and hecklers contained at least two elements: (i) a middle-class group totalling five or six and (ii) a working-class group totalling fifteen. By that time I had interviewed the first group on several occasions for long periods of one to two hours. Of the second group I interviewed eight of the main activists, including my two 'key' figures to whom I returned at least once a week over a period of several months. Initial success was difficult and not a little frightening – I was accorded some of the traditional stereotypes – but the major research difficulty proved to be the constant need to seek confirmation of what were presented as factual statements. There was a tendency towards gross distortion of numbers or of the consequences of particular events. Some of the latter were purely internal National Front affairs, and, as a non-National Front member regarded with a degree of suspicion and paranoia, difficult to document. Fortunately I was able to obtain an almost complete set of internal members' bulletins from June 1968 to late 1970 – the bulk of these from a friend who successfully 'joined' the National Front.

Inevitably the total picture is uneven. It is largely the product of over fifty semi-structured interviews with fourteen activists, a survey of the twenty-five local election addresses (ten in May 1969, thirteen in May 1970 and one in September 1970), twenty-six local bulletins, plus general election material for Jim Watson, the National Front candidate in Fettlerbridge West. In addition, one of the middle-class members has written a book and I was able to obtain a number of letters written by individual activists to each other. A further sample of material was the letters from the local National Front published by the local Fettler-bridge paper. Finally, during the 1970 General Election, Jim Watson held four factory meetings, of which I attended two, and one abortive open-air discussion which I also observed.[27]

It is worth recording the research methods adopted if only because it reveals something of the mechanisms of a small minority group. Just as members of mainstream parties hold stereotypes about the National Front, so any 'investigator' was stereotyped by National Front members. My presence provoked distortion and rumours about my role which revealed the existence of subgroups within the National Front as a whole. On at least two occasions in the midsummer of 1970, the National Front headquarters in London requested that local activists should not talk to outsiders about the movement. A later 'special bulletin' (mid-August 1970) from Martin Webster[28] purported to describe a spy calling on National Front members in the Yorkshire-Lancashire region. I was carefully questioned as to the comparability of Webster's 'character' with myself by two of my informants. Both seemed genuine in their belief in Webster's creation.

The fact that my informants continued to give long interviews (often to a tape recorder) indicated how the National Front core subdivided into small social cliques, which did not all share the same views about my role, or about the correct ideology and strategy of the National Front. One of the supposed functions of an appeal to a common threat is the binding effect exerted on group members. But demands for secrecy from Chesterton or local leaders were not sufficient to break my contacts. My two main informants felt I was 'alright' partly because they had criticisms of the local ruling clique in the National Front and wanted to discuss these and also because they were unaware of my links with local ethnic minorities.

Preconditions of Political Deviance: Problems of Definition

Deviance is inevitably relative. Usually the yardstick is that of formal legislative politics. The right, left and community fringe politicians can be labelled deviant in terms of their behaviour or their ideology. Part of the surprise of political activists and commentators at these deviant movements must be attributed to their ignorance of the extent of separation of formal political processes from the lives of large sections of the population, and to their inadequate conceptualisation of the beliefs and behaviour of the latter. It will be suggested that the 'political apathy of the working class' is not synonymous with political inactivity once different definitions of the word political are allowed. Of course it is easy for a writer to shift definitions in order to demolish straw men. But there is a sense in which the characteristics of the National Front sufficiently overlap both the formal boundaries *and* those more invisible political arenas of everyday life. Herein lies both the significance and dilemma of a political movement — to grow may be to formalise and risk isolation.

Talcott Parsons has argued that 'rightism' '. . . is at least as deeply rooted in the social structure and dynamics of our society as was socialism at an earlier stage.'[29] Major rearrangements of industrial and urban life are experienced unevenly and prompt partial fragmentation of cultural and moral value systems. Different kinds of strain seem to be apparent among those experiencing certain kinds of social mobility (up or down) as Runciman recognised in his later reflections on reference groups and social integration.[30] Significantly he referred to the study of working-class white support for George Wallace in Gary, Indiana. These people had a limited education but a middling income and shared both a deep cynicism of government and a sense of political powerlessness. They had '. . . done better than their fathers and were objectively fairly secure . . . had high aspirations without a sense of making progress . . . *believed that Negroes are unjustly making rapid strides forward* . . . helped out by a . . . government that had forgotten them.'[31]

When people who are isolated from formal politics make demands about their grievances ' . . . from the point of view of those who accept the consensus, the demands and concerns . . . appear at best to be non-political. At worst they appear as stupid, irrational or irresponsible.'[32] This isolation is seen as stemming primarily from broad *structural* alterations in the nature of formal politics. (How far it is possible to attribute part of this process to *value systems* is touched on in a later section.) We should not be trapped into conclusions about political inactivity. There is, for example, considerable evidence of political interest on the shop floor. What is clear, however, is that much of this is necessarily a kind of 'ad hocracy'[33] characterised within a wider interpretation as 'anomic,' i.e. where there is '. . . a lack of *moral* regulation over the wants and goals that individuals hold.'[34] This disorder is conceptualised as rooted in the inequalities of society as a whole — as 'normal' not pathological. It is, therefore, important to locate the National Front within the '. . . complementarity of subcultural distinctness *and* (my emphasis) total-culture coherence.'[35]

Part of the explanation, however, must consider cultural frameworks. Family life, the shop floor, clubs and pubs provide arenas for intense social interaction in which there exists almost no bureaucratic organisation or planning, but tensions between appeals to solidarity and the need for leadership, limited intellectualisation and an almost casual reliance on oral communication.[36] Problems can also arise from initial conceptions concerning the proper objects for study. Thus, in a discussion of the difficulties associated with understanding 'religiousness,' Towler has distinguished between institutional belief systems and 'common religion.'[37] A familiarity with the former seems to encourage an oversystemisation of the latter which might be better conceptualised as an 'assortment of themes'[38] not logically related to each other, but rather to those constitutional regularities of social life such as birth, marriage, crises and death.

Similarly, it may be *conceptually* useful to adopt the notion of a 'common politics' (cf. 'organic politics'[39]) without the formal coherence of a political party and ideology, which is nevertheless far from being anarchic. Individual sectors may not be able to *explain* their actions within a total framwork which is relatively consistent, but this need not preclude the *existence* of degrees of consistency in their 'common' politics. The relevance of the National Front may therefore lie in the extent to which its form of organisation as a new movement are resonant with sections of working-class life and its own 'cracker mottoes' can tap themes from 'common' politics.

Preconditions of Political Deviance: Status Politics?

Perhaps the most commonly used framework in an interpretation of the impact of major social changes on responses to ethnic groups is that concerned with 'status politics.'[40] Bell's major perspectives provide bases of comparison with Fettlerbridge, although it seems unlikely that the present study can separate 'interest' from status. The latter will be used as a descriptive label in order to assess the relevance of 'mass society' approaches, compared with, for example, that implied in the recently published Commission on the Consitution.[41]

The first feature of the 'status politics' approach is the characterisation of the 'masses' as disorganised and heterogeneous. But the American commentators (e.g. Lipset, Bell and Kornhauser[42]) were writing about a more fluid social structure subject to greater tensions. Fettlerbridge, although far from isolated from broader national trends, has retained a partial framework of identity because of the continued existence within the borough of villages first established in the eighteenth century. Nevertheless there have been more subtle demographic alterations as well as the obvious entry of immigrants from the Caribbean and Asia. In 1951 the population was 129,026 and almost totally white. Two decades later the overall total was still only 132,210 (est.) of which at least 12,000 were 'coloured immigrants.' Fettlerbridge thus contained both the physical ingredients for the continuance of specific social traditions and symbols of mass change. The fear of the 'mass' because of its association with inferiority is the second element in the 'status politics' approach. and this may well exist in Fettlerbridge.

The Commission on the Constitution examines differential cultural identification according to region and highlights the peculiarly strong feelings of cultural identity and exclusiveness in the Fettlerbridge area. Some 73 per cent[43] of inhabitants in Fettlerbridge's region had lived there all their lives, a percentage second only to the 82 per cent in Scotland, by contrast to the 44 per cent in Southeast England. Further evidence on regional identification indicated that the concept was both comprehensible and acceptable to a majority and that the Fettlerbridge (F.R.) was almost as strong in identification as those outposts of nationalism, Wales and Scotland. Table 1 summarises some points of comparison between F.R. and 'other parts of Britain.

Table 1 Comparison of 'Fettlerbridge region' with 'other parts of Britain'

	Average % (12 regions)	F.R. %	position	Lowest	Highest
'Feeling of difference in people'	37	48	2nd	15	53
'Particularly proud of Culture and Customs'	73	91	3rd	54	94

Source: *Commission on Constitution*, Research Paper No. 7, p. 49.

Bell's third perspective developed inferences about the likelihood of economic alienation as mass production came to dominate industrial processes. Tangential to this is Benewick's explanation of support for the British Union of Fascists[44] in conditions 'suitable to a movement with limited finances and manpower. Substandard and overcrowded housing, poor working conditions, limited incomes, and inadequate recreational facilities drove people to the diversions provided by the street-corner politicians.' But Fettlerbridge in the 1960s enjoyed a rate of unemployment of around 1 per cent and the more typical industrial unit is the small or medium-sized firm, often locally owned and imperfectly unionised. It was only in the mid-1960s that some of the larger engineering concerns became 'organised' in the trade union sense, and it may be that the very slowness and weakness of working-class organisation has facilitated the growth of anti-immigrant movements. 'Fettlerbridge man' is not yet 'mass production man' and the sources of his antipathy reside elsewhere.

Another explanation of 'deviant' political activity used by the most disparate of ideologies places responsibility upon the 'Crisis of Capitalism'. Movements such as the National Front are either 'the desperate resort of a dying capitalism'[45] or efforts to combat the 'world Jewish Internationalist conspiracy.'[46] Some of the ideological dialectic will be outlined in a later section, but it is not a prime concern of this paper to examine the role of ideology.

The final two 'cogs' in Bell's scheme involve the machinery of bureaucracy and politics: the inhabitants of mass society, the argument goes, become administrative units and political eunuchs, powerless and non-political. Over half of the sample interviewed for the Commission on the Constitution felt powerless in the face of government and in particular this view was shared by 'younger people, those with fewer years of education and those from working-class households . . .'[47] Comparability between the Commission and Bell's framework is more difficult in the area of political 'involvement' partly because of the spectrum, ranging from the 17 per cent who had contacted a local councillor to the 8 per cent who knew the date and place of council meetings, to the mere 0.05 per cent who were members of a reorganised local council.

In an attempt to focus more specifically on the convergent activities of some political minority movements since the late 1960s one clue may reside in 'The only "new" experience, going sharply counter to tradition . . . that of the coloured immigration of the 1950s and 60s.'[48] During the last decade there have also been five general elections, and a major reorganisation of local government, punctuated by large phases of attention to the 'problems' of immigration and race relations legislation. Some individuals and their social networks have not simply reacted to backstage sociological promptings but have themselves directed the course of events by their searchings for power. When, therefore,

therefore, the responses of National Front activists are examined they need to be related to promptings at a number of levels, not the least of which includes the attempts of politicians to use these same promptings for their own ends.

The 'status politics' emphasis on normative 'preconditions' accounts for far more political deviance (in the traditional sense) than actually occurs since only a limited number of people become members or active participants in movements such as the National Front. Consideration of three major membership types (the rank and file, the elite and the eccentrics) suggests that the looseness of entry criteria and the stress on activity permit at least temporary coexistence. So long as minimal stress is laid on ideological purity this situation is likely to continue. For many joiners the demands are much less constricting than formal political membership. They are caught up in activity for a wide range of reasons, only some of which are later reorganised into a rationalisation. For many of working-class background the initial steps may have been for much less organised reasons than those assumed by social scientists.

Political Motivation – Becoming a Member

The focus in this section is upon the self-reports of different types of member. The conflicting levels of political awareness seemed less significant than the rewards of friendship, marital solidarity and emotional release which were mentioned as being derived from membership. When there was mention of Rhodesia, West Indian Jehovah's Witnesses and Hitler, this seemed part of an attempt to organise what had initially been (for the rank and file and most of the eccentrics) an eclectic response.

Most generalisations about the political motivations of activists in mass social movements have referred to working-class or upper middle-class activists. An examination of National Front membership suggests a predominance of the lower middle-class and members of the skilled working class with branch variations emphasised in the contrasts between, for example, Worthing and Blackburn.[49] Benewick emphasises the part played by middle-class and professional people in the active segment of the BUF.[50] Whilst the solicitor, estate agent, chartered engineer, pharmaceutical chemist and maths lecturer elite in Fettlerbridge seems to confirm Benewick in matters of *control*, a substantial proportion of the *work* of the branch was carried out by people with occupations usually labelled 'working-class.'[51] Harris, for so many years a newspaper correspondent, and Harvey, merchant navy and sales representative, provide intermediate examples. On the other hand Midgley was a bus driver, Denton a textile spinner and Greenough a butcher. Of the regular active core of about twenty to thirty people, the occupations of twenty-four members could be identified. With the exclusion of the ten previously mentioned, the others were housewife (1), lorry driver/bus driver (3), semi-skilled engineer or mechanic (7), textile labourer (1), decorator (1) and laboratory technician (1). For any normal branch meeting there might be fifteen to twenty people present on a good night. At least two-thirds would represent the traditionally working-class occupations. One main pattern of recruitment in this respect seems to be the under-representation of the textile and chemical industries where the largest number of immigrants work and where general levels of job skills are lower than in engineering. National Front activists from the working class appear to have come from above the lowest skill levels — just that group where social and economic tensions might be greatest.

Political motivation by self-report is inevitably limited and partial, but insight can be gained as to how far motives have become independent of the original needs and perhaps submerged within the contemporary needs of the growing movement. Clear-cut categorisation of answers to open-ended interview situations is not possible but at least 'the *direction* that rationalisations take can permit us to understand the pressures under which motives operate.'[52] That it is worth accepting and using these 'directions' is underlined in the seemingly arid circularity of much of what passes for sociological explanation (cf. a recent text book on political sociology: [recruitment is determined] '... by the basic social and political attitudes of the individual, which are closely associated with his personal and social characteristics as well as with the social and political environment which forms the context of his political behaviour.'[52]

Five National Front 'joiners' have been chosen to represent the three different if overlapping types of member. The first is Pat Kiernan who offered to stand as a National Front candidate after hearing that a local Pakistani shopkeeper was standing in the same ward as a Liberal. Kiernan promised to take time off work during the campaign. In the event his election address was written for him — even the 'personal message' was the same as three others except for 'I have lived in Fettlerbridge all my life and will put your interests foremost.' He visited the ward once before voting, and most of his election addresses were distributed for him by the ageing but enthusiastic Harris, the National Front candidate in an adjacent ward. On polling day Kiernan appeared in the ward after work at about 6.00 p.m. to the fury of the ever-active Harris.

Pat Kiernan, a crane driver, had never been politically active before, knew nothing of council work, was unaware of the identity of half the thirteen National Front candidates and did not read literature about the National Front. That he stood at all was largely due to the energies of Malcolm Midgley the branch secretary, whose pressure was partially reinforced by the fact that Kiernan and Midgley, both in their twenties and single, shared membership in overlapping pub cliques.

224

Kiernan's intermittent, supposedly 'deviant,' activity therefore consisted of a series of naive fumblings around the fringes of local politics. He was used by the National Front because their central aims were for external publicity and internal coherence via involvement. As a loosely organised movement there were virtually no filters through which a candidate or his scrutineers had to pass, whilst the formal 'political' activity almost entirely revolved around the distribution of leaflets.

Woolton represented in the local National Front the small town, self-made man, from a local family with a small shop and known and liked by the immediate neighbourhood. Woolton and Webb grew up together but separated during secondary education. Both these men represent the calm and resolute determination of individuals who feel they have lost out on the changes in the world, feeling insufficiently recognised, they sought redress against 'the big battalions' (Woolton's phrase). Talk of coloured immigrants came *after* their lists of frustrations. There was a consistent pattern of status anxiety particularly in relation to occupation, and then an attempt to transfer this to the political arena in a none too logical way! 'I'm stuck as a chemist, fixed regulations, and fixed hours . . . I'm nowhere . . . you just can't express yourself because of the limitations of your surroundings.'

Similar observations were made by Woolton about Webb. 'Ronald now has his own firm because no-one could appreciate exactly how much depended on him and how much work he was doing . . . his intellect was beyond that of his bosses and so straight away I was on the same level as him . . .' Webb now describes himself as a chartered engineer and 'head of a firm.' The labour force seemed to consist of himself, wife, a married daughter and two or three others. Nevertheless he has a fairly new detached house in a small private development in a fashionable residential area of Fettlerbridge.

By the early 1960s Woolton and Webb had developed a close agreement about the dangers in the world, and were increasingly concerned to do something about them. In 1963 they joined the Anglo-Rhodesia Society because of their disgust at the 'shabby treatment accorded the Rhodesians.' I asked him 'Why Rhodesia?' and was told 'What else was there . . . this is our concern . . . Rhodesia is ours . . . our kin are having a raw deal . . . incompetent blacks are taking over in Africa simply for the sake of them being black . . .'

At about the time of UDI, Webb and Woolton met some white Rhodesians, liked them and decided to go on a holiday to Rhodesia 'to see for ourselves.' For three weeks in 1966 they toured the country and talked to 'the people' (whites) and found them to be '. . . a cut above the average you find around here . . . we could identify with them and trust them without knowing the details of the issue . . .'

Both men were aware of the League of Empire Loyalists but were only stimulated into joining an overtly political organisation in 1967 when Webb wrote off for a National Front pamphlet. 'He'd seen the address in a paper somewhere, and when he got their stuff he said, "These people are saying just what we've been saying." ' They joined via the London HQ and were put in touch with the local secretary – Malcolm Midgley. The latter plus Greenough, Denton and three or four others constituted the total paper membership of the National Front in late 1967. Webb and Woolton then visited a number of addresses in the Fettlerbridge area, from which brief survey the latter concluded '. . . there was no coherent idea or general view among them . . . they'd joined on a particular point and hadn't advanced from there . . . somehow we met Cornell [solicitor] and he gave the final stability and direction . . . the others would have blundered, though I admit they're absolutely essential . . .'

It was clear that there existed an uneasy tension between the middle-class elite, rank and file and eccentric members of the new movement. Most of the fourteen interviewees complained about other subgroups. Even the elite of five or six members did not form a cohesive unit within the National Front or a social group outside it. None of the latter had reason to fear the intrusion of the coloured immigrant within the occupational or domestic segments of their lives. On the other hand, all expressed a concern about their place in society and the differing ways in which they were being threatened.

In contrast, Mr and Mrs Gormley were unable to develop either the jargon-laden philosophy of Cornell or the homespun, self-help elitism of Woolton and Fanton. They subscribed to the 'theology' but more pragmatic responses cohered around the 'coloured immigrant' as 'cause' of a cluster of somehow related problems. Mrs Gormley, a grandmother in her early sixties was easily the most active of the rank and file and has risen since her response to National Front propaganda during April 1968 to the position of Chairman of the local branch (1972), and member of the National Front Directorate (1973). She is a thin woman who wears heavy facial make-up to hide skin disorders, wigs to compensate for recent hair loss, and generally bright clothes (red nail varnish, three large rings, pendant jewellery).

Her house is a neat council property on the corner of an estate in suburban Fettlerbridge, to which she moved when it was first built in 1940. Part of her explanation of involvement in the National Front came from professed feelings of being threatened by coloured people: '. . . there are lots of West Indians on this estate . . . some of their places are terrible, you can see them easy . . . most of my election nominees were from round here but I could have got them anywhere . . . like Elsie and Fred across the road . . . they share our views but they're not bothered about voting . . . just like me really . . .' It was all a 'conspiracy' by the Council as West Indian families were gradually being 'slipped into' particular estates, all the time getting nearer the Gormleys.

Economic changes reinforced their subjective mental maps of the estate. Mrs Gormley's shop job folded when the premises closed, her younger son was out of work for the first time in 1970 and Mr Gormley had been 'off on the sick' for a long period.

In the wide, privet-bordered roads near the Gormley's house a West Indian face was relatively rare. Yet on Sunday mornings two Jamaican women would canvass on behalf of the Jehovah's Witnesses. Some time early in 1969 Mrs Gormley discovered that her son had become an active worker for the Witnesses and had been spending his evenings doing much of the joinery work in the new Kingdom Hall. The fact that the West Indian woman and not her son had told her made the denouement all the more galling. There had followed a series of family crises about blood transfusions, voting, gift giving and sundry other facets of the religion which upset Mrs Gormley. After an ultimatum, the son and his wife agreed to withdraw from the church rather than lose contact with their parents. During the telling of this incident, Mrs Gormley had become excited as she explained two subsequent encounters with the same West Indian woman. 'I had the poker in my hand and I said "you rotten race of bloody people . . ." I've never been so angry in all my life . . . I just had to tell her . . . I'd have screamed if I hadn't had a go at her . . .'

Both Mr and Mrs Gormley had never before been so united over a political issue. Before joining the National Front in 1968, Mr Gormley had been an active Labour voter, whilst his wife had been in the Primrose League in the early 1930s in Oldham. She explained that her strongly pro-Tory family had been instrumental in her joining the forerunner of the Young Tories but '. . . I wasn't brought up in Fettlerbridge and so I wasn't "in" as you might say . . .' The husband and wife 'team' had found a new sense of purpose and, in the case of Mrs Gormley, a feeling of enhanced status at a time of life when options were beginning to run out. For them it was all talk of expansion and the success round the corner. They were caught up in the new awakening after Powell, and the conditions of minority group activity allowing nearly everyone a 'significant' role have compounded their determination to make the National Front succeed. It has to do well as a movement because they are so personally involved. Thus the familiar psychological mechanisms seem to operate, as each election produces a similar protest vote for the National Front. Hope is salvaged from the most pathetic performance. Like the religious missionaries so detested by her, Mrs Gormley is convinced that failure is the result of a lack of effort rather than the irrelevance of the message.

Within the pub culture of central Fettlerbridge, a number of constantly changing drinking cliques have established some persistence of identity through the continuance of one or two core members. 'Midgley's lot' was a varying collection of five or six, and part of the human scenery in the interconnecting work of saloon bars in the centre of town. When they emerged in particular forms of street politics in the late 1960s, some Fettlerbridge inhabitants were not surprised.

Typical of 'Midgley's lot' in style was Denton. He can be regarded as an 'eccentric' in contrast to the more central and regular activists of the elite and rank and file. Another eccentric category, not considered in this paper, consisted of two or three men in their seventies whose activities were concentrated more towards multiple membership of right-wing organisations, bill-posting and letter writing.

Denton had been a 'sympathetic activists' of the National Socialists since the late 1950s whilst in the Navy. During a Jordan rally in Trafalgar Square he had been 'beaten up by young Commies and Jews,' and then reprimanded by his commanding officer. Through the middle to late 1960s, with the dissolution of the National Socialists and his own exit from the Navy, he had merely 'kept in touch.' His explanations of activity included familiar rationalisations about coloured immigrants plus some notably more extreme items. He '. . . admired Hitler . . . not because of his death camps before he went off the handle . . . but what he did prior to war . . . I read *Mein Kampf* . . . it's very difficult to understand.' In Denton's invectives against 'bosses' at the mill his conclusions were held together by a racial rather than a class thread:

> '. . . When we're being laid off there'll be bloody wogs still on the job . . . you've got to work with them . . . but I can't touch one of them without shuddering, it may be just me . . . I can't help this . . . I don't care what people say, these sociologists and that . . . it just sends a shiver up my spine . . .'

Violence was present in many segments of his life. His 'record,' apart from the Trafalgar Square incident, included thunderous heckling of middle-aged ladies at Community Relations meetings, arrest and fines for drunken driving (April 1970) and for violent behaviour (June 1970). In November 1970 his wife took their son and left him, whilst early in 1971 he emigrated alone to Rhodesia. He seemed happiest exercising his Alsatian dogs which he had been breeding since leaving the Navy, and which he used in analogies about the dangers of interracial marriage. From mid-November 1969 to April 1970 he was effectively and officially the local National Front branch secretary. After this period a driving ban limited his activity whilst in mid-June after his arrest for violent behaviour he resigned from the organisation.

These examples of political motivation are held to be broadly representative of the range of membership. That they did not share the same social networks or official National Front ideology was apparent, but the activities of the most involved ensured that opportunities were increasingly available for the political socialisation of these disparate members. Their prior orientations meant a receptivity to the binding concern with the threat of the coloured immigrant. As the cliques and subgroups came to participate in electoral activity, social gatherings

228

and street politics, so a common fund of experiences began to be forged. Part of this process involved the fashioning of local interpretations of national ideology, not without puzzlement and dissatisfaction within the local organisation. In an attempt to throw some light on how the 'joiners' became 'members,' this paper now concentrates on the role of social events. Of course, a full account would need to examine formal and subterranean ideologies and the place of conflicts as sources of social control, but space precludes this.

It is sufficient to emphasise that the extent to which a particular member of the National Front was able to outline his or her ideology depended upon the nature of their involvement and their relative social status within the minority organisation. Many of the rank and file had joined not at the end of a long ideological equation which concluded with 'National Front,' but becaise of a single issue in society or in their personal lives, *and* because the local branch was active. Their late association with the National Front led some of them to begin to move away from a loose cluster of opinions and towards a more organised belief system, even an ideology. Continued activism seemed to be a function of personal and social influences, rather than a political standpoint. Members who remained active, did so primarily not because they 'believed' (in the sense of acceptance) but because they needed to believe in order to obtain other benefits which accrued from belonging. Theirs was a form of pragmatic politics rather than of any overarching philosophy. What really held a core together was their participation in local political arenas and their interaction with rival political activists.

Political Activity — the Maintenance of a Social Movement

This final section considers the significance of National Front political activity not primarily in relation to formal political criteria such as the strength of ward organisation or number of votes, but in order to arrive at conclusions concerning the degree to which (a) National Front activities were deviant and (b) definitions of deviance which were as much the product of the other actors in the political arena as the National Front, yet progressively embraced by the latter for reasons of social control.

Entry into electoral activity usually reaches an early euphoric peak and then declines, to be succeeded by increasing involvement in street politics similar perhaps to the processes involved in school gangs, soccer supporters' 'adventures' and club trips. This 'expressive' politics was supplemented by internal social controls often manufacturing new meanings from earlier experiences.

The typical approach of political scientists and 'ornithologists' is to survey the electoral performance of the National Front upon which generalisations are based about its 'political significance.' February 1974 witnessed the National Front's first use of the national media as a result of fielding over fifty general election candidates. In Fettler-bridge alone since 1969 there have been forty-six instances of the National Front contesting a ward election, as well as four general election candidates. October 1974 was the first time *both* Fettlerbridge constituencies had National Front candidates. Table 2 represents a comparison of local electoral performances over four successive years in the six wards most regularly contested. Proportionate and absolute support for the National Front in these and *all* other wards shows a massive *decline*, except for Valley Ward, in 1972. The reorganisation of local ward boundaries in 1973 precluded a continuing comparison but the three candidates in both County and District elections again experienced falling support, to such an extent that Mrs Gormley was beaten by a Communist in May 1973, an unprecedented experience for any local National Front candidate.

Table 2 National Front electoral performance at local level — selected Fettlerbridge wards

	National Front as % of total votes			
Ward	1969	1970	1971	1972
Eastside	14.0W	12.8	4.3	4.1
Hirst	16.7G	11.5	18.4G	3.2G
Pennine	15.0	12.8	7.6	5.8
Valley	14.0	8.9	4.7	6.1
Eastville	11.0	11.3		3.6
Estate	9.0	7.8G		6.3

G = Mrs Gormley   1973 = Eastside + Estate in County Elections 360 = 5.5%
                                        Estate in District Elections (3 elected per ward) 100 out of 7,183 votes cast
W = Webb   1972 = Joint candidate in Wilton Ward = 4.25%
                      1973 = Didn't stand
      February 1974 = General Election candidate, Fettlerbridge East. 796 votes = 1.9%

There may be some inverse relationship between the steady decline in electoral support and the injection of the local National Front into alternative activities. Elections did serve to engage the core of twenty to thirty activists for several weeks of frenzied leafletting but the peripheral younger elements clearly discernible during street marches were less enthusiastic. The elite sought to manufacture an image of a responsible political party to be accepted on the same level of credibility as its Conservative, Liberal and Labour rivals; on the other hand, participation of the rank and file in 'street politics' (i.e. marches and heckling) made fewer demands on fragile ideological and administrative resources. In the event the number of local election candidates per annum has almost halved since 1969-70, whilst the branch held its first public meetings, and hosted a gathering of National Front branches at a large march and rally in March 1973. In formal electoral terms the movement may have enjoyed its greatest impact during the Powell euphoria and the general election of 1970. Any appraisal of its overall political significance must, therefore, be founded in the processes of *internal* social control, and the perceptions of National Front activists concerning their more *informal* political excursions. The following section briefly considers (a) the role of status rewards, particularly as these affected the elite, (b) the meaning of 'social' activity – exemplified by Mrs Gormley and (c) street politics and the eccentrics.

In a general sense the elite have gained status wherever other local politicians have reacted to the National Front for 'causing' tensions, or in 1970 for 'influencing' the general election result in Fettlerbridge West. In September 1970 the presentation of gold badges 'for excellent service' went to fourteen National Front activists, including Jim Watson (London-based general election candidate for Fettlerbridge West), Malcolm Midgley, and Greenough (then local Treasurer). In *Spearhead* an article 'Local Polls show big National Front potential' (May 1970) Fettlerbridge received half of the space and glowing praise: 'The greatest organisation achievement was in Fettlerbridge . . . the work of a truly professional organisation which deserves our highest praise and in which the Webb and Midgley families in particular have rendered wonderful service.' Perhaps the top prize went to Webb – appointment to the National Directorate – announced at a branch meeting in August 1970.

During the 1968-70 period internal National Front bulletins talked of £1 to £3 raffles, leaflets and biro pens, whilst Webb showed slides of his trip to the Everest base camp. But as Fettlerbridge National Front used hundreds of pounds that year, it was clear that some alternative sources of finance had been established. Mrs Gormley, one of the few active women at that time, continued her social enthusiasms. An early high point came in December 1970 when she arranged a presentation for Mr and Mrs Webb at a buffet supper. Initial arrangements began in August and preoccupied her at least once a week for over three months. Eventually Webb received a pewter tankard and his wife a bouquet of flowers. Mrs Gormley wrote in a letter (December 1970) 'We had a lovely social evening the 8th December. Unfortunately the men had to go down to the Friendly & Trades . . . Powys, Cornell and some of Powy's friends, and Jim Merrick[54] from Bradford, brought a load of his members over . . . our lot tied them up in knows [i.e. the two principal speakers] all the big coloured henchmen were all there and the police were waiting outside but nothing happened sorry to say.'

Mrs Gormley and indeed the majority of the active core were becoming increasingly involved in 'expressive politics', i.e. '. . . a means to express how the actors feel about their situation.'[55] So that 'Social suggestion, not individual words and verification, becomes the stimulus of activity . . . This is not to suggest that signs or symbols in themselves have any magical force as narcotics. They are, rather, the only means by which groups not in a position to analyse a complex situation rationally may adjust themselves to it, through stereotypisation, over-simplification and reassurance.'[56] The goals of National Front action are not necessarily, therefore, the objective 'solutions' to the initial problems, but rather they are attained in the behaviour itself. From 1970 much of the political socialisation of National Front members moved increasingly from formal politics to the public halls and streets.

There had always been members who enjoyed visits to meetings of the United Nations Association, the Labour Party and the Community Relations Council, noisy heckling being their usual contribution. Brief examination of one indoor meeting provides some insight into the processes of socialisation. The September 1970 issue of *Candour* singled out seven events deemed to have won the National Front major publicity over the previous twelve months and '. . . the heckling of Dr David Pitt by activists in Fettlerbridge . . .' was singled out as helping to make the National Front 'a household word.' A meeting arranged by the CRC and Cooperative Education Department began at 2.45 p.m. on Saturday 7 February 1970 and ended in uproar, with the reading of the Riot Acts and arrests for assault two hours later. The local National Front bulletin announced proudly 'Race-Mixers Shattered.' Interpretations of the meeting were as muddled on the National Front as on the CRC side. The former seemed to derive their greatest pleasure simply from retelling particular incidents of how 'we showed 'em,' the overall impression being one of general euphoria that they had been sufficiently strong to call out so many police. The National Front 'stopped' an important speaker and caused ripples through Fettlerbridge, this being 'proof that our policies are taking effect when people sit up and take notice like that.' The Trades Club in fact witnessed very little of National Front policy, except in so far as this related to 'methods for disturbing meetings.' Participation had been the essential thing. To have been there was to have been baptised into extremism.

When this extremism becomes part of a complex interaction, with challenges from antagonistic movements ranging from the Communist Party to the International Socialists, and when the context shifts from the comparatively identifiable structure of an indoor meeting to a street march and a crowded open-air rally, problems of theory and method are compounded.

Butler and Pinto-Duschinsky summarised national National Front activities in the 1970 election as negligible ('. . . scarcely heard from except in their local press')[57] although they conceded that the electoral intervention of the National Front in Fettlerbridge West may have prevented a Conservative gain. The Lime Square meeting was '. . . almost an incident . . .'[58] The local press chose to play this down for a variety of reasons, although it was the largest election meeting of 1970 in Fettlerbridge and one in which white people were gathered in hundreds together with similarly large groups of Caribbean and Asian immigrants. The local paper provided 140 words and the regional daily 160.

The gathering of people took place because a maverick Tory (Powys) attempted what was almost a one man pressure group exercise. His efforts to secure a public platform for Powell were never practical but events carried him along, as the local Communist Party quickly produced leaflets asserting the central place of the National Front in the arrangements. The Communist activists, and some members of the Indian Workers Association, pre-empted Powys, spoke, and were assaulted by Denton before large numbers of police broke up the meeting. A collection of youths (including Greenough, the National Front Treasurer, who seemed to believe he was 'leading' them although he was just another body in the rush) ran out of the Square, and later there *was* an 'incident' outside a Pakistani cafe.

The National Front's general election candidate was driven around the Square before the meeting and then to canvassing in a distant ward. Individual National Front members present included Mr and Mrs Gormley, Greenough, Denton and one of the aged eccentrics, whilst Fanton 'watched' from his tutorial room 100 yards away. All were interviewed after having been observed, the consistent conclusion being that they were present individually, were not completely aware of each other, and did not constitute a coherent National Front presence. Jim Watson (the National Front candidate) declared that '. . . so far as I am aware none of our supporters was present.' *Spearhead* (August 1970) noted that 'sixty Indians invaded the meeting and set about everybody with hockey sticks,' whilst the Fettlerbridge *National Front Bulletin* for July 1970 noted how the meeting '. . . brought out the reds in force. Some of them armed with hockey sticks chased young Britons from Lime Square. The most significant thing was that of the 750 Communists present, 99.9 per cent were coloured.' No details were ever published about the arrest of Denton for to do so would have disrupted the manipulation of experience to the disadvantage of the growing movement.

National Front electoral activity was therefore important because

(1) It gave members something to do — the addressing and posting of leaflets, letters and the heckling provided immediate satisfactions.

(2) It occasioned interaction with the formal political worlds from which they were separated. In the ensuing process the emergence of

233

stereotypes of National Front deviance was contributory to an emergent identity. The small and disregarded were taking action and this was 'meaningful' because of the response.

(3) It anchored the street politics into perceptions of relevance and progress.

(4) It demonstrated the importance of the elite. Finance, knowledge of politics and legal requirements, and equipment, were all necessary for formal political excursions. The relationship between formal and organic politics was a shifting one as the growing movement pragmatically shifted from one event to the next. More crucially these different activities were functional for purposes of social control — how else could the solicitor, lecturer and chemist be impelled into activity with usherette and lorry driver?

Some Conclusions

The use of a largely ethnographic approach in the study of what is conventionally labelled a deviant political movement permits some modest concluding points. In particular it is worth exploring:

(a) how far the irrelevance of formal politics in the lives of *many* sections of the population is translated by *some* into a melange of cultural or regional nationalism. Is the English equivalent of the various Celtic oppositions to Westminster to be located in the National Front?

(b) whether the concept of deviance is rooted in structural and ideological arrangements rather than in particular inherent properties of specific acts and values. By using the self-reports of members it was possible to distinguish the presence of chance and pragmatism. The chief actors were not mere puppets within the normative cage of mass society analysts. They generally felt quite 'ordinary' and visibly enjoyed their excursions in expressive politics.

(c) how the tightrope which a political movement must walk stretches between electoral sophistication and bureaucratic clarity on the one hand and the 'break-outs' into common politics on the other. This ambivalence is necessary both in terms of recruitment and in social control as the diverse recruits stumble into more coherent explanations of their position. For in the last analysis membership meant not simply activity but meaning.

Some observers still suggest that Englishmen '. . . take their national identity for granted.' The Commission on the Constitution provides increasing evidence to the contrary. Part of the general distrust of government achieves expression via a kind of negative nationalism which in towns like Fettlerbridge seems to gain inputs, however fragmented they may be, of a regional cultural identity. Whilst some of the

National Front membership may be searching for status (the middle class), much of the rank and file's initial involvement may have originated as

'. . . an expression of their pain and powerlessness confronted by the decay and dereliction, not only of the familiar environment, but of their own lives too – an expression for which our society provides no outlet . . . something more complex and deep-rooted than what the metropolitan liberal evasively and easily dismisses as prejudice.'[60]

The reactions within formal political structures at a local level to the National Front resembles in some respects those to pressures such as the Fettlerbridge Pakistani Association. When spokesmen from the latter organised a petition concerning Islamic education their challenge was absorbed by political entrepreneurs, who translated the requests, thereby excluding the ethnic minorities from that mesh of formal and informal opinion – sounding which is part of the Fettlerbridge version of representative democracy. But in the case of the National Front it may be that their use of race is merely *a means* (always in danger of becoming *the end*) whereby the bewilderment of much larger sections of the population achieves expression.

When Mrs Gormley referred to her (formally) politically apathetic neighbours Elsie and Fred as 'just like me really,' she was probably nearer the truth about membership of the National Front, than in any other statement. If traditional political science is to assess more adequately the strength of this argument its practitioners will have to travel much closer to the 'Mrs Gormleys' of the National Front – only then can explanations be obtained about which 'ordinary' joiners become 'core members.' Part of this explanation may rest in discovering why people *need* that kind of expressive politics which prompted Mrs Gormley to reflect '. . . nothing happened – sorry to say.' Greater detail about what therefore constitutes 'something' in the politics of such movements may require greater use of the participant method.

In the last analysis the National Front is important partly because some aspects of its activity are racialist and prompted by assortments of ideas about groups characterised on the basis of colour. Herein are a number of taks for the political activist rather than the occupant of the armchairs of tertiary education. But more important still is the fact that small groups of people find it necessary to by-pass the supposedly civilised processes of western democracy. It is never enought to hurl out epithets, for these can assist in the transformation of the 'ordinary' man into a crank. Perhaps political analysis needs to break out and try a little common politics before it is too late.

NOTES

I am grateful to Bob Miles of the Research Unit on Ethnic Relations and to Roger King of Manchester Polytechnic for commenting on an earlier draft of this paper.

1.   D.W. Scott, *A Political Sociology of Minorities*, unpublished Ph.D. thesis, Bristol University, 1972.
2.   Fettlerbridge is a medium sized industrial town north of London. All local names are also pseudonyms.
3.   N. Polsky, *Hustlers, Beats and Others*, Penguin, Harmondsworth, 1971, p. 143.
4.   D. Butler and D. Stokes, *Political Change in Britain*, Macmillan, London, 1969.
5.   *Ibid.*, p. 14.
6.   R. Rose (ed.), *Studies in British Politics*, Macmillan, London, 1966, p. 174.
7.   See, for example, M. Rush and P. Althoff, *An Introduction to Political Sociology*, Nelson, London, 1971, pp. 10-13.
8.   E.J. Hobsbawm, *Primitive Rebels*, Manchester University Press, 1959, p. 2.
9.   W. MacKenzie, 'Political Science: between analysis and action,' *New Society*, 25 July 1974, p. 220.
10.   R. Rose, *Politics in England Today*, Faber, London, 1974, p. 38.
11.   F. Parkin, *Middle Class Radicalism*, Manchester University Press, 1968.
12.   R. Rose, *Politics in England Today*, p. 251.
13.   N. Deakin (ed.), *Colour and the British Electorate*, Pall Mall, London, 1965.
14.   D. Butler and M. Pinto-Duschinsky, *The British General Election of 1970*, Macmillan, London, 1971, p. 329.
15.   *Ibid.*, pp. 232-3.
16.   W.G. Runciman, *Relative Deprivation and Social Justice*, Penguin, Harmondsworth, 1972.
17.   E. Leach, 'Liberty Equality Fraternity,' *New Statesman*, 8 July 1966, Runciman does touch his forelock in the direction of participant observation in a postscript to the original material, *op. cit.*, p. 397.
18.   H. Beynon, *Working for Ford*, Allen Lane, London, 1973, pp. 202, 207.
19.   S.M. Miller and F. Riessman, 'Working Class Authoritarianism: A critique of Lipset,' *British Journal of Sociology*, vol. 12, 1961, pp. 263-76.
20.   See, for example, D. Barker, 'On the Patriotic Frontier,' *Guardian*, 2 June 1972; M. Walker, 'Open File,' *Guardian*, 17 June 1974; Bob Campbell, 'Who are the Ultra Right' (series of four articles), *Morning Star*, 30 February-1 March 1973; M. Hanna, *op. cit.*; as well as successive issues of *Red Mole, Socialist Worker, Private Eye* and the *Current Notes* of the Board of Deputies of British Jews, which all record 'sightings' of the different species, as do a number of anonymous pamphlets with a limited circulation.
21.   *British Sociological Association Notes*, no. 17, June 1974.
22.   See S.M. Lipset and E. Raab, *The Politics of Unreason*, Harper & Row, New York, 1970.
23.   I. Taylor and L. Taylor, *Politics and Deviance*, Penguin, Harmondsworth, 1973, p. 163 *et seq.*
24.   *Ibid.*, pp. 211-14.
25.   See, for example, W. Allen, *The Nazi Seizure of Power*, Eyre & Spottiswoode, London, 1966; R. Benewick, *Political Violence and Public Order*, Allen Lane, London, 1969; C. Cross, *The Fascists in Britain*, Barrie & Rockliff, London, 1961; and W. Mandle, *Anti-Semitism and the British Union of Fascists*, Longmans, London, 1968.

26.   N. Polsky, *op. cit.*, p. 128.
27.   I have attempted to document the activities of the local organisation after the fieldwork period and have used National Front correspondence and extensive photographic evidence throughout 1973.
28.   National activities organiser of the National Front.
29.   T. Parsons, *Politics and Social Structure*, Macmillan, Toronto, 1964, p. 94.
30.   W.G. Runciman, *op. cit.*, p. 391.
31.   T. Pettigrew, *Racially Separate or Together?*, McGraw-Hill, New York, 1971, p. 250.
32.   B. Hindess, *The Decline of Working-Class Politics*, MacGibbon & Kee, London, 1971, p. 145.
33.   H. Beynon, *op. cit.*, p. 318.
34.   J. Goldthorpe, 'Social Inequality and Social Integration in Modern Britain,' in Raynor, J. and Harden, J. (eds.), *Equality and City Schools*, Routledge and Kegan Paul, London, 1973, pp. 4-27.
35.   C.A. Valentine, *Culture and Poverty*, University of Chicago, 1970, p. 108.
36.   See, for example, J. Klein, *Samples from English Cultures*, vol. I, Routledge & Kegan Paul, London, 1965, pp. 206-14; and B. Jackson, *Working Class Community*, Routledge & Kegan Paul, London, 1965, pp. 39-68.
37.   R. Towler, *Homo Religiosus*, Constable, London, 1974, p. 148, '. . . beliefs and practices of an overly religious nature which are not under the domination of a prevailing religious institution.'
38.   Cf. R. Hoggart, *Uses of Literacy*, Penguin, Harmondsworth, 1960, p. 80, where he refers to 'cracker-mottoes.'
39.   C. Macinnes, *Times Educational Supplement*, 5 October 1973.
40.   See, S. Lipset, *Political Man*, Heinemann, London, 1960; and D. Bell, *The End of Ideology*, Free Press, New York, 1967.
41.   *Commission on the Constitution*, Research Paper no 7, HMSO, London, 1973.
42.   W. Kornhauser, *The Politics of Mass Society*, Routledge & Kegan Paul, London, 1965.
43.   The survey distinguished twelve major administrative regions. Sampling of 4,892 adults took place in mid-1970. There were 120 constituencies including 2 wards of a Fettlerbridge constituency with 27 respondents in each.
44.   In an attempt to avoid possible misinterpretation it is not the present intention of the author to suggest that there is an exact and direct relationship between inter-war fascism and movements such as the National Front. Convention requires comparisons which could be with the Communist Party. Those who are sensitive about these issues must take their pick.
45.   R. Neubauer, 'The Face of British Fascism,' *Red Mole*, 8-22 April 1971.
46.   A.K. Chesterton, *The New Unhappy Lords*, Candour, London, 1967.
47.   *Commission on the Constitution, op. cit.*, p. xi.
48.   T. Nairn, 'Enoch Powell: The New Right,' *New Left Review*, no. 61, May-June 1970, p. 17.
49.   M. Hanna, *loc. cit.*, p. 51.
50.   Benewick, *op. cit.*, p. 125.
51.   A feature perhaps underlined by the appearance as candidates in the 1972 and 1973 local elections of six newly active National Front members. Their occupations were catering assistant, driver, mechanic, textile worker and housewife (2).
52.   H. Toch, *The Social Psychology of Social Movements*, Methuen, London, 1971, p. 188.
53.   P. Althoff and M. Rush, *op. cit.*, p. 114.
54.   Founder of the British Campaign to Stop Immigration.
55.   J. Gusfield, *Symbolic Crusade*, University of Illinois, Urbana, 1966, p. 19.
56.   M. Edelman, *The Symbolic Uses of Politics*, University of Illinois, Urbana,

1967, pp. 40, 97.
57.   D. Butler and M. Pinto-Duschinsky, *op. cit.*, p. 112.
58.   *Ibid.*, p. 329.
59.   R. Rose, *Politics in England*, p. 63.
60.   J. Seabrook, *City Close-Up*, Penguin, Harmondsworth, 1973, p. 57.

9.   THE SUPPORT FOR ENOCH POWELL

Roger King and Michael Wood

It is surprising that Enoch Powell has been mostly ignored by political sociologists. Despite being one of the few politicians of the right to have achieved public prominence in Britain in recent years, scant attention has been paid by social scientists to the sources of Powell's appeal. Even fairly limited questions on the kind of groups that support Powell have rarely been raised, but generally left to newspapers and periodicals.

Answers to these questions may not only be interesting for providing insights into a leading politician, but an analysis of Powell's support could also be suggestive for some of political sociology's more recent concerns. For example, there would appear to be at least three fairly typical accounts of political behaviour in contemporary Britain that answers to the general question of 'who supports Powell?' might throw light on.

Firstly, much recent political commentary has focused on the idea of a newly discovered 'volatility' in the British electorate. Large-scale, rapid fluctuations in voting intentions in the last few years, as charted by the opinion polls, are seen as indicative of the crumbling of traditional class and party loyalties. Butler and Stokes have written that 'the increase in political volatility so manifest in the 1960s raises important questions about Britain's electoral system.' Their own evidence indicated that almost a third of the electorate changes its party allegiance between elections.[1] Studies of working-class Conservatism buttress such findings by revealing an increasingly less stable basis of party loyalty, especially among younger voters. Older, deferential support for Conservatism appears to be gradually eroding as parties come to be judged by their efficiency in government and in economic management.[2]

Consequently, we might ask whether Powell helps to forge new political alliances, either as beneficiary or part instigator, in this period of electoral flux. Powell's statements usually imply an appeal to a wider audience than traditional Toryism, as his support for the Labour Party as the February and October 1974 general elections illustrate. Is there any evidence that Powell attracts Labour voters? Does he affect the Conservatives electoral fortunes?

Secondly, although many political sociologists have been anxious to map variations in political alignments within western European societies,[3] regional differences in political behaviour in Britain are often discounted. The largely accepted model of the British political system during the 1960s conceived a relative uniformity of social and political attitudes, dividing almost solely on universalistic class lines.[4] Although Rose's work on Northern Ireland, Budge and Urwin on Scotland, and the writings of Cox and Morgan on Wales, have helped to qualify these ideas by pointing to more complex lines of political cleavage to be found at the periphery, possible non-class based political differences within the industrialised regions of England still tend to be ignored.[5]

However, as a member of parliament for Wolverhampton Southwest for over twenty years, Powell has been visibly associated with the West Midlands. Many of his speeches on immigration have included explicit reference to the problems of that region. If an analysis of Powell's admirers revealed that he attracts a substantially greater measure of support from the West Midlands than from any other region, this might provide a further corrective to over-simple characterisations of British political behaviour.

Finally a third area of interest that knowledge about Powell's support might illuminate centres around claims made by some social scientists that lower social status groups are especially prone to the appeal of 'extremist' politicians of both the left and right. Lipset's writings on 'working-class authoritarianism,' for example, suggest that working-class ethnic prejudice and the 'consistent' association between authoritarianism and lower class status,[6] has meant that extremist and intolerant movements in modern society are more likely to be based on the lower social classes than on the middle and upper classes. Lipset's claim that working-class individuals are more likely than individuals belonging to other classes 'to prefer extremist movements which suggest easy and quick solutions to social problems and have a rigid outlook'[7] rests, in part, on the results of a number of personality studies carried out by social psychologists in the 1950s and 1960s which linked authoritarianism and ethnocentrism with low occupational status. Whilst a number of variables related to such personality patterns, both Lipset and the 'authoritarian personality school' remark that education appears to be the strongest of all the various negative correlates. Lipset has written that 'there is consistent evidence that degree of formal education is highly correlated with undemocratic attitudes.'[8] T. Adorno's *The Authoritarian Personality* and similarly oriented studies of authoritarianism by Hyman and Sheatsley, and Kornhauser, Sheppard and Mayer, reveal a clearly consistent decline of authoritarianism with increasing exposure to formal education.[9]

More recently, Lipset and Raab have argued that the mass appeal of certain 'radical right' politicians in the United States derives in part from the moral conservatism ('the intolerance of groups and ideas which are different') of the less privileged.[10] Here, too, they assert that low socioeconomic and educational status correlates with intolerance. More specifically, they argue that prejudice against Negroes is clearly and independently associated with low formal education. 'The most prejudiced of all are the fundamentalists and those with strong

240

religious commitment who have not been educated beyond the eighth grade. However, a poorly educated Catholic or liberal Protestant will be more anti-Negro than a fundamentalist who went to college.'[11]

The relevance of their analysis for British society is not clear, and there are great difficulties in taking a set of questions formulated with one society particularly in mind and asking them in a different social and political environment. Nonetheless, studies of the incidence of colour prejudice in British society that are available suggest that similar processes may also be operating. Abrams, following his survey research on attitudes towards immigrants held by the white British population, maintains that, amongst other factors, length of full-time education is negatively associated with racial prejudice.[12] Consequently, it is interesting to investigate the degree of support that Powell, as a politician with clearly expressed anti-coloured views that have elicited demonstrations of working-class approval, receive from the lower social classes in comparison with other social groups. Does Powell tap those wellsprings of support that are also associated with ethnocentrism, authoritarianism and intolerance? Does level of formal education intervene as a negative constraint on the general level of his support?

Part of my answer to these questions must depend on what we know about Powell's admirers. But interpretations of the nature of the support that Powell attracts for his views, and its electoral importance, are often contradictory, differing not only over its composition but also its extent. For example, following the Conservative victory at the polls in 1970, the Louis Harris polling organisation argued that it was 'highly probable that on balance Powell helped the Conservative cause rather than damaged it,'[13] whilst *The Times* asserted that 'Powell was an unmitigated liability to Mr Heath.'[14] Other sources are equally divided. Bourne and Deakin, from an analysis of constituency 'swings' in the 1970 election, maintain that there was 'no substantial source of extra support for Powellite Conservatives.'[15] In *Powell and the 1970 Election*, however, Maurice Cowling writes that 'it is difficult to avoid the conclusion that Mr Powell's impact on the election was great,'[16] a view supported by Diana Spearman in the same book, who concludes that 'without the impact of Powell's speeches, although the victory would have been won, the majority would have been smaller.'[17]

Similar differences surround these writers' estimations of the source of Powell's support. In an early analysis of 'Enoch Powell's Postbag' in *New Society* Spearman suggests that 'the writers came from every social class and from every part of the country,'[18] repeating the assertion after a further analysis of his 1970 election letters of support that 'every social class is represented.'[19] Likewise, Cowling claims that 'Powell has adopted positions which divide the intellectual leaders of the Labour movement from the body of Labour voters.'[20] However, Spearman's and Cowling's remarks are relatively meaningless, providing no adequate test of the social representativesness of Powell's admirers.

Furthermore, Bourne and Deakin argue that 'the swing towards the Conservatives slowed up in areas of substantial immigrant settlement ... whilst there does not appear to have been any substantial compensating disadvantage for Labour in terms of alienation of traditional support.'21

These contradictions over the composition of Powell's support may well stem from the methods employed by the various writers. Spearman's analyses are based on letters of support sent to Powell and as such are likely to over-represent the letter writing middle class. Bourne and Deakin's account rests heavily on the notion of 'constituency swing,' an unreliable guide to individual attitudes.

One way to resolve these differing interpretations is to look at survey data. We have been fortunate in having access to an Opinion Research Centre national quota sample survey of 1,029 respondents taken immediately after the 1970 election. The survey elicited a wide array of political attitudes. This provides us with a sample that is more likely to be representative of the electorate at large than that available to Spearman, and a collection of replies that should be more indicative of individual attitudes than that gained by Bourne and Deakin's 'macro' analysis.22

A re-analysis of the data contained in the survey on Powell, correlated with key socioeconomic and political variables, proves highly suggestive, although this is not to claim that the data provides definitive answers to the questions we pose or, in fact, systematically 'tests' the theoretical propositions outlined above.23 But our findings do shed light on these concerns.

Findings

To begin with we propose to centre the analysis around responses to a single question. Respondents were asked to agree or disagree with the statement: 'He (Powell) is the only politician I really admire in Britain.' This is a serviceable, if not totally satisfactory, indicator of support for Powell. Twenty-five per cent of the respondents agreed with the statement whilst sixty-three per cent disagreed. These figures may underestimate the amount of admiration or support for Powell as dissenters to the statement that Powell 'is the *only* politician I really admire' (our italics) may well include supporters who share their admiration for Powell with other politicians. As such, the statement may be regarded as a fairly stringent test of Powell's support.

1 Socioeconomic Variables

Let us first look at socioeconomic variables for a breakdown of these responses. Table 1 shows a distinct tendency — nothing more — for favourable attitudes to Powell to correlate negatively with class as

Table 1

	Class			
	AB	C1	C2	DE
Only admire Powell	21% (28)	20% (37)	26% (91)	28% (100)

measured by the Registrar-General's classifications. The C2 and DE categories reveal the most extensive admiration for Powell.

However, the most striking correlation is with education. Table 2 allows us to state fairly confidently that the greater the period of formal education, the less likely an individual is to say that he admires Powell. While 58 per cent of those who left school at fourteen and under do not 'support' Powell, the corresponding figure for those leaving school after 18 is over 80 per cent.

Table 2

	Education				
	14-Under	15	16	17-18	19-Over
Only admire Powell	30% (131)	23% (65)	28% (39)	16% (13)	* *

Thus, it would appear at this stage, that support for Powell correlates with class and education variables in similar fashion to that discovered by the 'authoritarian personality' studies. Education in particular acts to suppress Powell's support. However, the problem of the relationship between the dependent variable and the independent variables has still to be resolved. More specifically, does education act as an intervening variable between class and admiration for Powell in the way that it appears as a determinant between class and authoritarianism? It may be not so much low class that is the cause of admiration for Powell but rather lack of education as a result of belonging to a low class which cause admiration for Powell.

Thus, taking the relationship between 'Admire Powell only' and class, controlling for education, we might expect the partial tables to vanish.[24] However, in order to check for interaction effects, the data was subjected to the A.I.D. algorithm.[25] The dependent variable was 'Admire

Powell only' and the independent (predictor) variables were education, work, sex, class and age. To achieve the most theoretically meaningful result we dichotomised the independent variables rather than leave the splitting to the programme. We show below the matrix of E^2 values for each independent dichotomy and then a tree showing the 'fission' process.

Table 3 Dependent variable — admire Powell only

Predictors	1	2	3
1. Sex	0.00001	0.00007	0.01298*
2. Age	0.00321	0.00049	0.00050
3. Class	0.01043*	0.00345*	0.00078
4. Education	0.02168	†	†
5. Work	†	0.00002	0.00002
N	905	760	145

* denotes unsuccessful candidate
† denotes predictor has variance in this group

DEPENDENT VARIABLE

Mean	x = 1.717	1.688	1.869
S.D.	o = 0.450	0.468	0.337

As can be seen, the programme made only one split, the second pair of branches being constructed from the largest pair of unsuccessful 'candidates.' We can see from the 'tree' that the input of class has an effect, otherwise not. The effect might be illustrated in terms of symbolic 'partial' tables.

Dependent Variable	High Education	Low Education
Admire Powell only	No class effect	Class effect

Consequently it appears that education does act as an intervening determinant between class and the level of support for Powell. Upper class individuals, with a low level of education, for example, are far more likely to support Powell than men or women with a higher level of education. Although the interaction effects are complex, and more complicated than some of the 'authoritarian personality' studies indicate, Powell's support appears subject to those influences that have

Table 4

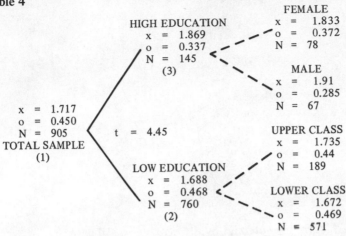

	FEMALE
HIGH EDUCATION	x = 1.833
x = 1.869	o = 0.372
o = 0.337	N = 78
N = 145	
(3)	MALE
	x = 1.91
	o = 0.285
	N = 67
x = 1.717	
o = 0.450	UPPER CLASS
N = 905	x = 1.735
TOTAL SAMPLE	o = 0.44
(1)	N = 189
t = 4.45	
	LOWER CLASS
LOW EDUCATION	x = 1.672
x = 1.688	o = 0.469
o = 0.468	N = 571
N = 760	
(2)	

The lower the mean value the more
likely a group admires Powell only.

In decreasing order of admiration for Powell

Lower Class	Upper Class	Female	Male
Low Education	Low Education	High Education	High Education

been closely associated with levels of authoritarianism and prejudice.

Further inferences may be drawn from the findings. Since it is well known that Labour voters are drawn disproportionately from the less well educated, these findings suggest that Powell could have been appealing to a substantial section of potential or actual Labour supporters. He could be attracting support across the party divide thus facilitating, or perhaps merely indicating, decreasing commitment to the established parties.

There is of course a further possibility. The Conservative Party traditionally attracts very substantial support from those of low socio-economic status. It is normally calculated that over one-third of the working class vote Conservative.[26] It would be quite plausible to suggest that the 30 per cent who left school before fourteen (see Table 2) are non-Labour identifiers. Powell's working-class support might come overwhelmingly from working-class Tories.

Nonetheless, we feel we have grounds for accepting the alternative line of thought — that Powell appeals to a sizeable section of Labour Party identifiers. In addition to any impressionistic evidence we may have, such as the dockers' marches in 1968 in support of Powell's anti-immigration speeches, the survey allows us to examine how far party

Table 5 Subjective political identification

	LAB	CON	LIB
Only admire Powell	21% (87)	30% (117)	14% (13)

Table 6 Party voted for, 1970

	LAB	CON	LIB
Only admire Powell	19% (72)	30% (130)	14% (13)

Table 7 Party last voted for by those who changed party

	LAB	CON	LIB
Only admire Powell	53% (21)	* *	42% (9)

identification affects attitudes to Powell. The figures in Table 5 indicate that Powell does cross party lines in the sense that over a fifth of those who identify with the Labour Party admire him.[27]

As we can see from Table 6, Powell's ability to tap this large reservoir of support seemed to be hindered by the strength of traditional party loyalties. Almost a fifth of those who still voted Labour in 1970 admired Powell. Nonetheless, even given the constraints of existing party loyalties, there is some evidence that Powell attratced support to the Tories in 1970. Of those who changed from Labour, 53 per cent admired Powell. This compares with the 25 per cent of the whole sample expressing favourable attitudes to Powell (see above). The numbers are fairly small and we are still left with the unresolved problem of whether defectors to the Conservatives may have been predisposed to admire Powell, or, equally, whether a change in voting intention occasioned support for Powell. Nonetheless, although the survey does not allow us to come to any firm conclusions, it would appear implausible that support for Powell follows a change in voting intention, especially as we have already indicated that Powell attracts support across the party divide.

2 Trade Unionism

Powell's ability to gather support in traditional working-class Labour groups is further indicated by the fact that trade union membership apparently makes little difference to attitudes towards him.

Table 8 Trade Union Membership

	Member	Non member
Only admire Powell	23%	25%

Table 8 indicates that 23 per cent of union members and 25 per cent of non-members professed admiration for him. Previous research suggests that union membership normally increases the propensity to exhibit left-wing political loyalties. Butler and Stokes, for example, despite their concern with qualifying such views, have written that 'the electoral weight of the trade unions is a recurring theme of political commentary in Britain. Some have seen in the division between trade union families and the rest of the electorate a pre-eminent basis of party loyalty.'[28] Their own sample was indicative. Seventy-three per cent of their trade union families voted Labour compared with 42 per cent of non-union families.[29]

Whilst Butler and Stokes point out that these sort of findings may overestimate the persuasive effect of trade unions on political allegiance — class and party inclination itself may account for much of the relationship between the trade unions and the Labour Party — our findings do suggest that support for Powell does cut across these traditional associations. As a right-wing politician we might expect trade unionists to be relatively hostile to him. The lack of marked antipathy throws up the idea that Powell may be playing a small part in eroding the political partisanship of trade union membership.

Nonetheless, we should not be too surprised at the inability of trade union membership to predict attitudes to Powell in our survey. As membership in trade unions has grown, becoming more obligatory and customary even for many white-collar occupations, unions may be less strongly associated with distinctive social and political attitudes. They cease to be self-selected groups of like-minded individuals and come to cover a large number of occupations without discrimination.[30]

As a consequence, although the term 'trade unionist' still retains its manual, left-wing imagery, it could still be possible that the trade union admirers of Powell in the sample were predominantly in white collar occupations favourably viewing a Conservative politician, and thereby

Table 9

		Class		
	AB	C1	C2	DE
T.U. Members				
Only admire Powell	* *	* *	23% (26)	30% (23)
Column Total	8% (20)	14% (36)	46% (115)	30% (76)
Non-Members				
Only admire Powell	23% (25)	21% (31)	27% (64)	27% (71)

weakening our proposition that Powell cuts across established lines of class cleavage.

But our findings show that almost a third (30 per cent) of trade unionists 'Powellites' were in the DE class category, the same total as the overall proportion of trade unionists in the DE category, suggesting that Powell's attraction is not confined to white collar Conservatives. Membership of a trade union has little effect in minimising the tendency for individuals in class DE to support Powell, and, as we can see from Table 9, only 27 per cent of the non-unionised DE group professed a favourable attitude to him. These findings confirm the results of the Abrams survey, which revealed that the prejudice scores of working-class people in trade unions was almost identical with the scores from working-class people not in trade unions.[31]

It appears reasonable to assume that Powell appeals to a substantial section of working-class opinion. Explanations for findings of this sort — working-class support for right wing politicians with radical proposals — are often difficult to make, especially when viewed against the often accepted 'rational interest' model of class-based political behaviour which equates working-class interests with left-wing policies and parties. Some political sociologists put forward the view that the authoritarian nature of subcultural relationships (in the family, for example) found in lower status groups, may give rise to 'extremist' political orientations.[32] Whilst it is extremely doubtful that Powell, with his commitment to parliamentary democracy, could be accurately labelled an extremist, he has sometimes been viewed as eliciting fanatical, and sometimes racialist, responses from those who admire him. Does our survey substantiate this proposition?

So far we have used admiration as an indicator of support for Powell, namely, favourable replies to the question 'He is the only politician I really admire in Britain.' The survey also contains two further sets of responses that could be used as indicators of support for Powell, and which, although shrouded in ambiguity, raise some interesting questions about the motivations of Powell's admirers.

The first is 'Powell Dangerous' — replies to the statement 'He is a fanatical and dangerous man.' And the second is 'Powell Racialist' — replies to the statement 'He has stirred up feelings between people of different races in Britain.'

'Powell Dangerous'

Neither question satisfactorily acts as an indicator of 'extremism' or 'racialism' but they are the only questions in the survey that tap the motivations of the respondents in respect of Powell. Given the moral opprobrium attached to such terms one could reasonably assume that admirers of Powell (and, of course, some who do not admire him), would disavow that he was a dangerous and fanatical man. In fact, a cross-tabulation of 'Powell Dangerous' with 'Powell Admire' does reveal that 85 per cent of his admirers did disagree with this statement (see Table 10).

Table 10

	Only admire Powell		
	Agree	Disagree	D.K.
Powell dangerous	12%	85%	3%

Table 11

	Class			
	AB	C1	C2	DE
Powell dangerous	19% (25)	24% (45)	26% (93)	28% (99)

However, as we can see from Table 11, the lower classes disproportionately think Powell is dangerous. Given our earlier findings that more members of the working class admire Powell this finding is surprising when taken with the pejorative implications of the question. It provokes two possible explanations. Firstly, the working class take a more clearly defined yet divided position in their view of Powell. They are prepared either explicitly to admire him *or* to think he is dangerous. Alternatively, and less plausibly, the working class, when compared with the other social classes, contain a great number of individuals who both support Powell *and* think he is dangerous. If this is so, some working-class admirers of Powell are not discouraged by their feeling that he is 'a fanatical and dangerous man.'

Powell 'Racialist'

Of course, it is conceivable that these findings are just random. But they do appear to be replicated by the 'racialist' variable. Similarly, and again unexpectedly, we have the finding that Powell is slightly more likely to be perceived as a man 'who stirs up feelings between people of different races' by those groups who admire him most, although the relationship is not quite so marked as it is for the 'Powell Dangerous' variable (see Table 12).

Table 12

	Class			
	AB	C1	C2	DE
Powell racialist	54% (71)	64% (122)	64% (227)	64% (228)

3 Region

A major theme that informs contemporary political analysis is that British society possesses a pattern of electoral behaviour without the sizeable regional wrinkles of the nineteenth century or of modern Continental societies. The secularisation of religious beliefs and the lack of large agricultural communities is viewed as having removed the foundation for the territorial variations found within the developing political societies of Europe, particularly since the secession of most of Ireland in the 1920s removed the most powerful non-class cleavages from British politics. Consequently, class provides the basis of political allegiance in all areas; responses to shared national controversies are the source of change in party popularity.[34]

There is obviously substance in much of this. Class still plays the primary role in shaping party identification in many parts of Britain. English electoral behaviour particularly displays a remarkable consistency in this respect. Nonetheless, it is easy to underestimate differences in political behaviour that do occur. Butler and Stokes point out that the persisting, uneven spread of party support between the regions tends to be obscured by the evenness of 'swing' in elections. Yet, as they write: 'if the electors in each constituency were to respond to national political influences in an identical way we would not see the same fraction of the electorate, or total vote, change hands between the parties in each constituency.' This would be so only if swing involved 'not identical fractions of the total vote of electorate in each constituency but a fraction proportional to the prior strength of the party.' As usually calculated it does not. Butler and Stokes' own analysis reveals distinctive patterns of support between regions, even when the class composition of the respective regions are allowed for. They found that throughout the 1960s[35] Labour's proportion of the support for the two main parties was, on average, 10 per cent higher in the North of England, Scotland and Wales, than it was in the Midlands and the South.

Political attitudes on particular issues, submerged within the broad sweep of electoral movements, may reveal even greater differences between locales. Certainly our survey strikingly suggests that a large part of Powell's support is to be found in one particular region. As Table 13 shows, while 25 per cent of the whole sample admire Powell (see above), in the West Midlands this figure rises to 42 per cent. In every other region the proportion is always below 30 per cent.

Table 13

			Region		
	Northeast	Yorks	E. Mids	E. Anglia	S. East
Only admire Powell	24%	16%	20%	29%	28%
	(22)	(13)	(14)	(14)	(37)
	G. London	S. West	Wales	W. Mids	N.W./Scot
	20%	22%	24%	42%	22%
	(32)	(16)	(10)	(48)	(20)

This is not too unexpected. At the time of the survey Powell was a long standing member for a West Midlands constituency. More particularly, his speeches on immigration towards the end of the 1960s were clearly aimed at articulating grievances and issues that were perceived as affecting the West Midlands more than other regions. At the same time, certain writers have pointed to the salience of the race issue in parts of the West Midlands, particularly the Birmingham area. Rex and Moore, for example, in their study of race relations in the Sparkbrook area of Birmingham write that 'race problems dominated public discussion' in Birmingham during the 1960s, mainly as a consequence of the housing situation and the deterioration of what were thought to be good residential areas becoming homes for coloured citizens.[36] The local Conservative organisations reflected these feelings. 'What surprised us most about the Conservative Party workers were their working-class accents . . . they were certainly not simply a white collar group . . . Above all, they felt that too little was being done about immigration and blamed the Labour Party for its evil consequences.'[37]

Similarly, Abrams' 1966 survey of attitudes to immigrants in five

English boroughs with a relatively high proportion of coloured residents (Lambeth, Ealing, Wolverhampton, Nottingham and Bradford) contained a higher level of prejudiced responses to certain statements in Wolverhampton than in the other boroughs. He writes, 'At least 60 per cent of the respondents thought that each of the three coloured groups took "more out of the country than they put into it"; in Wolverhampton the proportion was as high as 75 per cent.'[38]

More recently, Michael Mann has written in a similar vein.

'If happy, long-settled working-class neighbourhoods did ever exist near the centre of Birmingham, successive waves of immigration seem to have destroyed them. The residents most satisfied in these areas were the Irish and coloured people in the sample — 11 of the 14 living there liked doing so. Apart from them, under half the residents liked their area — a striking contrast to the residents of other areas . . . The English-born working class in Birmingham is being pushed outwards by its distaste for the recent immigrants to their old communities. As more obtain council houses on the fringe of Birmingham (and Rex and Moore show that their local political dominance enables many of them to do so), and as the more prosperous workers are able to afford to buy their own houses in the suburbs, the ones left are those who simply cannot move, because of the economics of housing. Feeling trapped, their hostility to the immigrants increases.'[39]

During the 1970 election campaign, Enoch Powell was one of the most popular Conservative speakers, and his views on immigration especially were highly publicised. The election results revealed a swing to the Conservatives of 4.7 per cent in the United Kingdom as a whole. The swing in the West Midlands connurbation — 6.1 per cent — was the largest of any region. It included a swing of 5.6 per cent in Birmingham itself, and over 9 per cent in the two Wolverhampton constituencies, including Powell's.[40] There may be no connection between Powell and these Conservative gains. The relationship is certainly hard to assess, especially as we find some West Midlands constituencies such as Smethwick, Selly Oak and All Saints showing lower than average swings.[41] Nonetheless, it is significant that those seats which showed the lowest swings to the Conservatives in Birmingham were those with the highest proportion of immigrants from the 'New Commonwealth.' All Saints (1.2 per cent swing to Labour), Handsworth (1 per cent swing to the Conservatives), and Selly Oak (1.1 per cent swing to the Conservatives) contained 13.8 per cent, 12.1 per cent and 7.9 per cent respectively. On the other hand, Hall Green (6.6 per cent to the Conservatives), Northfield (8.6 per cent to the Conservatives), Perry Barr (6.8 per cent to the Conservatives), Stetchford (7.1 per cent to the Conservatives), and Yardley (6.5 per cent to the Conservatives), contained 0.7 per cent, 0.4 per cent, 1.3 per cent and 0.7 per cent of immigrants from the 'New

Commonwealth' respectively.[42]

It appears likely, therefore, that Powell and the Conservative Party incurred the hostility of substantial sections of the immigrant population. If Powell was influential in securing electoral advantage for the Conservatives in the West Midlands, then he must have gained it from the white population. In areas of little immigration, the support Powell may have polled from working-class and lower middle-class groups, as indicated in our findings, translated itself into sizeable Conservative swings. Where constituencies contained large numbers of immigrants, Powell's appeal to such groups appears to have been nullified by immigrant hostility thus reducing his impact in terms of aggregate electoral advantage for the Conservatives.[43]

Some Additional Findings

1 Sex
Women working fulltime display a similar level of support for Powell to that of the males in the sample, although women who do not work exhibit quite a sharp decline compared to both.

Table 14

	Male	Sex Female WFT	Female
Only admire Powell	25% (124)	26% (115)	16% (16)

This finding accords with the Abrams survey findings which revealed that women, in all age groups, were consistently more tolerant than men, whilst the incidence of tolerance amongst women not working was even higher.[44] However, Abrams points out that many non-working women are either young or elderly, two groups in his survey found more likely to express tolerant attitudes. Similarly, in our survey an examination of the other social characteristics of these groups reveals that females who do not work are better educated than those females who do work and, as we have seen, admiration for Powell tends to decline with an increase in educational experience (see Table 2).

2 Age
Our survey also suggests that it is the middle aged who provide the greatest number of admirers of Powell as compared with other age groups.

The table indicates a curvilinear relationship with people in the age range 35-54 having the greatest propensity to say that they admire

Table 15

	18-20	21-24	Age 25-34	35-44
Only admire Powell	22% (14)	19% (16)	23% (42)	27% (50)
	45-54	55-64	65+	
	31% (60)	23% (36)	25% (33)	

Powell. Again, these findings tie in with the results of the Abrams survey. Here, 'the incidence of extreme prejudice was highest among people aged 45-54: it fell away on both sides of that dividing line so that the lowest levels of extreme prejudice were found among the young (i.e. under 35 years of age) and the elderly (i.e. aged 65 or over).'45

Comments on the 1970 Findings

Enoch Powell has distinctive views on issues other than race. He has, for example, forcibly expressed opinions on the desirability of market forces as the primary mechanism for the creation and distribution of economic resources. Whilst political intervention in the economy is not precluded, the emphasis in Powell's writings is to confine state action to monetarist policies that exclude direct attempts at controlling prices and incomes. Similarly, Powell has well publicised views on Northern Ireland, repeatedly arguing that Ulster is an integral part of the United Kingdom and should have greater representation at Westminster. His candidature and subsequent election as member for South Down at the October 1974 General Election highlights the strength of his commitment to the ultimate sovereignty of the British Parliament, and the belief that demands for Irish unity threaten Britain's social and political homogeneity. Likewise, whilst Powell may be reconciled to the abandonment of 'Greater Nationalism' and its colonial connotations, he remains wedded to the unbroken nationalism of the British homeland ('Little Englander'). Consequently, his opposition to British membership of the European Economic Community is based on what he sees as the concomitant decline in power of British political institutions.

Nonetheless, as Studler points out:

'his views on these issues have not taken hold among the public as have his views on immigration. In a September 1968 survey of public opinion on issues raised by Powell other than immigration, NOP found that although a substantial minority supported Powell's positions on decentralisation and prices and incomes policy, support for these issue positions themselves was not very strongly related to support for Powell as a political leader.'[46]

Similarly, Frankin and Inglehart found that support for Powell derives from concern with the single political issue of immigration policy, as opposed to other issues, including the Common Market.[47]

Unfortunately, it is not possible in our survey to confirm or reject the view that Powell is associated mainly with his views on race. However, it appears clear from our findings that support for Powell is correlated with similar factors normally associated in other survey work with prejudice, intolerance and ethnocentrism. The negative correlations with class and education on support for Powell, for example, together with the effects of sex and age, are typical of results from both the 'authoritarian personality' studies and the account by Abrams of the incidence of racial prejudice in Britain. It appears highly probable, therefore, that much of Powell's support is attracted by his views on immigration and that he is identified with his position on that issue.

With the relative disappearance of the immigration policy from his overall 'package' since 1970, does this indicate that Powell's support has diminished or changed its composition since that time? An examination of his support at the time of the February 1974 General Election, to which we now turn, may provide an answer.

General Election, February 1974

We have concentrated out attention so far on the support that Powell commanded in 1970. Since then Powell's speeches have indicated a change in emphasis in the positions he adopts, and appears to lay greater stress on the Northern Ireland and Common Market issues than he did in 1970 when his anti-immigration speeches received the most attention from the press. Furthermore, his allegiance to the Conservative Party has diminished to the extent that he now recommends support for the Labour Party on the grounds of its relative hostility to the Common Market. Has the pattern of admiration for Powell that we discovered in the 1970 sample, particularly his cross-class and cross-party appeal, been maintained?

We have again been fortunate in having access to survey material, a random sampling of over 1,500 respondents in three West Midland marginal constituencies on a range of electoral issues, undertaken by Marplan for the *Birmingham Evening Mail* during the February 1974 election campaign.[48] An analysis of the data it contains on Powell proves revealing. Besides its relative contemporaneity, this survey provides an indication of support for Powell in the region which revealed the highest admiration for him in our 1970 national sample.

Findings

It must be remembered, of course, that Powell did not seek re-election in February 1974, and, consequently, he remained less 'visible' than in the 1970 election campaign. Although his speeches for the 'Get Britain Out' movement towards the end of the campaign received prominent press attention, this survey was undertaken before these speeches. As such, our findings may slightly underestimate the general level of approval for him.

Nonetheless our findings revealed a high level of regard for Powell. Once again we have had to rely upon a relatively crude indicator to measure this. Respondents were given the names of six prominent politicians — Heath, Wilson, Powell, Thorpe, Whitelaw and Jenkins — and asked 'Which of these politicians do you think would make the best Prime Minister?'

Table 16

Best Prime Minister by Voting Intention

(i)   Birmingham Perry Barr

	Total %	Will vote Con %	Will vote Lab %	Will vote Lib %
Heath	24	55	1	4
Powell	22	19	16	30
Wilson	19	1	58	6
Thorpe	11	4	8	52
Whitelaw	10	16	2	6
Jenkins	6	3	11	2
D.K./None	8	2	4	*
	(528)	(194)	(145)	(50)

(ii)   Walsall South

	Total %	Will vote Con %	Will vote Lab %	Will vote Lib & others %
Wilson	26	*	58	12
Heath	24	57	*	13
Powell	19	18	18	23
Whitelaw	10	14	4	13
Thorpe	9	6	8	16
Jenkins	6	4	8	5
D.K./None	6	1	4	18
	(514)	(171)	(197)	(146)

(iii)   Bromsgrove and Redditch

	Total %	Will vote Con %	Will vote Lab %	Will vote Lib & others %
Heath	25	54	*	14
Wilson	19	*	55	7
Powell	17	20	14	16
Thorpe	13	5	9	24
Whitelaw	12	18	4	13
Jenkins	6	1	16	5
D.K./None	8	1	2	21
	(516)	(199)	(149)	(168)

256

As the table shows, not only was Powell generally the most popular candidate after Heath and Wilson, but in Perry Barr he ran ahead of the Labour Party leader by 3 per cent, only 2 per cent behind the then Prime Minister, Mr Heath, and with double the percentage of the Liberal Party leader. More specifically, correlations with voting intention reveal that Powell was the only politician whose support clearly crossed party lines. In Perry Barr, 19 per cent of Conservative voters, 16 per cent of Labour voters and 30 per cent of Liberals, preferred Powell. This compares with the much greater concentration of support for the other politicians within their own parties. Similarly, in Walsall South, he drew equally from Conservative and Labour identifiers (18 per cent from each), whilst it was only in Bromsgrove and Redditch that Powell captured substantially more support from Conservative voters (20 per cent compared with the 14 per cent of Labour voters). The overall picture suggests that Powell appears to have confirmed the findings of the 1970 survey by maintaining his appeal to a substantial section of Labour Party voters.

Table 17

Best Prime Minister by Class

	Powell %	Whitelaw %	Heath %	Others %	(N)
(i)	*Perry Barr*				
AB	*	*	*	*	*
C1	23	14	33	30	(75)
C2	16	8	17	59	(356)
DE	21	6	20	53	(165)
(ii)	*Bromsgrove and Redditch*				
AB	17	20	30	23	(65)
C1	16	14	35	35	(129)
C2	18	13	16	53	(194)
DE	16	*	25	53	(124)
(iii)	*Walsall South*				
AB	*	21	41	23	(54)
C1	22	16	33	29	(88)
C2	23	10	17	50	(188)
DE	17	*	20	60	(190)

The class composition of Powell's admirers reveals a similar pattern to that contained in the 1970 survey for the West Midlands. Powell attracts far more support from the C1, C2 and DE categories than he does from the ABs. On the other hand, we find that the preferences for the other two Conservative politicians in the survey — Heath and Whitelaw — were far more likely to come from the highest social groups. This is particularly noticeable for Whitelaw, who steadily loses support the further we descend the class scale.

Issues[49]

Table 18 Issues (in %)

	Perry Barr		Bromsgrove and Redditch		Walsall	
	All	Powell	All	Powell	All	Powell
Full employment	72	67	63	62	67	66
Higher pensions	39	34	30	26	32	40
Miners' pay	18	13	22	18	23	11
Inflation	54	48	63	67	55	51
Common Market	18	23	19	21	17	24
Industrial relations	19	14	32	32	26	19
Who governs Britain	19	13	19	17	19	25
Strikers payments	4	5	3	2	4	2
Better housing	29	24	20	21	29	23
Law & order	21	36	26	26	19	19

Finally, it is worth pointing out that at the time of the survey Powell's admirers were only marginally more likely to regard the Common Market issue as an important issue in the election, and their pattern of concern generally reflected that of the sample as a whole, with full employment and inflation having the most importance. If the very high swings to the Labour Party in many parts of the West Midlands that occurred in the February 1974 election are attributable in some part to the influence of Powell's decision to support the Labour Party, it appears probable that it was not the Common Market issue that proved decisive.[50] As Michael Steed has pointed out, if Powell helped to persuade many anti-coloured working-class voters to switch to the Conservatives in 1970, the dissociation of the Conservative Government from anti-immigration sentiments through such actions as the admission of the Ugandan Asians, and Powell's own estrangement from the Conservative Party, may have encouraged working-class anti-coloured voters to vote Labour on class and economic issues rather than Conservative on race.[51]

Conclusion

Finally, two points are worth making. Firstly, a remarkable aspect of Powell's support is its durability. The Birmingham speech of April 1968 established him as a potential party leader. Studler's analysis[52] of responses to Gallup questions on leading Conservatives found that from being the choice to succeed Edward Heath of 1 per cent of the public in a survey immediately preceeding his speech, he became the choice of 24 per cent in a survey soon afterwards. Six years later Powell enjoyed a level of support, at least in the West Midlands, that remained relatively undiminished from the days of his initial national impact. As we have seen, this appears as a consequence of his persisting association with race. The Common Market was no more salient as an issue for Powell's supporters than for the rest of the population.

Secondly, our findings confirm that Powell sustains cross-party appeal. Studler has written, on the basis of responses to NOP questions on choices for Prime Minister between June 1970 and March 1971, that 'Powell's popularity is not derived from traditional sources of support for the Conservative Party . . . Powell's popular support for the post of Prime Minister cut across normal party affiliations much more than did that of his two chief rivals for public favour, Heath and Wilson.'[53] It is clear from our more recent analysis of Powell's support that his ability to attract support from all the major parties remains unimpaired.

Appendix

Methodological note on the 1970 survey
The data are the results of a large quota sample (N = 1,029) carried out in 1970. The dearth of probability sample data exploring attitudes to Enoch Powell and our lack of facilities to mount such a survey ourselves meant that we were forced to rely on data of this type. Reanalysing this sort of data calls for some comment.

It would not have been appropriate for us to use any tests of significance. We do not intend here to rehearse the already very extensive controversy surrounding the use of significance testing.[1] But three points are worth making. In essentially exploratory data analysis there are no hypotheses to test. Secondly, it is circular to apply 'significance' tests to the same data that has already led one to formulate the hypothesis. There is still the problem, however, in multivariate analysis to know when to stop the elaboration. Clearly significance tests do provide a useful guard against partialling out indefinitely, long after it is clear that chance mechanisms are the most probable cause of the given (partial) tables. We have had to resort to arbitrary stopping rules mostly based upon our own intuitive feelings about the data. We were also unable to calculate confidence limits for any of the differences that we found or the statistics that we calculated.

Consequently, we would be very reluctant to generalise from our findings. They are presented because the results were intrinsically interesting and generate a number of hypotheses that might be usefully tested at some later date.

NOTES

The authors owe a special debt to Dr Michael Moran for his invaluable help and suggestions. We wish to express our gratitude, in addition, to Mr N. Spencer of Opinion Research Centre; Mr J. Hopkinson, editor, and Mr C. Lewis, assistant editor, of the *Birmingham Evening Mail*; and Mr J. Fuller, managing director of Marplan, for their aid and accessibility. Finally, we thank Mr W. Hallam, Mrs P.S. Arnold and Mr M. Newman without whose help this article could not have been written.

In all tables * = N less than 10.

1.   D. Butler and D. Stokes, *Political Change in Britain*, Penguin, London 1971, p. 355.
2.   See R.T. McKenzie and A. Silver, *Angels in Marble*, Heinemann, London, 1968; and E.A. Nordlinger, *The Working Class Tories*, London, 1967.
3.   See, for example, S. Lipset and S. Rokkan, *Party Systems and Voter Alignments*, Free Press, New Yorkm 1967; E. Allardt and S. Rokkan, *Mass Politics*, Free Press, New York, 1970; M. Dogan and R. Rose (eds.), *European Politics: A Reader*, Macmillan, London, 1971.
4.   See, for example, J. Blondel, *Voters, Parties, Leaders*, London, 1963; R. Alford, *Party and Society*, Rand McNally, Chicago, 1963; R. Rose, *Politics in England*, Faber, London, 1965.
5.   R. Rose, *Governing Without Consensus*, Faber, London, 1971; I. Budge and D. Urwin, *Scottish Political Behaviour*, Longmans, London, 1966; K. Cox, 'Geography, Social Contexts and Voting Behaviour in Wales 1861-1951,' in *Mass Politics*; D. Morgan, *Wales in British Politics, 1868-1922*; University of Wales Press, Cardiff, 1950.
6.   S. Lipset, *Political Man*, Heinemann, London, 1966, p. 105.
7.   *Ibid*., p. 100.
8.   *Ibid*., p. 109.
9.   T.W. Adorno *et al.*, *The Authoritarian Personality*, part 1, John Wiley, New York, 1964, p. 285; H. Hyman and P. Sheatsley, 'The authoritarian personality – a methodological critique,' in R. Christie and M. Jahoda (eds.), *Studies in the Scope and Method of 'The Authoritarian Personality'*, Free Press, New York, 1954, pp. 50-122; A. Kornhauser, K. Sheppard and A. Mayer, *When Labour Votes*, University Books, New York, 1956.
10.   S. Lipset and E. Raab, *The Politics of Unreason*, Heinemann, London, 1971, p. 30.

11.   *Ibid.*, pp. 434-7.
12.   M. Abrams, 'Attitudes of the British Public,' in E.J. Rose *et al., Colour and Citizenship*, Oxford University Press, London, 1969, pp. 556-7.
13.   Quoted in Robert Rhode James, *Ambitions and Realities: British Politics 1964-70*, Weidenfeld and Nicolson, London, 1972, p. 276.
14.   *The Times*, 15 June 1970. Also quoted in Rhode James, *op. cit.*, p. 276.
15.   N. Deakin and J. Bourne, 'Powell, the Minorities and the 1970 Election,' *Political Quarterly*, vol. 41, 1970, p. 409.
16.   M. Cowling, 'Mr Powell, Mr Heath and the Future,' in *Powell and the 1970 Election*, (ed. J. Wood), Elliot Right Way Books, London, 1970, p. 11.
17.   D. Spearman, 'Enoch Powell's Election Letters,' *ibid.*, p. 49.
18.   D. Spearman, 'Enoch Powell's Postbag,' *New Society*, vol. 11, no. 293, 9 May 1968, pp. 667-9.
19.   *Op. cit.*, p. 21.
20.   *Op. cit.*, p. 16.
21.   *Op. cit.*, p. 407.
22.   See our methodological note.
23.   See our methodological note.
24.   See P. Lazarsfeld and Kendall, 'Problems of Survey Analysis,' in R. Merton and P. Lazarsfeld, *Continuities in Political Research*, Free Press, London, 1960.
25.   Morgan and Sonquist, *The Detection of Interaction Effects*, Monograph 35, I.S.R. Survey Research Centre, University of Michigan, 1964.
26.   See, for example, R. Rose, *Politics in England,* p. 75.
27.   There is evidence suggesting that, if anything, Labour Party members may be slightly more prejudiced that Labour Party supporters. See, for example, M. Abrams, *op. cit.*, p. 559; and R. Schaefer, 'Party Affiliation and Prejudice in Britain,' *New Community*, vol. 2, no. 3, Summer 1973, pp. 296-9. Consequently, if Powell attracts support from the same sources as ethnocentrism and prejudice, and the rest of the survey findings indicate that he does, then he may well be attracting a sizeable number of committed Labour Party members and not just the 'floating' Labour Party supporter. This could be especially true of Powell's own bailiwick in the West Midlands. Abrams, for example, found that whilst Conservative supporters were normally more prejudiced than Labour or Liberal supporters, in Wolverhampton considerably more Labour than Conservative supporters gave a hostile response when asked: 'Suppose there are two workers, one coloured and one white, who do exactly the same work. If one, and only one, had to be declared redundant, should it be the coloured or the white worker?' (p. 575).
28.   *Op. cit.*, p. 190.
29.   *Op. cit.*, p. 195.
30.   This point is well made in G. Bain, D. Coates and V. Ellis, *Social Stratifica tion and Trade Unionism*, Heinemann, London, 1973, pp. 57-8.
31.   M. Abrams, *op. cit.*, p. 560.
32.   See S. Lipset, *Political Man*, p. 114.
33.   Nonetheless, despite its implausibility, quite a large proportion (23 per cent) of those who agree that Powell is a 'racialist' also admire him.
34.   See No. 4 above.
35.   S. Lipset, *op. cit.*, pp. 174-82.
36.   J. Rex and R. Moore, *Race, Community and Conflict*, Oxford University Press, 1967, pp. 19-20.
37.   *Ibid.*, p. 194.
38.   M. Abrams, *op. cit.*, p. 570.
39.   M. Mann, *Workers on the Move*, Cambridge University Press, 1973, pp. 151-4.
40.   D. Butler and M. Pinto-Duschinsky, *The British General Election of 1970*,

Macmillan, London, 1971, pp. 356-67.

41.   *Ibid.*, p. 362.

42.   *Ibid.*, p. 362.

43.   The introduction of test factors, although reducing the cell values to such small amounts that we do not include them here, reveals that it is only in the West Midlands that Powell attracts substantial support from the C1 category. Here, this group's attitudes appear much more like those of the working class, with the 40 per cent supporting Powell comparing with the 41 per cent and 50 per cent in the C2 and DE categories respectively. Again this ties in with the Abrams survey which found that, whilst there was more working-class than middle-class hostility to the idea of a coloured worker enhancing his status at the expense of the white competitor, 'there was proportionately most middle class hostility in Wolverhampton' (p. 578). Why this should be the case is difficult to explain, although it raises the possibility that the West Midland's historical association with Chamberlainite Conservatism − its appeal to a working-class alliance with Conservative manufacturers against aristocratic elites − may retain a contemporary virulence in the figure of Powell.

44.   M. Abrams, *op. cit.*, pp. 554-5; 559-50. For example, the level of 'tolerance' for women in the age groups 21-34, 35-54, and 55+, was 43 per cent, 38 per cent and 39 per cent respectively, compared with male scores of 31 per cent, 29 per cent and 30 per cent respectively. Similarly, whilst 41 per cent of women not working were tolerant, the figure fell to 36 per cent for those women who were working. The level of tolerance for men working was 29 per cent, while for those not working it rose to 33 per cent.

45.   *Ibid.*, p. 554.

46.   D. Studler, 'British Public Opinion, Colour Issues, and Enoch Powell: A Longitudinal Analysis,' *British Journal of Political Science*, 4, June 1974, p. 379.

47.   M. Franklin and R. Inglehart, 'The British Electorate and Enoch Powell: Dimensions in the Evaluation of a Political Personality,' *(unpublished manuscript)*.

48.   The survey was commissioned by the *Birmingham Evening Mail* for publication during the February 1974 election campaign, and undertaken for them by Marplan Ltd. It comprised two stages, although we have made use only of Stage 1 (conducted 16-17 February) as the questions on the 'Best Prime Minister' were omitted from Stage 2.

49.   Unfortunately, the survey did not include immigration as a possible issue.

50.   David Butler, writing in the *Sunday Times*, 3 March 1974, suggested that 'the West Midlands provide the really deviant case . . . It can be calculated that nationally Labour gained twenty seats net over what they would have won if new boundaries had been in force in 1970. No fewer than eight of those gains were in this Powell territory.'

51.   *Observer*, 3 March 1974.

52.   D. Studler, *op. cit.*, p. 379.

53.   *Ibid., loc. cit.*

NOTE TO APPENDIX

1.   See, for example, R.E. Henkel and D.E. Morrison (eds.), *The Significance Test Controversy*, Butterworths, London, 1970.

METHODOLOGICAL CONSIDERATIONS

10. PROBLEMS OF EMPIRICAL RESEARCH ON RACE IN BRITAIN

Colin Airey and Roger Jowell

Introduction

A fallacy implicit in the title of our chapter makes the task of writing it extremely difficult. There has never been a discreet subject called 'race' or 'race relations' with which empirical research in Britain (or anywhere else) could exclusively deal. As we have seen in preceding chapters, research on race relations concerns itself — by definition — with both majority and minority groups, or, in other words, with the whole of society. Moreover, it incorporates behavioural measurements, factual measurements and attitudinal measurements, all of which require chapters on their own to do them justice.

In any case, many of the problems faced by race researchers are inseparable from those faced by general population researchers. And over the last decade, all social researchers have had to take increasing account of the racial and cultural patterns woven into the fabric of our urban population. The vocabulary of race relations is fast being incorporated into the jargon of survey research: phrases such as immigrant concentration, language matching and ethnic stratification are now fairly commonplace in survey research usage. Almost no social scientific enquiry can afford any longer to ignore the patchy but pervasive changes in demographic and social structure caused by immigration to Britain during the 1960s.

In this chapter we can give only a shorthand review of some of the major problems and their solutions associated with research on race relations in Britain. Although British experience of race research is limited, there is a growing body of British source material and a wealth of information and experimental evidence from the United States, much of which can be transplanted to the British scene.

The problems we deal with concern mainly the design, organisation and conduct of survey research among minority ethnic groups in Britain; we refer also at the end of the chapter to some of the methodological problems involved in assessing and monitoring the extent of prejudice and discrimination among majority groups.

Structure of the Immigrant Populations

If colour alone was at the core of the study of British race relations, a great deal could be gleaned from American research of black-white relationships. But in Britain we have minority groups whose country of origin may well be more of a distinguishing characteristic than their colour. This conflict of research perspectives is discussed by Patterson (1974) and Banton (1967). Historically, however, much of minority ethnic research in Britain has been based (implicitly or explicitly) on the assumption that immigrants in this country form a group that has homogeneous problems and characteristics. Early reference to this putative group used descriptions such as 'dark strangers,' 'the alien wedge,' 'disappointed guests,' 'the coloured worker,' 'newcomers,' 'Commonwealth immigrants.' And early research saw race relations as a white-black problem of adjustment, with the implication that black people in Britain were more alike than different in background, culture and expectations.

Fortunately this view no longer prevails. Later research has been based on the overdue realisation that recent immigrants to this country have only three common features: first, most come from former British colonies; second, most are black or brown; third, most face varying degrees of prejudice and discrimination in their dealings with British natives. A breakdown of major recent immigration shows the heterogeneity of the 'group' conveniently described as Commonwealth immigrants:

FROM ASIA, principle countries of origin are: India, Pakistan, Bangladesh, Ceylon, Malaysia and Singapore. Many immigrants of Asian origin also come from: Kenya, Uganda and Guyana.
The principle Asian languages in Britain are: Gujarati, Bengali, Punjabi, Mirpuri, Hindi, Urdu, Singalese, Malay and Chinese languages.
Among immigrants from Cyprus, the two languages are Greek and Turkish.

FROM THE CARIBBEAN, principal countries of origin are: Jamaica, Trinidad, Tobago, Barbados and Guyana; minorities of West Indians also come to Britain from several other territories.

FROM AFRICA, principal countries of origin are: Nigeria, Ghana, Sierra Leone, Tanzania, Kenya, Uganda, Zambia and Rhodesia.
A host of different languages are spoken by the African immigrants in Britain.

The disparities of language, cultural background, colour and religious affiliation are dramatic. So are the contrasts between economic circumstances and educational backgrounds of the different nationalities who emigrate to Britain. So too are the differences in the reasons for immigration, the family patterns, the expectations, the intentions and the settlement patterns. All these differences create formidable problems for survey researchers in Britain, most of whom are fairly homogeneous in educational background, colour, language and class.

and many of whom have had little or no previous contact with the groups they seek to describe. The research procedures are therefore tortuous, time consuming and daunting.

Securing Maximum Cooperation

The problem of respondent cooperation in survey research generally is receiving increasing attention nowadays (e.g. Hodgson, 1974). Response rates among most groups in the population appear to be beginning to decline — a tendency attributed to various factors including public cynicism about the usefulness of survey research and concern about intrusion and interference into private lives. A further factor seems to be the changing employment structure, which causes more and more homes to be left empty during the working day.

Within most of the black communities in Britain, these problems are writ very large indeed. There is a growing body of opinion among minority group leaders that the resources currently devoted to survey research should be channelled instead into the furtherance of racial justice. Their argument runs along the following lines: enough research has been done to illuminate the principal problems; resources for race relations are limited; more research is a luxury; resources should therefore be concentrated instead on measures and agencies that will reduce racial prejudice and discrimination. Undoubtedly, this scepticism about the value of survey research filters through to minority communities and creates an atmosphere of hostility there that is not present in the rest of the population.

Worries about intrusion and privacy and also pronounced among minority groups, for understandable reasons. Race research in Britain is always conducted in the context of the general racial situation. Specifically, it is usually being undertaken by whites; it is often sponsored by Government departments or agencies rhat have also been responsible for the various Immigration Acts and the crackdowns on illegal immigration resulting from those Acts. There is real suspicion and fear about the motives of research in this context and accordingly a degree of alienation and vulnerability on the part of potential respondents. Fear of the consequences to black people of giving information led to the protests about the census from black leaders in 1971. But, in the census, cooperation is compulsory. In other research exercises it is not. So we must expect a degree of non-cooperation from minority groups because they feel under threat from officialdom. And, needless to say, it would be unethical and unacceptable for researchers to mask the fact that their studies are being sponsored by the Government when this is the case.

So non-response, and the potential biases it can produce, is of major concern to race researchers. How can it best be minimised?

First, any research cxercise among minority groups should have the

266

active support of opinion leaders within those groups. A sizeable research project recently foundered because this support was neither
sought nor given. Second, particularly when the research is being conducted by people to whom the minority culture is unknown or alien, it
needs the advice and participation of members of that minority group.
All too often research exercises have failed because researchers were
insufficiently aware of differences in family patterns, cultural norms
and social habits among certain minority groups. Third, the matching
of interviewers to respondents on ethnic and language criteria is always
advisable. And fourth, preliminary qualitative studies need to be more
protracted and more closely analysed in minority research than in any
research among whites. This is essential for getting the agenda and the
approach right and for ensuring that the questionnaire development
and phraseology are appropriate.

We return to the problems of interviewing and ethnic matching in
research among minority groups later. First, we consider the special
problems of locating and selecting the respondents who are to be the
subject of the interviews.

Sampling Minority Groups

Most household sampling operations in Britain make use of the electoral registers. But this method is inefficient for small minority groups
of any kind because they are not only thin on the ground but also
usually dispersed throughout the whole population. Sampling them
therefore usually involves difficulty, expense and wastage in interviewing resources.

Among ethnic minorities in Britain, the problems of sampling are
exacerbated by the apparent absence of large numbers of immigrants
from the electoral registers. This does not happen because Commonwealth immigrants are ineligible to vote: they acquire the right to do so
after a very short period of residence. Rather, it is probably connected
with the suspicions of officialdom and form-filling that we have already mentioned, and, in some areas, it may be because — as tenants —
immigrants do not receive the appropriate forms. Language difficulties
among certain groups also probably account for their low incidence
on the register.

Surveys of racial minorities cannot therefore be based on electoral
registers in the usual way without presenting unquantifiable deficiencies in the frame. Valuation lists are a theoretical alternative for household sampling and would be free of the biases inherent in the electoral
registers. But serious difficulties still arise in sampling from them and
the limitations of access imposed by some local authorities often mean
that they cannot be used.

Kish (1965) suggests other techniques for researchers seeking to
survey small minorities, one of which is *cumulative sampling*. This

involves either the use of omnibus surveys, where the cost of a large screening operation is shared by several users, or the gradual accumulation of eligible names and addresses over a number of *ad hoc* surveys. In practice, however, neither technique is much used, party because both involve a good deal of time and party because they are cumbersome and extremely difficult to plan for or cost accurately. Moreover, unless their sampling frames are specially stratified, they are unlikely to give each member of the target group an equal chance of selection.

Very occasionally, special lists exist that may be adequate as sampling frames for members of minority groups. This was the case with the Ugandan Asian refugees in 1972. Because a special Resettlement Board was created, and because the documentation was complete, a theoretically comprehensive sampling frame was available for a survey that was undertaken exclusively among this group. Even so, the lists went out of date very quickly and the quality of the lists in different areas was variable. Moreover, the degrees of cooperation received from local Boards were inconsistent. But uniquely in the documentation available on racial minorities in Britain, the lists were at least viable.

We know from census data that there are high concentrations of racial minority groups in relatively small sections of British connurbations. We know too that the proportion of these groups that lives outside the pockets is small. And this knowledge gives the first clue to the techniques most often used for race research among minority groups in Britain, because, as Kish points out, if we can find small strata that contain large portions of a rare population, it is efficient to increase their sampling fractions. In other words, if most of that rare population is located in small pockets of the total population, it should be sampled heavily. Large gains can accrue if over 90 per cent of the rare population is located within 10 per cent of the total population.

To start with, we need only a distribution map: standard census tables include a demographic analysis of the population of each Enumeration District in Britain, analysed by country of birth. New Commonwealth births, which are not perfectly correlated with ethnic groupings, are shown for twenty-five countries (ten African, five American, eight Asian and two European). It is therefore convenient to use Enumeration Districts (rather than wards or polling districts) as the basic sampling units. A sample of EDs can then be selected with probability of selection proportionate to the number of relevant immigrants within each unit. Each ED contains approximately 150 households or 300 adults and, being small, is usually fairly uniform in its racial characteristics. Maps are available from the office of Population Censuses and Surveys for each selected ED.

The scene is now set for the preamble to the sampling of the ethnic minorities to be covered in the survey. Having got the areas, we now have to find the households within each area that contain members of the appropriate group. This task invariably involves a field screening exercise to identify the final stage smpling units — usually a fixed number of relevant households within each of the EDs.

But even the screening process is beset with difficulties. The first is the almost insoluble problem of defining the required group. Country of birth is a fairly easy definition to apply, but it does not identify specific racial groups from each country. So the question of colour arises. What instructions does an interviewer need to follow to establish the racial characteristics of each household? First, he should exclude all white households, regardless of country of birth. Second, he should include all households with even one black immigrant among their members. And third, he should establish (for the later interview) the main home language of the household. All these requirements involve judgements by the interviewer on which the margin of error is incalculable.

Moreover, the standard survey definition of households (based on the regularity with which people living in the premises eat together) is not altogether appropriate for some immigrant groups. Among some Asian communities, for example, a high proportion of males still live singly or in groups and each should, ideally, be considered as constituting a separate household.

Finally, there is the problem of choosing the right type of enumerator to conduct the screening operation. The survey itself will usually be carried out by ethnically matched interviewers, but there are obvious practical difficulties in matching enumerators to an area whose characteristics are incompletely known. White enumerators tend to be used, and as a result problems of language may arise, as may problems of cooperation, from the very groups that are being sought. But screening is a demanding task in race research and there is great value in using experienced interviewers rather than recruiting and training a black field force especially for this task.

Screening, then, is always a messy process and is in some respects a less than rigorous sampling method. But it is the least deficient method so far evolved. Because of the practical problems it presents, however, it is unlikely that it meets Kish's criterion that the deficiencies of screening should be biased towards the inclusion of false positives (erroneous inclusions) rather than that of false negatives (erroneous exclusions).

Even so, the result of the process is a sample (albeit imperfect) of ethnic minority groups that can now be selected from for the interview proper.

Who Should Interview Whom?

There is substantial and persuasive evidence (principally from America but increasingly from Britain as well) to suggest that the best results are achieved if interviewers and respondents are ethnically matched.

Experimental work reported by Hyman (1954), Price and Searle (1961), Williams (1964) and Schuman and Converse (1971) has shown that apparently more accurate answers are achieved by interviewers of the same race as the respondent than by those of a different race. Black respondents generally give more 'socially acceptable' answers to white interviewers than they do to black interviewers.

In any case, where a respondent speaks little or no English, such matching is essential for a successful interview. No matter how severe the budgetary constraints, considerations both of response rate and of quality of response make ethnic matching a practical necessity in all research among ethnic minority groups. But how precise must the matching be?

The different island (and national) origins of West Indian residents in Britain frequently pose a dilemma. There is some evidence (Daniel, 1968) that problems occur, for example, in the relationship between former Barbadians and former Jamaicans. Other evidence (Rose, 1969) suggests that there are discrepancies in educational background between people from Jamaica and those from the islands of the East Caribbean. In a large study of West Indian groups, these points would have to be noted. But there are practical difficulties in successfully matching interviewer to respondent by island within the Caribbean, not least because the best medium for recruitment of West Indian interviewers is the *Jamaican Weekly Gleaner*, a newspaper published in Jamaica but widely read in this country.

Among the various Asian groups, our experience suggests that language matching is more important than matching by nationality or religion as a first criterion. Certainly it seems that the continental origins (African or Asian) are irrelevant and, perhaps more surprising, that differences in country of origin in the Indian subcontinent no longer create hostility between interviewer and respondent.

Clearly, within the Cypriot community, both Turkish and Greeks need to be recruited and precise matching would seem to be essential.

The major problems of language matching occur in relation to Asian immigrants, notably those from India, Pakistan and Bangladesh. In India itself there are fifteen official mother tongues and about 10 per cent of the population speak 'unofficial' languages. Thirty per cent of the population speak Hindi as their mother tongue and a further 20 per cent a Hindi-based language such as Urdu, Punjabi, Bihari or Rajasthani. A further 25 per cent, living in Southern India, speak one of the Dravidian tongues, the main one being Tamil. And further regional minorities speak Bengali, Gujarati and several other languages.

The pattern of emigration to Britain from India has produced a very different language pattern. Emigration has predominantly come from that part of the west of India from which the East African Indians originate. Consequently the major languages that the British researcher has to contend with are Gujarati, Urdu and Punjabi. Hindi is not commonly used in Britain, except in some cases as a *lingua franca*, and is generally a second-best alternative for interviews.

The proportion of Asian immigrants who speak virtually no English is very small. But a sizeable proportion have insufficient English to take part in a complicated interview. So language matching is necessary and is, in practice, facilitated by the fact that most applicants for interviewing from Asian groups speak two or more languages.

We show below an approximate breakdown of languages other than English spoken by a representative sample of adult Asian immigrants. The figures are based on a screening operation of nearly 40,000 households carried out during the spring of 1974, and are the product of white enumerators' assessments:

	Men %	Women %
English spoken as main language at home	22	26
English spoken fluently but not at home	49	29
	71	55

English not spoken fluently:

		Men	Women
Main language	Gujarati	2	7
	Bengali	2	*
	Urdu	9	9
	Punjabi	13	22
Others/no information		3	7

* = less than 0.5%

In the event, interviewers were matched to respondents on the basis of these data. But the fieldwork suggested that the white enumerators had considerably overstated the degree of fluency in English. As a result, about one-third of those reported as being fluent English-speakers were interviewed in one or other of the Asian languages.

Recruitment of Interviewers

As we have said, screening operations are most conveniently carried out by experienced interviewers, most of whom are white. But once a sample of households has been selected, there is the daunting prospect of acquiring enough interviewers in the right places of the appropriate ethnic origin or language to carry out the main interview.

Newspaper and magazine advertisements are still the most effective sources for recruitment. But personal contacts, official contacts such as local Community Relations Councils, and college noticeboards all provide valuable extra applications.

271

Whether press advertisements for particular racial groups infringe the provisions of the Race Relations Act we do not yet know. In practice, since we make use of the specialist minority press, the question does not arise: our advertisements in a number of Indian and Pakistani local and national newspapers give the qualifications required as 'able to interview in Gujarati or Urdu,' and so on. Similarly, in the West Indian press (*Jamaican Weekly Gleaner* and *West Indian World*) the advertisements refer to 'people able to work in the West Indian community.' Thus we never indicate overtly that we are seeking black applicants in case, in doing so, we contravene the Act.

The applicants we get from these advertisements differ considerably in terms of age, sex and working status from those who answer advertisements for white interviewers. The typical white interviewer is female, old enough for her children to be at school and not herself in full-time work. The variety among black interviewers is much greater. Among Asian groups, for example, a typical interviewer is male, young and working, so that all the interviewing has to be carried out at evenings and weekends. Among West Indian groups, male and female interviewers appear in roughly equal proportions, but again their average age is lower than for whites and they are usually in full-time jobs.

The preponderance of male interviewers creates some difficulties. Our experience suggests that where several interviews are being conducted in a household male interviewers can achieve successful interviews with both males and females. But where only one interview per household is required, the response rate for male interviewers among women is not so good. Generally, however, cooperation by male respondents is higher than by females. And response rates among Asian groups are higher than those among West Indian groups: in the former case, rates of over 80 per cent can be achieved, whereas it is difficult to achieve response rates of over 70 per cent among West Indian groups.

So far the bulk of training and supervision of minority group interviewers in this country has been conducted by experienced white fieldworkers and staff. The number of experienced black interviewers is currently too small for a senior supervisory group to have emerged. But the situation is beginning to change and it is hoped that the market research world will soon begin to have a policy for the recruitment and training of black interviewers.

Translating Questionnaires

The task of translating questionnaires from English to the respondent's language seems likely, in theory, to be straightforward. But in practice it is not. Improvised doorstep translations are inadequate, and professional translators and non-arabic script typewriters need therefore to be brought into service. Since translation inevitably involves interpretation it is always useful to get two translators to carry out the task independently and then agree on one version.

But some phrases cannot be translated happily from English to another language. For example, 'supplementary benefits,' 'rent allowances' and 'rebates' are generally comical when translated literally and best left in the original. Another problem is that some languages, for instance Punjabi, can be written in more than one script and the translator's script may be almost incomprehensible to the interviewer.

Interviews are only rarely carried out entirely in the appropriate Asian language. Some English is nearly always used, and, occasionally the whole interview is in English. It is preferable therefore to provide the interviewer with versions of the questionnaire that include questions in English as well as the appropriate language. But it is not feasible to include translations of more than one Asian language on the same questionnaire. If several languages are required, separate layouts and print runs are needed for each.

The White Problem

So far we have concentrated our attentions on minority group research. We now turn to a brief review of existing techniques for measuring the racial attitudes and behaviour patterns of the white majority in Britain.

A cruel reality in the measurement of prejudice is that the verb 'to be prejudiced' is very rarely used in the first person singular. This creates immediate problems for the survey researcher, who normally relies on respondents to be frank about their attitudes and views. Indirect measurements of racial prejudice are therefore necessary. The maxim quoted by Kaplan (1971): 'if you can measure it (directly), that ain't it,' applies more to race research than to most other forms of attitude research.

In trying to measure prejudice in a given population we are trying to measure an elusive abstraction. The results will tell us little or nothing about the incidence of racial discrimination: to discover that, we have to take behavioural measurements. They will tell us only that, at a given time and in a given place, a proportion of the population admits to attitudes that we think are associated with racial hostility. Many sceptics believe that even this limited objective is unattainable. Attitude measurements, they claim, do violence to the individuality of human minds and cannot encapsulate the conflicting sets of motivations, fears and preferences behind the views expressed by respondents. To an extent the critics are right: no one measurement of opinion can describe or explain the components of that opinion. The objectives of attitude measurement need to be extremely limited; the precision of the results will always be in question and will depend on a realistic selection of aims, on the quality of the measurement tools, and on the extent to which the object of the measurement is subject to accurate quantification in the first place.

What then are the principal tools for measuring racial attitudes? They fall into three main categories: opinion surveys, attitude scaling techniques and a variety of unstructured and disguised techniques.

At its simplest, the opinion survey consists of a series of questions asked of a representative sample of respondents and a documentation of cross-tabulated answers to those questions. The opinion poll is a cursory form of this type of survey, usually restricting itself to a handful of questions, the answers to which provide only scant information about prevailing attitudes. If the same questions are repeated at regular intervals, however, the answers can tell us a great deal about fluctuations in attitude. Sheatsley (1966) usefully illustrates this point in his use of poll series data to measure fluctuations in the 'white backlash' within the United States. His research provides persuasive evidence of how misleading individual poll data can be, but of how valuable they can be collectively over a period of time.

The development of scaling techniques – the second category of attitude measurements – has preoccupied many social scientists for half a century. The variety of such techniques ranges widely from social distance scales (Bogardus, 1925), the first of the *a priori* scaling methods, through psychophysical or rational scaling (Thurstone and associates, 1929), summated rating scales (Likert, 1932), the semantic differential method (Osgood, 1965), to the Guttman scale (Guttman, 1944), which appeared to be the logical conclusion of scaling theory. More recently, however, social scientists have devised further scaling techniques that rely on computer technology for their interpretation. Techniques such as factor analysis and automatic interaction detection (AID analysis) are all becomingly increasing familiar in British survey research. In practice these sophisticated methods achieve little more than the Thurstone and Likert scales were designed to achieve nearly forty years ago. But they achieve it more quickly, more efficiently and almost certainly more objectively.

No matter how sophisticated and well-tested these scaling techniques may be, they are subject to the strictures that apply to all other forms of attitude measurement. They involve an underestimation of the subtleties and contradictions in human minds; they are subject to rapid change – which itself needs to be measured – and they are not universally applicable. At their best they oversimplify reality; at their worst they distort it.

Many proponents of the third set of methods for measuring racial attitudes – unstructured techniques, such as free response interviews and group discussions – claim that their approach does not deserve these criticisms. They believe that the expressions of attitudes they derive are more spontaneous and therefore closer to reality than those derived from structured techniques. We do not agree. Unstructured methods are splendid devices for eliciting free ranging information on racial feelings, but they have the serious limitation of generating unquantifiable and irreproducible information. As a measurement device they are therefore inadequate. However, if they are used to complement structured techniques, the resultant story is a more graphic one than could be achieved by quantitative methods alone.

Even the more systematic disguised and projective techniques cannot overcome the problems of racial attitude measurement, although sentence completion tests, thematic apperception tests, doll play techniques, information and personality tests have all been used ingeniously in race research. The use of many of these techniques has contributed both to the development of survey research and to the theoretical work on race relations in America and Britain. But, like other measurements, though they add to our understanding of potential racial problems and tensions, they fail to capture precisely the abstract, complex and elusive qualities inherent in racial feeling and its causes.

Discrimination Testing

Measuring behaviour ought to be less difficult than measuring attitudes. But in race research, even this area of measurement has special problems, not least among which is that racial discrimination has been outlawed in Britain and America. Its direct measurement therefore usually involves an element of subterfuge by researchers.

Indirect measures of racial discrimination do not, however, involve such subterfuge. They consist, for example, of interviews with potential discriminators, such as employers, hoteliers and housing authorities, which ask about admission policies and practice. Without wishing to gainsay the method, we believe that it generally produces an understatement of discrimination. In any case, it is probably partly a measure of prejudice (or of the propensity to discriminate) rather than a discrete measure of discrimination, *per se*.

Conversely, interviews can be conducted with the potential targets of discrimination, eliciting information on their personal experiences of a colour bar. As Daniel (1968) points out, the subjective reports obtained by this method are surprisingly accurate when tested against objective measurements, nine out of every ten claims of job discrimination having been validated. But there are two weaknesses of the interview as an accurate device for establishing the levels of discrimination in society at large. The first is that it can understate discrimination, because many people do not expose themselves to the possibility of humiliation. This tendency may be a function both of experience and hearsay but, in any event, it applies unevenly within the employment field as a whole. The second weakness of an interview on these subjects is that it invariably has an attitudinal component, and the potential for over or understatement is always present. The evidence drawn from this technique therefore always requires validation by objective methods.

De facto discrimination can also be investigated by the analysis of any available records showing the racial composition of, say, employees within categories of firms, or tenants within local authority housing. But records generally reflect past rather than present behaviour patterns. And no investigation of them can identify whether the cause of discrepancies results from discrimination, from differences in eligibility criteria, or from small numbers of applications (for jobs, housing, etc.) from minority group members. Other related data sources may fill in some of the gaps, but the evidence will always be incomplete.

Accordingly, the measurement of discrimination usually relies on direct testing by some form of subterfuge. There are two principal types of tests, the first involving personal applications from carefully matched applicants of different races, and the second involving postal applications from similarly matched applicants. The main difference between the two is that the second measures the applicants' relative success rates in achieving interviews rather than in being offered employment. Both methods have been used (Daniel, 1968; Jowell & Prescott-Clarke, 1971; Macintosh Smith, 1974) and both methods have drawbacks.

Leaving aside the ethical questions of subterfuge (which we realise we should not), the obvious weakness of the personal approach, involving 'actor applicants,' is that the motivation to succeed may be different between the two matched applicants. There is no reason to expect that this process operates one way only: the white applicant may wish to prove that discrimination does not exist, the black applicant to prove the opposite. And any discrepancies in motivation are wholly incalculable. Moreover, personality differences between the matched applicants – in plausibility, in modesty, in their ability to sell themselves – present the same problem. Such characteristics may be randomly distributed between white and black actors, but only if the sample of actors is large enough, which is not usually the case. So the discrepancies here too are unquantifiable and uncontrollable.

These problems do not apply to postal applications. Differences in motivation and personality are invisible in letters; eligibility criteria can be identical; writing styles can be effectively neutralised. But two new problems come into play, neither of which applies to personal applications. First, for most jobs, written applications are neither sought nor made. Hardly any manual jobs and few clerical jobs depend on postal applications. Second, in 'inventing' suitably matched applicants, we cannot be sure that the *curricula vitae* in the letters are credible. The employer may regard the applicant's description of his job experience as implausible (for example, there are likely to be few Pakistani sales managers with ten years' experience in leading manufacturing firms all over Britain – a real example of an 'invented' applicant for one of the postal tests undertaken). And he may react in one of two ways: he may invite the applicant for interview just because he seems unusual, or reject the application through disbelief. Both reactions will create

276

biases, but, in the former case, a suitably briefed actor will perhaps be more credible than an impersonal letter.

Postscript

Our review of existing techniques of race research must appear gloomy and hypercritical. But we do not think that we have exaggerated any of the problems. It is clearly a peculiarly difficult and sensitive area of research and needs to be approached and interpreted with diffidence. Some of the problems it presents are being solved. Others are unlikely to be solved. The conclusion that we hope will be drawn from our research is that claims of accuracy or precision in the data collected on these subjects should be less extravagant than they have frequently been to date.

NOTES

Banton, M. (1967), *Race Relations*, Tavistock Publications, London.
Bogardus F. (1925), 'Measuring Social Distance,' *Journal of Applied Sociology*, vol. 9, pp. 299-308.
Daniel W.W. (1968), *Racial Discrimination in England*, Penguin.
Guttman L. (1944), 'A Basis for Scaling Quantitative Data,' *American Sociological Review*.
Hodgson P.B. (1974), 'Factors Affecting Response Rates – A Critical Evaluation,' *Proceedings of Esomar Congress*.
Hyman, H. *et al.* (1954), *Interviewing in Social Research*, University of Chicago Press, Chicago.
Jowell R.J. and Prescott-Clarke P.P (1971), 'Racial Discrimination & White Collar Workers in Britain,' in *The Prevention of Racial Discrimination in Britain* (ed. Abbott), OUP, pp. 175-193.
Kaplam A. (1971), 'Measurement in Behavioural Sciences,' *Research Methods and Insights* (ed. Franklin and Osborne), Wadsworth.
Kish L. (1965), *Survey Sampling*, John Wiley & Sons, New York.
Likert R. (1932), 'A Technique for the Measurement of Attitudes,' *Archives of Psychology*.
McIntosh N. and Smith D.J. (1974), 'The Extent of Racial Discrimination,' *PEP Broadsheet*, vol. XL, no. 547.
Osgood C.E. (1965), 'Cross Cultural Comparability in Attitude Measurements via Multi-Lingual Semantic Differentials,' in *Current Studies in Social Psychology* (ed. Steiner and Fishbein), Holt, Rinehart & Wilson, New York.
Patterson S. (1971), 'Immigrants and Minority Groups in British Society' in *The Prevention of Racial Discrimination in Britain* (ed. Abbott), OUP.
Price D.O. and Searles R. (1961), 'Some Effects of Interviewer Respondent Interaction on Responses in a Survey Situation,' *Proceedings of the Social Statistics Section of the American Statistical Association*.
Rose, E.J.B. *et al.* (1969), *Colour and Citizenship*, OUP.

Schuman H. and Converse J.M. (1971), 'The Effects of black and white interviewers on black response 1968,' *Public Opinion Quarterly*, XXXV, pp. 44-68.

Sheatsley P. (1966), 'White Attitudes towards the Negro,' *Daedalus*, vol. 95, no. 1, pp. 217-38.

Thurstone L.L. (1929), 'The Theory of Attitude Measurement,' *Psychological Review*.

Williams J.A. (1964), 'Interviewer Respondent Interaction,' *Sociometry*, vol. 27.

BIBLIOGRAPHY

Notes

This bibliography aims to provide a comprehensive list of studies employing sociological perspectives to examine the role of race in twentieth century British political life. In addition, it provides a selective list of General Studies on race relations in Britain though quite clearly it would be impossible and inappropriate to provide an exhaustive listing of such works in this volume. In particular, it should be noted that this General Section excludes a number of studies focusing on specific geographical areas published more than five years ago; these may be found in Sivanandan's *Coloured Immigrants in Britain*, (1969). The latter also contains a useful appendix of journals, periodicals and newsletters published by organisations and movements concerned with race relations and the politics of race.

Studies on race on Northern Ireland have been generally omitted but three bibliographies of research in this area are included.

Abbreviations have been avoided, but in order to save space, books published by the Oxford University Press (London) for the Institute of Race Relations have been referenced IRR/OUP.

Bibliographies

Commonwealth Institute, *Race Relations* (Selected readings for advanced study), Commonwealth Institute, London, 1968.

Sivanandan, A., *Coloured Immigrants in Britain: A Select Bibliography*, Institute of Race Relations, Special Series, London, 1969.

Sivanandan, A. and Evans, J.M., *Register of Research on Commonwealth Immigrants in Britain*, Institute of Race Relations Special Series, London, 1969.

Sivanandan, A., and Kelly, C., *Register of Research on Commonwealth Immigrants in Britain*, Institute of Race Relations Special Series, London, 1972.

United Kingdom Community Relations Commission, *Race Relations in Britain: Selected Bibliography with Emphasis on Commonwealth Immigrants*, Community Relations Commission, London, 1969.

Joint Conference on Research in Race Relations in Britain (Royal Anthropological Institute and Institute of Race Relations), Report, *Race*, vol. 3, no. 1, 1961.

Lehmann, P., *Anglo-Jewish Bibliography 1937-70*, Jewish Historical

Society of England, London, 1973.

Richmond, A.H., Race Relations — Britain, *International Social Science Bulletin*, vol. 10, no. 3, 1958.

Schmool, M. Register of Social Research on Anglo-Jewish Community, *Jewish Journal of Sociology*, vol. 10, no. 2, 1968.

Schmool, M., Register of Social Research on Anglo-Jewry 1968-71, *Jewish Journal of Sociology*, vol. 13, no. 2, 1971.

Northern Ireland

Rose, R., Ulster Politics: A Select Bibliography of Political Discord, *Political Studies*, vol. 20, no. 2, 1972.

Institute of Irish Studies, *Theses on Subjects relating to Ireland presented for Higher Degrees*, Queen's University, Belfast, 1968.

Northern Ireland Community Relations Commission, *Register of Research into the Irish Conflict*, Community Relations Commission, Belfast, 1972.

General Studies of Race Relations in Britain

Abbot, S., *The Prevention of Racial Discrimination in Britain*, Oxford University Press, London, 1971.

Allen, S., *New Minorities, Old Conflicts: Asian and West Indian migrants in Britain*, Random House, New York, 1971.

Banton, M., *Racial Minorities*, Fontana, London, 1972.

Baxter, P. and Sansom, B. (ed.), *Race and Social Differences*, Penguin Books, Harmondsworth, 1972.

Bermant, C.I., *The Cousinhood: The Anglo-Jewish Gentry*, Eyre & Spottiswoode, London, 1971.

Bermant, C.I., *Troubled Eden: an anatomy of British Jewry*, Basic Books, New York, 1970.

Bloom, L., *The Social Psychology of Race Relations*, Allen & Unwin, London, 1971.

Brown, J., *The Unmelting Pot — An English Town and its Immigrants*, Macmillan & Co., London, 1970.

Davison, R.B., *Commonwealth Immigrants*, OUP/IRR, London, 1964.

Deakin, N., *Colour, Citizenship and British Society*, Panther, London, 1970.

Desai, R., *Indian Immigrants in Britain*, OUP/IRR, London, 1963.

Duke, C., *Colour and Rehousing: a study of redevelopment in Leeds*, OUP/IRR, London, 1970.

Esch, S., see Gould, J.

Field, F. and Haikin, P., *Black Britons*, OUP/IRR, London, 1971.

Freedman, M. (ed.), *A Minority in Britain*, Vallentine Mitchell, London, 1955.

Garrard, J.A., *The English and Immigration. A comparative study of the Jewish Influx 1880-1910*, OUP/IRR, London, 1971.

Gould, J. and Esch, S., *Jewish Life in Modern Britain*, Routledge & Kegan Paul, London, 1964.

Griffith, J.A.G., *et al., Coloured Immigrants: Britain*, OUP/IRR, London, 1960.

Haikin, P., see Field, F.

Hill, C., *Immigration and Integration: a study of the settlement of coloured minorities in Britain*, Pergamon Press, Oxford, 1970.

Hill, M.J. and Issacharoff, R.M., *Community Action and Race Relations. A Study of community relations committees in Britain*, OUP/IRR, London, 1971.

Hiro, D., *Black British, White British*, Eyre & Spottiswoode, London 1971.

Humphrey, D. and John, A., *Because they're black*, Penguin Books, Harmondsworth, 1970.

Issacharoff, R., see Hill, M.J.

Jackson, J.A., *The Irish in Britain*, Routledge & Kegan Paul, London, 1963.

John, A., see Humphrey, D.

Krausz, E., *Leeds Jewry: Its History and Social Structure*, Heffer/ Jewish Historical Society, Cambridge, 1964.

Lawrence, D., *Black Migrants, White Natives*, Cambridge University Press, 1974.

Lipman, V.D. (ed.), *Three Centuries of Anglo-Jewish History*, Heffer/ Jewish Historical Society, Cambridge, 1961.

Little, K., *Negroes in Britain* (rev. ed.), Routledge & Kegan Paul, London, 1972.

Mason, P., *Race Relations*, Clarendon Press, OUP, 1970.

Mason, P., *Patterns of Dominance*, OUP (2nd impression), 1971.

Moore, R., see Rex, J.

Mullard, C., *Black Britain*, Allen & Unwin, London, 1973.

Ng. Kwee Choo, *The Chinese in London*, OUP/IRR, London, 1968.

Parekh, B. (ed.), *Colour, Culture and Consciousness. Immigrant Intellectuals in Britain*, Allen & Unwin, London, 1974.

Patterson, S., *Dark Strangers*, Tavistock, London, 1963.

Patterson, S., *Immigration and Race Relations in Britain 1960-67*, OUP/IRR, London, 1969.

Rex, J. and Moore, R., *Race, Community and Conflict*, OUP/IRR, London, 1967.

Rex, J., *Race Relations in Sociological Theory*, Weidenfeld & Nicolson, London, 1970.

Rex, J., *Race, Colonialism and the City*, Routledge & Kegan Paul, London, 1973.

Richmond, A.H., *Migration and Race Relations in an English City: A study of Bristol*, OUP/IRR, London, 1973.

Rose, E.J.B. *et al., Colour and Citizenship: a report on British race relations*, OUP/IRR, London, 1969.

Sherman, A.J., *Island Refuge: Britain and Refugees from the 3rd Reich 1933-39*, Paul Elek, London, 1973.
Walvin, J., *Black and White, the negro in English society 1553-1945*, Allen Lane, London, 1973.
Zubaida, S. (ed.), *Explanations in Sociology: Race and Racialism*, Tavistock Publications, London, 1970.
Zubrzycki, J., *Polish Immigrants in Britain*, Martinus Nijhoff, The Hague, 1956.

Bagley, C., 'Race Relations and theories of status consistency,' *Race*, vol. 11, no. 3, 1970.
Butterworth, E., 'Aspects of Race Relations in Bradford,' *Race*, vol. 6, no. 2, 1964.
Richmond, A.H., 'Housing and Racial Attitudes in Bristol,' *Race*, vol. 12, no. 1, 1970.
Dahya, B., 'Pakistanis in Britain: Transients or settlers,' *Race*, vol. 4, no. 3, 1973.
Drake, St. C., 'The "colour problem" in Britain: a study in social definitions,' *Sociological Review*, vol. 3, no. 2, 1955.

Drake, St. C., *Value Systems, social structure and race relations in the British Isles*, Ph.D. dissertation, University of Chicago, 1954.

Race in the British Social Structure

Bagley, C., *Social Structure and Prejudice in Five English Boroughs*, Institute of Race Relations Special Series, Research Publications Services, London, 1970.
Castles, S. and Kosack, G., *Immigrant Workers and Class Structure in Western Europe*, OUP/IRR, London, 1973.
Kosack, G., see Castles, S.
Krausz, E., *Ethnic Minorities in Britain*, McGibbon & Kee, London, 1971.

Cousins, F., 'Race Relations in Employment in the United Kingdom,' *International Labour Review*, vol. 102, no. 1, 1970.
Davies, P. and Newton, K., 'The Social Pattern of Immigrant Areas,' *Race*, vol. 14, no. 1, 1972.
Leech, K., 'Migration and the British Population 1955-62,' *Race*, vol. 11, no. 4, 1966.
Newton, K., see Davies, P.
Rose, R., 'Do the British Exist?', *New Community*, vol. 1, no. 4, 1972.
Ward, R.H., 'How Plural is Britain?', *New Community*, vol. 1, no. 4, 1972.

Brotz, H., *An Analysis of Social Stratification within Jewish Society in Britain*, Ph.D., London, 1951.

Carrier, J.W., *Working Class Jews in present day London: a sociological study*, M.Phil., London, LSE, 1969.

Race in British Politics

Beetham, D., *Transport and Turbans: A Comparative Study in Local Politics*, OUP/IRR, London, 1970.
Deakin, N. (ed.), *Colour and the British Electorate 1964*, Pall Mall Press, London, 1965.
Fiddick, P., see Smithies, B.
Foot, P., *Immigration and Race in British Politics*, Penguin Books, Harmondsworth, 1965.
Foot, P., *The Rise of Enoch Powell*, Penguin Books, Harmondsworth, 1969.
Lenton, J. *et al., Immigration, Race and Politics: a Birmingham View*, Bow Publications, London, 1966.
Prem, D.R., *The Parliamentary Leper: Colour and British Politics*, Everest Press, Delhi, 1966.
Smithies, B. and Fiddick, P., *Enoch Powell on Immigration*, Sphere Books Ltd., London, 1968.
Stacey, T., *Immigration and Enoch Powell*, Tom Stacey, 1970.
Wood, J. (ed.), *Powell and the 1970 Election*, Elliot Right Way Books, Kingswood, Surrey, 1970.

Aronsfield, C.C., 'Challenge to Socialist Brotherhood: British Dockers and Coloured Immigrants,' *Patterns of Prejudice*, vol. 2, no. 4, 1968.
Bourne, J., see Deakin, N.
Byrne, J., 'Smethwick by another name,' *Institute of Race Relations Newsletter*, February 1966.
Cohen, R., see May, R.
Deakin, N., 'Immigration and British Politics,' *Crucible*, May 1965.
Deakin, N., 'Britain — the 1966 Election,' *Institute of Race Relations Newsletter*, April 1966.
Deakin, N., 'British Voters and the Immigration Issue,' *Institute of Race Relations Newsletter*, March 1967.
Deakin, N., 'Enoch's Flood,' *Venture*, vol. 20, no. 4, 1969.
Deakin, N. and Bourne, J., 'Powell, the Minorities and the 1970 Election,' *Political Quarterly*, vol. 41, no. 4, 1970.
Franklin, M.N. and Inglehart, R., 'The British Electorate and Enoch Powell: Dimensions in the evaluation of a political personality,' *Mimeo*, University of Strathclyde, 1972.
Frasure, R.C., 'Constituency Racial Composition and the Attitudes of British M.P.s,' *Comparative Politics*, vol. 3, no. 2, 1971.
Inglehart, R., see Franklin, M.N.
IRR Newsletter, 'The Leyton By-Election in Retrospect,' *Institute of Race Relations Newsletter*, May/June 1965 (Supplement).

Katznelson, I., 'The Politics of Racial Suffering in Nottingham 1954-68,' *Race*, vol. 11, no. 4, 1970.

Kullmann, M., 'Notting Hill Hustings,' *New Left Review*, Jan.-Feb., 1960.

Kyle, K., 'North Kensington,' in Butler, D.E. and Rose, R., *The British General Election of 1959*, Macmillan & Co., London, 1960.

Labour Research Department, 'Powell and His Allies,' LRD Publications, 1969.

May, R. and Cohen, R., 'The Interaction between Race and Colonialism. A Case Study of the Liverpool Race Riots of 1919,' *Race and Class* (formerly *Race*), vol. 16, no. 2, 1974.

Moore, R., 'Labour and Colour,' *Venture*, vol. 20, no. 8, 1968.

Nandy, D., 'Immigrants and the Election,' *Labour Monthly*, October 1964.

Rex, J., 'The Race Relations Catastrophe,' in *Matters of Principle, Labour's Last Chance*, Penguin Special, Harmondsworth, 1968.

Rose, H., 'The Extreme Right and the Election Campaign,' *Race Today*, vol. 2, no. 8, 1970.

Rose, H., 'Race Relations in British Politics,' in Benewick, R. and Smith, T., *Direct Action and Democratic Politics*, George Allen & Unwin, London, 1972.

Singham, Ali, 'Immigration and the Election,' in Butler, D.E. and King, A., *The British General Election of 1964*, Macmillan & Co., London, 1965.

Williamson, J., 'Threat of Racialism in Britain,' *Political Affairs*, vol. 45, no. 1, 1966.

Sherman, A.J., *British Government policies towards refugees from the Third Reich 1933-39*, D.Phil., Oxford, 1971.

(See also: The Politics of Race Legislation; Race and Voting Behaviour; Fascist, Racialist and Anti-Immigrant Organisations; Minority Movements and Organisations.)

The Politics of Race Legislation

C.A.R.D., *The White Paper: A Spur to Racialism*, Campaign Against Racial Discrimination, London, 1965.

Foot, P., *Immigration and Race in British Politics*, Penguin Books, Harmondsworth, 1965.

Humphry, D. and Ward, M., *Passports and Politics*, Penguin Books, Harmondsworth, 1974.

Steele, D., *No Entry: The Background and Implications of the Commonwealth Immigrants Act, 1968*, Hurst, London, 1969.

Boston, R., 'How the Immigrants Act was passed,' *New Society*, vol. 11, no, 287, 1968.

Deakin, N., 'The Politics of the Commonwealth Immigrants Bill,' *Political Quarterly*, vol. 39, no. 1, 1968.

Deakin, N., 'The British Nationality Act of 1948: A brief study of the political myhtology of race relations,' *Race*, vol. 11, no. 1, 1969.

Deakin, N., 'Political Rights and Minority Groups,' *New Community*, vol. 1, no. 3, 1972.

Dummett, A. and Dummett, M., 'The Role of Government in Britain's Racial Crisis,' in Donnelly, L. (ed.), *Justice First*, Sheed & Ward, London, 1969.

Hindell, K., 'The Genesis of the Race Relations Bill,' *Political Quarterly*, vol. 36, no. 4, 1965.

Hogg, Q., 'Race Relations and Parliament,' *Race*, vol. 12, no. 1, 1970.

Kushnick, L., 'The Race Bill Battle,' *New Society*, vol. 11, no. 300, 1968.

Lester, A. and Deakin, N. (eds.), *Policies for Racial Enquiry*, Fabian Society, London, 1967.

Race Today, 'No Entry,' *Race Today*, March 1971.

Stephens, D., *Immigration and Race Relations*, Fabian Research Series 291, London.

(See also: Race in British Politics.)

Race and Voting Behaviour

Anwar, M., 'Pakistani Participation in the 1972 Rochdale By-Election,' *New Community*, vol. 2, no. 4, 1973.

Anwar, M., 'Pakistani Participation in the 1973 Rochdale Local Elections,' *New Community*, vol. 3, nos. 1-2, 1974.

Bentley, S., 'Intergroup Relations in Local Politics: Pakistanis and Bangladeshis,' *New Community*, vol. 2, no. 1, 1972-3.

Bourne, J., see Deakin, N.

Bristow, S., 'Up the Poll in Slough,' *Race Today*, vol. 3, no. 6, 1971.

Chaudri, J. and Dhesi, A., 'Caste in Immigrant Politics,' *Race Today*, vol. 1, no. 1, 1969.

Deakin, N. and Bourne, J., 'Powell, the Minorities and the 1970 Election,' *Political Quarterly*, vol. 41, no. 4, 1970.

Deakin, N. and Bourne, J., 'The Minorities and the General Election 1970,' *Race Today*, vol. 2, no. 7, 1970.

Dhesi, A., 'The Immigrant Vote: Asian Variants,' *Race Today*, vol. 2, no. 7, 1970.

Dhesi, A., see Chaudri, J.

Goldman, A.R., see Le Lohé, M.J.

Hanna, M., 'Where are the Coloured Tories?', *Crossbow*, May 1973.

Humphry, D., 'Organising the Black Vote,' *Race Today*, vol. 2, 1970.

John, D., 'Southall, Part II,' *Institute of Race Relations Newsletter*, April 1966.

Jupp, J., 'Immigrant Involvement in British and Australian Politics,'

Race, vol. 10, no. 3, 1969.

Le Lohé, M.J., 'By-Election in Bradford,' *Institute of Race Relations Newsletter*, April/May 1968.

Le Lohé, M.J. and Goldman, A.R., 'Race in Local Politics: The Rochdale Central Ward Election of 1968,' *Race*, vol. 10, no. 4, 1969.

Le Lohé, M.J., see Spiers, M.

Rose, H., 'The Coloured Margin,' *New Society*, vol. 15, no. 401, 1970.

Scott, D., 'West Pakistanis in Huddersfield: Aspects of Race Relations in Local Politics,' *New Community*, vol. 2, no. 1, 1972-3.

Spiers, M. and Le Lohé, M.J., 'Pakistanis in the Bradford Municipal Election of 1963,' *Political Studies*, vol. 12, 1965.

Steed, M., 'Borough Elections – May 1968,' *Institute of Race Relations Newsletter*, July, 1968.

Thomas, G., 'The Council Election in Southall – May 1968,' *Institute of Race Relations Newsletter*, July 1968.

(See also: Race in British Politics.)

Attitudes in the Host Community

Bagley, C., *Social Structure and Prejudice in Five English Boroughs*, Institute of Race Relations Special Series, London, 1970.

Banton, M., *White and Coloured: The Behaviour of British People Towards Coloured Immigrants*, Jonathan Cape, London, 1959.

Constantine, L., *Colour Bar*, Stanley Paul, London, 1954.

Daniel, W.W., *Racial Discrimination in England*, Penguin Books, Harmondsworth, 1968.

Dummett, A., *A Portrait of English Racism*, Penguin Books, Harmondsworth, 1973.

Garrard, J.A., *The English and Immigration: a comparative study of the Jewish Influx 1880-1910*, OUP/IRR, London, 1971.

Political and Economic Planning, *Report on Racial Discrimination*, P.E.P., London, 1968.

Robb, J.H., *Working-Class Anti-Semite: A Psychological Study in a London Borough*, Tavistock, London, 1954.

Tumin, M.M., *International and Intergenerational patterns of ethnocentrism: A Study of youth and adults in England, France and Germany*, Princeton University Press, New Jersey, 1961.

Aronsfeld, C.C., 'Challenge to Socialist Brotherhood: British Dockers and Coloured Immigrants,' *Patterns of Prejudice*, vol. 2, no. 4, 1968.

Bagley, C., 'Relative Deprivation of the Working Class Racialist,' *Institute of Race Relations Newsletter*, June 1968.

Bagley, C., 'Racial Prejudice and the "Conservative" personality: A British Sample,' *Political Studies*, vol. 18, no. 1, 1970.

Bagley, C., see Runciman, W.G.

Baker, P., 'Attitudes to Coloured People in Glasgow,' *Glasgow Survey*

Research Centre, 1970.

Bhatnagar, J.K., 'The Values and Attitudes of some Indian and British Students,' *Race*, vol. 9, no. 1, 1967.

Field, J., 'Race Relations and the Polls,' *Race Today*, vol. 1, no. 1, 1969.

Garrard, J.A., 'Parallels of Protest: English Reaction to Jewish and Commonwealth Immigration,' *Race*, vol. 9, no. 1, 1967.

Garrard, J.A., 'English Reactions to Immigrants: Now and Seventy Years Ago,' *Patterns of Prejudice*, vol. 1, no. 4, 1967.

Hartmann, P. and Husband, C., 'A British Scale for measuring white attitudes to Coloured People,' *Race*, vol. 14, no. 7, 1972.

Hebron, M. and Ridley, F., 'Characteristics associated with racial prejudice in adolescent boys,' *British Journal of Social and Clinical Psychology*, vol. 4, no. 2, 1965.

Hoogvelt, A.M.M., 'Ethnocentrism, Authoritarianism and Powellism,' *Race*, vol. 9, no. 1, 1969.

Husband, C., see Hartmann, P.

Kohler, D., 'Public Opinion and Illegal Immigrants,' *New Community*, vol. 2, no. 4, 1973.

Kohler, D., 'Public Opinion and the Uganda Asians,' *New Community*, vol. 2, no. 2, 1973.

Marsh, A., 'Tolerance and Pluralism in Britain: Perspectives in Social Psychology,' *New Community*, vol. 1, no. 4, 1972.

Race Today, 'Bradford's Mainstream Extremists,' *Race Today*, vol. 3, no. 5, 1971.

Richmond, A.H., 'Economic Insecurity and Stereotypes as Factors in Colour Prejudice,' *Sociological Review*, vol. 42, 1959.

Ridley, F., see Hebron, M.

Runciman, W.G. and Bagley, C., 'Status Consistency, Relative Deprivation and Attitudes to Immigrants,' *Sociology*, vol. 3, no. 3, 1969.

Schaefer, R.T., 'Party Affiliation and Prejudice in Britain,' *New Community*, vol. 2, no. 3, 1973.

Schaefer, R.T., 'Contacts between Immigrants and Englishmen,' *New Community*, vol. 4, no. 4, 1973.

Sharf, A., 'Nazi Racialism and British Opinion,' *Race*, vol. 5, no. 11, 1963.

Studlar, D.T., 'British Public Opinion, Colour Issues and Enoch Powell: A Longitudinal Analysis,' *British Journal of Political Science*, vol. 4, no. 3, 1974.

Thomas, G., 'The Integration of Immigrants: A Note on the views of some Local Government Officials,' *Race*, vol. 9, no. 2, 1967.

Warr, P.B. *et al.*, 'A British ethnocentrism scale,' *British Journal of Social and Clincial Psychology*, no. 6, 1967.

Burt, R.A., *Colour Prejudice in Great Britain*, B.A. Thesis, Princeton, 1960.

Attitudes of Minorities

Davison, J.L., see Tajfel, H.

Parekh, B. (ed.), *Colour, Culture and Consciousness: Immigrant Intellectuals in Britain*, George Allen & Unwin, London, 1974.

Political and Economic Planning, *Colonial Students in Britain*, P.E.P., London, 1955.

Richmond, A.H., *Colour Prejudice in Britain: A study of West Indian Workers in Liverpool, 1942-51*, Routledge & Kegan Paul, London, 1954.

Tajfel, H. and Davison, J.L. (eds.), *Disappointed Guests*, OUP/IRR, London, 1965.

Azim Tariq, 'Race and Repatriation – An Asian Viewpoint,' (Survey) *Race Today*, vol. 3, no. 5, 1971.

Bagley, C., 'A Survey of Problems reported by Indian and Pakistani Immigrants in Britain,' *Race*, vol. 11, no. 1, 1969.

Bhatnagar, J.K., 'The Values and Attitudes of Some Indian and British Students,' *Race*, vol. 9, no. 1, 1967.

Hiro, D., 'The Coloured Man's View of the British,' *New Society*, vol. 11, no. 282, 1968.

Lyon, M., 'Ethnic Minority Problems: An Overview of some Recent Research,' *New Community*, vol. 2, no. 4, 1973.

Singham, A.W., 'The Political Socialisation of Marginal Groups,' *International Journal of Comparative Sociology*, vol. 8, no. 2, 1967.

Fiscian, C.E., *Minority Group Prejudice: A Study of Some Sociological and Psychological Correlates of anti-English prejudice amongst West Indian Immigrants in London*, Ph.D. Thesis, London, 1960.

Fascist, Racialist and Anti-Immigrant Organisations

Benewick, R.J., *The Fascist Movement in Britain*, Allen Lane, Penguin Press, London, 1972. (First published as 'Political Violence and Public Order,' Allen Lane, Penguin Press, London, 1969.)

Cross, C., *The Fascists in Britain*, Barrie & Rockcliff, London, 1961.

Mandle, W.F., *Anti-Semitism and the British Union of Fascists*, Longmans Green, London, 1968.

Thayer, G., *The British Political Fringe*, Anthony Blond, London, 1965.

Armitage, J., 'The National Front in Huddersfield,' *Race Today*, vol. 3, no. 10, 1971.

Aronsfeld, C.C., 'The English Rights Association,' *Wiener Library Bulletin*, vol. 20, no. 4, 1966.

Aronsfeld, C.C., 'The Britons Publishing Society,' *Weiner Library Bulletin*, vol. 20, no. 3, 1966.

Benewick, R.J., 'Mosley's Anti-Semitism, 1933-39,' *Weiner Library Bulletin*, nos. 3-4, 1959.

Cross, C., 'Britain's Racialists,' *New Society*, vol. 5, no. 140, 1965.

Eysenck, H.J. and Coulter, T.T., 'The Personality and Attitudes of Working-Class British Communists and Fascists,' *Journal of Social Psychology*, vol. 87, no. 1, 1972.

Fountain, N., 'The Front,' *New Society*, vol. 13, no. 340, 1969.

Hanna, M., 'The Rise of the National Front,' (The National Front and other right-wing Organisations), *New Community*, vol. 3, nos. 1-2, 1974.

IRR, 'Post-Fascists and Neo-Nazis in Britain Today,' *Institute of Race Relations Newsletter*, November, 1972.

Manchester University Liberal Society Study Group, *Anti-Immigrant Organisations*, Union of Liberal Students, London, 1966.

Mandle, W.F., 'The Leadership of the British Union of Fascists,' *Australian Journal of Politics and History*, December 1966.

Race Today, 'Bradford's Mainstream Extremists,' *Race Today*, vol. 3, no. 5, 1971.

Race Today, 'Pressure Groups at the Polls: The British Campaign to Stop Immigration,' *Race Today*, vol. 4, no. 6, 1972.

Richardson, C. and Lethbridge, J., 'The Anti-Immigrant Vote in Bradford,' *Race Today*, vol. 4, no. 4, 1972.

Rose, H., 'The Extreme Right and the Election Campaign,' *Race Today*, vol. 2, no. 8, 1970.

Skidelsky, R., 'Great Britain,' in Woolf, S.J. (ed.), *European Fascism*, Weidenfeld & Nicolson, London, 1968.

The Racial Preservation Society, *Weiner Library Bulletin*, vol. 20, no. 3, 1966.

Biddle, R.J., *The Western European 'Right.' A comparison of the National Front and the Monday Club within a framework of the European 'Right.'*, M.A., Essex, 1971.

Minority Movements and Organisations

Dummett, M., *Immigrant Organisations*, IRR, London, 1968.

Heineman, B.W., *The Politics of the Powerless: A Study of the Campaign Against Racial Discrimination, 1964-67*, OUP, London, 1972.

The Times, *The Black Man in Search of Power: A Survey of the Black Revolution across the World*, by the Times News Team, Nelson, London, 1968.

Dummett, M., 'CARD Reconsidered,' *Race Today*, February, 1973.

Fitzherbert, K., 'Immigrant Self-Help: The West Indians,' *New Society*, vol. 13, no. 337, 1969.

Glean, M., 'Whatever happened to CARD?', *Race Today*, January 1973.

Hiro, D., 'Immigrant Self-Help: Indians and Pakistanis,' *New Society*, vol. 13, no. 337, 1969.

Karadia, C., 'The Black People's Alliance,' *Institute of Race Relations Newsletter*, June 1968.

Kirby, A., 'Black Consciousness,' in Benewick, R. and Smith, T. (eds.), *Direct Action and Democratic Politics*, George Allen & Unwin, London, 1972.

Lewis, G.K., 'Protest among Immigrants,' *Political Quarterly*, vol. 40, no. 4, 1969.

Macdonald, R.J., 'Dr Harold Arundel Moody and the League of Coloured Peoples, 1931-47. A Retrospective View,' *Race*, vol. 14, no. 3, 1973.

Manley, D., 'The Formal Associations of a Negro Community in Britain,' *Social and Economic Studies*, vol. 4, no. 3, 1955.

Bentley, S., *The Structure of leadership among Indians, Pakistanis and West Indians in Britain*, M.Sc., Bradford, 1971.

Heineman, Jr., B.W., *The Politics of Race: A Study of the Campaign Against Racial Discrimination*, B. Litt. Thesis, Oxford, 1967.

Kinder, C., *West Indians in Moss Side: The Effectiveness of Voluntary Organisations in Integrating West Indians*, B. Litt. Thesis, Oxford, 1966.

Race and Industrial Relations

Beetham, D., *Transport and Turbans: A comparative study in Local Politics*, OUP/IRR, London, 1970.

Brooks, D., *Race and Labour in London Transport*, OUP/IRR, London, forthcoming.

Dewitt, J., *Indian Workers' Associations in Britain*, OUP/IRR, London, 1969.

Hubble, K., *Race Jobs and the Law in Britain*, Allen Lane, Penguin Press, London, 1968.

McPherson, K. and Gaitskell, J., *Immigrants and Employment: Two Case Studies in East London and Croydon*, IRR Special Series/RPS Ltd, 1969.

Marsh, P., *The Anatomy of a Strike: Unions, Employers and Punjabi Workers in a Southall Factory*, IRR Special Series/RPS Ltd, 1967.

Patterson, S., *Immigrants in Industry*, OUP, London, 1968.

Wright, P., *The Coloured Worker in British Industry*, OUP/IRR, London, 1968.

Bidwell, S., 'Coloured Workers and Unions: Are some unions more generous than others in their acceptance of coloured workers? or is area important?', *Race Today*, vol. 1, no. 1, 1969.

Brooks, D. and Singh, K., 'Race Relations, Industrial Relations and

Pluralism,' *New Community*, vol. 1, no. 4, 1972.

Campaign Against Racial Discrimination, *Memorandum of Evidence presented to the Royal Commission on Trade Unions and Employers Associations*, CARD, London, 1966.

Cohen, B. and Jenner, P., 'The Employment of Immigrants: A Case Study within the Wool Industry,' *Race*, vol. 10, no. 1, 1968.

Davison, C. and Finch, P., 'What Happened at Woolf's: The Story of the Southall Strike,' London Industrial Shop Stewards' Defence Committee, London, 1966.

Davison, R.B., 'Immigration and Unemployment in the United Kingdom, 1955-62,' *The British Journal of Industrial Relations*, vol. 1, no. 1, 1963.

De Trafford, D.H., 'Racial Integration in the Field of Employment,' *Journal of the Royal Society of Arts*, vol. 116, no. 5141, 1968.

Finch, P., see Davison, C.

Foot, P., 'The Strike at Courtaulds, Preston – 24 May to 12 June 1965,' *Institute of Race Relations Newsletter*, July 1965.

Hattingh, I., 'Race Relations and the Engineering Industry,' Engineering Employers' Federation, London, 1967.

Hepple, B., 'The Position of Coloured Workers in British Industry,' National Committee for Commonwealth Immigrants, London, 1967.

Jenner, P., see Cohen, B.

Jowell, R. and Prescott-Clarke, P., 'Racial Discrimination and White Collar Workers in Britain,' *Race*, vol. 10, no. 4, 1970.

Patterson, S., 'Immigrants and Employment,' *Political Quarterly*, vol. 39, no. 1, 1968.

Prescott-Clarke, P., see Jowell, R.

Radin, B., 'Coloured Workers and the British Trade Unions,' *Race*, vol. 8, no. 2, 1966.

Reid, J., 'Employment of Negroes in Manchester,' *Sociological Review*, vol. 4, no. 2, 1956.

Richmond, A.H., 'Relation between Skill and Adjustment of a Group of West Indian Negro Workers in England,' *Occupational Psychology*, vol. 25, no. 3, 1951.

Singh, K., see Brooks, D.

Stephens, L., 'Employment of Coloured Workers: the Birmingham Area,' Institute of Personnel Management, London, 1956.

Torode, J.A., 'Race Moves in on the Unions,' *New Society*, vol. 5, no. 142, 1965.

Race and the Police

G.B. House of Commons Select Committee on Race Relations and Immigration Reports. Police and Immigrant Relations, vols. 1-3, HMSO, London, 1972.

Humphrey, D., *Police Power and Black People*, Panther Books, London,

1972.
Lambert, J.R., Crime, *Police and Race Relations: A Study in Birmingham*, OUP/IRR, London, 1970.

Banton, M., 'The Definition of the Police Role,' *New Community*, vol. 3, no. 3, 1974.
Chase, L., 'West Indians and the Police,' *New Community*, vol. 3, no. 3, 1974.
Judge, A., 'The Police and the Coloured Communities, *New Community*, vol. 3, no. 3, 1974.
Lambert, J.R., 'Race Relations: The Role of the Police,' in Zubaida, S. (ed.), *Exploration in Sociology – Race and Racialism*, Tavistock, London, 1970.
Lambert, J.R., 'Police Immigrant Relations: A Critique of the Select Committee on Race,' *New Community*, vol. 3, no. 3, 1974.
Pearson, N., ' "Colour" and the Police,' *The Criminologist*, vol. 3, no. 10, 1968.
Race Today, 'Immigrants and the Police,' *Race Today*, vol. 1, no. 2, 1969.
Rose, H., 'The Police and the Coloured Communities,' *Institute of Race Relations Newsletter*, October 1968.
Sington, D., 'The Policeman and the Immigrant,' *New Society*, vol. 7, no. 178, 1966.
Tobias, J.J., 'Police-Immigrant Relations in England 1880-1910,' *New Community*, vol. 3, no. 3, 1974.

Comparative Studies

Böhning, W.R., *The Migration of Workers in the United Kingdom and the European Community*, OUP/IRR, London, 1972.
Castles, S. and Kosack, G., *Immigrant Workers and Class Structure in Western Europe*, OUP, London, 1973.
Katznelson, I., *Black Men, White Cities*, OUP, London, 1973.
Kosack, G., see Castles, S.
Tumin, M.M., *International and Intergenerational patterns of ethnocentrism: A Study of youth and adults in England, France and Germany*, Princeton University Press, New Jersey, 1961.

Bagley, C., 'Racialism and Pluralism: A dimensional analysis of forty-eight Countries,' *Race*, vol. 13, no. 3, 1972.
Grimshaw, A.D., 'Factors Contributing to Colour Violence in the United States and Britain,' *Race*, vol. 3, no. 3, 1962.
Jupp, J., 'Immigrant Involvement in British and Australian Politics,' *Race*, vol. 10, no. 3, 1969.
Lyon, M.L., 'Race and Ethnicity in Pluralistic Societies: A Comparison of Minorities in the United Kingdom and the United States,' *New*

Community, vol. 1, no. 4, 1972.
Rose, R., 'Race Problems in the United States and the United Kingdom,' *Venture*, vol. 17, no. 3, 1965.

Race and the Mass Media

Sharf, A., *The British Press and the Jews under Nazi Rule*, OUP, London, 1964.

Bagley, C., 'Race Relations and the Press: An Empirical Analysis,' *Race*, vol. 15, no. 1, 1973.
Harman, N., 'Good Race Relations make Bad News,' *Crossbow*, May 1972.
Hartman, P. and Husband, C., 'The Mass Media and Racial Conflict,' *Race*, vol. 12, no. 3, 1971.

Opinion Polls

Opinion Poll data on race relations, immigration, repatriation, and so on, are to be found in the following survey reports:

Gallup Political Index
Report no. 23, November 1961; no. 24, December 1961; no. 44, September 1963; no. 52, July 1964; no. 53, August 1964; no. 64, August 1965; no. 67, November 1965; no. 69, January 1966; no. 88, August 1967; no. 90, October 1967; no. 92, December 1967; no. 95, March 1968; no. 96, April 1968; no. 97, May 1968; no. 98, June 1968; no. 104, December 1968; no. 106, February 1969; no. 110, June 1969; no. 118, February 1970; no. 128, March 1971; no. 135, October 1971; no. 146, September 1972; no. 158, September 1973.
Gallup Survey, Institute of Race Relations Newsletter, August 1961.
Gallup Survey, Institute of Race Relations Newsletter, April-May, 1968.

National Opinion Polls
Political Bulletin: March 1965; August 1965; March 1968; September 1968; October 1968; December 1968; November 1969; November 1970; October 1973; Special Supplement on Race Relations, April-May 1968 and May 1971.

Miscellaneous: Race Relations Research in Britain

Abbott, S., 'Race Studies in Britain,' *Social Science Information*, February 1971.
Allen, S., 'Plural Society and Conflict,' *New Community*, vol. 1, no. 5, 1972.

Banton, M., 'The Future of Race Relations Research in Britain: the establishment of a multi-disciplinary research unit,' *Race*, vol. 15, no. 2, 1973.

Cohen, P.C., 'The Study of Immigrants,' *Jewish Journal of Sociology*, vol. 7, no. 2, 1965.

Hughes, E.C., 'Race Relations and the Sociological Imagination,' *Race* vol. 5, no. 3, 1964.

Krausz, E., 'Locating Minority Populations: a research problem,' *Race*, vol. 10, no. 3, 1969.

Krausz, E., 'Acculturation and Pluralism: A clarification of concepts,' *New Community*, vol. 1, no. 4, 1972.

Rex, J., 'The Future of Race Relations Research in Britain: Sociological Research and the politics of Racial Justice,' *Race*, vol. 14, no. 4, 1973.

Sivanandan, A., 'Race, Class and Power: an outline for study,' *Race*, vol. 14, no. 4, 1973.

Current Research

Ahmed, M., Political perceptions of Pakistani immigrants in Britain, Dept. of Politics, University of Nottingham.

Axford, B., Race and political participation in Britain, Dept. of Politics, University of Southampton.

Bagley, C., Racialist attitudes in teenagers, Centre for Social Research, University of Sussex.

Beechey, V., Ideology of Racism, Oxford.

Bridges, L., Race and Politics, Dept. of Political Science, University of Birmingham.

Duncan, N.C., Changing attitudes towards immigration as reflected in British Party Policy and local constituency politics, University of Manchester.

Hallam, W., Immigration and Race Relations in Bolton, Dept. of Social Science, Manchester Polytechnic.

Hill, B., Fabian thought on racial and ethnic issues 1885-1914, Dept. of Economic History, University of Sheffield.

Hopper, E., Some Structural and attitudinal correlates of prejudice towards coloured people, London School of Economics.

Jackson, R., Political Socialisation with special reference to English and Asian children in secondary schools, Inst. of Education, University of London.

Kokosalikis, N., Ideology and Community: the Jewish Community in Liverpool, Dept. of Sociology, University of Liverpool.

Le Lohé, M.J., Voting Behaviour of ethnic minorities in the N.E., Post-Graduate School of Social Studies, University of Bradford.

Lyon, M.H., Origins of Racialism in Britain, Dept. of Sociology, University of Aberdeen.

Lunn, K.J., The Marconi Scandal: a study of anti-semitism in Britain, Dept. of Sociology, University of Sheffield.
Mountstephen, J.L., Social History of Black militancy in Britain, Dept. of Economic History, University of Sheffield.
Phizakalea, A.-M., The Political Socialisation of West Indian Adolescents in Britain, Dept. of Politics, University of Exeter.
Scott, D.W., Field Study of immigrant groups, their organisation and involvement in the politics of an English town, University of Bristol.
Webster, Y., Racial Identity and White and Black Racism, Dept. of Sociology, University of Warwick.

Periodicals and Journals

Community Forum	Northern Ireland Community Relations Commission
New Community	Community Relations Commission
Patterns of Prejudice	Institute of Jewish Affairs
Race and Class (formerly Race)	Institute of Race Relations
Race Today	Institute of Race Relations
Race Relations	Race Relations Board
Race Relations Abstracts	Institute of Race Relations
Race Relations Bulletin	Runnymede Trust
Runnymede Trust Newsletter	Runnymede Trust

NOTES ON CONTRIBUTORS

COLIN AIREY is Managing Director of the Centre for Sample Surveys, an organisation associated with Social and Community Planning Research. He has been engaged on various projects on racial attitudes and discrimination in Britain.

GEOFFREY ALDERMAN is a Lecturer in History at Royal Holloway College, London. He has written *The Railway Interest* (1973) and various articles on Victorian transport in the *Historical Journal* and *Maritime History*. He was also commissioned to write the *History of Hackney Downs School* (1972). His present research interests concern the part played by Jews in British politics since Emancipation, and in particular the changing political views of British Jewry, and the 'Jewish vote.'

BARRIE AXFORD is a Lecturer in Politics at Oxford Polytechnic. He is currently engaged on a study of political socialisation amongst black youth, and is also co-author of a forthcoming book on political leadership.

ALAN BRIER is a Lecturer in Politics at the University of Southampton. He is co-author of *Computers and the Social Sciences* (1974) and has published articles in *Political Studies, Public Administration, the International Journal of Community Development* and *Youth and Society* on the Liberal Party and decision making in local government. His current research interests include West African politics and sociological theories of the state and he is engaged on a study (with Professor P.A.R. Calvert) of world-wide revolutionary incidents.

IVOR CREWE is a Senior Lecturer in the Department of Government at the University of Essex and Director of the SSRC Survey Archive. He is the co-author of *Social Survey of the Civil Service* (1969) and has written several articles on British electoral behaviour. At present he is engaged (with Bo Sarlvik) on a national survey study of political attitudes and electoral behaviour at the two general elections of 1974.

ROGER JOWELL is Co-Director of Social and Community Planning Research, which has been involved in various projects on racial attitudes and discrimination in Britain. He has published research papers on race relations in Britain in *Race* and *Race Today* and contributed chapters to S. Abbott (ed.), *The Prevention of Racial Discrimination in*

Britain (1971) and to Peter Watson (ed.), *Psychology and Race* (1973).

ROGER KING is Senior Lecturer in Sociology in the Faculty of Social Science at Manchester Polytechnic. His main research interests lie in right wing political movements and he is co-editor of a forthcoming book on British right-wing policies.

DANIEL LAWRENCE is a Lecturer in the Department of Sociology at the University of Nottingham. He has recently published *Black Migrants: White Natives* (1974), a study of race relations in Nottingham.

MICHEL LE LOHÉ is Lecturer in Politics and Chairman of the Post-graduate School of Studies on Social Sciences at the University of Bradford. He is the author of a number of articles and reports on the electoral behaviour of immigrant groups in Bradford, including the chapter on Bradford in L.J. Sharpe (ed.), *Voting in Cities* (1967).

SARAH NELSON is a Graduate Student in the Department of Politics at the University of Strathclyde. She is engaged on a doctoral thesis on perceptions of the conflict in Northern Ireland amongst Loyalist political groups.

ANNE-MARIE PHIZAKALEA has recently joined the SSRC Unit on Ethnic Relations at the University of Bristol as a member of a research team concerned with the relationship between identity, structure and ideology in social movements. She was formerly a Teaching Assistant in the Department of Politics at the University of Strathclyde.

BARRY SCHUTZ is Assistant Professor in Political Science and Director of the Third World Studies Programme at Fort Lewis College, Durango, Colorado. He has published numerous papers on European nationalism in Rhodesia, in *Comparative Politics* (1968), the *Canadian Journal of African Studies* (1973), as well as in David Chanaiwa (ed.), *African and European Nationalism in Rhodesia* (forthcoming) and Hasu Patel and Ashley Dixon (eds.), *Society and Politics in Rhodesia* (forthcoming). His research will be reported in two forthcoming books, *White Rhodesia: South African Foundations of a Fragment Regime* and (with Douglas Scott), *Conflict and Change in Fragment Regimes: Northern Ireland and Rhodesia*.

DOUGLAS SCOTT, JR. is Assistant Professor in the Department of Political Science at the University of California, Los Angeles, and a Program Director (Community Studies and Local Government) of its Survey Research Center. His doctoral thesis was a comparative study of 'segmented pluralism' in Britain and other smaller European democracies and he has published numerous articles and papers on communal conflict in Northern Ireland and Rhodesia from the perspective of 'fragment theory'.

DUNCAN SCOTT is a Lecturer in the Department of Youth Studies at the University of Manchester. He has published various articles in *New Community* on race relations in the United States and in British local politics. His contribution to the *Yearbook* is based on his Ph.D. thesis on 'Ethnic Politics in an Industrial Town.' His current research interests include the politics of race and ethnic relations and urban youth education outside schools.

MICHAEL WOOD was a Lecturer in Sociology in the Department of Social Science at Manchester Polytechnic before joining the Social Science Research Council as a Scientific Officer. He has a special interest in computer applications in the social sciences.